CHRISTOPHER HIBBERT

THE RISE
AND FALL OF
THE HOUSE
OF
MEDICI

ALLEN LANE

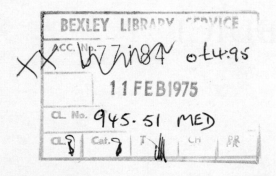

FOR EVE WEISS
AND IN MEMORY OF
ROBERTO

CONTENTS

PART ONE · IL QUATTROCENTO

CONTENTS

CONTENTS

PART FOUR · 1537–1743

LIST OF ILLUSTRATIONS

Maps and Genealogical Tables by Leo Vernon

AUTHOR'S NOTE

ALTHOUGH THERE are very many books on the lives and times of the Medici, not since the appearance of Colonel G.F.Young's two-volume work in 1909 has there been a full-length study in English devoted to the history of the whole family from the rise of the Medici bank in the late fourteenth century under the guidance of Giovanni di Bicci de' Medici to the death of the last of the Medici Grand Dukes of Tuscany, Gian Gastone, in 1737. This book is an attempt to supply such a study and to offer a reliable alternative, based on the fruits of modern research, to Colonel Young's work, which Ferdinand Schevill has described as 'the subjective divagations of a sentimentalist with a mind above history'.

I cannot pretend to be an expert in any of the wide-ranging fields covered in the book; and I am, of course, deeply indebted to those writers and scholars upon whose publications I have been able to rely. I would like to mention in particular Sir Harold Acton, Miss Eve Borsook, Professor Eric Cochrane, Mr Vincent Cronin, Professor J.R.Hale, Dr George Holmes, Professor Lauro Martines, Marchesa Iris Origo, Marchese Ridolfi, Professor Raymond de Roover, Professor Nicolai Rubinstein and Mr Ferdinand Schevill. I am also extremely grateful to Dr Brian Moloney of the Department of Italian in the University of Leeds and to Dr George Holmes of St Catherine's College, Oxford, for having read the book in proof and for having made several valuable suggestions for its improvement. Parts of the book have also been read by Signor Fabio Naldi who has been good enough to place his wide knowledge of Tuscan topography and architecture at my disposal. For their great kindness and help when I was working in Florence I want to thank Signorina Patrizia Naldi and the staffs of the Biblioteca Nazionale Centrale and of the Museo di Firenze Com'Era.

For their help in a variety of other ways I am much indebted to Dr Roberto Bruni, Mrs Maurice Hill, Mrs Geraldine Norman, Conte

13

AUTHOR'S NOTE

Francesco Papafava, Mrs John Rae, Mrs Joan St George Saunders, Mr Meaburn Staniland and the staffs of the British Museum, the London Library and the Bodleian Library, Oxford.

Finally I want to say how grateful I am, once again, to my friends Mr Hamish Francis and Mr George Walker for having read the proofs, and to my wife for having compiled the index.

C.H.

SWITZERLAND

KINGDOM OF
HUNGARY

Bellinzona

Aosta
Como
DUCHY OF SAVOY
Turin
Asti
D. OF MILAN
Milan
DUCHY OF MILAN
Parma
Modena
D. OF MODENA
Bologna
EMILIA
Fivizzano
Forli
REP. OF GENOA
Genoa
Monaco
Nice
Pisa
Florence
REP. OF FLORENCE
Siena
REP. OF SIENA
ELBA

Bassano
Padua
Mantua
D. OF MANTUA
R. PO
R. PO
D. OF FERRARA
Ferrara
Ravenna
R. OF SAN MARINO
Rimini
Urbino
THE MARCHES
Ancona
Perugia
Assisi
UMBRIA
R. TIBER
PATRIMONY OF ST. PETER

Trieste
ISTRIA
Venice
VENETIAN REPUBLIC
Zara
DALMATIA
Split
Ragusa
Cattaro

OTTOMAN
EMPIRE

Ligurian Sea

CORSICA

Tyrrhenian Sea

Civitavecchia
Ostia
Rome
ABRUZZI
MOLISE
Pescara

Adriatic Sea

CAPITANATA
CAMPANIA
Capua
Naples
Salerno
PRINCIPATI
BASILICATA
APULIA
Bari
Brindisi
Taranto
Otranto

SARDINIA

KINGDOM
OF THE
CALABRIA
Castiglione
LIPARI IS.
TWO SICILIES
Palermo
Messina
Reggio
SICILY
Catania
Syracuse

Italy circa 1490
D – Duchy M – Marquisate R – Republic

0   25   50   75   100   125   150   Miles

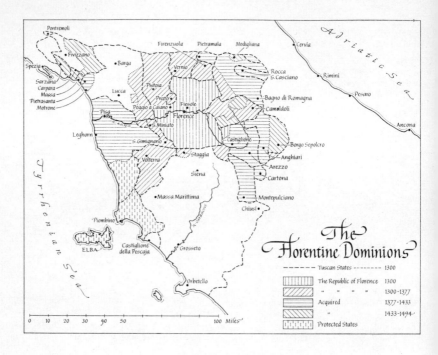

Pontremoli
Firenzuola Pietramala Modigliana
Adriatic Sea
Cervia
Fivizzano
Spezia
Barga
Vernio
Rocca
S.Casciano
Rimini
Sarzana
Carrara
Massa
Pietrasanta
Metrone
Lucca
Pistoia
Prato
Poggio a Caiano
Fiesole
Bagno di Romagna
Camaldoli
Pesaro
Pisa
Florence
Ancona
Leghorn
S.Miniato
S.Gimignano
Castiglione
Borgo Sepolcro
Volterra
Staggia
Anghiari
Siena
Arezzo
Cartona
Massa Marittima
Montepulciano
Chiusi
Piombino
ELBA
Castiglione
della Pescaja
Grosseto
Tyrrhenian Sea
Orbetello

The
Florentine Dominions

- - - - - Tuscan States - - - - - 1300
The Republic of Florence 1300
"   "   "   "   1300-1377
Acquired   1377-1433
"   1433-1494
Protected States

0 10 20 30 40 50   100 Miles

PART ONE

Il Quattrocento

FLORENCE AND THE FLORENTINES

*'A Florentine who is not a merchant ...
enjoys no esteem whatever'*

ONE SEPTEMBER morning in 1433, a thin man with a hooked nose and sallow skin could have been seen walking towards the steps of the Palazzo della Signoria in Florence.[1] His name was Cosimo de' Medici; and he was said to be one of the richest men in the world. As he entered the palace gate an official came up to him and asked him to wait in the courtyard: he would be taken up to the Council Chamber as soon as the meeting being held there was over. A few minutes later the captain of the guard told him to follow him up the stairs; but, instead of being shown into the Council Chamber, Cosimo de' Medici was escorted up into the bell-tower and pushed into a cramped cell known as the Alberghettino – the Little Inn – the door of which was shut and locked behind him. Through the narrow slit of its single window, so he later recorded, he looked down upon the city.

It was a city of squares and towers, of busy, narrow, twisting streets, of fortress-like palaces with massive stone walls and over-hanging balconies, of old churches whose façades were covered with geometrical patterns in black and white and green and pink, of abbeys and convents, nunneries, hospitals and crowded tenements, all enclosed by a high brick and stone crenellated wall beyond which the countryside stretched to the green surrounding hills. Inside that long wall there were well over 50,000 inhabitants, less than there were in

Paris, Naples, Venice and Milan, but more than in most other European cities, including London – though it was impossible to be sure of the exact number, births being recorded by the haphazard method of dropping beans into a box, a black bean for a boy, a white one for a girl.

For administrative purposes the city was divided into four *quartieri* and each *quartiere* was in turn divided into four wards which were named after heraldic emblems. Every *quartiere* had its own peculiar character, distinguished by the trades that were carried on there and by the palaces of the rich families whose children, servants, retainers and guards could be seen talking and playing round the *loggie*, the colonnaded open-air meeting grounds where business was also discussed.

The busiest parts of the city were the area around the stone bridge, the Ponte Vecchio, which spanned the Arno at its narrowest point and was lined on both sides with butchers' shops and houses;[2] the neighbourhood of the Orsanmichele, the communal granary, where in summer the bankers set up their green cloth-covered tables in the street and the silk merchants had their counting-houses;[3] and the Mercato Vecchio, the big square where once the Roman Forum had stood.[4] Here, in the Mercato Vecchio, the Old Market, were the shops of the drapers and the second-hand-clothes dealers, the booths of the fishmongers, the bakers and the fruit and vegetable merchants, the houses of the feather merchants and the stationers, and of the candle-makers where, in rooms smoky with incense to smother the smell of wax, prostitutes entertained their customers. On open counters in the market, bales of silk and barrels of grain, corn and leather goods were exposed for sale, shielded by awnings from the burning sun. Here also out in the open barbers shaved beards and clipped hair; tailors stitched cloth in shaded doorways; servants and housewives gathered round the booths of the cooked-food merchants; bakers pushed platters of dough into the communal oven; and furniture makers and goldsmiths displayed their wares. Town-criers marched about calling out the news of the day and broadcasting advertisements; ragged beggars held out their wooden bowls; children played dice on the flagstones and in winter patted the snow into the shape of lions, the heraldic emblem of the city. Animals roamed everywhere: dogs wearing silver collars; pigs and geese rooting about in doorways; occasionally even a deer or a chamois would come running down from the hills and clatter through the square.

Not many years before, though Dante had denounced their luxurious manners, the Florentines seem to have frowned upon any untoward display of wealth. They had dressed very simply, the standard costume for all men who were artisans being an ankle-length gown of dark-coloured cloth, buttoned down the front like a cassock. Their houses, too, had been unassuming. Even those of the richest families had been furnished with plain wooden tables and the most uninviting beds. The walls were generally whitewashed, tapestries being unpacked from chests to be displayed on special occasions only; floors were of bare stone, rarely covered with anything other than reed matting; the shuttered windows were usually made of oiled cotton. Glass and majolica ornaments were few and discreet; silverware was produced from the sideboard, or from a locked cupboard in the master's room, for none but the honoured guest; and few families yet had forks. In more recent years, however, though the Florentines continued to enjoy a reputation for frugality, they had become noticeably less abstemious and restrained. The stone houses of the well-to-do still presented a severe, even forbidding appearance to the street; but behind the glazed and curtained windows of the upper storeys, the rooms were frequently carpeted, the walls painted with murals, hung with tapestries, religious pictures and occasionally concave looking-glasses to reflect light onto a table or desk. Fireplaces were much more common so that on cold winter nights warming-pans and *scaldini* – earthenware jars filled with hot charcoal – were not so necessary. Much of the furniture was painted or decorated with marquetry. The canopied beds, standing on raised platforms and surrounded by footboards, were very large – often twelve feet wide – big enough for four people or even more to sleep in them side by side, lying naked beneath the linen sheets and breathing in air made sweet by scent or by herbs burning slowly in pierced globes hanging from the ceiling.

Over their trunk hose and jacket men still wore the *lucco*, the dark ankle-length gown with long, wide sleeves and a hood attached to the neck; but many young men now preferred more gaily coloured clothes – a pink cape, perhaps, worn with a satin jacket, white stockings shot with silver lace, a velvet cap with a feather in the brim, scented gloves, golden rings and a golden chain, a jewelled dagger and a sword. There were sumptuary laws as there were elsewhere in Europe; but no one paid them much attention. Certainly the women did not. An official, who was ordered to compel women to obey the laws, submitted a characteristic report of his failure:

In obedience to the orders you gave me, I went out to look for forbidden ornaments on the women and was met with arguments such as are not to be found in any book of laws. There was one woman with the edge of her hood fringed out in lace and twined round her head. My assistant said to her, 'What is your name? You have a hood with lace fringes.' But the woman removed the laced fringe which was attached to the hood with a pin, and said it was merely a wreath. Further along we met a woman with many buttons in front of her dress; and my assistant said to her, 'You are not allowed to wear buttons.' But she replied, 'These are not buttons. They are studs. Look, they have no loops, and there are no buttonholes.' Then my assistant, supposing he had caught a culprit at last, went up to another woman and said to her, 'You are wearing ermine.' And he took out his book to write down her name. 'You cannot take down my name,' the woman protested. 'This is not ermine. It is the fur of a suckling.' 'What do you mean, suckling?' 'A kind of animal.'

To the dismay of many an austere churchman, the wives of Florentine merchants were, indeed, renowned for their sumptuous clothes, their elegance, their pale skin and fair hair. If their hair was too dark they dyed it or wore a wig of white or yellow silk; if their skin was too olive they bleached it; if their cheeks were too rosy they powdered them. And they walked the streets in all manner of styles and colours, in dresses of silk and velvet, often adorned with sparkling jewels and silver buttons; in winter they wore damask and fur, showing off prized features of a wardrobe which might well have cost far more than their husband's house. Unmarried girls of good family were not, of course, allowed such freedom, rarely being seen in the streets at all, except on their way to Mass, and then always heavily veiled. In some households young and precious daughters were not allowed out at all; they had to read Mass in their own bedrooms and to take exercise in their father's garden or in the family *loggia*. When it was time for marriage their parents or guardians made all the arrangements, of which the amount of the dowry was the most significant.

Many dowries included foreign slaves whose importation had been officially authorized in 1336 after an outbreak of plague had led to a serious shortage of native servants. These slaves were generally Greeks, Turks or Russians, Circassians or Tartars, the Tartars being preferred by some households because they worked harder, the Circassians by others because they were better looking and better tempered. All were expected to be fully occupied from morning to night, as Fra Bernardino, a travelling preacher from Siena, urged housewives to remember for their own good:

It there sweeping to be done? Then make your slave sweep. Are there pots to be scoured? Then make her scour them. Are there vegetables to be cleaned or fruit to be peeled? Then set her to them. Laundry? Hand it to her. Make her look after the children and everything else. If you don't get her used to doing all the work, she will become a lazy little lump of flesh. Don't give her any time off, I tell you. As long as you keep her on the go, she won't waste her time leaning out of the window.

Bought quite cheaply in the markets at Venice and Genoa, the slaves were usually young female children who spent the rest of their lives in bondage. An owner had complete power over them 'to have, hold, sell, alienate, exchange, enjoy, rent or unrent, dispose of by will, judge soul and body and do with in perpetuity whatsoever may please him and his heirs, and no man may gainsay him'. They were, in fact, considered as chattels, and classed in inventories with domestic animals. Many of them became pregnant by their masters: the correspondence of the time is full of disputes arising from such inconvenience; and the foundling hospitals were continually being presented with little bundles of swarthy or Slavic-looking babies.

At least the slave, hard as she was worked, could generally be sure of eating well, for although she had few legal rights and was often dismissed in documents as a creature of little importance, she was regarded as one of the family and treated as such. In hard times she was certainly better off than the very poor native Florentines who were sometimes reduced to a diet of dried figs or bread made with oak bark. If she belonged to a moderately prosperous family she could look forward to sharing their evening meal of garlic-flavoured *pasta*, *ravioli* in broth, liver sausage or black pudding, goat's milk cheese, fruit and wine, with an occasional pigeon or a piece of meat, usually lamb, on a Sunday. For the richer merchants, of course, there was more exotic fare. Excessive indulgence was forbidden by sumptuary laws; but, as with clothes, the laws were flagrantly disregarded and the most was made of every loophole. If the main course was to consist of no more than 'roast with pie', well, then, everything that could possibly be desired was tossed into the pie, from pork and ham to eggs, dates and almonds. An honoured guest of a well-to-do citizen might be offered first of all a melon, then *ravioli*, *tortellini* or *lasagne*, then a *berlingozzo*, a cake made of flour, eggs and sugar, then a few slices of boiled capon, roast chicken and guinea fowl, followed by spiced veal, or pork jelly, thrushes, tench, pike, eel or trout, boiled kid, pigeon, partridge, turtle-dove or peacock. For vegetables there was usually a choice of broad beans, onions, spinach, carrots, leeks, peas and beetroot. Finally there might be rice cooked in milk of almonds and served with sugar and honey, or *pinocchiato*, a pudding made out of pine kernels, or little jellies made of almond-milk, coloured with saffron and modelled in the shape of animals or human figures. Everything was strongly flavoured. A chicken *minestra* would be spiced with ginger and pounded almonds, as well as cinnamon and cloves, and sprinkled with cheese or even sugar. Into a fish pie would go olive oil, orange and lemon juice, pepper, salt, cloves, parsley, nutmegs, saffron, dates, raisins, powdered bay leaves and marjoram. The red sauce known as *savore sanguino* contained not only meat, wine, raisins, cinnamon and sandal, but also sumac which is now used only for tanning. In summer the main meal of the day in the families of most well-to-do merchants would be served just before dusk at a trestle table near to the open garden door, the guests sitting on straight-backed chairs or, more likely, on benches or the lids of chests, while musicians played softly in a far corner of the room.

From such households as these came the men who ruled Florence. Theoretically every member of the city's several guilds, the *arti*, had a say in its government; but this was far from being the case in practice. There were twenty-one guilds in all, seven major ones and fourteen minor. Of the seven major guilds that of the lawyers, the *Arte dei Giudici e Notai*, enjoyed the highest prestige; next in importance were the guilds of the wool, silk and cloth merchants, the *Arte della Lana*, the *Arte di Por Santa Maria* and the *Arte di Calimala* which took its name from the streets where the cloth warehouses were to be found.[5] Emerging as a rival to these in riches and consequence was the *Arte del Cambio*, the bankers' guild, though bankers still suffered from the condemnation of the Church as usurers and felt obliged to adopt certain customs and euphemisms in an attempt to disguise the true nature of their transactions. The *Arte dei Medici, Speziali e Merciai* was the guild of the doctors, the apothecaries and the shopkeepers, of merchants who sold spices, dyes and medicines, and of certain artists and craftsmen, like painters who, buying their colours from members of the guild, were themselves admitted to it. The seventh major guild, the *Arte dei Vaccai e Pellicciai*, looked after the interests of both dealers and craftsmen in animal skins and fur.

The minor guilds were those of such relatively humble tradesmen as butchers, tanners, leatherworkers, smiths, cooks, stonemasons, joiners, vintners and innkeepers, tailors, armourers and bakers. But while a member of the *Arte della Lana* would look down upon the *Arte dei Fabbri*, the smiths, in their turn, could feel superior to tens of thousands of those ordinary workers in the wool and silk trades, the weavers, spinners and dyers, the combers and beaters who, like carters and boatmen, labourers, pedlars and all those who had no permanent workshop, did not belong to a guild at all and – though they constituted more than three-quarters of the population of the city – were not allowed to form one. Such deprivation had in the past caused bitterness and occasional outbursts of violence. In the summer of 1378, the lowest class of woollen workers, known as the *ciompi* – because of the clogs they wore in the wash-houses – rose in revolt, protesting that their wages were scarcely sufficient to keep their families from starvation. Shouting, 'Down with the traitors who allow us to starve!' they sacked the houses of those merchants whom they condemned as their oppressors, forced them and their elected officials to flee for their lives, and demanded the right to form three new guilds of their own. The right could not in the circumstances be denied them; but they did not enjoy it for long. The jealousy of their fellow workers in other trades, combined with the power and money of their employers, soon destroyed the *ciompi*'s short-lived guilds. By 1382 the twenty-one original guilds were once more in undisputed control of the city; and by the re-enactment of the Ordinances of Justice of 1293, which had defined the constitution of Florence as an independent republic, these guilds resumed their manipulation of the government.

The government was formed in this way: the names of all those members of the guilds aged thirty or over who were eligible for election to office were placed in eight leather bags known as *borse*. Every two months these bags were taken from the sacristy of the church of Santa Croce where they were kept;[6] and, in a short ceremony to which any citizen who cared to watch it was admitted, names were drawn out at random. Men known to be in debt were declared ineligible for office; so were those who had served a recent term or were related to men whose names had already been drawn. The citizens eventually selected were known for the next two months as *Priori*; and the government which they constituted was known as the *Signoria*. There were never more than nine men in the *Signoria*, six of them representing the major guilds, two of them the minor guilds. The ninth became *Gonfaloniere*, temporary standard-bearer of the Republic and custodian of the city's banner – a red lily on a white field. Immediately upon their election all the *Priori* were required to leave their homes and move into the Palazzo della Signoria where they were obliged to remain for their two-month term of office; they were paid a modest salary to cover their expenses and enjoyed the services of a large staff of green-liveried servants as well as a *Buffone* who told them funny stories and sang for them when they were having their excellent meals. They wore splendid crimson coats lined with ermine and with ermine collars and cuffs, the *Gonfaloniere's* coat being distinguished from the others by its embroidery of golden stars.

In enacting legislation and formulating foreign policy, the *Signoria* were required to consult two other elected councils known as *Collegi*, one the *Dodici Buonomini*, consisting of twelve citizens, the other, the *Sedici Gonfalonieri*, comprising sixteen. Other councils, such as the Ten of War, the Eight of Security and the Six of Commerce, were elected from time to time as the circumstances of the Republic demanded. There were in addition various permanent officials, notably the Chancellor, who was customarily a distinguished man of letters; the *Notaio delle Riformagioni*, who promulgated the decrees of the *Signoria*; and the *Podestà*, a kind of Lord Chief Justice, a foreigner usually of noble birth who lived at the palace, which was also a prison, later known as the Bargello.[7]

In times of trouble the great bell of the *Signoria* would be tolled in the campanile of their Palazzo. Because of its deep, mooing tone it was known as the *Vacca*; and as its penetrating boom sounded throughout Florence all male citizens over the age of fourteen were expected to gather in their respective wards and then to march behind their banners to the Piazza della Signoria to form a *Parlamento*. Usually on such occasions the citizens, having affirmed that two-thirds of their number were present, were asked to approve the establishment of an emergency committee, a *Balìa*, which was granted full powers to deal with the crisis.

The Florentines were inordinately proud of this system which, upheld by them as a guarantee of their much vaunted freedom, they were ever ready to compare favourably with the forms of government to be found in other less fortunate Italian states. Venice, admittedly, was also a republic, but it was a republic in which, so its detractors soon pointed out, various noble families played a part in government which would have been impossible for such families under the constitution of Florence. Florence's great rival, Milan, was under the firm rule of a tyrannical duke, Filippo Maria Visconti. The Papal States, a disorderly array of petty tyrannies which sprawled across the peninsula from Rome to the Adriatic, were in a condition approaching anarchy; while the Kingdom of Naples and Sicily was being torn apart by the rival factions of the Houses of Anjou and Aragon.

Compared with these other states, Florence certainly seemed fortunate to enjoy so commendably stable and democratic a government. But in practice the government was not democratic at all. Not only were the ordinary workers, the *Minuto Popolo*, successfully excluded from it; not only were the nobles, the *Grandi*, similarly denied representation in the councils of the Republic; but the whole process of election to those councils was controlled by a few of the richest merchant families who contrived to ensure that only the names of reliable supporters found their way into the *borse*, or, when this proved impossible, that a *Parlamento* should be summoned and a *Balìa* appointed to 'reform' the *borse*, thus disposing of any unreliable *Priori* who might have been elected to the *Signoria*. In fact, it was a government carried on mainly by the rich and almost exclusively in their interests.

To the Florentine merchant, money had a quite extraordinary significance. To be rich was to be honourable, to be poor disgraced. According to that characteristic Renaissance man, Leon Battista Alberti, the philosopher, poet, athlete, painter, musician and architect, who came from one of Florence's oldest merchant families,[8] no one who was poor would ever 'find it easy to acquire honour and fame by means of his virtues'; poverty 'threw virtue into the shadows' and subjected it to a 'hidden and obscure misery'. Matteo Palmieri, another Florentine philosopher of old merchant stock, agreed with this view. In his opinion only the successful merchant who traded on a large scale was worthy of regard and honour: provided the lowest orders of society earned enough to keep them in food from day to day, then they had enough and should not expect to have more. Gregorio Dati, one of Florence's international silk merchants, went so far as to say, 'A Florentine who is not a merchant, who has not travelled through the world, seeing foreign nations and peoples and then returned to Florence with some wealth, is a man who enjoys no esteem whatsoever.'

By common consent it was agreed that the trade from which the merchant's riches were derived must be both 'comely and grand'. Quickly made fortunes were highly suspect; so were those made from dealing in 'ugly trades', from 'socially inferior skills', from 'low callings, suitable for wage earners'. Trade on an imposing scale and in fine merchandise, however, was not only a credit to the merchant who carried it on but also to the Republic itself which derived such benefit from it.

Having acquired riches the merchant must not be chary of spending them. He must have a fine palazzo and a commodious family *loggia*, a pleasant country villa and a private chapel. He must provide his family with suitably expensive if not unduly flamboyant clothes, and be ready to provide his daughters with handsome dowries. He must be generous in his donations to the building of churches and convents not only for the glory of God but also for the honour of his descendants and of Florence. If he were rich enough he would gain additional prestige by lending money to the Republic. Giovanni Rucellai, whose enormous fortune was based on the famous Florentine red dye, the *oricello*, from which his family derived their name, declared that he had done himself much more honour 'by having spent money well than by having earned it'; he had also derived deeper satisfaction in spending it, especially the money he had spent on his palazzo, a splendid edifice designed by Alberti.[9]

But to be a rich and munificent merchant in a respectable way of business was not in itself sufficient to gain esteem in Florentine society. Ideally a good marriage was also required; so was a tradition of family service to the Republic. Indeed, no one could pretend to high social rank who did not hold or had not held some public office. This was impressed upon the sons of merchants from their earliest years; and a family whose name did not feature on the parchment lists of former *Priori*, all of whom had been carefully recorded since 1282, was almost beyond the pale. The venerated and enormously rich patrician, Niccolò da Uzzano, kept one of these lists hanging on the wall of his study so that, when the candidature of someone unknown to him was canvassed, he could immediately satisfy himself that he was not a parvenu.[10]

The Medici were not parvenus. Yet, compared with many of their rivals, they were not an ancient family either. In later years all manner of legends gained currency.

II

THE RISE OF THE MEDICI

'Always keep out of the public eye'

IT WAS said that the Medici were descended from one Averardo, a
brave knight who had fought under the banner of Charlemagne.
This Averardo had once passed through Tuscany on his way to
Rome, and in the district to the north of Florence known as the
Mugello he had come upon a savage giant, the terror of the poor
peasants of the neighbourhood. He had done battle with the monster
and had killed him. In the fight his shield had been dented in several
places by the heavy blows of the giant's ferociously wielded mace;
and Charlemagne had rewarded Averardo's bravery by allowing
him to commemorate his great victory by representing the dents on
his coat-of-arms by red balls or *palle* on a field of gold – ever afterwards the insignia of the Medici.[1] More prosaically, and rather more
probably, others maintained that these red balls represented pills or
cupping-glasses, the Medici – as their name suggested – having
originally been doctors or apothecaries, descendants of a charcoal
burner who had moved into Florence from the Mugello. Yet others
had it that the balls represented coins, the traditional emblems of
pawnbrokers.

What at least was certain was that in more recent years the Medici
had been leading lives of quiet respectability in Florence, prospering
as the city prospered, and occasionally occupying public office. The
first member of the family to become *Gonfaloniere* was one Ardingo
de' Medici who was elected to that office in 1296. His brother Guccio
also became *Gonfaloniere* three years later and had the distinction of
being buried in a fourth-century sarcophagus which was placed out-

30

side the black and white octagonal church of San Giovanni Battista, known as the Baptistery. Another Medici, Cosimo's great-great grandfather, Averardo, was elected *Gonfaloniere* in 1314; but thereafter the family appear to have suffered a decline. One of Averardo's grandsons, Filigno di Conte de' Medici, lamented this decline in a short book of memoirs he wrote for his children. He was pleased to say that the family still owned several small houses in Florence, as well as two palazzi, an inn, and 'the half of a palazzo with houses round it' at Cafaggiolo in the Mugello. They were still quite well off, but not nearly as rich as once they had been; while their social position, though 'still considerable, ought to have been higher'. Gone were the days when it 'used to be said, "You are like one of the Medici", and every man feared [them]'.

A cousin of Filigno, Salvestro de' Medici, reclaimed the family's prestige by being elected *Gonfaloniere* in 1370 and again in 1378, the year of the riots of the *ciompi*. Salvestro was known to be in sympathy with the *ciompi* and for a time his reputation blossomed in the light of their success. But their ultimate failure ruined him; and thereafter the Medici, whose name was now inevitably associated with the party of the people, were regarded with suspicion by many of the leading families of the city.

It was a suspicion which Cosimo's father, Giovanni di Bicci de' Medici, had always been anxious to allay. He had not been born rich: the little money left by his own father had had to be divided between a widow and five sons. And having made his own fortune, Giovanni was determined not to put it in jeopardy. His sympathies, like Salvestro's, were supposed to be with the *Minuto Popolo* and he consequently enjoyed much popularity with them. Yet he was a man of the utmost discretion, acutely aware of the danger of arousing the Florentines' notorious distrust of overtly ambitious citizens, anxious to remain as far as possible out of the public eye while making money in his rapidly expanding banking business.

He enjoyed the reputation of a kind man, honest, understanding and humane; yet no one could mistake the worldly-wise shrewdness in his hooded eyes nor the determined set of his large chin. He was never eloquent, but in his talk there were occasional flashes of wit which were rendered all the more disarming by the habitually lugubrious expression of his pale face. Although his riches had been increased by the handsome dowry which his wife, Piccarda Bueri, had brought into the family, he lived with her and his two sons, Cosimo and Lorenzo, in a modest house in the Via Larga before moving to a slightly larger but still unpretentious house in the Piazza del Duomo not far from the unfinished cathedral of Santa Maria del Fiore.[2] Giovanni would have preferred to avoid public life altogether, as many minor merchants contrived to do; he would ideally have liked to divide his time between his house in Florence and his country villa, between his office in the Piazza del Duomo and his bank in the Via Porta Rossa[3] near the present Mercato Nuovo.[4] But in Florence, as one of his grandsons was to say, rich merchants did not prosper without taking a share in the government.

So Giovanni reluctantly accepted office as one of the *Priori* in the *Signoria* in 1402, in 1408 and again in 1411; and in 1421, for the statutory two-month period, he occupied the office of *Gonfaloniere*. For the rest he appeared content to sit in the shadows of his counting-house, contributing generously to public funds and private charities, investing in land in the surrounding countryside, adopting no more definite a political stance than one of moderate opposition to the civic aspirations of the dispossessed *Grandi* – whose banker he was nevertheless happy to be – and allowing the rich Albizzi family to exercise control of the government through their friends and nominees in the *Signoria*.

It had to be agreed even by their political opponents that this period of rule by the Albizzi and their associates had not so far been particularly unpopular in Florence, coinciding as it did with a time of relative prosperity. It had been a harsh rule to be sure: opposition to it had been rigorously crushed; malcontents and rivals had been arrested, banished, impoverished, even executed. But Florentine territories had gradually and continually expanded. Before the Albizzi came to power these territories already stretched far beyond the walls of the city and included the towns of Pistoia, Volterra, and Prato which was bought from the Queen of Naples in 1351. But since they had successfully taken over the government, the Albizzi had not only gained possession of Arezzo; they had also opened up a passage to the sea by capturing Pisa and its port, Porto Pisano, in 1406, and in 1421 they had bought Leghorn from the Genoese.

The acquisition of these ports – celebrated at Pisa by the launching of the first Florentine armed galley – immensely increased the wealth of the Republic, and gave a new impetus to the trade in wool and cloth upon which its prosperity had long depended. From England and the Low Countries, as well as from the hills and valleys of Tuscany, vast quantities of wool had for generations come into Florence to be refined, dyed and re-exported. Before the Black Death the industry was believed to have supported as many as 30,000 people. This explained the importance and influence of the *Arte di Calimala* and the *Arte della Lana*, the cloth and wool trade guilds, which for so long had played an essential part in the government of the city and had been responsible for the construction of so many of its finest buildings. The building of the Cathedral of Santa Maria del Fiore, for instance, had been entrusted to officials of the *Arte della Lana* whose emblem of a lamb was a notable feature on its walls.

The owner of two wool workshops in Florence, Giovanni di Bicci de' Medici was a member of the *Arte della Lana*; but, since his main interest was banking, he was also a member of the *Arte del Cambio*, a guild whose prestige had been increasing ever since 1252 when the bankers of the city had issued a beautiful small gold coin, stamped on its reverse side with the city's Latin name, Florentia, and on the obverse with its emblem, the lily.[5] This was the famous *fiorino d'oro* which became internationally known as the flower, the florence or the florin. It contained fifty-four grains of fine gold, and in terms of purchasing power the florin of the 1430s might be considered the equivalent of about £20 today: certainly a man could live very comfortably indeed on an annual income of 150 florins; a small house and garden in the city could be rented for about thirty-five florins a year; a handsome palazzo could be bought for a thousand; a maidservant would cost him no more than ten florins a year and a slave could be bought for fifty. The florin had rapidly gained universal confidence and was soon in common use throughout Europe, to the great credit of the city of its origin and to the banking houses which conducted business there. In 1422 there were two million golden florins in circulation and seventy-two bankers and bill-brokers in the neighbourhood of the Mercato Vecchio. One of the most prosperous and certainly the most rapidly expanding of these businesses was that of the Medici.

An office in Rome had been established in the previous century by Giovanni's distant cousin, Vieri di Cambio de' Medici; there were also branches in Venice and Genoa, Naples and Gaeta. Giovanni de' Medici, who had begun his career as an apprentice to his cousin Vieri, opened a new branch in Geneva, a second branch in Rome, and, as a consequence of the growth in trade following the conquest of Pisa, established correspondents in Bruges and London. But Giovanni's success as a banker was not so much due to the prosperity of the Florentine wool trade as to his friendship with the Pope.

It seemed a most improbable friendship, for Baldassare Cossa, who was elected Pope in 1410, was not at all the sort of man with whom a rather staid and provident banker might be expected to associate. Sensual, adventurous, unscrupulous and highly superstitious, Baldassare Cossa came of an old Neapolitan family and had once been a pirate. When he decided to enter the Church it appeared to those who knew him best that he sought further adventure rather than the service of God. Adventures he certainly had.

The Church at this time was in a deplorable condition with a pope at Avignon contesting the rival claims of a pope at Rome. In an attempt to end this 'great schism', which was dividing Europe into rival camps, a Council had met at Pisa in 1409. The Council's solution had been to depose both the Avignon pope, Benedict XIII, and the Italian pope, Gregory XII, and to elect a new pope, Alexander V, who promptly adjourned the Council. Since neither of the previous rivals was prepared to accept the verdict of the Council there were now three popes instead of two, a situation which was not improved when Alexander V died and Baldassare Cossa succeeded him, choosing the title of Pope John XXIII. In a fresh attempt to resolve the difficulty, the German Emperor Sigismund summoned a new Council at Constance, and towards the end of 1414 Pope John left for

Constance, apparently taking with him a representative of the Medici bank as his financial adviser.

By this time the Medici were well established as the Pope's bankers. Other Florentine banking houses, notably the Alberti, the Ricci and the Spini, had acted as financial agents for the Curia in the past; and the amount of business which the Medici had conducted at Rome was relatively small, though Giovanni had much increased its volume while he was working there between 1386 and 1397. During the pontificate of John XXIII, however, it was the Medici who were most closely associated with the affairs of the Curia. It was said that they had helped to secure this position for themselves by providing the Pope with the money – 10,000 ducats – with which he had purchased his cardinal's hat; certainly, while he had been Cardinal Legate at Bologna from 1403 until 1410 he had constantly been in correspondence with Giovanni, with whom he had conducted a great deal of business and to whom he referred as 'my very dear friend'.

After Cardinal Cossa's election as Pope the Medici had begun to enjoy an exceptionally profitable relationship with the Papal Chamber, by which the Curia's revenues were collected and disbursed. They had also been the principal backers of John XXIII during his war with King Ladislaus of Naples who supported the claims of Gregory XII one of the two rival popes; and when Pope John made peace with King Ladislaus in June 1412 it was again the Medici who played the main part in finding the 95,000 florins which were to be paid to the King of Naples under the terms of the treaty. Two valuable mitres, as well as a quantity of papal plate, were handed over to one of the Rome branches of the Medici bank as a pledge. This sort of transaction was not to Giovanni's taste; but it was a small and necessary price to pay for the enormous profits to be made from the handling of papal finances. How truly immense these profits were may be judged from the fact that over half the astonishing profits of the Medici bank now came from the two Rome branches.

At the Council of Constance, however, the Medici suffered a setback. Pope John arrived at Constance at the end of October 1414 to find himself accused of all kinds of crimes including heresy, simony, tyranny, the murder by poison of Alexander V and the seduction of no fewer than two hundred of the ladies of Bologna. After escaping from Constance disguised as a layman with a cross-bow slung over his shoulder, he was betrayed and brought back to face the Council, which deposed both him and Benedict XIII, accepted the resignation of Gregory XII, and elected a new pope, Martin V.

Pope John, ill and destitute, was held prisoner for three years in the Castle of Heidelberg until the Medici once more came to his help by arranging, through their Venetian branch, to pay a ransom for his release of 38,500 Rhenish gulden. Accompanied by Bartolomeo de' Bardi (soon to become the Medici's manager in Rome), the deposed Pope made his way to Florence where Giovanni de' Medici welcomed him, provided him with a home for the remaining few months of his life, and interceded on his behalf with Martin V, who agreed to appoint him Cardinal-Bishop of Tusculum.

Martin V was then also living in Florence where he remained for two years at the monastery of Santa Maria Novella.[6] He was a gentle, simple man, but his relations with the Medici were not as close and friendly as Giovanni would have liked. There was trouble over a pearl-encrusted mitre which had come into Medici hands at the time of Pope John's flight from Constance and which was only returned to the papal chancellor after Giovanni had been threatened with excommunication. There was trouble, too, over Pope John's will, under the terms of which the Medici received a finger of St John the Baptist which the testator, whose trust in relics was unbounded, had carried with him always. Later there was a quarrel over Pope John's tomb in the Baptistery, which contained upon its base the words '*Ioannes Quondam Papa XXIII*', an inscription which Pope Martin V considered an affront to his own authority.

On 9 September 1420 Pope Martin left Florence for Rome accompanied by twelve cardinals. An immense procession of the city's officials, representatives of the guilds and the colleges, and uniformed standard-bearers escorted him to the Porta di San Pier Gattolini where he gave them all his apostolic blessing. He then rode out of the city to the convent of San Gaggio. Here 'he got down from his horse', so a contemporary chronicler reported, 'and asked for all the nuns of the convent to be brought before him. He blessed them one after the other and kissed them on the forehead over their veils.'

Giovanni de' Medici, who had accompanied the procession as one of the four *Cavalieri*, those honoured citizens of Florence who had the right to wear golden spurs, watched him depart and cannot have felt other than concerned that his bank's relationship with the Papacy had become so strained. The Medici were not entirely excluded from curial business, but they no longer enjoyed the special privileges they had had in the time of Pope John XXIII. Now it was their ancient rivals, the Spini, who were favoured by the Papal Chamber.[7] But towards the end of 1420 the Spini company suddenly failed and were forced into bankruptcy. Soon afterwards the Medici manager in Rome took over their business, and his bank recovered its former position. Within a few years, indeed, the Medici bank became not only the most successful commercial enterprise in Italy, but the most profitable family business in the whole of Europe. For this as much credit was due to the elder son as to the father.

Cosimo had been born on 27 September 1389, the day upon which are commemorated the early Christian martyrs, Cosmas and Damian, the patron saints of physicians, whom he was often to have introduced into paintings commissioned by him or painted in his honour. He had received his early education at the school of the Camaldolese monastery of Santa Maria degli Angeli, where he had begun to learn German and French as well as Latin and a smattering of Hebrew, Greek and Arabic.[8] Later, together with the young sons of other rich Florentine families, he had attended the lectures and lessons of Roberto de' Rossi, one of the leading scholars of the day and himself a member of an old and wealthy Florentine family. Under Roberto de' Rossi's enlightened guidance, and thereafter in discussion groups at the Santa Maria degli Angeli monastery which he continued to attend in his middle age, Cosimo acquired and developed that deep respect for classical learning and classical ideals, combined with an interest in man's life on earth which was to remain with him for ever. He became, in fact, a humanist.

He was not as learned as many other humanists in his circle, though Pope Pius II, who had a very low opinion of Florentines in general, condemning them as 'traders, a sordid populace who can be persuaded to nothing noble', allowed that Cosimo was a highly cultured, clever and knowledgeable man, 'more lettered than merchants are wont to be'. Certainly there were few Florentine humanists with a wider knowledge of classical manuscripts which he began to collect at an early age, and there were scarcely any who were more intensely concerned with the importance of humanistic ideals in the conduct of public life. Although he himself never became a master of those arts and disciplines, such as rhetoric, which the humanist was taught to practise, he never questioned the right of those who did master them to occupy the most honoured positions in Florentine society. Most of them, after all, came from the same sort of background as himself. But in one important respect Cosimo was different, as his father had always urged him to be, from most of the humanists of Florence: he seemed anxious to remain, as far as possible, out of the public eye.

He was rarely to be seen walking the streets of the city, never with more than one servant in attendance, and always quietly dressed, scrupulous in giving the wall to older citizens and 'showing the utmost deference to the magistrates'. He left it to the scions of other rich families to play the parts of paladins: at a big tournament in the Piazza Santa Croce in 1428,[9] when Lorenzo, son of the great Palla Strozzi,[10] won the victor's laurels, Cosimo was not even mentioned as having been present, nor was any other member of his family. When people came to him for help or to ask his advice about some business matter, he would listen to them carefully and quietly and then tell them what he thought in a few, short words, almost brusquely, as though unwilling to commit himself to friendship. Ordinary people liked him, though, and trusted him; and, even in later years, when age had withered his sallow features giving them a sardonic twist, when his curt and often ambiguous observations assumed an increasingly sarcastic and derisive note, there was something in his manner that commanded affection rather than awe.

He was still in his early twenties when he married Contessina de' Bardi, eldest daughter of Giovanni de' Bardi, one of his father's

THE RISE OF THE MEDICI

partners in the Rome branch of their bank. The Bardi were an old Florentine family and had once been immensely rich; but, like the Peruzzi and Acciaiuoli families, they had lent far more than was ever repaid to various rulers, including King Edward III of England and Robert, the Angevin King of Naples, so that they had consequently fallen on hard times. The dowry which Contessina was able to bring to her husband was therefore not a large one, although it included the Palazzo Bardi, the family palace in the Via de' Bardi, a street whose houses had once all belonged to her family.¹¹ She and Cosimo moved into the palace, whose rooms were soon unobtrusively decorated with the Medici insignia; and it was here that their first child, Piero, was born – in accordance with the hopes of a well-wisher who had written to Cosimo, 'God preserve you and arrange that the first night you sleep with your noble and illustrious wife, you may conceive a male child.'

Contessina appears to have been a rather unimaginative, fussy, managing woman. Fond of good food, fat, capable and cheerful, she was also domestic and unsociable. Far more scantily educated than her granddaughters were to be, she was, like many another Florentine wife, denied access to her husband's study. Cosimo was quite fond of her; but he was never in the least uxorious, and bore his long partings from her with equanimity, writing to her seldom.

The first of these partings appears to have occurred in 1414 when, at the age of twenty-five, Cosimo is reported by his friend, the bookseller Vespasiano da Bisticci, as having left for the Council of Constance with Pope John XXIII. He was away for two years, travelling from city to city north of the Alps after Pope John's deposition, and visiting the various branches of the family bank in Germany, France and Flanders. He was back in Florence at the time of Pope John's death; but soon afterwards went down to Rome as branch manager, leaving his wife behind in the Palazzo Bardi to look after their son, Piero, and Piero's younger brother, Giovanni.

Cosimo was manager in Rome for over three years, making occasional visits to Florence but living most of the time in a house at Tivoli where he was looked after by a slave-girl whom he called Maddalena. One of his agents had bought this girl for him in Venice, having established that she was 'a sound virgin, free from disease and aged about twenty-one'. Cosimo was attracted by her, shared his bed with her; and she bore him a son. As was usual in such unexceptional cases the son, who was christened Carlo, was brought up with Contessina's sons and given a suitably thorough classical education. A young man of markedly Circassian appearance, he entered the Church and, through his father's influence, became Rector of Prato and Protonotary Apostolic.[12]

While Cosimo remained in business at Rome, he was able to avoid arousing the jealousy of his family's rivals and enemies in Florence; but soon after his return his obvious capacity and his supposed support of the *Popolo Minuto* against the *Magnati* reawakened the Albizzi's suspicions of his family.

His father, always so wary and discreet, had throughout his life maintained his reputation for modesty and moderation. When the Albizzi approached him with plans to tighten the hold of the existing oligarchy on the government of the Republic, he declined to co-operate with them. But as soon as the Albizzi's opponents, learning of this refusal, endeavoured to gain Giovanni's support for a more positive resistance to the oligarchy, he replied that he had no intention of helping to bring about a change of government and that, in any case, he was too busy with his own business affairs. Likewise, when the Albizzi proposed to reform the iniquitous Florentine tax system by introducing a new kind of income and property tax known as the *catasto*, Giovanni, after greeting the proposal with the utmost caution, eventually agreed to support it but with so many conditions and reservations that his actual attitude towards it was clouded by ambiguity.

All his life he had been at pains to behave like this, never to give cause for jealousy, always to avoid commitment; and as he lay dying he urged his two sons to follow his example. Be inoffensive to the rich and strong, he advised them, while being consistently charitable to the poor and weak.

Do not appear to give advice, but put your views forward discreetly in conversation. Be wary of going to the Palazzo della Signoria; wait to be summoned, and when you *are* summoned, do what you are asked to do and never display any pride should you receive a lot of votes ... Avoid litigation and political controversy, and always keep out of the public eye ...

When the time came, Cosimo was to give his own sons similar advice; but, despite his apparent modesty and the guarded reticence of his manner, he was far more ambitious than his father and was determined to put his money to different uses. The Albizzi watched his progress with suspicion and concern.

III

ENEMIES OF THE ALBIZZI

'He has emblazoned even the monks'
privies with his balls'

THE HEAD of the Albizzi family, Rinaldo di Messer Maso, was a haughty, proud, impulsive man, reactionary and priggish.[1] He had proved his worth as a soldier and a diplomat, and was firmly resolved both to maintain the power of the oligarchy – if necessary by halving the number of the lesser guilds – and to defeat Florence's rivals in battle. He had already pushed the *Signoria* into an inconclusive war with Milan; and in 1429 he urged a war with Lucca which had sided with Milan against Florence, her ancient enemy and principal competitor in the silk trade. The idea of conquering Lucca was popular in the city; and Cosimo himself was later to lament that its rich territories, stretching from the mountains to the coast, remained stubbornly independent despite all attempts to subjugate them by force. But he doubted that the moment was propitious for war; and, although he consented to serve on the emergency committee, the Ten of War, he did so with evident reluctance, hinting that under the direction of the Albizzi the Florentine army could not possibly win. His caution was justified. The Lucchesi appealed to Milan for help, and, in response to their request, Duke Filippo Maria Visconti dispatched to Lucca the great *condottiere*, Francesco Sforza. The Florentine mercenaries were no match for Sforza, whom the *Signoria* were reduced to buying off with a bribe of 50,000 florins and when this merely led to the Duke of Milan finding another talented general for the Lucchesi – Niccolò Piccinino – the Ten of

War were driven to devising a complicated plan to divert the river Serchio and thus sweep away Lucca's ramparts by a sudden inundation of water. This plan also failed as its critics had predicted: the garrison rushed out of Lucca at night, pulled down the Florentines' dam and sent the waters cascading into the enemy camp. By the autumn of 1430 Cosimo had decided that it would be unwise to remain associated any longer with the conduct of the disastrous and enormously expensive campaign. So, making the excuse that he wished to let others have their turn serving on the war committee, he left Florence for Verona.

In his absence his enemies spread rumours in Florence that he was using his enormous wealth to overthrow the government by hiring *condottieri* to invade the Republic. There were those who believed these rumours; and there were many more who, while not believing them, were prepared to use them as an excuse for ridding Florence of an over-successful rival. A deputation of disgruntled *Grandi* and *Magnati* called upon the elderly Niccolò da Uzzano, the most respected statesman in Florence, to seek his advice and enlist his support in their proposed attack on Cosimo. Niccolò received the deputation at his palace in the Via de' Bardi; he listened to them politely, but was wary and discouraging: even if it were possible to get rid of the Medici, would it really be desirable to increase thereby the power of the Albizzi who might even become tyrants like the Visconti of Milan? Besides, it might very well not be possible to get rid of them. If it came to a contest between the adherents of the two families, it was doubtful that the Albizzi would get the best of it. The *Minuto Popolo*, grateful for past favours, were still on the Medici's side. They had other supporters too: several of the most prominent families in the city, the Tornabuoni and the Portinari amongst them, were closely associated with them in various business undertakings; other families were indebted to them for loans and gifts; yet others were linked to them by marriage – the Bardi by Contessina's marriage to Cosimo, the Cavalcanti and Malespini by his brother, Lorenzo's, marriage to Ginevra Cavalcanti.[2] Moreover, in the close-knit circle of the humanists, Cosimo had numerous friends, whereas Rinaldo degli Albizzi – an outspoken not to say bigoted critic of the new classical learning as being inimical to the Christian faith – had many enemies.

Niccolò Niccoli, Carlo Marsuppini, Poggio Bracciolini, Leonardo Bruni and Ambrogio Traversari were all close friends of Cosimo and each one of them was already an influential figure in Florentine society. They were all remarkable men. Niccolò Niccoli, the handsome, aesthetic son of a rich Florentine wool merchant, was at sixty-six the oldest. A most fastidious, exquisitely dressed and almost excessively neat dilettante, he had never cared for trade and had exhausted his inherited fortune on a beautiful house and a magnificent collection of books and manuscripts, medals, coins, intaglios, cameos and vases which 'no distinguished visitor to Florence ever failed to inspect'. He had begun this collection when Cosimo, twenty-five years younger than he, was a child; and, as Cosimo grew up, he had been inspired by it to make a similar collection of his own. They had once planned to go to the Holy Land together in search of Greek manuscripts; but a journey for such a purpose had not commended itself to Giovanni de' Medici, who had packed off his son into the bank before he caught any other fanciful ideas from Niccolò. For Niccolò's devotion to classical antiquity was an obsession. He eventually amassed eight hundred books, by far the largest library of his day, and was adding new volumes to his shelves up to the day of his death, selling off land and borrowing money from Cosimo in order to do so. He never wrote a book himself, since he never managed to finish a paragraph that wholly satisfied his exacting taste; but he did develop a cursive script which enabled his scribes to copy out manuscripts quickly, neatly and elegantly and which became the basis for the italic type used by the early Italian printers. He became an object of curiosity to visitors to Florence, who looked out for his dignified figure as he passed gracefully down the street but who were warned that he could be very brusque, ill-tempered and dismissive. The only person of whom he himself appeared to be in awe was his termagant of a mistress whom he had taken over from one of his five brothers, much to the annoyance of the rest of the family. One day two of these brothers, enraged by the girl's brash ill-temper, bundled her out of the house and gave her a good thrashing. Niccolò, to whose sensitive ears even the 'squeaking of a trapped mouse' was intolerable, burst into tears at her screams.

Many of Niccolò's manuscripts were discovered for him by his friend Poggio Bracciolini, who was to achieve lasting fame as a scholar, orator, essayist, historian, satirist and author of a collection of humorous and indecent tales, the *Facetiae*. Born in a village near Florence in 1380, he was the son of an impoverished apothecary, and came to the city as a boy with only a few coins in his pocket. He contrived to get a place at the Studio Fiorentino,[3] the university which had been founded in 1321 after the Pope's excommunication of Bologna and which Cosimo, as one of its trustees, had helped to extend by pressing for the employment of professors of moral philosophy, rhetoric and poetry in addition to those already teaching grammar, law, logic, astrology, surgery and medicine. Poggio studied law, entered the guild of notaries and obtained employment as a writer of apostolic letters at the Curia. He went with Pope John XXIII to the Council of Constance and, some years later, accompanied Cosimo on a holiday to Ostia where they made an archaeological study of the area. Resourceful, charming, cheerful, convivial, humorous, highly intelligent and not above bribing monks whose assistance could not otherwise be procured, he was immediately and remarkably successful as Niccolò Niccoli's agent in seeking out manuscripts in Germany, France and Switzerland. He brought all manner of treasures to light, discovering whole masterpieces long since lost and the full texts of what had previously been known only in mutilated copies. In the library of one Swiss monastery, for instance, which was housed in a dingy, dirty dungeon at the bottom of a tower, he found Lucretius's *De rerum natura*, a history by Ammianus Marcellinus, a book on cookery by Apicius and an important work on Roman education by Quintilian.

Texts which could not be purchased he copied out in an exquisite, easily-read and well-spaced hand, using as his model the eleventh-century Carolingian script rather than the tiresome, clumsy Gothic handwriting which had superseded it. When Cosimo de' Medici saw Poggio's script he decided to have all his own books copied in a similar manner. It was also admired by the early Italian printers who used it as a basis for their Roman type, just as they had used Niccolò Niccoli's cursive script for their italic. In Poggio's script lay the origins of modern handwriting and of modern printing.

Poggio, however, was not one of those humanists who became so involved in study they lost their taste for life. He loved eating and drinking, making jokes and making love. Ideally he liked to work in the company of pretty girls. He told Niccolò Niccoli how one day, when he was copying an inscription, he had broken off to feast his eye on two girls who were watching him. Niccolò had been rather shocked; but Poggio replied that whenever he was working he would always choose to have well-shaped girls beside him 'rather than a long-horned buffalo'. He had several mistresses and, by his own admission, fourteen illegitimate children for whom he could afford to care well; with his business sense, and through his connection with the Curia, he had been able to make a great deal of money. It was not until he was fifty-five that he decided to get married. Then, characteristically, he chose a pretty girl of eighteen who brought him a handsome dowry with which he purchased a palazzo where, in due course, six more of his children were born.

Like Poggio, Leonardo Bruni, another of Cosimo's humanist friends, had come to Florence as a poor young boy, had studied law at the Studio Fiorentino and, having obtained employment at the Curia, had amassed a fortune. But he was far more intense and earnest than Poggio, sharp-nosed, alert, inclined to be arrogant and, so a fellow humanist said of him, 'unbelievably eloquent'. He strongly disapproved of Niccolò Niccoli's having a mistress; and Poggio he considered to be really depraved. He himself had abandoned the idea of a career in the Church in order to marry a respectable, and extremely rich, young woman. Thereafter he devoted himself to writing, translating, and to playing his due part in the civic life of Florence, a city which he urged men to consider as the successor of the ancient republics and of which he was to become – and tenaciously to remain – Chancellor. So exalted was his reputation that an envoy from the King of Spain was once seen to fall on his knees before his magnificently red-robed figure.

An equally honourable but far more modest and saintly man was

Ambrogio Traversari, to whom Cosimo was devoted. A little monk who never ate meat, Traversari had come to Florence from the Romagna, where his family owned large estates, and had entered the austere Camaldolite Order of which he had just become Vicar-General. He was a formidable scholar who had taught himself Hebrew, and was as much at his ease in translating Greek as Latin. So rapidly, indeed, could he translate Greek into the most polished Latin that Niccolò Niccoli, who could write as quickly as any man in Florence, could not keep up with his dictation. For Cosimo, who was just three years older than he was, he translated all of Diogenes Laertius's works overcoming his modesty to include the most impure passages with the rest. Cosimo was a frequent visitor to his rooms at Santa Maria degli Angeli, and was soon to have cause to feel deeply grateful for his firm friendship in his imminent clash with the Albizzi.

Also seen frequently at the monastery of Santa Maria degli Angeli was Carlo Marsuppini, a scholar from a noble family of Arezzo, who had been appointed lecturer in rhetoric and poetry at the University. At the age of thirty-two he was the youngest of Cosimo's humanist friends; but his learning was already renowned – during the course of one single celebrated lecture he contrived to quote from every known Greek and Latin author. He was considerably less prolific than Bruni but, not as fastidious as Niccolò Niccoli, he did manage to produce one or two Latin translations from the Greek, some epigrams and poetry, and a funeral oration for Cosimo's mother.

Marsuppini's bitter rival at the University was a young man of his own age, Francesco Filelfo, who was born at Tolentino near Ancona where his parents, both Florentines, were then living. Before he was twenty he had already gained a reputation as a classical scholar that enabled him to obtain an important diplomatic appointment in the Venetian service at Constantinople. Here he married the pretty daughter of his Greek tutor, John Chrysoloras, whose brother, Emmanuel Chrysoloras, had been Professor of Greek at the University of Florence. Filelfo himself came to teach in Florence at the invitation of Niccolò Niccoli who was, at first, delighted by his versatility and energy. Filelfo rushed from lecture to lecture, talking from dawn to dusk and with equal facility about Cicero and Terence,

Homer and Livy, Thucydides and Xenophon. He also lectured on moral philosophy, and once a week in the Cathedral gave a public discourse on Dante. In addition to these activities he found time to write numerous epigrams and odes, speeches and histories, and to undertake translations whenever these promised to be sufficiently profitable. But after a time Niccolò Niccoli began to regret ever having asked the bustling young man with the Byzantine beard to come to Florence. Filelfo proved to be vain, ill-tempered, insolent, avaricious, prodigal and spiteful. Cosimo's friends took to avoiding him, and in his quarrels with Carlo Marsuppini they took his rival's side. Filelfo then courted the Albizzi and offered them his services as a master of invective. Cosimo, who had greeted him warmly on his arrival in Florence and had offered to pay his rent, was to become the most virulently savaged of all his victims.

Yet so long as the other humanists in Florence remained his friends and, what was even more important, so long as Niccolò da Uzzano was alive, Cosimo had no reason to fear that the Albizzi could mobilize forces strong enough to ruin him. Even though he was generally sympathetic towards the political views of the Albizzi, Niccolò da Uzzano had always respected the Medici and had actually been moved to tears at the funeral of Cosimo's father. But in 1432 Niccolò himself died and, thereafter, Rinaldo degli Albizzi's anti-Medicean plot quickly matured. Malicious stories about Cosimo, many doubtless inspired by Filelfo, began to circulate in the streets of Florence: he dressed so plainly, it was said, only the more easily to avoid accusations about his ill-gotten riches; his supposed sympathy for the people was no more than the calculated duplicity of the self-seeker; had he not been heard to say that the people never did anything honest except for their own advantage or out of fear? His well-publicized donations to religious charities and building funds were utter hypocrisy, the conscience-money of a usurer, given with an eye to his family's glory and nothing more; did he not always make sure that the Medici insignia were prominently displayed on any building that he had paid for? Why, he had emblazoned 'even the monks' privies with his balls'! One night in the early months of 1433 the doors of Cosimo's palace were smeared with blood.

Once again, as in the autumn of 1430 when he had gone to Verona, Cosimo withdrew from Florence, this time to his estate il Trebbio in the Mugello where he stayed for several months.[4] Meantime, he discreetly transferred huge sums of money from his bank in Florence to his branches in Rome and Naples, giving orders for bags of coins to be desposited for safe keeping with the Benedictine hermits of San Miniato al Monte and the Dominican friars of San Marco, where they would be safe from confiscation should the Albizzi move against him.

While Cosimo was away in the country, Rinaldo degli Albizzi set about manipulating the elections to the new *Signoria* which was due to meet in September. He completed the work with unobtrusive skill. Of the nine *Priori* chosen, seven were definitely prepared to support him, while only two, Bartolommeo Spini and Jacopo Berlinghieri, were believed to be possible Medici adherents. The man elected as *Gonfaloniere* was Bernardo Guadagni whose debts Rinaldo had settled in order to render him eligible for office.[5]

During the first week in September, Cosimo who was still in the Mugello, received an urgent summons from Guadagni to return to the city immediately. There were, he was told, 'some important decisions to be made'. He decided to face them.

Cosimo arrived back in Florence on 4 September 1433. That afternoon he went to the Palazzo della Signoria to see the *Gonfaloniere*, Bernardo Guadagni, who was evasive and uncommunicative: the 'important decisions' which had necessitated Cosimo's return from the Mugello would be discussed when the *Signoria* met in council three days later; in the meantime there was no way of accounting for the rumours of impending trouble which had been circulating in the city for the past few days.

After leaving the *Gonfaloniere*, Cosimo went to see one of the *Priori* whom he believed to be a friend and from whom he received the same kind of vague reassurance. He then went to his bank, no doubt to arrange for the transfer of further sums from Florence. After that he could do nothing but await the imminent meeting of the *Signoria*.

When he arrived at the Palazzo della Signoria on the morning of 7 September the session had already begun. As the captain of the guard escorted him up the stairs, he passed the shut door of the Council Chamber. Soon after being locked inside his little cell he was told that he had been 'arrested on good grounds, as would be soon made clear'.

Two days later, on 9 September, the huge *Vacca* boomed in the belfry above his head to call the citizens of Florence to a *Parlamento* in the Piazza. As the low, mooing notes of the bell sounded through the city, crowds of people began to converge upon the Piazza in response to its summons; but armed supporters of the Albizzi halted them at the entrances to the square and all those who were known to be, or suspected of being, Medici adherents were denied entry. Looking down from the window of his cell, Cosimo afterwards claimed to have counted no more than twenty-three heads in front of the *ringhiera*, the ground-floor stone terrace upon which the *Priori* were standing. In the name of the *Signoria* these few citizens were asked by the *Notaio delle Riformagioni* if they agreed to the establishment of a *Balìa*, a committee of two hundred members 'to reform the city for the good of the people'. Obediently they gave their approval and a *Balìa* was accordingly appointed.

Although Rinaldo degli Albizzi now seemed to be in full control of the government, the *Balìa* could not be persuaded to recommend the execution of Cosimo as he strongly urged it to do. Its discussions were apparently stormy and indecisive, some members supporting the proposal that Cosimo should be beheaded, others arguing that banishment would be punishment enough, one or two suggesting that the prisoner ought to be released. It was clear that many members of the *Balìa* were reluctant to go to the extremes advocated by the Albizzi not only for fear of the violent disapproval of those thousands of Florentines who, though for the moment intimidated, still looked to the Medici as their champions, but also because his arrest had already called forth strong protests from abroad. The Marquis of Ferrara, a customer of the Medici bank, had intervened on Cosimo's behalf. The Venetian Republic, also financially indebted to him, had immediately dispatched three ambassadors to Florence who did all in their power to secure his release; and if, after a heated talk with Rinaldo, they failed to do so, their arrival in Florence, as Cosimo said himself, had 'a great effect on those who were in favour of executing' him. Rinaldo also had a visit from Cosimo's old friend, Ambrogio Traversari, Vicar-General of the Camaldolite Order, and supposedly the representative of an even more influential customer of the Medici bank, Eugenius IV, the austere son of a Venetian merchant, who had succeeded Martin V as Pope two years before. By this time Rinaldo had succeeded in bringing a charge of treason against Cosimo by having two of his supporters tortured on the rack. One of these, Niccolò Tinucci, a celebrated notary and occasional poet, had been forced by the city rackmaster to confess that Cosimo had intended to enlist foreign help in bringing about a revolution in the city. Neither Traversari nor the Venetian ambassadors believed in this confession; nor did most of the citizens of Florence. Rinaldo, indeed, was gradually being forced to conclude that he would have to be content with a sentence of banishment rather than the death penalty which his henchman Francesco Filelfo was so insistently demanding.

In his cell in the tower of the Palazzo della Signoria, Cosimo had been allowed to see a few selected visitors, in addition to Ambrogio Traversari. He had also been permitted to have his meals brought over from the Palazzo Bardi as he was afraid of being poisoned. But the greatest care was taken to ensure that he neither received nor gave any messages, and that no communications passed between him and his bank: an official watched over the cooking, carrying and serving of his food, while a guard remained within earshot when he was talking to his visitors. But the guard, Federigo Malavolti, was sympathetic: messages *did* pass out of the cell, and bribes *were* offered and accepted. The *Gonfaloniere* himself, the impecunious Bernardo Guadagni, readily pocketed a thousand florins as soon as they were offered to him – he was a feeble fellow, Cosimo afterwards commented derisively, as he could have had ten thousand or more if he had asked for them. Anyway, in return for the relatively modest bribe, Guadagni announced that he had suddenly been taken so ill that he could no longer participate in the council's deliberations; he delegated his vote to another *Priore*, Mariotto Baldovinetti, who, equally impecunious, had also received a bribe from the Medici coffers.

As well as having to contend with former supporters who had now been suborned, with powerful foreign customers of the Medici bank, with faithful friends of the Medici family who were growing more outspoken every day, and with the gradual desertion of such influential moderates as Palla Strozzi, the Albizzi had also to face the possibility of an armed uprising. For as soon as he heard of the arrest, Cosimo's brother, Lorenzo, and various other members of the family had rushed out to the Mugello to raise troops to release him. At the same time preparations had been made to assemble a small army of Medici adherents at Cafaggiolo; and the *condottiere*, Niccolò da Tolentino, believed to have received money through Cosimo's friend, Neri Capponi, had moved down with a band of mercenaries from Pisa to Lastra. Niccolò da Tolentino remained at Lastra for fear that his further advance would result in a tumult in Florence during which Cosimo might be assassinated; but there could be no doubt that he played an important part in Rinaldo degli Albizzi's ultimate decision to abandon hope of having his tiresome prisoner condemned to death.

On 28 September it was decided that Cosimo should be banished for ten years to Padua, that his wily cousin, Averardo, should be sent to Naples, also for ten years, and that his brother, Lorenzo, a quieter and less offensive figure, should be exiled for five years to Venice. All of them, together with the rest of the family, excepting only the Vieri branch, were declared to be *Grandi* and thus excluded from office in Florence for ever. Subsequently the leaders of their party in Florence, Puccio and Giovanni Pucci, were banished to Aquila for ten years;[6] while the two *Priori* who had not followed the Albizzi line during the meetings of the *Signoria* were denied the rewards, in the way of sinecures and appointments of both profit and honour, that were given to all the rest.

When Cosimo, whose many virtues seem not to have included physical courage, was summoned before the *Signoria* to hear the decree of banishment read out to him, he evidently made a rather abject reply. He protested that he had never frequented the Palazzo della Signoria except when summoned, that he had 'always declined to be nominated an official', that far from inciting any Tuscan city to rebel against the government of Florence he had helped to buy several by providing loans to raise troops to conquer them. However, he declared,

As you have decided I am to go to Padua, I declare that I am content to go, and to stay wherever you command, not only in the Trevisian state, but should you send me to live among the Arabs, or any other people alien to our customs, I would go most willingly. As disaster comes to me by your orders, I accept it as a boon, and as a benefit to me and my belongings ... Every trouble will be easy to bear as long as I know that my adversity will bring peace and happiness to the city ... One thing I beg of you, O Signori, that seeing you intend to preserve my life you take care that it should not be taken by wicked citizens, and thus you be put to shame ... Have a care that those who stand outside in the Piazza with arms in their hands anxiously desiring my blood, should not have their way with me. My pain would be small, but you would earn perpetual infamy.

Anxious as he was himself that there should be no uncontrollable violence, the *Signoria* gave orders that their prisoner should be spirited from Florence under cover of night through the Porta San Gallo. He was to be escorted by armed guard to the frontier, and there left to make his own way to Padua by way of Ferrara.

IV

EXILES AND MASTERS

'He is King in all but name'

ON HIS journey into exile, Cosimo was met with compliments rather than reproach. At Ferrara he was warmly welcomed and splendidly entertained by the Marquis; at Padua he was greeted as an honoured guest by the authorities who were obviously delighted to have so distinguished and so rich an exile amongst them. For rich he still certainly was, all the attempts of Rinaldo degli Albizzi to bankrupt him while in prison having failed. 'One should either not lift a finger against the mighty,' Rinaldo commented gloomily to his friends, 'or, if one does, one must do it thoroughly.' He was forced to recognize that, although he had succeeded in temporarily re-moving his enemy from Florence, his own position in the city was now far from secure.

After spending two months in Padua, Cosimo secured permission to join his brother in Venice where he was offered rooms in the monastery of San Giorgio Maggiore. Here he settled down comfort-ably and, no doubt influenced by the knowledge that it was a monas-tery for which Pope Eugenius – having once been a friar there – had much affection, he announced that he would pay for a much-needed new library.[1] He commissioned a design from the young Florentine architect, Michelozzo Michelozzi, who had accompanied him to Venice, the buildings in Florence on which he was working for Cosimo having been brought to a temporary halt.

While in Venice, Cosimo was kept fully and regularly informed of the changing situation in Florence where his supporters were con-tinually plotting the downfall of the Albizzi. At the beginning of

February 1434, the eloquent and highly cultivated Agnolo Acciaiuoli,[2] who had criticized the Albizzi's dictatorial methods, was arrested and sentenced to ten years' banishment to Cosenza. A few weeks later a distant relative of Cosimo, Mario Bartolommeo de' Medici, who was suspected of trying to undermine the Albizzi's foreign policy, was also arrested and banished for ten years.

Cosimo himself warily avoided implication in these conspiracies. He knew that every month the Albizzi were becoming more and more unpopular in Florence and that both Venice and Rome favoured the return of the Medici. He was comforted to learn that since the Medici's departure no other bankers could be found to supply the government 'with so much as a pistachio nut'. By the late summer of 1434, after a decisive defeat by Milanese mercenaries of Florentine troops at Imola, feelings against the government had run so high that a majority of known Medici supporters were elected to the *Signoria*. One of these, Niccolò di Cocco, became *Gonfaloniere*.

Had it not been for the objections of the immensely rich Palla Strozzi, who, since the death of Niccolò da Uzzano, had been the most respected and influential of the moderates in the oligarchy, Rinaldo would have used violence to prevent this new *Signoria* meeting; but he was persuaded to allow the members to enter into office on the understanding that they would be forcibly ejected from the Palazzo della Signoria at the first suggestion that the Medici should be asked to return. Determined not to be browbeaten, the *Signoria* took advantage of Rinaldo's temporary absence from Florence in September to issue the invitation which he dreaded; and, upon his return to the city, they summoned him to their Palazzo. Suspecting that he would be arrested and thrown into the Alberghettino as Cosimo had been, and believing that he had the support of several prominent citizens – including Palla Strozzi, Giovanni Guicciardini,[3] Ridolfo Peruzzi[4] and Niccolò Barbardori[5] – Rinaldo ignored the summons, hurried to his palace, called his remaining adherents to arms and gave orders to the captain of his five-hundred-strong bodyguard to occupy the church of San Pier Scheraggio[6] opposite the Palazzo della Signoria and to prepare to take possession of the Palazzo itself. The guard on the door of the Palazzo was offered as many ducats as would fill his helmet to open the door for Rinaldo's men should the *Signoria* instruct him to lock it.

On the morning of 25 September, Rinaldo's troops began to take up their positions. But the *Signoria* were not to be caught unawares. They brought their own troops into the Piazza, ordered others to march up and down through the streets, and made preparations to withstand a siege by having provisions brought into the Palazzo. They then shut and barricaded the gates, and summoned reinforcements from the surrounding districts. To gain time while these reinforcements were being assembled, they also sent two *Priori* to enter into negotiations with the Albizzi and called upon the services of another far more powerful intermediary who had now arrived in Florence, Pope Eugenius IV.

Having quarrelled with the powerful Colonna family, to which his predecessor, Martin V, had belonged, Pope Eugenius had been driven from Rome by a rampaging mob and had fled to Florence where he was given shelter in the monastery of Santa Maria Novella. Here he was known to have spoken sympathetically of the Medici and to have entertained the hope that a strong government in Florence might ally itself with Venice and help him return to Rome, backed by Medici money. On the afternoon of 26 September, the Pope's representative, Cardinal Vitelleschi, left Santa Maria Novella to find Rinaldo and to bring him back to the monastery for discussions with his Holiness.

By now Rinaldo's situation was becoming desperate. He had succeeded in occupying the Piazza Sant' Apollinare and in closing all entrances to it as preliminary measures before seizing the Bargello, attacking the Piazza della Signoria and burning all the houses of the Medici as well as those of their principal supporters. But although numerous mercenaries, promised the prospect of plunder rather than pay, had been enlisted outside Florence, they were slow in arriving; and many of Rinaldo's troops already inside the city were gradually deserting him. Worst of all, Giovanni Guicciardini, whose support he had deemed essential to his success, now declared that he was prepared to do no more than ensure that his brother, Piero, a known Medici adherent, would not back up the *Signoria*; while Palla Strozzi, who had previously indicated that his five hundred personal men-at-arms would be at Rinaldo's disposal, changed his mind, rode into the Piazza Sant' Apollinare with merely two servants in attendance and then, having spoken briefly to Rinaldo, rode quickly off again. Rinaldo's main supporter, Ridolfo Peruzzi, also began to waver, accepted a summons to appear before the *Signoria* and, having wasted time in fruitless discussions with them, urged Rinaldo to accept Cardinal Vitelleschi's invitation to go to talk to the Pope at Santa Maria Novella.

Accompanied by Peruzzi and Barbadori, and followed by a disorderly squad of armed supporters, Rinaldo rode off to see the Pope soon after six o'clock in the evening. As they approached the houses of the Martelli family, whose senior members were close friends and sometimes business associates of the Medici, an attempt was made to block their way. Fighting broke out, several men were badly wounded, and after the Martelli's guards had been driven back inside their walls, Rinaldo had the utmost difficulty in inducing his men to follow him to Santa Maria Novella rather than to break into the Palazzo Martelli and plunder it.[7] When at last they arrived grumbling before the monastery they sat down in the Piazza, obviously unwilling to wait there long.

Few of them did wait long. Night had long since fallen when Rinaldo emerged from the monastery to find only a small group of them still sitting in the Piazza. It was clear that his spirit was broken. The Pope, so commanding in appearance and manner, so skilled in argument, had persuaded him of the futility of further resistance to the wishes of the *Signoria* which were also, so Rinaldo was informed, the wishes of the Curia. Little reassured by the Pope's promise to do what he could to protect the Albizzi from the vengeance of their opponents, Rinaldo returned to his palazzo.

Two days later, for a full hour, the huge *Vacca* in the tower of the Palazzo della Signoria was tolled to summon the citizens to a *Parlamento*. As the people gathered in the Piazza, which was ringed by troops, Cardinal Vitelleschi and two other representatives of the Pope appeared on the *ringhiera*. Soon afterwards, to the clamorous welcome of fanfares, they were joined there by all the members of the *Signoria* and the officials of the Republic, including the *Notaio delle Riformagioni* who in the time-honoured way called out, 'O, people of Florence, are you content that a *Balìa* shall be set up to reform your city for the good of the people?' The crowd obediently gave their consent; and a *Balìa* of three hundred and fifty citizens was accordingly elected. The sentence of banishment passed on the Medici was immediately revoked, and the family were commended for their good behaviour during the time of their exile from which they were now formally recalled.

On the same day, 28 September 1434, Cosimo left Venice with an escort of three hundred Venetian soldiers; and a few days later, cheered by the peasants in the villages through which he passed, he arrived at his villa at Careggi in time for dinner.[8] The grounds were crowded with welcoming people. There were crowds, too, along the road leading into Florence, and in the city itself masses of people were waiting in the streets, hoping to witness the triumphal return of the Medici to their palace. For fear of uproar, the *Signoria* sent an urgent request to Cosimo not to enter the city that day, but to wait until nightfall. So, after sunset, accompanied by his brother, Lorenzo, one servant and a mace-bearer from the city, he re-entered Florence by a small gateway near the Bargello. He spent the night in a room which had been specially prepared for him in the Palazzo della Signoria; and the next morning, after visiting the Pope to thank him for all he had done for him, he returned to the Palazzo Bardi to the tumultuous cheers of the crowds gathered in the streets 'as though he were returning from a great victory'.

Already sentences had been passed on his opponents. Rinaldo degli Albizzi, his sons and descendants were all banished from Florence – so were branches of several other families, and, in some cases, families in their entirety, in accordance with the custom of considering a crime as much a collective as a personal responsibility. Included in the decrees of banishment were members of the Peruzzi, Guasconi, Guadagni and Guicciardini families, Niccolò Barbadori, and Matteo Strozzi. Indeed, so many well-known names – over seventy in all – appeared in the list of exiles that someone complained to Cosimo that he was almost emptying Florence of its leading citizens. His typically brusque and sardonic reply was, 'Seven or eight yards of scarlet will make a new citizen.'

Rather than risk sharing the fate of the Albizzi upon Cosimo's return, Francesco Filelfo had already fled to Siena where, in the service of the Visconti, he wrote a stream of slanderous abuse of the Medici, incited the Florentines to rise up against them, and even, so it seems, helped to hire a Greek assassin to murder Cosimo. Few regretted the departure from Florence of this tiresome, vain and cantankerous scholar. But many lamented the banishment to Padua of the revered and honest Palla Strozzi, who had never given his full support to the Albizzi and had ultimately abandoned them altogether. Cosimo, however, recognizing that his position in Florence would be more secure if Palla Strozzi, so enormously rich and so dangerously impressionable, were to be compelled to leave, decided not to risk his being pardoned. When asked to put in a good word for him for the sake of past friendship, he did so in a characteristically ambivalent manner, raising no protest when the decision to banish him was finally taken. He apparently comforted himself with the thought that Palla Strozzi would be much happier in Padua where, free from the temptation to meddle in politics, which were not his *métier*, he would settle down contentedly – as, in fact, he did – to a life of quiet study, conversation and bibliomania.

There were to be many times during the next few years when Cosimo had good cause to wish that he could have been left to such a life himself. To assume power in many another Italian state, where executions rather than banishments were commonplace punishments and where the ruler was supported and protected by a powerful army, would have been comparatively simple. But executions and military dictatorships were not in the Florentine tradition, and Florentine tradition was not to be flouted. If Cosimo were to rule successfully, he must appear scarcely to rule at all; if changes in the political structure were to be made, they must be changes calculated to arouse the least offence. Had it been possible to control and expand his bank without political influence he might, perhaps, have been content to remain even further in the background than he actually contrived to do. For he derived the greatest satisfaction from his business, saying that even if it were possible to procure money and possessions with a magic wand he would still continue to work as a banker. But as his father had been forced to recognize, a rich merchant in Florence was ill-advised to try to avoid public office. Even so, Cosimo succeeded in remaining the most powerful man in Florence for years without ever appearing to be much more than an extremely prosperous, generous and approachable banker, prepared to undertake whatever political or diplomatic duties were imposed upon him, and to help direct the financial policies of the State. He acted with the greatest skill to preserve his power, his friend, Vespasiano da Bisticci the bookseller, wrote. 'And whenever he wished to achieve something, he saw to it, in order to escape envy as much as possible, that the initiative appeared to come from others and not from him.' Unable to disguise his enormous wealth, he paid tax at a far higher rate than anyone else in Florence; but, like all rich men of prudence, he kept special accounts which, by exaggerating bad debts, showed his taxable income to be much lower than it was. So no one was quite sure just how rich he was. He was *Gonfaloniere* no more than three times in his entire life; he never considered the possibility of assuming a more obviously permanent control over the government, nor of offending Florentine susceptibilities by attempting any basic reform of the far from satisfactory constitution, other than by establishing a new council known as the *Consiglio Maggiore*, which was intended to have absolute control over national security and taxation and which later developed into the Council of One Hundred, the *Cento*. He scrupulously avoided display and ostentation of any kind, riding a mule rather than a horse, and when it suited him to do so, allowing the vain and talkative, flamboyant and ambitious but not over-intelligent Luca Pitti to appear to be the most powerful man in the Republic.

All was not, of course, as it seemed to be. Though the constitutional institutions and offices of the State remained as before, opponents of the Medici were conveniently excluded from election to the *Signoria* in times of political or military stress by the selection of candidates being entrusted to carefully chosen commissioners known as *Accoppiatori*. A majority of these *Accoppiatori* had links with the

Medici party to which such prominent citizens as Agnolo Acciaiuoli, now recalled from exile, lent their support and of which the wily, eloquent Puccio Pucci, a brilliant organizer raised by Cosimo from the artisan class, was the acknowledged manager. The party was constantly enlarging its base. At Pucci's suggestion the *Grandi* were now all declared *Popolani* which gratified the nobles, who were thus theoretically rendered eligible for election to office, while pleasing the *Popolo Minuto* who chose to interpret the measure as commendably democratic. The people were given greater satisfaction when it was seen that the most talented amongst them, despite their humble origins, were now considered, for the first time in the history of Florence, worthy of holding official positions in the State, though care was taken to ensure that this process did not go too far. The old noble families were still prevented from exercising any real power; and well over three-quarters of the population remained without any political rights at all. Of the 159 newly qualified citizens from the Santa Maria Novella quarter whose names were placed in the *borse* in 1453, no less than 145 were sons, grandsons or brothers of men who had been considered eligible for office in 1449.

Within a few years the Medici party was so strongly rooted – if always loosely knit – and so firmly identified with the interests of Florence as a whole that Cosimo had no need to suppress the voices of opposition. His erstwhile friend, Neri Capponi, old-fashioned and staunchly republican, was permitted to give occasional utterance to his concern about Cosimo's insidiously growing power. So was Giannozzo Manetti, a rich and scholarly merchant who was frequently employed on diplomatic missions. But neither of them had the backing of a party, and both soon departed from the scene: Capponi died in 1455, while Manetti, protesting that he was being ruined by the monstrously heavy taxes levied on his fortune, chose to leave Florence for Naples.

Although the practice was not as widespread as his critics afterwards maintained, there seems little doubt that Cosimo's party did on occasion use the Florence taxation system to break their enemies. Certainly the taxation officers – in the lists of whose names Puccio Pucci figures prominently – were not noted for their impartiality when assessing the taxes due from critics of the regime. Nor did the party managers – who were often used by Cosimo to do unpleasant work with which he did not want to be associated – shrink from buying up at bargain prices the estates of men banished from the Republic, or from making personal fortunes, as Puccio Pucci did, from buying and selling government stock.

For such reasons, though outspoken opposition was rare, the Medici party was far from universally popular; and in troubled times its position was very precarious. In 1458, indeed, it seemed on the verge of dissolution. In January of that year, following a long period of economic stagnation, the merchants and landowners of Florence were horrified to learn that they were to be assessed for a new *catasto*. Then, in the early summer, there was talk of a change in the constitution; there were rumours, too, that opponents of the change had been arrested and tortured to elicit confessions of conspiracy. Feelings in Florence ran so high that Cosimo rented a house in Pavia through the Milanese branch of his bank and prepared to move there with his wife should the situation grow more menacing. His daughter-in-law took his grandchild to his villa at Cafaggiolo, which he had had surrounded by walls and towers for just such an emergency.

On 10 August, the *Gonfalionere*, Luca Pitti, felt obliged to call a complaisant *Parlamento* into existence in the Piazza della Signoria which he prudently filled with mercenary troops and armed supporters of the regime. The members of the *Signoria* walked out of their palace, in their crimson, ermine-lined cloaks, to stand on the *ringhiera*. The *Notaio delle Riformagioni* read out the text of a law creating a new *Balìa*; then, following the ancient precedent, he asked the people in the square below whether they approved its creation. He 'repeated the question three times; but since the *Notaio* had a very weak voice, only a few understood what he was saying and there were not many voices to answer yea'. Nevertheless the few were enough; the *Balìa* was approved; 'the *Signoria* returned to the palace, the citizens to their workshops and the mercenaries to their billets'.

The *Balìa* thereupon immediately introduced those measures which the Medici party had proposed. The powers of the *Accoppiatori* were confirmed for a further ten years, so that the drawing of lots for election to public offices continued to be a mere formality. The power of the *Gonfaloniere* was at the same time much increased. Luca Pitti, whose tenure of that office was shortly to expire, had himself elected one of the ten *Accoppiatori*, while Cosimo's elder son, Piero de' Medici, became another. As supporters of the Medici paraded through the streets, shouting slogans and waving banners, Cosimo's family returned to Florence. The supremacy of their party was now assured and Cosimo himself recognized as the undisputed patriarch of Florence. He was now 'master of the country', in the words of Aeneas Silvius de' Piccolomini who became Pope Pius II in 1458. 'Political questions are settled at his house. The man he chooses holds office ... He it is who decides peace and war and controls the laws ... He is King in everything but name.' Foreign rulers were advised to communicate with him personally and not to waste their time by approaching anyone else in Florence when any important decision was required. As the Florentine historian, Francesco Guicciardini, observed, 'He had a reputation such as probably no private citizen has ever enjoyed from the fall of Rome to our own day.'

ARCHBISHOPS AND ARCHITECTS

*'Never shall I be able to give God enough to set
him down in my books as a debtor'*

NOTHING CONTRIBUTED more lustre to Cosimo's prestige in
the early years of his power than the General Council of the
Greek Orthodox and Roman Catholic Churches which he
helped to persuade his friend, Pope Eugenius IV, to transfer to
Florence in 1439.

Apparently irreconcilable differences, mainly doctrinal, had kept
the two great Churches of Christendom at loggerheads for six centuries; and, within the last two centuries, ever since the soldiers of the
Fourth Crusade had sacked Constantinople at the instigation of their
Venetian paymasters, the quarrel had grown more bitter. But now
that the Ottoman Turks, who had been gnawing at the Eastern
Empire for generations, were almost at the gates of Constantinople,
Pope Eugenius realized that the chances of reconciliation had never
been better. The Eastern Emperor, John Paleologus, had appealed for
help in the name of Christ, and was even prepared to make submission to the Pope if soldiers and seamen from the Catholic west
would help to save Byzantium from impending calamity. The Pope
accordingly decided to summon a Great Council to meet in Italy
without further delay.

He did not only have the unity of the Church in mind. There was
already another Council in session at Bâle; and this Council, called
into existence by the German Emperor, had proposed various reforms in the Church and propounded doctrines which the Pope was

64

not prepared to accept. He had, therefore, attempted to dissolve it. Declining to disperse, the obstinate delegates at Bâle had proclaimed their intention both of making radical changes in the finances of the Curia and of coming to terms with the Eastern Church. But the Pope was not prepared to listen patiently to suggestions of a reduction in papal income; and as for any settlement with the Eastern Church, he was determined to make it himself. So, to put an end to the messages passing between Bâle and Constantinople, the Pope issued an invitation to the Eastern Emperor to come to meet him at Ferrara.

Towards the end of 1437 John Paleologus sailed for Venice, accompanied by the Patriarch of Constantinople and their attendant bishops, theologians, scholars, interpreters and officials – a huge concourse of delegates, seven hundred strong. The great assembly began their deliberations at Ferrara on 8 January 1438. The town was overcrowded and very cold; there were disagreements about precedence; there were quarrels about rites. The Catholic bishop refused to allow the Greeks to celebrate Mass in their own way in his churches; the Patriarch expressed his strongest disapproval of the ban; the Pope was edgy and ill at ease. There were reports that his enemies were hatching plots against him in nearby Bologna, a city which theoretically formed part of the Papal States but which, after declaring itself independent, was now under the lordship of the Bentivoglio family. The Pope was further worried by his embarrassing shortage of money. He had to pledge his towering medieval castle at Assisi as security for the large sums he had borrowed. But even so, he was obliged to stop paying the expenses of his numerous Greek guests.

Cosimo heard of the troubles at Ferrara with satisfaction. He had been much annoyed when that city had been chosen in preference to Florence as a meeting-place for the Council. Any city that acted as host to so important a conference would benefit not merely financially but politically and culturally too. If unity between the Churches were to be achieved this could not but reflect honour upon the place where Christendom was once again made whole. Besides, closer contact with the rulers of the Eastern Empire might well bring much new business to the bankers, traders and merchants of Florence, while conversation with the Greek scholars in the Emperor's entourage would be a relaxation and a delight. When plague broke out in Ferrara towards the end of the year, Cosimo's hopes were fulfilled. His brother, Lorenzo, arrived in the city with assurances that Florence was a much healthier place, that there was ample accommodation there for which no charge whatsoever would be made, and that the Council could avail itself of a loan of 1500 florins a month for as long as the delegates remained in session. Lorenzo's offer was immediately accepted, and preparations were made for leaving Ferrara at once.

The entry into Florence of the Eastern Emperor and his enormous train of attendants was not as impressive as the city's officials had planned. A fierce winter storm of torrential rain drove the thousands of expectant observers off the streets and brought them down from the roof-tops where they had clustered to watch the great procession pass by. The banners and standards lay bedraggled beneath the window-sills; the sounds of the trumpet blasts were carried away by the wind. Cosimo, who had himself been elected *Gonfaloniere* for the occasion, confessed himself much relieved when the city's guests were safely installed in their lodgings.

The Pope and his suite were lodged in the monastery of Santa Maria Novella; the Patriarch was given apartments in the Palazzo Ferranti in the Borgo Pinti; the Eastern Emperor and his attendants moved into the palaces and houses of the exiled Peruzzi family where they were presented with wine and candles, crystallized fruits, marzipan and sweetmeats. The meetings of Council committees were held in Santa Maria Novella, while full sessions took place in Santa Croce.

Attending these sessions as a spectator, Vespasiano da Bisticci was profoundly impressed by the learned speeches and the skilful manner in which the interpreters translated Greek into Latin and Latin into Greek. Yet, as the days passed, it became only too clear that little headway was being made and that tempers on both sides were becoming excessively frayed. A principal point at dispute concerned the origin and nature of the third Person of the Trinity, the Greek opinion in this matter being strongly contested by the Pope's spokesman and his principal adviser, Ambrogio Traversari. Ancient texts

66

were produced, and the Greeks' arguments confounded when a nervous delegate, alarmed by a passage which he recognized as being unfavourable to their case, attempted to scratch it out but in his haste and anxiety scratched out a different one. The Emperor endeavoured to compose the uproar which this attempted fraud produced by suggesting that other and more authoritative manuscripts should be fetched from Constantinople, a proposal that brought forth from a Roman cardinal the magisterial rebuke, 'Sire, when you go to war you should take your arms with you, not send for them in the middle of the battle.'

To the Florentine citizens, however, the Council proved a delightful spectacle. The sight of the bearded men from Constantinople walking through the streets in their astonishingly opulent clothes and their bizarre head-dresses, attended by Moorish and Mongol servants and accompanied by strange animals, was a never-ending source of interest as well as an inspiration to many a Florentine painter from Gentile da Fabriano to Benozzo Gozzoli.

Ultimately, after lengthy private discussions between Traversari and the patient and clever Johannes Bessarion, Archbishop of Nicaea, a compromise on the delicate subject of the Holy Ghost was reached; and this opened the way for agreement on other matters, including the partial authority of the Papacy over the Eastern Church. The crucial document setting forth the terms of the oecumenical compromise was solemnly signed on 5 July 1439; and the following day, during a ceremony in the Cathedral, this dramatic pronouncement was made: 'Let the heavens rejoice and the earth exult, for the wall which divided the Western and Eastern Churches has fallen. Peace and concord have returned.'

The words were spoken by Cardinal Cesarini in Latin, and by Archbishop Bessarion in Greek. Then the Italian cardinal and the Greek archbishop embraced each other and, joined by all the other prelates and the Eastern Emperor, they knelt before the Pope. Afterwards their message to the Christian world, celebrating the triumph of reason, was inscribed on one of the great stone pillars which were to support the Cathedral dome.

But the concord thus joyfully celebrated was of brief duration. No sooner had the delegates returned home to Constantinople than the agreement reached in Florence was so strongly denounced that it had to be abandoned; and the Emperor was to find that the protestations of sympathy and promises of help against the Turk which he had received in Italy were to count for little. Fourteen years later the Sultan's janissaries were to clamber over the smoking walls of Constantinople and the severed head of its last Emperor was to be displayed to the jeers of its conquerors at the top of a column of porphyry.

Yet for Florence, as Cosimo had foreseen, the Council had far happier consequences. As well as profiting the trade of the city, it was an important influence on what was already being spoken of as the *Rinascimento*. The presence of so many Greek scholars in Florence provided an incalculable stimulus to the quickening interest in classical texts and classical history, in classical art and philosophy, and particularly in the study of Plato, that great hero of the humanists, for so long overshadowed by his pupil, Aristotle. Bessarion, whose lodgings had been crowded night after night with Greek and Italian scholars, was prevailed upon to remain in Italy where he was created a cardinal and Archbishop of Siponto. Gemistos Plethon, the great authority on Plato, who had travelled from Constantinople with Bessarion, also agreed to remain in Florence for a time before going home to die in his own country.

Cosimo, who had listened to Plethon's lectures on Plato with the closest attention, was inspired to found in Florence an academy for Platonic studies and to devote much more time to these studies himself. Plethon's return home and Cosimo's subsequent preoccupation with other matters had led to his plans being postponed for a time; but, some years later, when Cosimo adopted the son of one of his physicians, a young medical student named Marsilio Ficino, they were revived. Ficino's enthusiasm for Plato prompted Cosimo to pay for his further education and afterwards to offer to instal him in the villa known as Montevecchio where, in the peace of the country, the young man was to study Greek and to translate all Plato into Latin.[1] Ficino eagerly accepted the offer and, as he grew older and more learned, Cosimo would call him over from Montevecchio to the nearby villa of Careggi, and either alone or with other friends, such as the Greek scholar, John Argyropoulos, whom Cosimo persuaded to come to Florence in 1456, they would discuss philosophical questions far into the night. From these foundations grew the Platonic Academy which was to have so profound an influence upon the development of European thought.

As well as firing Cosimo with the ambition to found a Platonic Academy, the Council of Florence had also enabled him to make several marvellous additions to his library, which was beginning to be recognized as one of the most valuable in the world. For years past, his agents all over Europe and in the Near East had been buying on his instructions rare and important books and manuscripts when-ever they became available, particularly in German monasteries where the monks were supposed to have little idea of their worth. In 1437 the death of Niccolò Niccoli, who was deeply in Cosimo's debt, placed eight hundred more volumes in his hands. The religious books he gave to the monastery of San Marco; the others he kept for himself. Open to all his friends who cared to study there, it was the first library of its kind in Europe, and a generation later served as a model for the Vatican Library in Rome. Constantly increased by Cosimo and his heirs, it was eventually to contain no less than ten thousand *codices* of Latin and Greek authors, hundreds of priceless manuscripts from the time of Dante and Petrarch as well as others from Florence's remoter past.[2]

While spending immense sums on his library, Cosimo also followed his father's example in lavishing money upon the adorn-ment of Florence. Giovanni di Bicci had never much cared for books. Indeed, according to an inventory of his possessions made in 1418, he only owned three books altogether, a Latin life of St Margaret, a sermon by Fra Giovanni also in Latin, and a copy of the Gospels in Italian. But he had always recognized that the honour of the city, and the personal credit of the rich citizen who cared for honour, demanded donations to public building and to the enrichment of buildings already in existence.

The first important project with which Giovanni may have become involved was the provision of new doors for San Giovanni Battista. The Baptistery, '*il mio bel Giovanni*' as Dante called it, was already at least two hundred and fifty years old.[3] Its southern doors, depicting scenes from the life of the saint to whom the church was dedicated, were made by Andrea Pisano in 1330; and in 1402, a year of plague, it had been decided to provide new doors for the northern front as a votive offering, a plea to God not to repeat that dreadful visitation of 1348 when so many thousands of citizens had died in a fearful epidemic that had swept northwards across Europe from Naples. The doors were to be cast in bronze of the most exquisite workmanship, and seven of the leading artists of the day had each been asked to submit a design for a competition of which Giovanni di Bicci de' Medici was probably one of the judges.

The design was to be for a bronze panel representing the sacrifice of Isaac; and, when all the works had been handed in, the judges decided to give special consideration to the submissions of three young artists, all of them in their twenties, Jacopo della Quercia from Siena, Lorenzo Ghiberti and Filippo Brunelleschi, both Florentines. After lengthy deliberations the choice fell upon Ghiberti and Brunelleschi; but when these two were asked to collaborate, the suggestion so annoyed the fiery-tempered Brunelleschi that he stormed out of Florence and went to study architecture in Rome, handing the bronze he had made to Cosimo de' Medici who afterwards placed it in the old sacristy at San Lorenzo where it was displayed behind the altar.

Ghiberti, to whom the sole responsibility was now entrusted, was highly versatile, as a true Renaissance artist was required to be. Trained as a goldsmith, he was painter and architect as well as sculptor. He designed windows for the cathedral of Santa Maria del Fiore as well as golden tiaras for Martin V and Eugenius IV, the gold setting for a cornelian cameo depicting Apollo and Marsyas which belonged to Giovanni de' Medici, and, for Cosimo, a reliquary for the bones of three now forgotten martyrs. At the time of his first commission for the Baptistery he was twenty-three; he was to be seventy-three before his work there was completed. A most exacting

70

perfectionist, he cast and re-cast panel after panel before he was satisfied that the reliefs were as perfect as he could make them, exasperating his assistants by his exhausting, relentless, wearisome striving 'to imitate nature to the utmost'. After twenty-two years' work the doors were finished at last; and, in celebration of so important an event, the *Priori* came out in procession from the Palazzo della Signoria – an exodus permitted them only upon the most solemn occasions – to pay their respects to the artist and his great work.[4] No sooner was the ceremony over, however, than Ghiberti returned to his foundry in the Via Bufalini opposite the hospital of Santa Maria Nuova,[5] and immediately began to work on another set of doors for the eastern front of the Baptistery. He settled down to his task with that same determination to produce an unsurpassable masterpiece as he had brought to the earlier commission. After a further twenty-eight years' work, a frail old man close to death, he was forced reluctantly to conclude that he could make no further improvement. The gilded bronze panels, representing scenes from stories in the Old Testament, were mounted at last, in 1456, in the eastern door of the Baptistery where Michelangelo was later to stand transfixed in wonderment before them and to declare that they were 'fit to be the gates of Paradise'.[6]

Giovanni de' Medici, himself an old man even before Ghiberti's first doors were finished, had by then, together with his son, Cosimo, arranged for the Baptistery to be provided with another masterpiece, the monument to his friend, Pope John XXIII.[7] He had also concerned himself with the building and endowing of the Ospedale degli Innocenti, a hospital for the foundlings of Florence built for the *Arte di Por Santa Maria*,[8] and with the restoration and enlargement of San Lorenzo which, consecrated by St Ambrose in 393, was now falling into ruins. Eight of the leading men of the parish of San Lorenzo agreed to pay for the building of a family chapel, Giovanni undertaking to pay not only for a Medici chapel but also for the sacristy. This work, as also the Ospedale degli Innocenti, was entrusted to Brunelleschi, who had now returned from Rome anxious to display his newly acquired talents and to show Ghiberti how much more there was to art than the casting of bronze panels. His church of San

Lorenzo, which became the family church of the Medici and was later to be enriched with their tombs, is one of the masterpieces of the early Renaissance.[9]

Brunelleschi's most important commission, however, was to provide the massive dome for the cathedral. Men had almost despaired of this ever being done, since the space to be crowned – 138 feet in diameter – was so great. But Brunelleschi, who had made a careful study of the Pantheon and other buildings in Rome, insisted that it could be executed perfectly well and without scaffolding. The committee appointed by the Masons' guild to consider the problem were highly sceptical, particularly as Brunelleschi, petulant and ill-tempered as always, declined to explain to them how he intended to set about the task, insisting that the matter must be left entirely in his hands and that no board of untrained busybodies should be given the opportunity of interfering with his design. The story is told that at one of the committee's inconclusive meetings, Brunelleschi produced an egg, announcing that only he knew how to make it stand on its end: when all the others had confessed their failure to do so, he cracked its top on the table and left it standing there. 'But we could all have done that,' they protested. 'Yes,' replied Brunelleschi crossly, 'and you would say just that if I told you how I propose to build the dome.' On a later occasion Brunelleschi became so obstreperous that the committee gave orders for him to be forcibly removed from their presence. Attendants seized him, carried him out of the palace and dropped him on his back in the Piazza. Thereafter people pointed him out to each other in the streets, shouting, 'There goes the madman!'

Ultimately, after numerous other architects had been consulted and various ideas, such as a dome made of pumice-stone, had been rejected, the Committee gave way and in 1420 Brunelleschi was entrusted with the complicated task. To his exasperation, however, he was required to accept the collaboration of Ghiberti, whose assistance in the early stages was probably more useful to Brunelleschi than Brunelleschi would ever allow or posterity would recognize.

Sixteen years later the dome, as much an extraordinary feat of engineering as of architecture, was finished; and on 25 March 1436 the Feast of the Annunciation, the first day of the year according to the idiosyncratic Florentine calendar, it was consecrated in a splendid five-hour ceremony.[10] A wooden walk, raised on stilts, hung with banners and garlands and covered by a scarlet canopy, was constructed between the Pope's apartments in the monastery of Santa Maria Novella and the door of the Cathedral. At the appointed hour the Pope appeared, clothed in white and wearing his jewelled tiara, and began the slow procession along the carpet which had been laid over the raised boards beneath the canopy. He was followed by seven cardinals, by thirty-seven bishops and archbishops, and by the leading officials of the city led by the *Gonfaloniere* and the *Priori*. At the sound of the choir singing their hymn of praise many of the spectators were seen to be in tears.

After his father's death Cosimo continued to pour Medici money into the building, restoration and embellishment of churches, convents and charitable institutions all over Florence and in the surrounding countryside, as though determined to leave his mark on Tuscany. 'I know the humours of my city,' he once remarked to his friend, Vespasiano da Bisticci. 'Before fifty years have passed we shall be expelled, but my buildings will remain.' First of all, as a member of a committee of four appointed by the *Arte del Cambio*, he had a share in commissioning Ghiberti to make a statue of St Matthew, patron of bankers, for one of the fourteen niches on the outside walls of Orsanmichele which had each been adopted by a guild.[11] In paying for the work, Cosimo contributed more than his fellow bankers, as befitted his wealth, but only slightly more, in accordance with his accustomed discretion. After Orsanmichele, the novices' dormitory and chapel at Santa Croce,[12] the choir of Santissima Annunziata,[13] the library of the now demolished church of San Bartolommeo, the monastery known as La Badia at San Domenico di Fiesole – where Cosimo had his own room[14] – and San Girolamo nei Monti at Fiesole, all appear to have benefited from Cosimo's munificence and from his undoubted knowledge of architectural matters, to which even the leading craftsmen and designers seem to have deferred. Cosimo was also responsible apparently for the restoration of a college for Florentine students in Paris, the renovation of the church of Santo Spirito in Jerusalem and for additions to the Franciscan monastery at Assisi. The year after the completion of the Cathedral dome he undoubtedly provided funds for Michelozzo to rebuild the monastery of San Marco; this was a charitable enterprise which, according to Vespasiano da Bisticci, Cosimo was induced to undertake by Pope Eugenius IV whom he had consulted at a time when his conscience troubled him. He eventually spent the enormous sum of 40,000 ducats on this Dominican monastery, whose exacting, ascetic and intimidating Prior, Antonio Pierozzi – known as Antonino because he was so small – became Archbishop of Florence in 1445, and in 1523 a saint. Antonino was one of Cosimo's closest friends, and the two men could often be found talking together, and with other members of the community, in the large cell which Cosimo reserved for his own private use and to which he retreated by himself when feeling the need for quiet reflection. They often talked, so it was said, of usury and how that besetting sin of a banker's life might be expiated. The Church's ruling was that the usurer might obtain forgiveness only by restoring during his lifetime, or at his death, all that he had gained unrighteously; and cases were known of penitent bankers who had appalled their heirs by stipulating in their wills that the first charge upon their assets must be the payment of full restitution. The distribution of charity was an insufficient atonement; but practical churchmen were quick to suggest that it was a help; and no doubt Cosimo considered it to be so. Certainly he paid out enormous sums. According to his grandson, who came upon an account book covering the thirty-eight years 1434 to 1471, 'the incredible sum of 663,755 florins' had been spent on 'buildings, charities and taxes'. So generous was Cosimo towards San Marco, indeed, that the friars 'in their modesty' felt obliged to protest. But Cosimo passed over their complaints. 'Never,' he used to say, 'shall I be able to give God enough to set him down in my books as a debtor.' He subscribed money to endow the monastery when the restoration was completed, presented the friars with vestments, chalices and illustrated missals, as well as most of Niccolò Niccoli's library, and employed numerous scribes to copy out *codices* to add to their collection.[15]

74

When the work on San Marco was finished, Cosimo decided to build a new palazzo for his own family. He had moved some years before from the Palazzo Bardi to his father's house in the Piazza del Duomo which he had improved and extended; but while this old family house might have been large enough for his family's personal needs, it was far too small for his business which urgently required new store-rooms and counting-houses. As the site for the new building he chose the corner of the Via Larga, the widest street in the city, and the Via de' Gori which lay beneath the northern wall of the church of San Giovannino degli Scolopi.[16] The architect he selected was the brilliant, cantankerous Filippo Brunelleschi whose work on the nave of the nearby church of San Lorenzo was now almost completed. But when he saw Brunelleschi's plans and wooden model he thought them altogether too splendid and ornate, and rejected them as tactfully as he could. All the buildings which he had commissioned, and which he liked to consider as much his own works as those of the architects who had designed them, were quiet, restrained, composed and unemphatic and he wished his own palace to be the same. So, setting Brunelleschi's plans aside, he turned instead to the younger architect, Michelozzo Michelozzi, a decision which so angered Brunelleschi that, in a bout of fury, he smashed his model 'into a thousand pieces'.

Michelozzo was also a Florentine by birth, the son of a tailor whose family originally came from Burgundy. Formerly a pupil of Donatello, Michelozzo had already made a name for himself as a sculptor of exceptional promise, notably as the executor of the tomb for John XXIII in the Baptistery. His designs were less grand than those of Brunelleschi, much more in tune with Cosimo's taste for spacious simplicity and restraint of colour. Envy, Cosimo used often to say, was a weed that should not be watered; and he was anxious to ensure that the Palazzo Medici should give no offence to any of his critics. Since it was to contain offices and counting-houses for the family's business interests as well as private apartments it could not, of course, be too small. Cosimo's enemies, naturally, vastly exaggerating his intentions, condemned the palazzo as a monument to his greed. 'He has begun a palace which throws even the Colosseum at

Rome into the shade,' wrote one of them. 'Who would not build magnificently if he could do so with other people's money?' Yet when compared with other palaces which were to be built within the next two decades, such as the Palazzo Rucellai and the formidable Palazzo Pitti, the Medici Palace was far from grandiose. In the middle of the fifteenth century it was considered to be worth about 5,000 florins. Certainly, as time passed and it was altered and enlarged by both Cosimo's descendants and the Riccardi family into whose hands it eventually passed, the palace took on a more imposing appearance; but in the beginning it was remarkable less for its grandeur than for its originality. The days had passed when town houses had also to be fortresses with towers at the corners and machicolated battlements overhanging the street; but not until Michelozzo set to work on the Palazzo Medici had a house appeared in Florence which combined the delicacy of early Italian Gothic with the calm, considered stateliness of the classic taste.[17]

The walls of the ground floor were faced with those massive rough-hewn stones which give the effect known as *rustica* and which Michelozzo used so as 'to unite an appearance of solidity and strength, with the light and shadow so essential to beauty under the glare of an Italian sun'. Originally, there were no windows at ground level on the Via Larga front, the fortress-like appearance being broken only by a huge arched gateway. But above the gateway, where the family were to live, the sombre effect was softened by rows of arched windows, flanked by columns Doric on the first floor, Corinthian on the second, the whole being overhung by a cornice eight feet high, the top of which towered, like the cornices of classical Rome, in a powerful line over the Via Larga. Facing the Via de' Gori there was an open loggia, the arches of which were later filled in by those curved, barred windows known as 'kneeling windows' which were designed by Michelangelo. On the corner of the loggia was one of those beautiful iron lamps made by Niccolò Grosso, who was known as '*il Caparra*',[18] and above it the Medici arms carved in stone, with Cosimo's personal device of three peacocks' feathers, signifying the three virtues he most admired – temperance, prudence and fortitude – sprouting from the shield.

Before the Palazzo Medici was finished, Michelozzo began work on another house for Cosimo, a new villa in the Mugello. Cosimo never tired of country life. Whenever possible he left Florence to spend as long as he could at Il Trebbio or at his beloved villa of Careggi where he was able to read in peace, go out and perform those country tasks from which he derived such solace, pruning his vines and tending his olives, planting mulberry and almond trees, and talking to the country people from whom he acquired those peasant proverbs and fables with which, on his return to the city, he enlivened his own conversation. Here at Careggi he could talk to his friends without the irritation of constant interruption; he could summon his young protégé, the little, clever, ugly Marsilio Ficino, to come over from the villa of Montevecchio to keep him company, to have a meal with him, or perhaps to play chess, the only game Cosimo ever did play. He wrote to Ficino in one characteristic letter in 1462,

Yesterday I arrived at Careggi not so much for the purpose of improving my fields as myself. Let me see you, Marsilio, as soon as possible. Bring with you the book of our favourite Plato, which I presume you have now translated into Latin according to your promise; for there is no employment to which I so ardently devote myself as to discover the true road to happiness. Do come then, and do not forget to bring with you the Orphean lyre.

Cosimo had no intention of leaving Careggi; but he wanted another villa, more remote, one which would serve as a place of retreat in times of trouble or plague and which would help to bind the country people of the Mugello more closely to his family. He chose a site at Cafaggiolo where the Medici had owned land for generations; and here, to Michelozzo's designs, a new villa began to take shape in 1451.[19]

A few years later Michelozzo began work on yet another Medici villa. This was at Fiesole where Cosimo's son, Giovanni, chose to reconstruct the castle-like villa known as Belcanto.[20] The land around it was steep and stony, useless for farming, as Cosimo disapprovingly observed, cross with his son for spending so much money merely to enjoy a view. But, as Giovanni protested, that was the whole point of Fiesole. His villa there would be built for pleasure alone: on summer evenings he and his family and friends would be able to sit upon the shaded terrace looking down upon the roofs of Florence.

But this was not Cosimo's idea of a pleasant outlook. As he told Giovanni, he far preferred looking out from the windows at Cafaggiolo where all the surrounding land belonged to him. Besides, he was growing old, too old to think about new houses. When work on the Villa Medici at Fiesole was finished in 1463 he was seventy-four. For thirty difficult years he had been controlling the foreign policy of the Republic and the strain had weighed heavily upon him.

❧ VI ❧

WAR AND PEACE

'Rencine? Rencine? Where is Rencine?'

COSIMO'S SUPREME importance as arbiter of Florence's foreign policy had never been in doubt. Official correspondence was conducted through the *Signoria*; but no important decision was ever reached without reference to the Medici Palace. Foreign ambassadors were frequently to be seen passing through the gateway; Florentine ambassadors invariably called upon Cosimo before taking up their appointments.

For years his main preoccupation had been Milan. Patiently, doggedly, he had done all he could to persuade the Florentines that their standard policy of hostility to the Duchy was misguided and inexpedient, that they would be far better off with the Milanese as their friends even at the cost of antagonizing their traditional allies, the Venetians. At the beginning of the century Venice had enormously increased her possessions by conquering Verona, Vicenza, Padua, Belluno and Feltre, and, after defeating the Turkish fleet, had extended the frontiers of the Most Serene Republic far down the Dalmatian coast. In those years Florence had been thankful to have so powerful and rich an ally in her festering quarrel with Milan whose Duke, Filippo Maria Visconti, had been encouraged to make war on Florence by friends of the exiled Albizzi.

This Visconti was widely believed to be mad and was certainly unbalanced. He had been known on summer days to strip the rich clothes from his grotesquely fat and dirty body and to roll about naked in his garden. So ugly that he refused to have his portrait painted, so weak on his deformed legs that he could not rise from his chair without leaning on a page; so nervous that he had been known to scream at the sight of a naked sword; so frightened of thunder that he had a sound-proof room built in his palace; so fond of practical jokes that he would suddenly produce a snake from his sleeve when talking to an unsuspecting courtier, he was also wilful, secretive and inordinately suspicious. Nevertheless, he was undeniably an astute politician who, during the thirty-five years of his rule, succeeded in recovering much of the territory in Lombardy which his father had conquered but which had been lost while he was still a boy. His attempts to extend the Duchy southwards into Tuscany were not, however, so successful, despite assurances from the Albizzi and other Florentine exiles that he had merely to appear in force in the territories of the Republic for the people to take up arms against their oppressors, the Medici. His invading forces were defeated in 1437 at the battle of Barga; they were thwarted again in 1438. And in June 1440 one of his most talented *condottieri*, Niccolò Piccinino, was routed by an army of Florentine mercenaries in a savage battle near Anghiari on the Arno. After this defeat, Piccinino and the remnants of his army marched quickly out of Tuscany, followed by the Albizzi whose hopes of returning to power were finally dashed. Rinaldo degli Albizzi rode dispiritedly off on a pilgrimage to the Holy Land, while the Florentines took possession of large tracts of lands in the mountainous district of the Cesentino, formerly the domain of an anachronistic feudal lord who had misguidedly joined forces with the Milanese.

At the time of his setback at Anghiari, Duke Filippo Maria Visconti was forty-eight. He had been married twice, first to the rich widow of one of his father's *condottieri* whom he charged with adultery and had executed, then to a younger woman whom he had locked up after a dog had howled on their wedding night. By neither wife did he have a child; but a mistress bore him a daughter whom he called Bianca. This Bianca had many suitors but none more persistent than Francesco Sforza.

Francesco Sforza, too, was illegitimate. His father, an illiterate peasant from the Romagna whose name was Giacomo Attendolo, had been kidnapped by a gang of adventurers. After the death of

(*above*). Cosimo di Giovanni de' Medici, *Pater Patriae*, 1389–1464, by Pontormo.

(*right*). Giovanni di Bicci de' Medici, 1360–1429, by Bronzino.

ero di Cosimo de' Medici, 'il Gottoso', 1416–1469, by Mino da Fiesole.

4 (*top left*). Giovanni di Cosimo de' Medici, 1424–1463, by Mino da Fiesole.

5 (*top right*). Giuliano di Piero de' Medici, 1453–1478, by Botticelli.

6 and 7 (*above*). Lorenzo di Piero de' Medici, 'il Magnifico', 1449–1492.
Left a painted terracotta by Verrocchio. *Right* anonymous painting.

A detail of *The Procession of the Magi*, the mural by Gozzoli in the chapel in the Medici Palace.
gestions about the identity of the various figures are given on pages 110–11;
the man on the horse on the far right has also been identified as Piero de' Medici, Gozzoli's patron.
zzoli left no room for doubt as to his own identity by painting his name on his hat.

9 (*above*). Botticelli's *Adoration of the Magi*. As suggested on page 109 the young man with the sword
the left is probably intended to represent Lorenzo the Magnificent. The possible identity of the othe
figures is given on page 320. The man on the extreme right is usually taken to be Botticelli himself.

10 (*opposite above*). The courtyard of the Medici Palace was designed by Michelozzo Michelozzi.
It is described on page 90.

11. Botticelli's *Young Woman*, though formerly supposed to represent either Clarice Orsini or
Simonetta Vespucci, is more likely to be a portrait of Fioretta Gorini, mistress of Giuliano de' Medic
and mother of Giulio who later became Pope Clement VII.

PIERO·DI·LORENZO·DI·PIERO·DE·MEDICI·

12 (*top left*). Piero di Lorenzo de' Medici, 1471–1503, by Bronzino.

13 (*top right*). Girolamo Savonarola, 1452–1498, by Fra Bartolommeo.

14. The cloister of San Marco. Michelozzo was commissioned to rebuild this monastery by Cosimo de' Medici. Savonarola became Prior here in 1491.

(*top*). King Charles VIII's army entering Florence on 17 November 1494,
[Gr]anacci. A corner of the Medici Palace can be seen on the left.

[T]he execution of Savonarola in the Piazza della Signoria on 23 May 1498, by an unknown artist.

17. The Medici villa il Trebbio by Giusto Utens. Cosimo retreated to this villa during the anti-Medicean plot of 1433. It later passed into the hands of Giovanni delle Bande Nere.

18. The Medici villa at Cafaggiolo by Giusto Utens. It was rebuilt for Cosimo by Michelozzo on an estate which the family had owned for generations. One of the towers has since been demolished.

their leader he himself had taken command of them, had adopted the name of Sforza and, before being drowned in the Pescara River while trying to save the life of a young page, had led his men into battle in the service of both Naples and the Pope. At the age of twenty-two, in 1424, Francesco had succeeded his father in command of what was by then one of the best trained bands of mercenaries in Italy, and had subsequently shown exceptional military skill in fighting for the Visconti, the Venetians, the Pope and anyone else prepared to pay the high price he demanded for his services. He was an extremely strong, amiable, down-to-earth man, blunt of speech, with a big, honest face and the simple tastes of a man accustomed to the rough life of a camp. Pope Pius II later wrote of him:

He was very tall and bore himself with great dignity. His expression was serious, his way of speaking quiet, his manner gracious, his character in general such as became a prince. He appeared the only man of our time whom Fortune loved. He had great physical and intellectual gifts. He married a lady of great beauty, rank and virtue by whom he had a family of very handsome children [eight in all, as well as eleven illegitimate children]. He was rarely ill. There was nothing he greatly desired which he did not obtain.

To the annoyance of his occasional employer, the Duke of Milan, he had already carved out a small empire for himself in the Marches; but his ambitions were far from satisfied by that. By marrying Bianca he might, upon her father's death, succeed to the great Duchy of Milan.

Visconti did not much care for the idea of having this peasant's bastard as a son-in-law; but Sforza was not only the best soldier in Italy but a political force of consequence. So in November 1441 the Duke at last agreed to the marriage, giving his daughter Pontremoli and Cremona to present to her bridegroom as a dowry and making some rather indeterminate promises about the succession to the Duchy of Milan.

Visconti promises being notoriously unreliable, it came as no surprise when, upon Duke Filippo Maria's death six years later, it was learned that he had nominated Alfonso, the Aragonese King of Naples, as his heir. Italy was now plunged into uproar. The Duke of

Orleans also put forward a claim to the Duchy of Milan as a son of Valentina Visconti. At the same time the German Emperor asserted his ancient rights to Milan; while Venice announced that she would brook no interference in her own claims in Lombardy. As Francesco Sforza prepared to march to take possession of what he considered to be his rightful inheritance, the Milanese – attempting to settle the problem to their own satisfaction – declared themselves masters of their city and re-established their old republic.

In Florence, Cosimo watched the crisis develop with an alert and anxious eye. He had met Francesco Sforza several years before, and had been deeply impressed by his manner and the force of his personality. The friendship then begun had since become more intimate and had been much strengthened by the generous loans which Sforza, in constant financial difficulties, had little difficulty in raising from the Medici bank. As well as lending him money and ensuring that he received additional subsidies from Florentine taxpayers, Cosimo exercised all the political and diplomatic influence he could bring to bear on his behalf. And it was, in fact, largely through Cosimo's endeavours that Sforza, after three years of warfare and diplomatic negotiations, triumphantly entered Milan as Duke in March 1450.

Cosimo's unremitting support of Sforza had aroused much angry criticism in Florence, particularly from two of the city's most prominent citizens, Neri Capponi, who had played an important part in the defeat of Piccinino at Anghiari, and Giannozzo Manetti, the distinguished diplomat. Protests became even more outspoken when, to the extreme annoyance of Naples and Venice, Cosimo recognized Sforza as Lord of Milan before any other state had done so. It was outrageous, so opponents of the Medicean regime maintained, that Florentines should be taxed for the sake of an erstwhile *condottiere*, now a self-proclaimed duke, the declared enemy of a sister republic which was a traditional ally. Was not Cosimo's anxiety to back Sforza dictated by fear of losing the huge sums of money he had lent him, and by his expectations of having a more profitable and stable relationship with a despot than he could hope to have with a republic?

Cosimo argued that Venice could no longer be considered a

reliable ally: her interests in the Levant clashed with those of Florence; her territorial possessions in the eastern Mediterranean made her an enemy of Turkey with whose empire Florence enjoyed a mutually profitable trade; her shipping was a tiresome rival of Florence's growing fleet. On the other hand, Milan in the firm grasp of the grateful Sforza would prove an enormously valuable ally both against the encroachments of Venice and in Florence's still unfulfilled ambition to gain possession of Lucca. Above all, an alliance of Florence with Sforza was the one sure way of bringing peace to Italy, and without peace the commerce of the city could never hope to thrive. Cosimo's arguments were strongly and ably supported by Nicodemo Tranchedini da Pontremoli, Sforza's clever and persuasive ambassador in Florence who was to remain there for seventeen years.

It was some time, however, before these arguments gained much favour. But when the Venetians reacted against Cosimo's policy by allying themselves with the King of Naples and threatening an invasion of Tuscany, Cosimo saw his opportunity to overcome the Florentines' prejudices. Making one of his rare appearances at the Palazzo della Signoria, where Venetian ambassadors had gone to protest and issue warnings against the proposed alliance with Milan, he intervened personally in the debate to condemn their government as aggressors. He was not a gifted orator; but his words were clear, strong and effective. In August Florence's formal alliance with Milan was signed.

Its repercussions were widespread and immediate: the Venetians urged the German Emperor to break up the new alliance; the Eastern Emperor was induced to withdraw the privileges of all Florentine merchants who were simultaneously expelled from Naples and Venice; Venetian agents were paid to intensify anti-Medicean feeling in Florence. Cosimo countered by closing down the Venetian branch of his firm and opening a new branch in Milan. At the same time, through those of his managers involved in the eastern trade, he managed to obtain concessions from the Turks in order to compensate Florentine merchants for the privileges withdrawn by the Greeks; and he made diplomatic overtures to Florence's traditional friend,

France, so as to offset the advantages which Venice and Naples might have gained by approaching the German Emperor.

The negotiations at the French court required exceptional skill, for neither Cosimo nor Sforza wanted to precipitate French intervention in Italy, which both recognized to be almost inevitable once France and England had settled their differences. Rather did they hope to ingratiate themselves in Paris by making indeterminate offers of assistance should the French King, Charles VII, decide to insist upon Angevin claims to the Kingdom of Naples. The delicate discussions were left to Cosimo's charming and capable friend, Agnolo Acciaiuoli, who by cajolery, flattery, and that grandiloquent rhetoric so relished by connoisseurs of Renaissance diplomacy made a most favourable impression upon the conceited, ambitious and erratic King of France. In April 1452, at Montil-les-Tours, a treaty was signed: France undertook to come to the help of Florence and Milan should they be attacked; Sforza was recognized as Duke of Milan; and, in return, Charles VII was assured that there would be no interference from either Florence or Milan if he decided to move against Naples.

Provoked by this treaty – and anxious to break up the new alliance while France was still preoccupied with England – Venice and Naples both declared war on Florence and Milan; and King Alfonso's illegitimate son, Don Ferrante, marched on Tuscany. The Florentines listened to the news of his approach with the greatest alarm; crowds of citizens rushed to Cosimo's palace, demanding to know what was to be done to save the city from attack; one frantic merchant burst into his room, shouting 'Rencine has fallen! Rencine has fallen!' Cosimo, affecting never to have heard of this small town inside the Tuscan border, coolly replied, 'Rencine? Rencine? Where is Rencine?'

He was not nearly as confident as he took pains to appear. Feeling in the city was running high against him. The alliance with Milan was proving not merely a dangerous experiment, but an excessively expensive one as well; for Florence was having to pay for Sforza's defences as well as her own, and the oppressively burdensome taxes, so Sforza's agent in Florence reported to Milan, were daily increasing the number of Cosimo's enemies. Agnolo Acciaiuoli was sent hurrying back to France to enlist the help of Charles VII; but the French, with the English rampaging around Bordeaux, were for the moment reluctant to commit themselves to action on another front.

Cosimo fell ill and took to his bed; demands for peace became insistent; several of his leading supporters took the precaution of keeping away from his palace. Then, to the immense relief of the Medicean party, there came good news from France: Acciaiuoli had succeeded in persuading René of Anjou to come to the help of the alliance in exchange for reciprocal support of driving Alfonso's Aragonese brood out of Naples. The intervention of a rough, marauding French army, which alarmed its allies even more than its enemies, followed by the Turks' capture of Constantinople in May 1453, brought hopes of peace in Italy at last. These hopes were realized at Lodi in April 1454. And four months later, as the Turkish menace grew ever more threatening, Florence, Milan, the Pope and Venice drew together in a Most Holy League formed to guarantee the status quo within Italy and to withstand aggression from without.

Peace had come none too soon for Cosimo. 'The citizens have raised a great clamour about the new taxes,' the Venetian ambassador reported;

and, as never before, have uttered abusive words against Cosimo ... Two hundred respected families, who lived on the revenues of their possessions are in a bad way, their properties having been sold in order to enable them to pay their taxes. When this imposition was levied, Cosimo had to announce that no one need complain because he would advance the money required and would not reclaim it until it suited everyone concerned. In order to retain popular favour, he has had to distribute many bushels of corn every day amongst the poor who were crying out and grumbling because of the rise in prices.

Cosimo's patient and far-sighted policy was, however, at last rewarded with success. Venice had been checked and was now too concerned with the Turks to pose any further threat to Tuscany; Sforza, firm ally of Florence, was universally accepted as Duke of Milan. The treaty, of which Naples, too, was a signatory, offered the first real hope of a general peace that Italy had had for more than fifty years.

Cosimo was too much of a realist, of course, to suppose that the kind of loose alliance of Italian states which had now been formed was likely to endure. But for Florence, at least, so long as Cosimo lived, there were to be no more costly, unprofitable wars.

Nor was there to be any question of Florence joining the crusade against the Turks which the Pope preached with such fervour after the fall of Constantinople. As both the acknowledged arbiter of Italian policy and the papal banker, Cosimo was one of the first recipients of the Pope's appeal. He was asked to supply two galleys, equipped and manned, which were to be launched against the Turks in return for indulgences for the Florentines' immortal souls. Tactfully and guardedly, he replied to the request, making the excuse which he and his descendants were to find so useful:

When you solemnly speak of our immortal life to come, who can be so unimaginative as not to be uplifted by your words, not to glimpse the glory of his own immortality? ... But with regard to your present proposition, most blessed Father ... you write to me not as a private man who is satisfied with the mediocre dignity of a citizen, but as though I were a reigning prince ... You well know how limited is the power of a private citizen in a free state under popular government.

Other Italian states replied to the Pope's appeal with similar evasions. Only the Venetians, who stood to profit in this life as well as in the next by the successful outcome of a Holy War, were more forthcoming. Undeterred, the Pope determined to sail under the banner of the Cross; but before he could put to sea he died of malaria. The Medici bank officially lamented his loss, and transferred their attentions to his successor.

As a banker, Cosimo was quite as astute as his father; and under his direction the family business continued to expand. Noted for his brilliance as an organizer, for his astonishingly retentive memory, and for a tireless industry that sometimes kept him working all

through the night, Cosimo was also well known for the unquestion-
ing loyalty he demanded and obtained from his branch managers
who, wisely chosen and closely supervised, were expected to remit
to Florence regular and lengthy reports of their activities and who
received, in return, a generous share of profits. Finding his father's
associates, the Bardi, too old-fashioned in their methods, he took in
as partners two brilliant young men, Antonio di Messer Francesco
Salutati, manager of the Rome branch, and Giovanni d'Amerigo
Benci, manager at Geneva. And with their help the business grew
more rapidly than ever until the trade mark of the Medici bank – ✠ –
the bank's motto, '*Col Nome di Dio e di Bona Ventura*', and Medici
representatives could be found in almost every important capital and
commercial centre in Europe: London, Naples, Cologne, Geneva,
Lyons, Bâle, Avignon, Bruges, Antwerp, Lübeck, Ancona, Bologna,
Rome, Pisa and Venice. Some branches of the bank were quite small;
others were no more than temporary establishments, catering for the
trade of some passing fair or council. None of them had a large staff.
In 1470 the average number of men employed at the various branches
was between nine and ten, cashiers being paid about forty florins a
year, apprentices twenty. Even so, many of the Medici establishments
were amongst the largest commercial enterprises in their respective
cities, and their managers, as well as being astute men of business,
were also political agents of the Florentine Republic. The branch in
Milan, for example, was a kind of ministry of finance housed in a
palazzo made available to the bank by the Duke, Francesco Sforza,
and greatly enlarged at Cosimo's expense to the designs of Michelozzo. The branch in Rome, which followed the peregrinations of the
Curia, enjoyed a comparable prestige and was even more profitable.
As Cosimo's father had cultivated Baldassare Cossa, the future Pope
John XXIII, so Cosimo himself had cultivated Tommaso Parentucelli, the Tuscan doctor's son who became Bishop of Bologna and
finally Pope Nicholas V. Parentucelli, who as a young man had been
forced by poverty to leave the University of Bologna and to accept
work as tutor in Florence to the children of Rinaldo degli Albizzi
and Palla Strozzi, had distinguished himself at the Council of
Florence after which he had given invaluable advice to Cosimo on

the development of the Medici library. A friendly, witty man of great learning, of whom his friend and fellow humanist, Aeneas Silvius de' Piccolomini, used to say, 'What he does not know is outside the range of human knowledge', Parentucelli had seemed to Cosimo a man worth backing. He had appreciated his orderly mind, his discreet yet purposeful manner; and when asked for a loan he had had no hesitation in granting the Bishop all that was required. On the Bishop's becoming Pope, these close links with the Medici bank had been maintained to their mutual advantage. Nicholas V's friend Piccolomini, who was elected Pope in 1458 and chose the title Pius II, kept up the papal tradition of friendship with the Medici and continued to entrust them with the Curia's financial affairs. When he came to Florence in 1469 he stayed as a matter of course at the Palazzo Medici, where he and Cosimo seem to have become quite intimate. When bidding him good-bye, Cosimo

tried to kiss the Pope's foot, but because he was crippled with gout was unable to bend. He laughed and said, 'Two Florentines named Papa and Lupo returning from the country met in the Piazza and offered each other their hands and a kiss. But they were both very fat and there was such corporosity (if I may use that word) on both sides that they could only touch their stomachs. Gout now denies me what corpulence refused them.'

As well as undertaking all the customary services of a bank, the Medici houses undertook all manner of commissions for their customers, supplying tapestries, sacred relics, horses and slaves, painted panels from the fairs at Antwerp, choir boys from Douai and Cambrai for the choir of St John in Lateran, and even, on one occasion, a giraffe. They were also importers and exporters of all manner of spices, of silk and wool and cloth. They dealt in pepper and sugar, olive oil, citrus fruits, almonds, furs, brocades, dyes, jewellery, and above all, in alum, a transparent mineral salt essential to the manufacture of fast, vivid dyes and widely used in glassmaking and tanning. Up till 1460 nearly all European supplies of alum came from Asia Minor, the most productive mines near Smyrna being controlled by the Genoese until 1455 and thereafter by the Turks. But in 1460 huge new deposits were discovered at

Tolfa near Civitavecchia in the Papal States, where thousands of tons of alum had been deposited by vapours emitted from extinct volcanoes. No commercial concern was better placed than the Medici to exploit this valuable find. So, in 1466 the bank signed an agreement with the Pope which gave them and their partners in the Societas Aluminum the right to work these enormously profitable mines and to sell their products abroad.

Some years later the French historian, Philippe de Commines, described the bank not merely as the most profitable organization in Europe but as the greatest commercial house that there had ever been anywhere. 'The Medici name gave their servants and agents so much credit,' Commines wrote, 'that what I have seen in Flanders and England almost passes belief.'

✤ VII ✤

ARTISTS AND MOURNERS

'Too large a house now for so small a family'

ON PASSING through the archway in the Via Larga, the
visitor to the Medici Palace entered a charming and graceful
inner courtyard, a square, arcaded *cortile* with pillars supporting a sweep of arches above which were eight marble medallions,
several of them copies of cameos and the reverse side of medals in the
Medici collection. Under the arcades were classical busts, statues,
columns, inscriptions and Roman sarcophagi including the fourth-
century stone coffin used for Cosimo's great-great-great-great grandfather's cousin, Guccio de' Medici, who had been *Gonfaloniere* in
1299. Perhaps there already, and certainly there later, were Donatello's
bronze statue of *David*[1] and his *Judith Slaying Holofernes*.[2]

Donatello was born in Florence in 1386, the son of Niccolo di
Betto Bardi, a merchant who had been ruined by his support of the
Albizzi. Like Ghiberti he had been trained as a goldsmith and had
worked for a time in Ghiberti's studio, but rather than work on the
Baptistery doors he had left with Brunelleschi for Rome where he
studied classical art while working in a goldsmith's shop. On his
return to Florence he turned his hand to all manner of work, as happy
to execute a coat-of-arms for a chimney-piece, or a small bronze panel
in low relief, as he was to carve a big marble figure. He received
commissions for work in the Cathedral, in Giotto's campanile, in
Orsanmichele and in the Basilica of San Lorenzo where he later
designed the bronze pulpits. But although his works were much
admired – his marble *St George* at Orsanmichele, in particular, was
recognized as a masterpiece – it was not until his bronze *David* was

90

completed that his genius and originality were fully understood. His other statues, like all statues of his time, had been made to occupy a particular position in a building as an architectural motif or ornamentation, whereas the *David* was not only an astonishingly beautiful and emotive work of art, it was also a remarkable innovation, the first free-standing figure cast in bronze since classical times.

Some of his contemporaries found it shocking. That Donatello was a homosexual was bad enough; that he should have portrayed the young male form so lovingly, realistically and sensually, with so obvious a delight in the flesh, was outrageous. To Cosimo such objections seemed wholly unreasonable, obtusely at variance with those classical Greek ideals which were Donatello's inspiration. In his own devotion to the humanist spirit, Cosimo had accepted the dedication of Antonio Beccadelli's *Hermaphroditus* which, in the manner of Catullus, celebrates the pleasures of homosexual love. In the same spirit he honoured the genius of Donatello and the ancient art that had inspired it.

Cosimo grew deeply attached to Donatello, for whom he assumed a kind of paternal responsibility. He saw to it that he was never short of work, either by giving him commissions himself or by recommending him to his friends. With the work that Donatello did for the Medici collection such as a bronze head of Contessina de' Medici, Cosimo was never disappointed; for, as Giorgio Vasari said, 'Donatello loved Cosimo so well that he could understand all he wanted, and he never let him down.' With other patrons, however, Donatello was not so fortunate. One of these, a Genoese merchant who had commissioned a bronze head on Cosimo's recommendation, complained, when Donatello had finished it, that it was much too expensive. The dispute was referred to Cosimo who, having had the bronze carried up to the roof of the Medici Palace and placed in a good light against the blue of the sky, suggested that the price the merchant was offering was really not enough. The Genoese insisted that, on the contrary, it was more than generous, adding that since Donatello had finished the work in a month, the cost worked out at over half a florin a day. Infuriated by this remark, protesting that the merchant was obviously more accustomed to bargaining for beans than bronzes, Donatello knocked it off the parapet into the street where it was 'shattered into a thousand pieces'. The mortified merchant offered Donatello twice as much if he would do the head again, but neither his promises nor Cosimo's entreaties could persuaded him to do so.

Donatello was not really interested in money. In his studio he put what he earned into a wicker basket which hung by a cord from the ceiling; and all his workmen and apprentices and even his friends were allowed to help themselves to what they needed without asking him. Nor was he interested in clothes. Cosimo, distressed by the simple not to say ragged attire in which he walked about the streets, gave him a smart suit with a red cloak and cap as a present one feast day. But Donatello wore them for a few days only, before putting his old clothes back on again. When he was too old to work he was given a small farm on the Medici estates near Cafaggiolo; but he did not like it there. He was muddled by the accounts and irritated by the peasant who worked the land for him and who kept complaining about the wind that had blown the roof off his dovecot, or about the authorities that had confiscated his cattle because the taxes had not been paid, or about the storm that had ruined his fruit and vines. Donatello begged that the farm should be taken back into the family estate. This was done and he was given instead the income that he ought to have received from it. 'Donatello was more than satisfied with this arrangement,' so Vasari said, 'and, as a friend and servant of the Medici family, he lived carefree and happy all the rest of his life.'

While Donatello was carving statues and medallions for the Medici Palace, Fra Filippo Lippi was also there painting pictures. Twenty years younger than Donatello, Fra Filippo was born in Florence, the son of a butcher who died when Filippo was a child. His mother also being dead, he was placed at the age of sixteen as a novice in the community of the Carmelite friars of Santa Maria del Carmine.[3] But he had not the least taste for the religious life, and the only benefit he seems to have derived from his time with the Carmelites was a desire to emulate the great Masaccio whom he saw at work in their chapel of the Brancacci. Indeed, his interest in art appeared to the friars to be Fra Filippo's one virtue. He was a liar, a drunkard, a lecher and a fraud; and his superiors were profoundly relieved when he left the convent, abandoned his vows and was seized by Barbary pirates off the coast of Ancona while out sailing with some friends. On escaping from his chains he made for Naples, then returned to Florence where his lovely altarpiece for the nuns of Sant' Ambrogio brought his remarkable gifts to the attention of Cosimo de' Medici. Disregarding his reputation both as whore-monger and scrounger, Cosimo asked him to work for him and it was at the Medici Palace that several of his earlier masterpieces were produced, including the *Coronation of the Virgin*.[4] Later Cosimo obtained work for him at Prato where, in frescoes painted on the walls of the chapel of the high altar in the church of St Stephen, Filippo introduced a portrait of the Rector of the church, Cosimo's natural son, Carlo.

It was while working on an altarpiece for the nuns of Santa Margherita in Prato that Fra Filippo's lustful eye fell upon one of the young novices, Lucrezia, the daugher of Francesco Buti of Florence. He made advances to her and, having persuaded the nuns to allow him to use her as a model for the Madonna in his painting, he seduced her and carried her off. She bore him a son, Filippino; and Cosimo, thinking it was high time the father settled down, obtained a dispensation for him to marry from the Pope to whom he had tact-fully presented some small examples of Fra Filippo's work.

Filippo's lechery had already caused Cosimo a good deal of difficulty in Florence. When seized by feelings of unassuageable lust, Filippo found it quite impossible to concentrate on his work and would repeatedly slip away from his studio in the Medici Palace, hurry through the courtyard and disappear down the Via Larga in search of a woman. Eventually Cosimo, whose methodical practice it was always to obtain an artist's agreement to finish a commissioned work for a settled price on an agreed date, locked Lippi up in his room, telling him that he would not be let out again until the picture he was engaged upon was finished. Lippi thereupon got hold of a pair of scissors, cut up the coverings of his bed into strips, tied them together, and, using them as rope, climbed down into the street and ran away. Having found him and persuaded him to come back, Cosimo was so thankful that he 'resolved in future to try to keep a hold on him by affection and kindness and to allow him to come and go as he pleased'. Cosimo was often heard to say thereafter that artists must always be treated with respect, that they should never be considered mere journeymen as they were by most other patrons of his time.

An artist whom it was difficult not to treat with respect was Giovanni da Fiesole, known as Fra Angelico, a small and saintly friar whom Cosimo evidently commissioned to paint frescoes on the walls of the chapter-house, cloisters and corridors of San Marco. He was born at Vicchio in the Mugello in 1387 and christened Guido. On becoming a novice in the monastery of San Domenico at Fiesole in 1407 he took the name of Giovanni. After a time spent at Cortona, where he painted the frescoes in the Dominican monastery, he returned to Fiesole in 1418; and it was not until 1436, when he was nearly fifty, that he came to Florence and was asked to take up his brushes again by Cosimo. Thereafter Cosimo took a deep interest in his work, giving him 'much help, and advice with regard to the details' of *The Crucifixion*,[5] which was painted for the Chapter House, and choosing as the subject for the frescoes in the Medici cell the Adoration of the Magi, whose example in laying down their crowns at the manger in Bethlehem Cosimo liked to have 'always before his eyes for his own guidance as a ruler'.[6]

Every morning before he began work on *The Crucifixion*, as on every other morning before starting to paint one of those religious subjects to which he devoted the rest of his life, Fra Angelico would kneel in prayer. And each day, as on every other day when painting a picture of Christ suffering on the Cross, he would be so overcome by emotion that the tears would pour down his cheeks. He was a man of the utmost simplicity, modesty and holiness; his fellow friars never once saw him angry. Cosimo once said, 'Every painter paints himself.' Looking upon the faces and attitudes of the figures in the painting of Fra Angelico it was impossible not to believe that this was so.

When Fra Angelico died in 1455, Cosimo's health was failing fast.

Often totally incapacitated by arthritis and gout, he had to be carried about the house and would cry out as though in agony as he approached a doorway. 'Why do you scream so?' his wife once asked him, 'Nothing has happened.' 'If anything *had* happened,' he replied, 'it wouldn't be any *use* crying out.'

Over the years he had become increasingly sardonic, ever more terse and caustic. It was said that when his old friend the Archbishop asked him to introduce a measure making it illegal for priests to gamble, he had riposted with curt cynicism, 'Better to begin by forbidding them loaded dice.' A visitor to Florence at this time noticed how drawn and ill and unhappy he looked; and his declining years were, indeed, clouded by sadness. His eldest son, Piero, now forty years old, had never been strong and was not expected to survive him long, if at all. Cosimo's hopes were centred in his second, his favourite son, Giovanni, for whom Michelozzo had been asked to build the Villa Medici on the slopes of Fiesole.

Giovanni was thirty-seven when work began on the villa in 1458. An able, shrewd and cheerful man, he was ill-favoured in appearance with the large Medici nose, a lumpy swelling between his eyebrows and a skin troubled by eczema. Very fond of women, he was also a dedicated trencherman and extremely fat. He was a good judge of painting; he loved music; and was so taken with the ribald wit of the Florentine barber, Burchiello, that even after Burchiello's talents for burlesque had been turned against the Medici, he invited him to come to entertain him while he was taking a cure at the sulphur baths at Pietrolo. But although so cheerful and carefree, Giovanni was a conscientious citizen and a capable businessman, carefully trained by his father who relied on him more and more after the death of the bank's general manager, Giovanni d'Amerigo Benci.

Having worked for a time in the Ferrara branch of the family bank, Giovanni became a *Priore* in the *Signoria* in 1454, and in the following year served as ambassador to the Curia, where he seems to have spent a large part of his time eating and drinking with the more worldly cardinals. Like his father he had bought a Circassian slave girl from the market in Venice, a 'delightfully pretty girl aged about seventeen or eighteen ... with black hair, delicate features, vivacious and intelligent'. Yet he was evidently quite fond of his wife, Ginevra degli Albizzi, and he loved their only child, Cosimino. Cosimo, too, was devoted to this little boy. There is a story related by his contemporary, Lodovico Carbone of Ferrara, that one day, when Cosimo was discussing some matter of state with an embassy from Lucca, the boy walked into the room with a bundle of sticks, interrupting the conference to ask his grandfather to make him a whistle. Much to the annoyance of the Lucchese delegates, the meeting was promptly adjourned while Cosimo set to work; and no further business was discussed until the whistle had been made to the boy's satisfaction. 'I must say, Sir,' the leader of the delegation felt constrained to protest when recalled to Cosimo's presence, 'we cannot be other than surprised at your behaviour. We have come to you representing our commune to treat of grave matters, and you desert us to devote your time to a child.'

'Oh, my lords,' Cosimo replied, not in the least abashed, throwing his arms round the ambassadors' shoulders. 'Are you not also fathers and grandfathers? You must not be surprised that I should have made a whistle. It's a good thing that the boy didn't ask me to play it for him; because I would have done that too.'

To his grandfather's infinite sorrow, this beloved boy died in 1461 shortly before his sixth birthday. And two years later Giovanni himself, having steadfastly refused to diet to lessen his great weight, died of a heart attack. Cosimo never recovered from the shock. As his servants carried him through the big rooms of the Medici Palace, which at the height of his career had contained a household of fifty people, he was heard repeatedly to murmur, 'Too large a house now for so small a family.' At his villa at Careggi he spent long hours in silence. Why did he spend so much time alone, without speaking, his wife wanted to know. 'When we are going away, you spend a fortnight preparing for the move,' he replied. 'So, since I have soon to go from this life to another, don't you understand how much I have to think about.' On another occasion she asked him why he sat so long with his eyes shut. His reply on this occasion was briefer and even more resigned: 'To get them used to it.'

In the early summer of 1464, Francesco Sforza's envoy in Florence,

Nicodemo Tranchedini, went to call upon him. He had been there often in the past, and once had found Cosimo and both his sons in bed together, all suffering from gout and each one as ill-tempered as the other. But Cosimo was weary now rather than irritable, almost despairing. As well as gout and arthritis he was 'afflicted with suppression of urine which caused frequent fever'. 'Nicodemo mio,' he said to his visitor, 'I can bear no more. I feel myself failing and am ready to go.' Two months later, on 1 August, he died. He was in his seventy-sixth year. A few days before, he had insisted on getting out of bed and, fully dressed, making his confession to the Prior of San Lorenzo. 'After which he caused Mass to be said,' so his son Piero told his two surviving grandsons,

making the responses as though he were quite well. Afterwards being asked to make profession of his faith, he said the creed word for word, repeated the confession himself, and then received the Holy Sacrament, doing so with the most perfect devotion, having first asked pardon of everyone for any wrongs he had done them.

There *were* those he had wronged, as he well knew. Had he been more lenient, more forebearing he could never have won for himself so much power and wealth. He had never thought it prudent to pardon or to allow back to Florence those rivals whom the *Signoria* had banished in 1434; he had not hesitated to ruin families or businesses that had appeared to threaten his own; he had always been careful to ensure that his own family's friends were given profitable or honourable appointments which the Medici's opponents were rigorously denied. Yet to the Florentines as a whole, to those fellow citizens who had due cause to feel grateful for all he had done for them and for their city, he died revered and sincerely lamented, honoured for his generosity, his political acumen and the wide range of his many accomplishments. As his friend, Vespasiano da Bisticci, wrote of him, his knowledge, taste and versatility were truly remarkable.

When giving audience to a scholar he discoursed concerning letters; in the company of theologians he showed his acquaintance with theology, a branch of learning always studied by him with delight. So also with regard to philosophy. Astrologers found him well versed in their science, for he had a certain faith in astrology, and employed it to guide him on certain private occasions. Musicians in like manner perceived his mastery of music, wherein he took great pleasure. The same was true about sculpture and painting; both of these arts he understood completely, and showed much favour to all worthy craftsmen. In architecture he was a consummate judge; and without his opinion and advice no public building of any importance was begun or carried to completion.

Some years before the *Signoria*, of which he was not at that time even a member, had described him as '*Capo della Repubblica*'; now they passed a public decree conferring upon him the title *Pater Patriae* – a title once accorded to Cicero – and they ordered that the words should be inscribed upon his tomb.

They would have liked to have built a tomb at least as magnificent as that which his family had had made for Pope John XXIII in the Baptistery. But on his deathbed he had requested that he should be buried without 'any pomp or demonstration'.

His father had made a similar request; but the request had been ignored. Giovanni di Bicci de' Medici's body had been carried to the church of San Lorenzo in an open coffin followed by his sons, accompanied by twenty-eight other Medici and a long procession of foreign ambassadors and Florentine officials, to be buried in the centre of the old sacristy in a tomb which was later to be far more extravagantly ornamented than he himself would have considered appropriate.[7] Cosimo's funeral was conducted rather more quietly yet it, too, was imposing enough. After a long and solemn ceremony in the basilica of San Lorenzo, which glittered with innumerable candles, his remains were interred below a marble memorial which was surmounted by a circle of serpentine and porphyry decorated with the Medici arms and placed at the foot of the altar. Since San Lorenzo is the basilica of St Ambrose and contains many martyrs' relics beneath the altar, the Church's rules did not allow the body to be buried in the nave immediately below the memorial. So it was placed in the vault; but, so as to join the tomb to the porphyry and serpentine memorial, a massive stone pillar, eight feet square, was placed between them. On this pillar are the words 'Piero has placed this here to the memory of his father.'[8]

PART TWO

1464-1492

VIII

PIERO THE GOUTY

'When it is a matter of acquiring worthy or strange objects
he does not look at the price'

P IERO WAS forty-eight years old when he became head of the
family. The perpetual ill health which had afflicted him since
early manhood, and which had been responsible for his nick-
ame, *'il Gottoso'* ('the Gouty'), had prevented him from taking as
ctive a part in either the business of the bank or the affairs of Florence
s would otherwise have been expected of the heir to the Medici
ortune. He had, however, served as a *Priore* in 1448, had been
lorentine ambassador in Milan, Venice and Paris, and in 1461 had been
lected *Gonfaloniere*, the last Medici ever to be elected to that office.

Despite the drooping eyelids which gave his face a rather sleepy
ppearance and the swollen glands in his neck, he was better looking
ian his brother Giovanni, while his determined chin and thin, set
iouth suggested a character well able to withstand the almost con-
ant pain he suffered from his arthritic joints as well as the irritation
f eczema. Indeed, his nature displayed little of the edgy irritability
o often associated with prolonged illness. He was considerate,
atient and courteous. Though there were many who regretted a
ertain coldness in his manner and doubted his capacity to rule with
is father's authority, those who knew him well both liked and
spected him.

As a banker he did not have his father's flair, but he was scru-
ilously methodical. Characteristically he had noted in the most
xact detail the amount expended on Cosimo's funeral, the kinds of

Masses that had been paid for, the amount of black cloth given to the women of the family for veils and kerchiefs, the sums of money given to servants and slaves for mourning clothes, the numbers of candles and weight of wax. This care for detail was combined with qualities that had made him an excellent diplomat. In France, in fact, King Louis XI had been so taken with him that, soon after he became head of the family, he was granted permission to decorate one of the balls of the Medici arms with three of the lilies of the House of Valois.

That most Florentines were prepared for the moment to accord to Piero the privileges and respect enjoyed by his father was due partly at least to the wife he had married and the five attractive, healthy children she had borne him. For Lucrezia Tornabuoni was a remarkable woman, charming and spirited, profoundly religious and highly accomplished. Her family, formerly Tornaquinci, had once been a noble one; but in order to evade the disadvantages attaching to their birth they had changed their name, altered their arms and abandoned their former pretensions. They were still rich; their palace in what is now one of the main streets in Florence was a splendid one; the delightful murals illustrating the lives of St John the Baptist and the Virgin by Domenico Bigordi Ghirlandaio in the choir of Santa Maria Novella – which display the astute and wary features of several members of the family – were paid for with Tornabuoni money.[1]

Lucrezia herself was not content with patronage. She was a poet of more than moderate ability. Since her interests were largely theological, most of her poems were hymns or translations into verse of Holy Writ. But they displayed a depth of feeling as well as a literary quality rarely to be found in such compositions. Neither her spiritual bent nor her intellectual leanings, however, prevented her from being an admirable wife and mother. Both her husband and her children as well as her father-in-law, all seem to have adored her.

There were three daughters, Maria, Bianca and Lucrezia, known as Nannina. They were all to be married well, Maria to Leopetto Rossi, Bianca to Guglielmo de' Pazzi, and Lucrezia to the scholarly Bernardo Rucellai. There were also two sons; Lorenzo, who was fifteen when his grandfather died, and Giuliano who was eleven. Both of them promised to be distinguished men.

Lorenzo, in particular, was precociously gifted. He did not share the good looks which – rare in the Medici – his father and younger brother both enjoyed. But his sallow, irregular features were powerful and arresting; and though his movements were jerky and ungainly, he was tall, strong and athletic. His education, thorough and wide-ranging, had been supervised at first by Gentile Becchi, the Latinist and diplomat, and later by Cristoforo Landino, translator of Aristotle and commentator on Dante, and Marsilio Ficino, his grandfather's protégé and friend, whose allowance his father continued to pay. By the time Lorenzo was fifteen he was already being entrusted with responsibilities that most boys of his age would have found daunting. He was sent on diplomatic missions to Pisa to meet Federigo, the second son of King Ferrante of Naples; to Milan to represent his father at the marriage of King Ferrante's elder son to Francesco Sforza's daughter, Ippolita; to Bologna for conversations with its leading citizen, Giovanni Bentivoglio; to Venice to be received by the Doge; to Ferrara to stay with the Este family; to Naples to see King Ferrante. And in 1466 he went to Rome to congratulate the new Pope, Paul II, on his accession, to discuss the contract for the alum mines at Tolfa, and to try to make up for the neglect of business studies in his humanistic education by discussing the activities of the Roman branch of the bank with his uncle, Giovanni Tornabuoni, its manager. While in Rome he received a letter from his father which might well have been addressed to a diplomat of the most varied experience.

To the Medici's supporters in Florence it seemed by then that Piero himself was in need of just as much help and advice as Lorenzo. Ever since Cosimo's death the ambitious, ingratiating and plausible Luca Pitti had been endeavouring to achieve that power and influence in the city which seemed to him the just deserts of his talents. Piero he considered a wholly unworthy successor to the great Cosimo. So did the distinguished diplomat, Cosimo's former friend and ambassador to France, Agnolo Acciaiuoli, who had been a persistent critic of the Medici during the last years of Cosimo's life, maintaining that old age had reduced the father, as illness had reduced the son, 'to such cowardice that they avoided anything that might cause them trouble or worry'. In their increasingly outspoken attack on the Medici, Luca Pitti and Agnolo Acciaiuoli had recently been joined by the Archbishop of Florence's brother Dietisalvi Neroni, Florence's first resident ambassador in Venice and later ambassador in Milan. Between them these three men constituted a formidable opposition to the Medici; and, as the weeks passed, Florence became divided into two opposing camps, the Party of the Hill, comprising the supporters of Luca Pitti – whose huge palace on the high ground of the Oltrarno beyond the Ponte Vecchio was now almost finished – and the Party of the Plain, those who remained faithful to the occupants of the Medici Palace on the lower ground in the Via Larga. The Party of the Hill gained much support from the merchant class when Piero, having ordered a survey of his business assets in order to discover 'in how many feet of water he was standing', was so concerned by the subsequent report that he ill-advisedly called in many long outstanding debts to the family bank which Cosimo had left undisturbed. The numerous bankruptcies which almost immediately followed were naturally blamed upon Piero, although he did his best to help several of those who had been hardest hit. It was not, however, until the Party of the Hill was joined by a more energetic and more determined opponent of the Medici that it appeared strong enough to drive Piero out of Florence as his father had been driven out some forty years before.

This forceful recruit to the Party of the Hill was Niccolò Soderini an expert orator and a member of one of the oldest and proudes families in Florence. Soderini vehemently attacked the device of the *Accoppiatori*, by which the Medici had so conveniently packed th *Signoria* with their friends and adherents, and advocated a return t the election by lot as practised in the earlier days of the Republic His idealism and rhetoric triumphed. The *Accoppiatori* were abolished and, amongst the names of the *Priori* elected to the *Signoria* i November 1465 was that of Niccolò Soderini who was immediatel elected *Gonfaloniere*. He was accompanied to the Palazzo dell Signoria by a crowd of admirers who placed a wreath of olive leave around his head.

After this triumphant inauguration, Soderini's term of office w:

a humiliating anti-climax. The reforms which he had promised and now eagerly proposed were regarded with distaste by the *Collegi*, who discussed them unenthusiastically and set them aside. At the beginning of January 1466, their short time of office over, he and the other *Priori* dejectedly left the Palazzo della Signoria on which was posted a placard with the words, 'Nine Fools are out'. Soderini returned to his own palazzo convinced – as Pitti, Acciaiuoli and Neroni were all now convinced – that the only chance of success against the Medici lay in armed rebellion.

For several weeks nothing was done; and then, on 8 March, the Medici's great ally, Francesco Sforza, died in Milan, leaving several sons, the eldest of whom, Galeazzo Maria, was an unstable young man of strange tastes and weird behaviour. Piero, nevertheless, argued that the continuance of the Milanese alliance was essential to Florence's future prosperity. The Party of the Hill, on the other hand, insisted that the city should now return to its old friendship with Venice. Out of this dispute the attempted *coup* was born.

Pitti, Soderini and their friends secretly approached the Venetians for help in ridding Florence of the Medici. They also made overtures to Borso d'Este, the genial and ostentatious Duke of Ferrara who had recently erected a large statue of himself in the city's main square. Duke Borso agreed to help them by sending troops across the frontier under command of his brother Ercole. These troops were to advance on Florence, while other forces were to seize Piero, together with his two sons, and to have them all hastily executed on some convenient charge. A good opportunity to carry out this plan presented itself in August when Piero fell ill and was carried in a litter out of Florence to the villa of Careggi.

Scarcely had he arrived at Careggi than a messenger came to the villa with an urgent warning from his friend Giovanni Bentivoglio of Bologna of the approaching danger. Piero immediately ordered his servants to lift him out of bed and to carry him back to Florence, sending Lorenzo on ahead to prepare for his arrival. Galloping back to the city, Lorenzo came upon some of the armed conspirators loitering on the road near the villa of Dietisalvi Neroni's brother, the Archbishop. Not recognizing him, they let him pass by; but as soon as he was out of sight he sent word back to his father, warning him to make for Florence by a different and little-used road.

The sudden and unexpected return of the Medici to Florence on the afternoon of 27 August so alarmed the leading conspirators that they immediately lost their nerve. Luca Pitti hurried down to the Medici Palace to beg Piero's forgiveness, and to swear that he would 'live or die' with him; the others mustered their armed supporters, but could not decide what orders to give them. Piero, by contrast, appeared wholly in control of the situation and of himself. He summoned his men to arms, sent messages for help to Milan and made arrangements for the accession to power of a firmly pro-Medici *Signoria* at the next elections due to be held on 2 September.

This *Signoria*, chosen in compliance with Medicean prompting, called for a *Parlamento*. A few hundred well-disposed citizens entered the Piazza which was lined with three thousand troops, amongst whom Lorenzo de' Medici rode up and down on his horse. The *Parlamento* obediently agreed to a *Balìa*; and the troubles were suddenly over. The republican reaction was defeated, and the power of the Medici confirmed.

Soderini, Dietisalvi and Acciaiuoli were all banished from Florence. In recognition of his tardy submission Luca Pitti, old and humiliated, was pardoned in the expectation that this erstwhile friend of Cosimo would be reclaimed as an ally, an expectation realized when Luca's daughter was married to Giovanni Tornabuoni, a close relative of Piero's wife. Yet, in exile in Venice, Luca Pitti's two fellow conspirators, Neroni and Soderini, continued to plot against the Medici. They succeeded in persuading the Doge and the Council that feeling against the family was running high in Florence and that, were a Venetian army to attack the city, the enemies of the family within the walls would rise up in arms to support it. Accordingly, in May 1467, Bartolommeo Colleoni, the famous *condottiere* who, after twice deserting them for the Milanese, had been appointed by the Venetians captain-general of the Serene Republic for life, was paid to march towards the Tuscan frontier. Once again Piero reacted quickly. Summoning help from both Milan and Naples, he mustered a Florentine army to oppose Colleoni's advance. The Florentine mercenaries came upon the Venetian army in the territory of the tiny state of Imola, and there they decisively defeated it. Piero's control over the government of Florence was thus firmly secured.

While defending his family from their rivals within the city walls and the city itself from her enemies outside them, Piero continued the family tradition of munificence. He paid for a splendid tabernacle for the miraculous crucifix in the church of San Miniato al Monte,[2] and commissioned an even more magnificent tabernacle for the church of Santissima Annunziata which bore on its base the vainglorious inscription: '*Costò fior. 4 mila el marmo solo* The marble alone cost 4,000 florins'.[3] At the same time he added numerous ancient coins to the collection assembled by his father, bought great numbers of rare manuscript books for the Medici Library, and had many volumes copied out for him and brilliantly illuminated. Antonio Averlino Filarete was told that Piero spent hours looking at these books, turning over the pages 'as if they were a pile of gold':

One day he may simply want for his pleasure to let his eye pass along these volumes to while away the time and give recreation to the eye. The next day, then, so I am told, he will take out some of the effigies and images of all the Emperors and Worthies of the past, some made of gold, some of silver, some of bronze, of precious stones or of marble and other materials which are wonderful to behold ... The next day he would look at his jewels and precious stones of which he had a marvellous quantity of great value, some engraved, others not. He takes great pleasure and delight in looking at these and in discussing their various excellencies. The next day, perhaps, he will inspect his vases of gold and silver and other precious material and praise their noble worth and the skill of the masters who wrought them. All in all when it is a matter of acquiring worthy or strange objects he does not look at the price.

Like his father, Piero was anxious to be considered the friend as well as the patron of artists. And just as Cosimo, so Antonio Benavieni wrote, 'bestowed both honours and countless rewards' on Donatello during his active life, so Piero continued to honour and reward the sculptor in his old age and at his death. It had been one of Donatello's last requests that he should be buried near Cosimo in the church of San Lorenzo. Piero ensured that this request was fulfilled and undertook to bear the cost of his interment in the crypt next to Cosimo's tomb. When the coffin was carried there, it was followed by the Medici and thousands of the mourning citizens of Florence.

Many of the artists in this long procession were already at work, or were shortly to embark upon work, for Piero de' Medici. One of these was Luca della Robbia, soon to be elected president of the sculptors' guild. Born in Florence in 1400 he had achieved lasting fame with the beautiful singing-gallery in the cathedral which he finished in 1428.[4] Then, having been commissioned by the *Signoria* to complete the series of reliefs begun by Giotto and Andrea Pisano on the northern side of the campanile,[5] he had been asked to make some oval terracotta reliefs for the walls of Piero's study in the Medici Palace and some tiles for the floor, 'a new thing and most excellent for summer'.[6]

Another old artist in the funeral procession to San Lorenzo was Paolo di Doni, then aged sixty-nine. He, too, was a Florentine, a shy, withdrawn man with a passion for animals, particularly for birds, pictures of which filled his house and which earned him his nickname – Uccello. Several of his pictures of birds and of other animals, painted in tempera on canvas, were bought by the Medici to hang on the walls of their palace; and, some years before Donatello's death, Piero asked Uccello to paint a picture in three panels of the rout of San Romano, to commemorate Florence's victory over the Sienese in 1432 in the days of the Albizzi. This picture, in which the horses seem to dominate the action, was hung in Lorenzo's bedroom next to two other Uccellos, a scene from the legend of Paris and a picture of lions fighting dragons.[7]

Soon after the *Rout of San Romano* was finished, Piero bestowed his patronage on yet another Florentine artist who was asked to paint three large pictures for the Medici Palace. This was Antonio di Jacobo Benci, known as Pollaiuolo because his father was a poulterer. A sculptor, engraver, jeweller and enameller as well as a painter, he recommended himself to Piero by his skill in portraying the naked figure, a skill which he had perfected by spending hours in the most meticulous dissection of corpses. Piero ordered from him two of the twelve *Labours of Hercules* – the slaying of the Nemean lion and the destruction of the Hydra of Lernae – and a portrayal of Hercules's subsequent conquest of the Libyan giant, Antaeus.[8] In them Hercules, a symbol of courage on the official seal of the *Signoria*, was to be shown 'larger than life', as a Greek god rather than, in the manner of earlier times, a medieval warrior in shining armour.

In adapting classical mythology to celebrate the virtues and triumphs of Florence and of her rulers, no artist was more in sympathy with Piero's ideas than Alessandro di Mariano Filipepi, known as Botticelli. At the time of Donatello's death, he was twenty-two years old. The sickly son of a Florentine tanner in a poor way of business in the Via Nuova Borg' Ognissanti, Botticelli had probably derived his nickname (which means Little Barrel) from an elder brother, a *batiloro* – a beater of gold leaf used for picture frames – who agreed to relieve their father of responsibility for him. On leaving school Botticelli had been apprenticed to Fra Filippo Lippi; but soon afterwards had been invited to live at the Medici Palace where Piero and Lucrezia Tornabuoni treated him as one of their own family. In the *Madonna of the Magnificat*, which he painted soon after Donatello's death, he appears to have introduced both sons of the house as angels kneeling before the Madonna, Giuliano with seraphic features and thick, curly hair shaped so that an appealing curl fell down across his brow, the more swarthy Lorenzo, who was only five years younger than the artist, with his idealized features in profile and in shadow.[9]

In the *Adoration of the Magi*, however, which Botticelli painted as one of those family group pictures with a religious theme so favoured by Renaissance artists, Lorenzo – if the traditional identification can be accepted – appears in a stronger light and more exposed position. This picture was commissioned by Piero's friend Guaspare di Zanobi del Lama, for the church of Santa Maria Novella, perhaps as a votive offering after the Medici's escape from the danger of assassination and the threat of exile by the conspirators of 1466.[10] Although other members of his family occupy more prominent positions, the picture certainly seems to have been intended as a tribute to Lorenzo, just as *Fortitude*, which Botticelli afterwards painted for the Council of the

Arte della Mercanzia, appears to have been painted as a tribute to Piero.

Fortitude was one of six panels representing the virtues of Charity, Justice, Faith, Temperance and Fortitude which the commercial tribunal, the *Mercanzia*, had commissioned for their hall. It was originally intended that all the panels should be done by Antonio Pollaiuolo's younger brother, Piero, but Piero de' Medici induced Tommaso Soderini to persuade his colleagues on the Council to give the commission for at least one of the panels to Botticelli. Botticelli responded by producing a *Fortitude* which was taken to be an allegorical representation of the steadfast character of his friend and patron.[11]

Shortly before Botticelli completed this painting, another artist began work at the Medici Palace on a series of frescoes for the chapel on the first floor. This was Benozzo Gozzoli, also a native of Florence, who had worked on the Baptistery's bronze doors under the direction of Ghiberti and who had later acted as assistant to Fra Angelico. In the Medici chapel for months on end Gozzoli worked by lamplight, gradually producing round the walls of the chancel, above an ornamented border of the Medici device of a diamond ring and the motto 'semper', two huge pictures depicting groups of angels rejoicing in the birth of Christ and gazing upon Filippo Lippi's painting of *The Virgin Adoring the Child* which was placed above the altar.[12]

Around the walls of the main body of the chapel, Gozzoli painted a memorial to the history of the Medici family in what purported to be a representation of the journey of the three Magi to Bethlehem, modelling several of his groups on Gentile da Fabriano's altarpiece, *Adoration of the Magi*, which was painted for the altar of the Chapel of Onofrio Strozzi in Santa Trinità.[13]

It used to be confidently asserted that, as a celebration of the great Council of Florence of 1439 which had helped to make Florence a leading centre of European culture, the artist chose as his three Magi John Paleologus, the Emperor of the East, distinguished by his splendid robes, his melancholy bearded face and his unique turbaned crown; the Patriarch of Constantinople, a venerable white-bearded figure, also wearing a distinctive head-dress, and riding a mule; and the ten-year-old heir of the Medici family – whose grandfather was instrumental in bringing these great men from the east to Florence – Lorenzo de' Medici, gorgeously attired and riding a magnificently caparisoned horse whose trappings are covered with the seven balls of the family's emblem. It seems more likely, however, that the subject of the painting was suggested to Piero by the great pageants of the Three Kings which traditionally took place in Florence on the feast of Epiphany and in which members of the Medici family habitually took part. In 1446 Cosimo himself had made an appearance in a specially memorable Magi pageant which Michelozzo had helped to design. Certainly many of the men who took part in that spectacular cavalcade are depicted in Gozzoli's painting, most of them wearing the round, flat-topped cap favoured by scholars of the day and invariably to be seen in portraits of Cosimo *Pater Patriae*. Mingling with them are the bearded Greek scholars from Constantinople, several of them – like Argyropoulos and Chalcondylas – now settled in Florence at the instigation and expense of the Medici. Between two of these Gozzoli has painted himself, and lest there should be any doubt as to *his* identity he has boldly inscribed his name upon his hat. Preceding him are other members of his patron's family – Piero's younger son, Giuliano, a negro walking in front of him with a bow; Cosimo *Pater Patriae*, the trappings of his horse decorated with the Medici arms and his own personal emblem of three peacocks' feathers; Cosimo's brother, Lorenzo, wearing a conical hat and riding a mule; and his patron, Piero himself, hatless as he is usually depicted. Also there are three handsome girls on horseback, dressed alike with tall plumes in their hats, no doubt intended to represent Piero's three daughters.[14]

As in the case of other pictures which he commissioned, Piero took great interest in the painting of this picture, instructing Gozzoli to use the brightest colours and to make the clothes as rich and brilliant as possible. Gozzoli agreed to do so, adding that he would need a great deal of gold and ultramarine paint, so would Piero advance him the money? When the painting was nearly finished, Piero objected that the angels were too obtrusive. Gozzoli did not think so:

I have put in only two seraphim, one is in a corner among the clouds; nothing but the tips of his wings is visible, and he is so well hidden and so well covered by clouds that he does not spoil the picture at all, but on the contrary adds beauty to it ... The other seraph is on the far side of the altar, also hidden in a similar way. Ruberto Martegli has seen them and said there is no cause to make a fuss about them. However, I will do as you ask. Two small clouds will obliterate them both.

It is probable that Piero did not live to see this fresco finished. He had been ill since the beginning of 1469, and his last months were troubled ones. Groups of citizens, claiming to be acting on his authority, took to marauding through streets by day and night, ill-treating and threatening passers-by whom they accused of being opponents of the Medici and extorting money from them. Piero acted with that forceful determination which so often surprised those who supposed his ill-health had wasted his spirit, and who mistook for weakness his respect for the constitution of the state. He ordered the ringleaders to be brought to his room and, from his bed, up-braided them for their misdeeds; he warned them that, should their excesses continue, he would have members of various exiled families recalled to Florence to help control them. The violence immediately subsided and the marauding ceased; but before the end of the year Piero was dead. He was buried next to his brother, Giovanni, in the old sacristry of San Lorenzo. Over his body and that of their uncle his sons placed a porphyry sarcophagus, ornamented with acanthus leaves, designed for the Medici by Donatello's most brilliant pupil, Andrea del Verrocchio.[15]

✤ IX ✤

THE YOUNG LORENZO

'A naturally joyful nature'

LORENZO WAS now twenty, strong, virile, clever and inex-
haustibly energetic, the brilliant paladin of the Medici house,
the first such heir it had ever had. His straight, thick, dark hair,
parted in the middle, fell almost to his shoulders; his long flattened
nose, which had no sense of smell, looked as though it had been
broken and badly set; his heavy jaw jutted forward so that his lower
lip almost enclosed the upper; the eyebrows above his big, dark,
penetrating eyes were irregular and bumpy; he was quite strikingly
ugly. His voice was cracked, nasal and high-pitched. Yet when he
talked his face was so animated, his manner so arresting, his long
slender hands so expressive that few noticed his defects.

To his every activity he brought a marvellously infectious zest.
As Marsilio Ficino, said, he had a 'naturally joyful nature'. With
equal enthusiasm he played *calcio*, a fast game like football with
twenty-seven players on each side, and *palloni*, a ball-game played in
a court with gloved hands. He went out hunting and hawking. In a
voice not very tuneful, he sang at table and he sang in the saddle; once,
so one of his friends recorded, he kept singing and telling jokes
throughout a journey of thirty miles, keeping the rest of the company
in spirits as high as his own. He composed many of his songs himself,
and some of them were outrageously lewd. He had a strong taste for
bawdy, for sexual innuendo and ribald stories. He also shared his
contemporaries' taste for those boisterous practical jokes which later
generations were to find so heartless, even cruel. The story is told that
one night when a tiresome, bibulous doctor was drunker than usual,

Lorenzo suggested that two friends should bundle him off to the country, lock him up in a remote farmhouse and spread the rumour that he was dead. The rumour was accepted as the truth; and when the doctor escaped and returned home, pale and bedraggled, his wife believed him to be a ghost and refused to let him in.

Yet Lorenzo was renowned amongst his friends for his kindness and consideration. Responsive, affectionate and *simpatico*, he had a rare gift for friendship and a deep love of animals, particularly of horses. He generally fed his own horse, Morello, himself; and when he did not, the animal, who greeted his master's arrival by neighing and stamping his feet, would fret so much that he became ill. But although he spent so much time riding and hunting in the country, in gardening at Careggi, in supervising his farms in the Mugello, in raising herds of cows, breeding racehorses for the *palio*, rearing Calabrian pigs at Careggi and Sicilian pheasants at Poggio a Caiano, breeding rabbits and experimenting in the manufacture of cheeses, he derived quite as much pleasure from the activities he pursued in Florence, reading, writing, talking, studying Plato, playing the lyre, making architectural drawings and making love. He was astonishingly versatile; and he liked it to be known that he was. It had to be admitted that he was vain and intensely competitive. He could be very angry when beaten at a game or outwitted in some intellectual exercise.

When he was nineteen, it was decided that it was time for him to marry. The bride selected for him was Clarice Orsini, the daughter of Jacopo Orsini of Monterotondo, a sixteen-year-old heiress from Rome. Lorenzo's mother travelled to Rome to inspect the girl on the pretext of visiting her brothers, Giovanni and Francesco Tornabuoni, who looked after the Medici bank in Rome. Lucrezia caught her first glimpse of Clarice as she and her mother were on their way to St Peter's. The girl was wearing a *lenzuolo* in the Roman fashion so Lucrezia could not see her properly, but 'she seemed to be handsome, fair and tall'. The next time Lucrezia saw her she was still unable to inspect her figure as she would have liked, 'since Roman women [were] always entirely covered up'; but, so far as she could judge it in its tight bodice, her bosom seemed to be well-shaped; and her hands were 'long and delicate'. Her face was 'rather round but not unattractive, her throat fairly elegant but rather too thin'. She certainly had a 'nice complexion'. Her hair, Lucrezia noticed now, was not really fair – no women in Rome were so blessed – but reddish.

'She does not carry her head well, as our girls do, but pokes it forward,' Lucrezia concluded her report. 'I think she is shy . . . Yet, altogether I think the girl is a good deal above the average.' Of course, she added, she could not be compared with her own three daughters who were, indeed, not only better-looking but, as Florentines, far better-educated than any Roman girl could expect to be. Nevertheless, Lucrezia hoped that with her evident modesty and good manners Clarice would soon learn Florentine customs.

The Florentines themselves did not entirely approve of the match. It had never before been the custom for even the richest merchant families of the city to look outside Tuscany for brides and bridegrooms for their children; and the Medici had previously been content to ally themselves with families of their own sort. Lorenzo was well aware of the advantages of this himself. All his sisters married rich and influential Florentines; and two of his daughters were subsequently required to follow their example, one by marrying a Ridolfi,[1] the other a Salviati.[2] A third daughter, Luigia, was to be betrothed as a little girl to Giovanni, the younger son of his uncle, Pierfrancesco, with whose branch of the family Lorenzo and his father had quarrelled over the proper division of Cosimo's fortune. The dispute had been settled by the time of the betrothal; but Lorenzo was determined to strengthen the renewed ties by a marriage within the family. And, although the marriage never took place, as Luigia died before she was twelve, the friendship between the two branches was not broken again so long as Lorenzo lived.

Yet while Lorenzo understood the importance of marriage alliances between Florentine families, he recognized that there were good reasons for breaking the traditional rule and marrying an Orsini. Not only would he thus avoid arousing any jealousy in Florentine houses where there were marriageable daughters whom he had rejected, but he would be contriving an alliance with a family of far-ranging influence. The Orsini, soldiers and ecclesiastics by profession for countless generations, had huge estates within the Kingdom of Naples as well as north of Rome; they could raise soldiers as well as money; and in Clarice's maternal uncle, Cardinal Latino, they had a firm foothold in the Curia. Lorenzo would naturally have preferred a better-looking and more intellectual bride from a less feudal and enclosed background. But, having succeeded in catching sight of her one day at Mass, he agreed that she was acceptable; and, once a dowry of 6,000 florins was settled, he married her by proxy in Rome, represented by a distant cousin, Filippo de' Medici, Archbishop of Pisa.

To reconcile the Florentines to this unwelcome event, a splendid tournament was held on 7 February 1469, a tournament which was to cost 10,000 ducats and was to be one of the finest spectacles which they had ever seen, a worthy subject for that charming fifteenth-century Italian poem, Luigi Pulci's *La Giostra di Lorenzo de' Medici*.

The scene was the Piazza Santa Croce, where in the February sunshine the spectators, crowded onto roofs and balconies, peered down from windows and parapets to catch a glimpse of the beautiful Lucrezia Donati as she was escorted to the panoplied throne reserved for the 'Queen of the Tournament', and to admire the eighteen representatives of the *jeunesse dorée* of Florentine society who were to play the part of the knights. Preceded by heralds, standard-bearers, fifers, trumpeters, and accompanied by pages and men-at-arms, the knights paraded through the Piazza to the enthusiastic cheers of their thousands of supporters. All of them were magnificently clothed and most had elaborate armour and helmets specially made for the occasion, displays of beauty being more highly regarded on these occasions than demonstrations of reckless courage and strength: although Federigo da Montefeltro lost his eye in one, Italian tournaments were not the savage, bloody spectacle enjoyed in Germany.

None of the knights looked finer than Lorenzo de' Medici, who wore a cape of white silk, bordered in scarlet, under a velvet surcoat, and a silk scarf embroidered with roses, some withered, others blooming, and emblazoned with the spirited motto, worked in pearls: LE TEMPS REVIENT. There were pearls also in his black velvet cap as well as rubies and a big diamond framed by a plume of gold thread. His white charger, which was draped in red and white pearl-encrusted velvet, was a gift from the King of Naples; another charger, which he rode for the jousting, was presented to him by Duke Borso d'Este of Ferrara; his suit of armour came from the Duke of Milan. There was a large diamond in the middle of his shield; his helmet was surmounted by three tall blue feathers; his standard bore a device of a bay tree, one half withered, the other a brilliant green with the same motto, written in pearls, that appeared on his scarf. By way of compliment to him as heir to their host rather than in true recognition of unparalleled prowess, the judges, who included the famous *condottiere*, Roberto da Sanseverino, awarded Lorenzo the first prize and presented him with a helmet inlaid with silver and surmounted by a figure of Mars.

Four months later, in June 1469, Clarice Orsini, whom this great tournament had been designed to honour, arrived in Florence for the wedding celebrations. There were to be no less than five huge banquets at the Medici Palace where for weeks past presents of game and poultry, wine and wax, cakes and jellies, sweetmeats, marzipan and sugared almonds had been arriving from all over Tuscany, and where row upon row of tables were set out along the loggia and in the courtyard and gardens of the palace. The celebrations began on the Sunday morning when the bride, who had been escorted from Rome by Giuliano, emerged from the Palazzo Alessandri in the Borgo San Piero riding the white horse that the bridegroom had been given by the King of Naples.[3] Followed by a long procession of maids-of-honour and attendants, she rode in her white-and-gold brocade dress to the Medici Palace. Here, as she entered through the archway, an olive branch – traditionally displayed as a sign that there was to be a wedding in the family – was lowered over her head to the strains of festive music from an orchestra in the courtyard. As was customary at Florentine weddings, the guests were separated according to their age and sex. At Clarice's table in the loggia overlooking the garden were young married women; at Lorenzo's table in the hall were young men; on the balcony above the loggia, Lucrezia presided over the banquet for the older women; while the men of

Piero's generation and their elders dined in the courtyard in the middle of which were big copper coolers full of Tuscan wine. Each dish was heralded by a flourish of trumpets, and, though the 'food and drink were as modest and simple as befitted a marriage', it was estimated that by the time the last banquet was over five thousand pounds of sweetmeats had been consumed and more than three hundred barrels of wine – mostly *trebbiano* and *vernaccia* – had been drunk. After the banquets the guests were entertained by music and dancing on a stage hung with tapestries and enclosed by curtains embroidered with the Medici and Orsini arms.

For three days the feasting and dancing, the displays and theatricals continued, until, on the Tuesday morning, the bride went to the basilica of San Lorenzo to hear Mass, carrying 'a little book of Our Lady, a wonderful book written in letters of gold on dark blue paper and covered with crystal and graven silver'.

How beautiful is youth – as Lorenzo wrote in one of his poems – youth which is so soon over and gone; let him who would be happy, seize the moment; for tomorrow may never come:

> *Quant'è bella giovenezza*
> *Che si fugge tuttavia!*
> *Chi vuol esser lieto, sia;*
> *Di doman non c'è certezza.*

Lorenzo's young contemporaries eagerly followed his advice. There were dances by day and firework parties at night. Lorenzo himself would be up at dawn, riding out into the forest, his long-bow slung on his back. After dark, he would join groups of his friends, roaming the streets by moonlight and serenading with songs and verses the girls at the palace windows. Once, at two o'clock on a cold winter morning (Lorenzo himself was on a visit to Pisa at the time, and was told this by his friend Filippo Corsini), a great crowd of them gathered in the snow outside the palace of Marietta, the delightful, wayward, orphaned daughter of Lorenzo di Palla Strozzi. By the light of flaming torches, and with much singing, shouting,

blowing of trumpets and piping of flutes, they began hurling snow-
balls at her window. Marietta threw it open;

and what a triumph when one of the besiegers succeeded in flinging snow
upon the maiden's face, as white as the snow itself ... Moreover, Marietta
herself, so graceful and so skilled in this game, and beautiful, as everyone
knows, acquitted herself with very great honour.

The early years of Lorenzo's inheritance were notable in Florence
for a succession of entertainments: pageants, tournaments, masques,
spectacles and parades; musical festivals, revels, dances and amuse-
ments of every kind. For generations, indeed, Florence had been
famous all over Europe for such festivities. No city had more
spectacular nor more numerous public entertainments. Thanks to
the statutes of the various trade guilds there were no more than about
275 working-days in a year, so that the people had plenty of opportunity to enjoy themselves. There were carnivals, horse races and
football games, dances in the Mercato Vecchio, mock battles in the
Piazza Santa Croce and water displays beneath the bridges of the
Arno. Sometimes the Piazza della Signoria would be turned into a
circus or a hunting-field; wild animals would be let loose; boars
would be goaded by lances; and the Commune's lions would be
brought out of their cage behind the Palazzo and incited – rarely
successfully – to set upon dogs. On one occasion at least these
escapades got out of hand: three men were killed by a rampaging
buffalo, and afterwards a mare was set loose among stallions, a sight
which one citizen thought the 'most marvellous entertainment for
girls to behold', but which in the opinion of another, more respectable diarist, 'much displeased decent and well-behaved people'.

One of the most popular of all Florentine festivals was that of
Calendimaggio, May Day. For this, the young men got up early to
hang branches of flowering shrubs, decorated with ribbons and
sugared nuts, on the doors of their sweethearts' houses; and the girls,
wearing pretty frocks and carrying flowers and leaves, danced to the
music of lutes in the Piazza Santa Trinità. Then there was the festival
of St John the Baptist, patron of the city, when all the shops were
decorated with streamers and banners; when riderless horses, with

spiked iron balls hanging at their sides, raced from Porta al Prato down
the Via della Vigna through the Mercato Vecchio and the Corso to
Porta alla Croce; when processions of canons and choristers, of
citizens dressed as angels and saints, and of huge decorated chariots
passed through the streets bearing the Cathedral's sacred relics, which
included a thorn of the Holy Crown, a nail of the Holy Cross, and the
thumb of St John; when the Piazza del Duomo was covered with
blue canopies emblazoned with silver stars beneath which votive
offerings of painted wax were taken to the Baptistery; and when, in
the Piazza della Signoria, the most elaborate gilded castles, symboliz-
ing the towns which were subject to Florence, were carried on wagons
past the banners fluttering on the balcony of the Palazzo.

The Lenten festivals were naturally more sombre. On the Wednes-
day of Passion Week, the Matins of Darkness was held in the Cathedral. All the lights, save a single candle on the altar, were snuffed out;
and in the gloom the clergy and congregation ritually beat on the
floor with willow rods. On Maundy Thursday, the Archbishop
washed the feet of the poor. And on Good Friday, at three o'clock
in the afternoon, the vergers of all the churches and convents went
out into the streets with wooden clappers summoning the people to
kneel and pray wherever they were and whatever they were doing.
Afterwards Christ's funeral was enacted, through streets hung with
black. A long procession of monks carried a cross and a scourging
post, a crown of thorns, a spear and a sponge, together with every
object mentioned in the stories of the Passion, from hammers and
nails to purple robe and dice. Behind them was borne the figure of
the dead Christ beneath a canopy of black velvet and gold; then came
the Virgin Mary, clothed in black, a white handkerchief in her hand.
The next day, Holy Saturday, all was bright once more. The black
cloth was stripped from the altar of the Cathedral and replaced with
gold. The Archbishop sang *Gloria in Excelsis*; and as doves released
from the Cathedral fluttered to the rooftops of the Piazza del Duomo,
the bells in the campanile and all over Florence rang out triumphantly.

Lorenzo and Giuliano delighted in all these festivities, in helping to
design the tableaux, the backcloths and trappings, the sculptures and
armour, the costumes of the performers and the elaborate harnesses

and disguises of the scented animals. They delighted, too, in composing dramas and pageants into which were introduced those classical allusions so treasured by their contemporaries; and in discussing with scholars and poets the speeches which were to be delivered, the songs which were to be sung, the extravagant verse expositions of the allegorical masques.

Every distinguished visitor to the city was sure to be entertained extravagantly during his stay. Thus, when a great procession of noblemen from the south rode into Florence on 22 June 1473 as escort to the King of Naples's daughter, Eleonora, who was on her way to be married to Duke Ercole of Ferrara, the Florentines eagerly seized the opportunity to welcome them in their customary style. They cheered and clapped as the Princess, dressed in black velvet and adorned with 'numberless pearls and jewels', rode through the Porta Romana, across the Ponte Vecchio and up to the Palazzo della Signoria where she received an address from the assembled *Priori* before proceeding to the Medici Palace to have dinner with Lorenzo, Giuliano and their numerous guests. The next day a masque and brilliant procession were followed by a firework display; and on 24 June there was a *fête champêtre* on the Prato, the meadow which stretched down to the banks of the Arno, where the guests ate strawberries, walked in the green grass by the water's edge, and danced in the sunlight, jumping and leaping about in the energetic Florentine manner.

These festivities, splendid and exciting as they were, were not exceptional. But it was everywhere agreed that the tournament held in Florence in 1475 was unique. An even more impressive spectacle than the *giostra* of 1469, this tournament was held in honour of Giuliano, by then twenty-two years old, tall, dark-haired, athletic and universally admired. Giuliano's *giostra* took place in the Piazza Santa Croce where once again the lovely Lucrezia Donati was crowned 'Queen of the Tournament', as she had been in 1469, and where the even more strikingly beautiful Simonetta Cattaneo, the consumptive, dying young wife of Marco Vespucci, a woman with whom Giuliano himself was said to be deeply in love, was led to the throne of the 'Queen of Beauty'. Giuliano appeared before her wearing her favour on one of a series of specially designed costumes which were believed to have cost in all no less than 8000 florins. His standard, designed by Botticelli, depicted Pallas, goddess of wisdom and war, in a golden tunic and armed with spear and shield, looking upon Cupid who stood bound to the bole of an olive tree with his bow and broken arrow at his feet. Like his brother in the previous contest, Giuliano was awarded the first prize which he accepted in a helmet, designed in anticipation of his victory, by Verrocchio.

This famous tournament was the inspiration for the earliest literary masterpiece in Italian of Angelo Ambrogini, known from his birth-place as Poliziano, the son of a distinguished Tuscan lawyer who, as a warm supporter of the Medici family, had been murdered by con-spirators plotting the death of Piero. Shortly after his father's murder, Poliziano had been brought to Florence and his education paid for by the Medici: he had studied Latin under Cristoforo Landino, Greek under Argyropulos and Andronicos Kallistos, and philosophy under Marsilio Ficino. He was invited to stay for as long as he liked at the Medici Palace, and later given a villa by the family. By the time he was eighteen he was a classical scholar of formidable learning and a poet of extraordinarily precocious talent. His *Stanze della Giostra di Giuliano de' Medici* established him as the finest Italian poet since Boccaccio.

The tributes which Poliziano paid to Giuliano and, more parti-cularly, to Lorenzo were not merely the courtly allusions which every generous patron might well have felt his due. Lorenzo was, indeed, 'the laurel who sheltered the birds that sang in the Tuscan spring'. To his villas at Fiesole, Cafaggiolo and Careggi he invited artists, writers and scholars to talk with him, to read aloud with him, to listen to music, to discuss classical texts and philosophical mysteries. Sometimes the company met at the Abbey of Camaldoli[4] where, for four days in 1468, Lorenzo and Giuliano discussed such matters as man's highest vocation, the nature of the *summum bonum* and the philosophic doctrines to be found in the *Aeneid*, with various members of the Platonic Academy including Marsilio Ficino, Cristoforo Landino, Leon Battista Alberti and three merchants of intellectual tastes, Alamanno Rinuccini, and Donato and Piero Acciaiuoli.

'The second day after my father's death,' so Lorenzo recorded in his memoirs, 'the principal men of the city came to our house to console us and to encourage me to take on myself the care of the State, as my father and grandfather had done.' Among the leaders of the delegation was Tommaso Soderini, who had opposed his brother Niccolò's attempted *coup* against Piero, and who, as the husband of a Tornabuoni, liked to think of Lorenzo as his nephew. With him were several members of the Pitti family who, at a meeting of about seven hundred supporters of the existing regime held at the convent of Sant' Antonio the day before, had made amends for Luca Pitti's part in the *coup* by strongly supporting Soderini in his call for a unified request to Lorenzo. Lorenzo listened to the delegation with becoming modesty. 'Their proposal was naturally against my youthful instincts,' he protested,

and, considering that the burden and danger were great, I consented to it unwillingly. But I did so in order to protect our friends and property; since it fares ill in Florence with anyone who is rich but does not have any share in government.

Lorenzo's evident reluctance was understandable. He was not yet twenty-one, had been married for no more than six months, and would naturally have preferred to have spent more time than his new responsibilities would permit upon those pleasures which he pursued with such vigorous intensity. But he was a conscientious and ambitious young man who had already made up his mind that to decline the challenge of public life would be not merely selfish but unwise. Even without the advice of his dutiful, sensible and gifted mother who still had, and was always to have, great influence over him, he would never have attempted to avoid his family responsibilities. Although he agreed with becoming diffidence to assume his father's authority, he had already written to the Duke of Milan asking for the continuation of that support which the Sforzas had extended to the Medici since the time of his grandfather.

Duke Francesco's successor, Galeazzo Maria Sforza, was now firmly established in Milan, a competent ruler with an increasingly sinister reputation for acts of appalling viciousness and cruelty. His enemies said that he had raped the wives and daughters of numerous Milanese nobles; that he took sadistic pleasure in devising tortures for men who had offended him; that he supervised these tortures himself and pulled limbs apart with his own hands; that he delighted in the moans of dying men and in the sight of corpses. Advocates of the Milanese alliance dismissed such stories as malicious inventions but they could not deny that the Duke was both prodigiously extravagant and ineffably vain. When he made a state visit to Florence in 1471, he arrived with an enormous retinue of advisers, attendants, servants and soldiers, including five hundred infantry, a hundred knights and fifty grooms in liveries of cloth of silver, each leading a war-horse saddled in gold brocade and with golden stirrups and bridles embroidered with silk. The Duke also brought with him his trumpeters and drummers, his huntsmen and falconers, his falcons and his hounds. His wife and daughters and their ladies were carried into the city in twelve gold-brocaded litters.

It was all very fine, the Florentines conceded, but they were not unduly impressed. They could have put on a much better show themselves, one of them commented, had they wanted to. And even the Duke himself had to admit that, although the Medici lived in much simpler style that the Sforzas, although Lorenzo chose to wear such plain, dark-coloured clothes, there was little in Milan to compare with the treasures assembled within the walls of the Medici Palace. For, despite all his arrogance and outbursts of psychopathic inhumanity, Duke Galeazzo Maria Sforza was a man of some learning and much discernment. He had a genuine regard for the arts and scholarship for which Florence was so justly renowned; he also developed a deep respect for his young host who was already doing so much to foster them.

It was a respect that others were being taught to share. Piero had no sooner died when yet another attempt had been made to destroy the power and influence of the Medici. Thinking to take advantage of the youth and inexperience of the new head of the family, the conspirators who had attempted to overthrow Piero in 1466 and had since been living in exile assembled an army and, under the leadership of Dietisalvi Neroni, seized Prato. But that was the limit of their success. Their hopes of help from clandestine supporters in Florence and from Ferrara dwindled away as Lorenzo, and a *Signoria* well disposed towards him, acted as quickly and decisively as Piero had done under the earlier threat. A force of Florentine mercenaries was immediately dispatched to retake Prato; the conspirators were dispersed; and the authority of the Medicean regime was once again secure.

Lorenzo's personal position in that regime was not yet openly acknowledged. When, for instance, Pope Paul II died the next year, a deputation was sent to Rome by the *Signoria* to offer his successor, Sixtus IV, the city's congratulations. Lorenzo was invited to be one of the delegates, but he had no greater privileges nor higher status than any other member of the embassy: Florence was still, in name, a republic; and its citizens remained anxious that it should continue to appear to be so. It was recognized nevertheless that Lorenzo, by his birth, merited special treatment. Too young to be a member of the *Cento*, he was admitted as a member by special decree. He was also admitted to the *Balià* and kept busy with important affairs of state as though he were already a highly experienced politician, writing numerous letters to foreign ambassadors and princes and playing a leading part in the deliberations of the councils.

The influential position he had already achieved for himself by 1472 was demonstrated well enough when there was trouble in Volterra, one of the most restless and independent of those Tuscan towns which, while self-governing except as regards foreign policy, still had to render an annual tribute to Florence. The trouble arose over a contract for mining alum in a cave in the neighbourhood of Volterra; the contract had been granted to a consortium comprising three Florentines, three Sienese and two Volterrans. There was strong feeling amongst the people of Volterra that this consortium had gained its profitable contract by fraud. They therefore elected magistrates who seized the mine and dismissed the men who were operating it. Lorenzo was not a member of the consortium nor does he appear to have had any control over it; but when the commune of Volterra asked him to arbitrate in the dispute, he was sufficiently well disposed towards the consortium to decide that control of the mine must be handed back to its members. The two Volterran members, Inghirami and Riccobaldi, delighted and encouraged by his decision, promptly marched back to the mine with an armed escort and declared themselves representatives of the rightful owners. It was an invitation to violence, and violence immediately broke out. There were savage riots in which several people were killed; the dead body of Inghirami was thrown out of a window onto the square below; and the Florentine *Capitano* of Volterra had cause to feel grateful that he had not been thrown out with him.

Lorenzo was now determined that the uprising must be put down by force. His orders had been disobeyed. Some of those in whose favour he had pronounced had been savagely murdered, and the Volterran rebels had been joined by Florentine exiles who were urging them to join them in an attack on the Medici. A majority of the *Signoria* were of the opinion that to use force was both provocative and unnecessary. This was also the opinion of the Bishop of Volterra. But Lorenzo would not listen. The Volterrans were notoriously turbulent and should be taught a lesson; if they were not, other Tuscan towns might follow their example. His advice was taken. An army, led by Federigo da Montefeltro, Duke of Urbino, and composed of mercenaries in Florentine pay, marched towards Volterra, whose citizens looked frantically about for allies, but in vain. They even went so far as to offer their town to the King of Naples if only he would save them from Florence, but apart from a little help from Siena and Piombino no comforting response was received from anywhere. After a month's siege the town surrendered. Lorenzo wrote a letter expressing his relief that it had all ended so satisfactorily; but he wrote too soon.

By the time his letter reached Volterra the town was being wildly plundered. No one afterwards discovered how it was that the terms of surrender were so blatantly violated. Some said that the mercenaries employed by the Volterrans had opened the gates to the Duke of Urbino's men in order to help them plunder the town. By whatever means they entered it, the Duke's men were soon pillaging Volterra, breaking into houses and shops, murdering men and raping women. Some reports had it that the Duke himself, having found and stolen a rare polyglot Bible, made no efforts to control them; others claimed that he did have several of his soldiers hanged but that this was no deterrent. In any case, it was many hours before the uproar died down and by then hundreds of people were dead or mutilated, and whole streets were ransacked and in ruins. The horror of the scene of devastation was heightened by the effects of a landslip caused by torrential rain.

On learning what had happened Lorenzo immediately rode over to Volterra. He did what he could to reassure the people that his fellow citizens in Florence profoundly regretted the outrages, and he distributed money to those who had suffered loss. His regret was obviously sincere; but it was impossible to overlook the fact that it was he who had advocated the use of force, that it was he who had employed the Duke of Urbino, that it was he who had approved the restoration of the mines to the original *concessionaires*, and that it was he who had pressed for the withdrawal of Volterra's rights of self-government. And in Volterra these things are not forgotten even to this day.

X

THE POPE AND THE PAZZI

'Do what you wish provided there be no killing'

RANCESCO DELLA Rovere, to whom Lorenzo had offered
Florence's congratulations on his election in 1471 as Pope Sixtus
IV, was a big, gruff, toothless man with a massive head, a small,
squashed nose and an intimidating expression. Born in a poor fishing
community near Savona, he had entered the Franciscan order at a
very early age and, thanks to a highly developed gift for preaching, a
taste for learning and piety, some charm and much ambition, he was
made general of the order before he was fifty and a cardinal three
years later. Since then he had been unremitting in granting favours,
offices, money, lands and power to innumerable relations of dubious
merit of whom his sister's family were the most demanding. Six of
his nephews were made cardinals, and for those who were not in the
Church he endeavoured to find profitable lordships in the Papal
States.

One of these nephews, the witty, amiable and ostentatious Piero
Riario, was created Patriarch of Constantinople, Abbot of St Ambrose,
Bishop of Treviso, Mende, Spalato and Senigallia as well as Archbishop of Florence. Another nephew, Girolamo Riario, whom many
believed to be, in fact, his son, was even more importunate. A fat,
uncouth, rowdy young man, Girolamo had his eye on Imola as a
base from which to build up larger estates in the Romagna. This
small town between Bologna and Forlì had recently been sold by
Taddeo Manfredi to the Duke of Milan whose natural daughter,
Caterina Sforza, seemed to the Pope an ideal bride for Girolamo.
Negotations were immediately opened and the Medici bank in Rome

was asked to raise the 40,000 ducats necessary for the purchase of Imola.

Lorenzo was much disturbed by this request. So far, his relations with the Pope had been perfectly cordial. He had been greeted 'very honourably' in Rome where he had been assured that the Medici were to remain bankers to the Curia and agents for the alum mines at Tolfa. He had been presented with two marble heads, one of Augustus, the other of Agrippa; and he had been offered various treasures from the collections of Paul II, including intaglios, cameos, vases and cups in semi-precious stones, which he was able to buy at a most reasonable price. Lorenzo was naturally anxious that this promising start to his association with the new Pope should not be undermined; but he also recognized that the strategically placed town of Imola, which dominated the road from Rimini to Bologna and which he had hoped to buy himself for Florence, must on no account fall into the hands of the Pope. So when the application for a loan was placed before him he made excuses for not granting it. Undeterred, the Pope turned to the Medici's leading rivals as Florentine bankers in Rome, the Pazzi, who were delighted to be of service and to obtain the coveted Curial account.

Having settled Girolamo comfortably at Imola, the Pope now turned his attention to another nephew, Giovanni della Rovere, who, although Prefect of Rome and Lord of Mondovi in Piedmont, was still anxious to get the same sort of foothold in the Romagna as his cousin had done. Sixtus obligingly fixed this for him by arranging a marriage with the eldest daughter of Duke Federigo of Urbino, which not only brought the territorial influence of the Pope closer than ever to the Florentine frontier, but also detached a highly successful *condottiere* from Florentine service.

By now, relations between Lorenzo and the Curia were growing excessively strained; and when the Pope endeavoured to dislodge Niccolò Vitelli from Città di Castello, a town near the Florentine outpost of Borgo San Sepolcro – which had been bought in Cosimo's day with funds confiscated from a Jewish pawnbroker – Florence and the Papacy came close to war. Lorenzo raised 6,000 men to help defend Vitelli, which the Pope considered the grossest effrontery;

and after Vitelli, despite this assistance, had been forced to surrender, he was given an honourable welcome in Florence, which antagonized Sixtus even more.

There was yet further trouble in 1474 when Piero Riario died, worn out by his relentless enjoyment of the rich benefices his uncle had bestowed upon him; and the Archbishopric of Florence became vacant once more. Lorenzo succeeded in having his brother-in-law, Rinaldo Orsini, appointed Riario's successor; but he could not prevent the Pope nominating Francesco Salviati as Archbishop of Pisa, even though an undertaking had been given that no appointments to ecclesiastical benefices within the Republic should be made without the agreement of the *Signoria*. Since the Pope chose to ignore this undertaking, Lorenzo declined to admit Salviati into Tuscany; and for three years Salviati was kept waiting in Rome, frustrated, embittered and ready to lend his support to any anti-Medicean plot which might be proposed to him.

Lorenzo had other dangerous enemies in Rome. In order to maintain the uncertain peace in north Italy, he had proposed a mutual alliance between Florence, Milan and Venice. But, far from achieving peace, the proposal almost provoked another war, for the Pope angrily condemned the new league as aimed at himself, while King Ferrante of Naples was deeply suspicious of an alliance which had been formed without his being consulted and which seemed to threaten his interests in the Adriatic. The Pope and the King of Naples, whose traditional antagonism to the Papacy had been noticeably softened by the marriage of one of King Ferrante's illegitimate daughters to Leonardo della Rovere – another nephew from the Pope's seemingly inexhaustible supply – were now thrown closer than ever together in mutual distrust of the young upstart from Florence.

Lorenzo's difficulties were made all the more complicated when on St Stephen's Day, 1476, his firm ally, Galeazzo Maria Sforza, was stabbed to death by three young assassins on his way to Mass. For Galeazzo Maria's son was a small boy of seven. His mother declared herself Regent; but a disorderly gaggle of uncles clamoured for their brother's succession. And until their quarrel was settled, Lorenzo could hope for no help from Milan against the conspirators now gathering to destroy him.

Three of these conspirators met in Rome during the early weeks of the new year, 1477. They were Girolamo Riario, whose ambitions were far from satisfied by the lordship of Imola; Francesco Salviati, the disgruntled Archbishop-designate of Pisa, who hoped to obtain the more distinguished Archbishopric of Florence; and Francesco de' Pazzi, manager of the Pazzi family bank in Rome, a small, fidgety young man of 'great arrogance and pretensions', who thought that the time had now come for the Pazzi to take over as rulers of Florence from the Medici.

The Pazzi were a much older family than the Medici.[1] One of their forebears, Pazzo de' Pazzi, had been on the First Crusade and had returned to Florence with some flints from the altar of the Holy Sepulchre at Jerusalem which were deposited in the church of Sant' Apostoli.[2] They had loftily scorned trade up till the beginning of the thirteenth century; but in 1342 they had renounced their ancient lineage so as to be declared *popolani* and thus render themselves qualified for government office. They had subsequently made a fortune in banking. The head of the family in the early fifteenth century was Andrea de' Pazzi who spent a sizable part of that fortune in commissioning Brunelleschi to build the Pazzi Chapel next to Santa Croce.[3] His son, Piero, spent a good deal more of it on a fine library. But Piero's brother, Jacopo, who succeeded him in 1464, was not so concerned to spend money as to conserve it.

Indeed, Jacopo was a tight-fisted old man, noted throughout Florence for his passion for gambling, and for losing his temper when he did not win. He thought the chances of a successful *coup d'état* were so slight that he was 'colder than ice' when his young relative, Francesco, apprised him of the plot being hatched in Rome. Besides, Guglielmo, one of his ten nephews, was Lorenzo's brother-in-law, and he himself was on good terms with the Medici, even though Lorenzo's rule threatened to continue to exclude his family from any real authority in the State. To be sure, like the rest of his family, he had been extremely annoyed when Lorenzo interfered in the matter of Giovanni Borromeo's fortune. A Pazzi had married a daughter of this Borromeo and had naturally expected to inherit at least a good part of her family's money; but when the father died a new law was passed – supposedly at the instigation of the Medici – which enabled his estate to pass to his nephews, who were known to be Medici supporters, rather than to his daughter and her husband, who were not. But Jacopo de' Pazzi did not consider the Borromeo affair sufficient grounds for taking the inordinate risks involved in staging a *coup d'état*.

Supposing, however, that if he could produce evidence of strong military support the old man might yet be won over, Francesco de' Pazzi now approached Gian Battista da Montesecco, a *condottiere* who had done good work in the past in the service of the Curia. Montesecco, a rough soldier not given to intrigue, was not immediately forthcoming. He explained that he was employed by the Pope and his nephew, Girolamo Riario, lord of Imola, and could do nothing without their blessing. Francesco reassured him that it was in the very interests of the Pope that he was acting; as for Girolamo Riario, he was a party to the plot; so was Francesco Salviati, Archbishop of Pisa. Montesecco was still not convinced, neither that day, nor on a later occasion when both Francesco de' Pazzi and Salviati pressed their arguments upon him again, assuring him that Lorenzo had behaved abominably towards the Pope, that Girolamo Riario's rule in Imola was 'not worth a bean' so long as Lorenzo lived, that the Medici rule was detested by the Florentines who would rise up in arms against their present rulers at the slightest encouragement.

'My lords,' said Montesecco dubiously, according to his own account, 'beware of what you do. Florence is a big affair.'

'We know the position of affairs in Florence a great deal better than you do,' the Archbishop objected, evidently growing impatient with the stubborn soldier. 'There is no more doubt that our plan will succeed than that we are all sitting here now. The first essential is to enlist the support of Messer Jacopo de' Pazzi ... When we have him the thing is done.'

Slowly Montesecco began to give ground, and finally agreed to join the conspirators provided the Pope gave them his blessing. So it was agreed that the Archbishop and Riario should take him to see Pope Sixtus.

At the subsequent audience the Pope confirmed to Montesecco that it was, indeed, his wish that 'this matter of Florence' should be taken immediately in hand.

'But this matter, Holy Father, may turn out ill without the death of Lorenzo and Giuliano, and perhaps of others.'

'I do not wish the death of anyone on any account since it does not accord with our office to consent to such a thing. Though Lorenzo is a villain, and behaves ill towards us, yet we do not on any account desire his death, but only a change in the government.'

'All that we can do shall be done to see that Lorenzo does not die,' Girolamo said. 'But should he die, will Your Holiness pardon him who did it?'

'You are an oaf. I tell you I do not want anyone killed, just a change in the government. And I repeat to you, Gian Battista, that I strongly desire this change and that Lorenzo, who is a villain and a *furfante* [a despicable rascal], does not esteem us. Once he is out of Florence we could do whatever we like with the Republic and that would be very pleasing to us.'

'Your Holiness speaks true. Be content, therefore, that we shall do everything possible to bring this about.'

'Go, and do what you wish, provided there be no killing.'

'Holy Father, are you content that we steer this ship? And that we will steer it well?' Salviati asked.

'I am content.'

The Pope rose, assured them of 'every assistance by way of men-at-arms or otherwise as might be necessary', then dismissed them.

The three men left the room, as convinced as they were when they entered it that they would have to kill both Lorenzo and Giuliano if their plan were to succeed; and that the Pope, despite all that he had said to the contrary, would condone murder if murder were necessary.

Encouraged by the interview, Montesecco set about enlisting the military forces that would be required and left for the Romagna to discuss the tactics of the *coup* with various fellow *condottieri* in Tolentino, Imola and Città di Castello. He then rode across the Appenines to Florence to give Lorenzo assurances of Girolamo Riario's friendship and good will.

Lorenzo was in mourning for one of Clarice's relations when Montesecco arrived at Cafaggiolo; but he was amiable, talkative and attractive as ever. He spoke of Riario in the most friendly way; and Montesecco, captivated by his charm, began to regret the unpleasant task he had agreed to perform. Lorenzo accompanied him back to Florence where, in his room at the Albergo della Campagna, Montesecco had a visit from Jacopo de' Pazzi for whom he had letters from both Riario and the Archbishop.

Jacopo was as gloomy, cross and pessimistic as ever. 'They are going to break their necks,' he told Montesecco. 'I understand what is going on here better than they do. I do not want to listen to you. I do not want to hear any more about it.'

When he learned what Montesecco had to relate about the audience with the Pope, however, his mood gradually changed; and before long he was a whole-hearted, not to say enthusiastic, supporter of the plot, ready to take an active part in its development. He suggested that the best way of carrying out the assassinations would be to find some pretext for separating the two brothers, then to kill them both as far as possible simultaneously. For this purpose it was decided to invite Lorenzo to Rome and to assassinate him there while Giuliano was disposed of in Florence. But Lorenzo declined the invitation to Rome; so the conspirators had to conceive a plan for killing both brothers on their home ground, preferably when they were off their guard enjoying some entertainment.

An inducement for the Medici to give a suitable entertainment at which the murders could be done was to be provided by the arrival in the district of Raffaele Riario, the Pope's seventeen-year-old great-nephew, who was studying at the University of Pisa and who had just been made a cardinal. He was to be invited to come to stay at Jacopo de' Pazzi's villa at Montughi near Florence from where he was to make his presence known by letter to Lorenzo, who was then staying with his brother at the Medici villa at Fiesole. An opportunity to kill both the Medici either by dagger or by poison would surely present itself, if not at Montughi then at Fiesole.

On receipt of the young cardinal's letter, Lorenzo immediately invited him to Fiesole; and on the appointed day he rode over to Montughi with his son, Piero, and Poliziano, intending to accompany the cardinal and his suite back to Fiesole for a dinner party. Lorenzo apologized for his brother's being unable to come with them: he had hurt his leg in an accident and had had to stay at home in bed, and would unfortunately not be able to come down to dinner. So the conspirators decided that they must change their plans, and wait until Giuliano was better again.

It was now arranged that the murders should take place in Florence. Cardinal Raffaele Riario had asked if he might see the treasures at the Medici Palace about which he had heard so much, and had suggested that the following Sunday would be a suitable day as he could combine his visit to the Palace with High Mass in the Cathedral. Lorenzo immediately agreed to this suggestion and made preparations for a banquet to be given in honour of his guest, issuing invitations to numerous distinguished Florentines as well as to the ambassadors of Milan, Venice, Naples and Ferrara. Meantime, his enemies laid their plans to kill him and his brother while they were at the banquet. But at the last moment the conspirators' plans had to be changed once again: it was learned that Giuliano did not expect to be sufficiently recovered to attend the banquet after all. As well as his injured leg he was now suffering from 'an inflammation of the eyes'.

So many people had by now been apprised of the intended assassinations that it seemed to the Pazzi too dangerous to delay them any longer lest the secret leak out. Moreover, the troops whom Montesecco had arranged to have concentrated at various strategic points around the city would by dusk have arrived beneath the walls. If the Medici could not be killed together at the banquet, they would have to be dispatched in the Cathedral during Mass, an occasion which other assassins had found ideal. Giuliano could be stabbed by Francesco de' Pazzi, assisted by Bernardo Bandini Baroncelli, an adventurer anxious to make some money quickly, having dissipated fortune and being deeply in debt to the Pazzi with whom he had formerly been associated in business. At the same time Lorenzo could be cut down by Montesecco. But this idea was abhorrent to Montesecco. Before he had met Lorenzo he had succeeded in persuading himself that to kill him was all in the way of a soldier's duty; but since he had first spoken to him, he had been growing increasingly disgusted with his appointed task. Now he saw an opportunity to escape it altogether by protesting that his conscience would not allow him to 'add sacrilege to murder'; he could not bring himself to kill a man in cold blood in a place where 'God would see him'. Fortunately for the conspirators less scrupulous assassins immediately presented themselves in the persons of two lean, embittered priests, Antonio Maffei, a Volterran who hated Lorenzo for the part he had played in suppressing the recent uprising in his native town, and Stefano da Bagnone, tutor to Jacopo de' Pazzi's illegitimate daughter. Being priests they could not be expected to be as reliable with a dagger as Montesecco, but there were two of them and if they caught Lorenzo unawares they should between them be able to deliver a mortal blow before he could defend himself.

It was settled that the time to strike at both brothers would be at the sounding of the sanctuary bell, presumably when it was rung at the elevation of the Host. This moment would be ideal, not only because the sound of the bell and the celebrant's gesture would provide unmistakable signals which all the assassins would hear and see, but also because the eyes of the victims, and of the congregation generally would be downcast in reverence when the first blows were struck. As soon as the murders had been committed, Archbishop Salviati and Jacopo di Poggio Bracciolini, the ambitious, extravagant, impoverished son of the humanist who had been Cosimo's friend together with a large party of armed supporters were to march upon the Palazzo della Signoria, seize the government and kill any of the *Priori* who might attempt to resist them.

Towards eleven o'clock on that Sunday morning, 26 April 1478 young Raffaele Riario rode into Florence from Montughi and dismounted in the *cortile* of the Medici Palace. He was taken upstair to the apartments on the first floor which had been set aside for hi use and there he changed into his cardinal's vestments. When he wa ready he went downstairs again where, at the foot of the staircase, he was met by Lorenzo who accompanied him to the Cathedral. On their way they were joined by Archbishop Salviati who did not, however, enter the building, excusing himself on the grounds that he had to go and see his mother who, so he said, was seriously ill. Lorenzo took the Cardinal up to the High Altar and left him there, walking across to a group of friends in the ambulatory. There were no chairs in the nave and the large congregation moved about freely.

Giuliano had not yet arrived, so Francesco de' Pazzi and Baroncelli hurried back to the Medici Palace to fetch him. They discovered that he had decided not to go to Mass after all as his leg was still troubling him; but at length he was persuaded to change his mind, and he limped down the Via Larga towards the Cathedral. In the street Francesco de' Pazzi threw his arm round him as though in playful affection, remarking that he seemed to have grown quite fat during his illness, squeezing his body to ensure that he wore no armour under his shirt. His fingers felt the unprotected flesh. He noticed also with relief that Giuliano wore no sword.

As they entered the Cathedral, Francesco de' Pazzi and Baroncelli made for the northern side of the choir. Giuliano politely followed them. They stopped close to the door that leads out into the Via de' Servi. Lorenzo was still standing in the ambulatory on the other side of the High Altar, beyond Ghiberti's wooden screen which then separated it from the choir. His friend Poliziano was near him; so were four other friends, Filippo Strozzi, Antonio Ridolfi, Lorenzo Cavalcanti and Francesco Nori, formerly manager of the Medici bank in Lyons. The two priests, Maffei and Stefano, were immediately behind him.

At the sound of the sacristy bell, the priests snatched their daggers from their robes. Inexpertly, Maffei placed his hand on Lorenzo's shoulder, as though to steady himself or to make sure of his aim. As Lorenzo turned, he felt the dagger's point against his neck. Maffei lunged forward, and the tip of the dagger cut into the tensed flesh. Lorenzo leapt away, tearing off his cloak as he did so and wrapping it around his arm as a shield. He drew his sword, slashed at the two priests who, unnerved by his fast reaction, were beaten back without difficulty. Then he vaulted over the altar rail and dashed headlong for the new sacristy.

Giuliano's mutilated body was already on the floor. At the sound of the sacristy bell he had dutifully lowered his head, and Baroncelli, crying out, 'Take that, traitor!', had brought his dagger down in a ferocious blow that almost split his skull in two. Francesco de' Pazzi thereupon stabbed him with such frenzy, plunging the blade time and again into the unresisting body, that he even drove the point of the dagger through his own thigh. Giuliano fell to his knees while his two assailants continued to rain savage blows upon him, slashing and stabbing until the corpse was rent by nineteen wounds.

As Giuliano's blood poured over the floor, Baroncelli leapt over the body and made for the new sacristy, striking down Francesco Nori whom he killed with a single blow, and wounding Lorenzo Cavalcanti in the arm. But before he could reach the heavy bronze doors of the sacristy Lorenzo had dashed through them, and Poliziano with some other of his friends, had managed to get them shut. 'Giuliano? Is he safe?' Lorenzo kept asking; but no one answered him. While Antonio Ridolfi sucked the wound in Lorenzo's neck, in case the priests' daggers had been poisoned, another friend, Sigismondo della Stufa, who had escaped with them into the sacristy, clambered up the ladder into della Robbia's choir loft to look down into the Cathedral.

The congregation was in uproar. People were shouting that the dome had fallen in. Lorenzo's brother-in-law, Guglielmo de' Pazzi was loudly proclaiming his innocence. Giuliano still lay where he had fallen. Raffaele Riario stood transfixed, as though in shocked dismay, by the High Altar. The two priests who had attacked Lorenzo, together with Giuliano's assassins, had all apparently escaped. Lorenzo was bustled away by his friends to the Medici Palace

Meanwhile Archbishop Salviati and the other conspirators had gone as planned to the Palazzo della Signoria with their armed supporters, most of them villainous-looking mercenaries from Perugia disguised as his suite. Salviati informed the *Gonfaloniere* Cesare Petrucci, that he had an urgent message for him from the Pope. Petrucci, who was in the middle of dinner, gave orders for the

Archbishop and his attendants to be admitted. Salviati himself was shown into a reception room, while the Perugians were placed in nearby offices, the doors of which were closed behind them. The Archbishop's other companions, including Jacopo di Poggio Bracciolini, were left outside in the corridor.

Having completed his dinner, Petrucci came out to receive Salviati who by now was so nervous he was trembling. The Archbishop delivered what he claimed to be the Pope's message in a thick and mumbling voice, almost incoherently, changing colour alarmingly, and glancing round from time to time at the door. Petrucci, having listened to him for a few moments only, called out the guard, whereupon Salviati rushed from the room, shouting to his own men that the moment to strike had come. The response to his cries, however, were muffled shouts and bangings; for, on assuming office as *Gonfaloniere*, Petrucci had had the rooms of the Palazzo della Signoria fitted with special catches which could not be operated from the inside. The Perugians were, for the moment, effectively imprisoned.

As they hammered on the doors, Jacopo do Poggio Bracciolini rushed at the *Gonfaloniere* who caught him by the hair and threw him to the ground. Then, shouting for the *Priori* to follow him and for the *Vacca* to be tolled, the strong and energetic *Gonfaloniere* snatched up an iron cooking-spit as the nearest weapon to hand and rushed at the Archbishop and his companions who were quickly beaten to the ground. The notes of the great bell were by then booming through the city as the people poured into the Piazza. Members of the Pazzi family and small groups of their supporters rode up and down through the streets shouting, '*Libertà! Libertà! Popolo e Libertà! Abasso i Medici! Abasso le palle! Libertà! Libertà!*' But although some of the people in the crowd joined in these shouts, most of them responded insistently with, '*Vivano le palle! Vivano le palle! Palle! Palle! Palle!*'

A group of about fifty armed Medici supporters burst into the Palazzo della Signoria, and, joined by the palace guard, attacked the Perugians. Having killed them all, they rushed out into the Piazza again, bearing the dripping heads of their victims on the ends of lances and swords. News of Giuliano's murder had by now reached the Palace where immediately a rope was tied round Jacopo di

Poggio's neck, the other end was fixed to a transom and his body was hurled from a window. Archbishop Salviati was treated in the same way. So, too, was Francesco de' Pazzi who, still bleeding profusely from the thigh, had been dragged from his hiding place in the family palace and stripped naked. Two of the Archbishop's companions were strangled, and their bodies also hurled out. All five bodies were left dangling above the heads of the surging mob in the Piazza, twisting and swaying in the shadows beneath the machicolations of the northern wall. Poliziano, who was in the Piazza at the time, recorded the gruesome fact that as the Archbishop rolled and struggled at the end of his rope, his eyes goggling in his head, he fixed his teeth into Francesco de' Pazzi's naked body.

Following the fierce lead of the executioners in the Palazzo della Signoria, hundreds of people now ran through the streets, seeking out other conspirators or any unpopular citizen who could conveniently be charged with complicity in the plot. They swarmed beneath the windows of the Medici Palace, demanding to see Lorenzo who appeared before them, his neck in bandages, his brocade waistcoat covered with blood, to assure them that he was only slightly injured and to beg them not to wreak vengeance on those whom they merely suspected of murder. He urged them to save their energy to resist the enemies of the State who had engineered the conspiracy, and who would now undoubtedly attack the city that had thwarted it.

If the people cheered his words, they did not heed them. They attacked the conspirators, and those whom they chose to accuse of conspiracy, killing some, mutilating others, and dragging their remains through the streets. For several days the rioting continued, country people pouring into the city to see what pleasures or rewards were to be had, until some eighty people had been killed.

Few of those involved in the attempted *coup* escaped punishment. The young cardinal, Raffaele Riario, who had stood as though stunned by the High Altar during the uproar in the Cathedral until led to a safe place inside the old sacristy, was rescued by Lorenzo who sent some of his servants to bring him back to the Medici Palace. After the rioting was over, Lorenzo had him escorted in disguise to Rome where, to the end of his days, so it was said, his face never lost the pallor which the ghastly events he had witnessed had imposed upon it. Raffaele Maffei, a brother of the priest who had tried to murder Lorenzo, and Averardo Salviati, a relative of the Archbishop, were also saved from the mob through Lorenzo's intervention. But with the one exception of a certain Napoleone Francesi, whose complicity in the plot was in any case by no means clear, not one of the known conspirators escaped either public or private vengeance. Jacopo de' Pazzi, so overcome by despair at the failure of the plot that he boxed his own ears and threw himself to the floor in despair and rage, managed to escape from the city to the village of Castagno; but the villagers recognized him and brought him back to Florence where, after being tortured, he was stripped naked and strung from a window of the Palazzo della Signoria next to the Archbishop. Later, he was buried in Santa Croce; but the people, blaming the subsequent heavy rains upon his evil spirit, dug up the body and threw it into a ditch in an apple orchard. From here also it was later removed, to be dragged through the streets by a mob shouting, 'Make way for the great knight!' It was then propped against the door of the Pazzi Palace where, to the accompaniment of obscene jokes and cries of 'Open! Your master wishes to enter!' its decomposing head was used as a knocker. Eventually, the putrid corpse was thrown into the Arno from which it was fished by a gang of children who strung it up on the branch of a willow tree, flogged it and tossed it back into the water again.

The two priests, Antonio Maffei and Stefano da Bagnone, were also discovered in hiding. Both were castrated, then hanged. Renato de' Pazzi, Jacopo's brother, who was found in a house in the Mugello, was also executed, being hanged in a peasant's grey smock 'as if to make a masquerade', though his involvement in the plot was never established. Other members of his family escaped with terms of imprisonment in the dungeons of Volterra, though Lorenzo's sister's husband, Guglielmo de' Pazzi, who seems to have been innocent, was merely confined to his villa.

Montesecco, one of the last of the conspirators to be taken, was discovered on 1 May. He was closely questioned under torture and gave a detailed account of the origins of the conspiracy and of the Pope's involvement in it. All the information which he could give having been forced out of him, he was, as a soldier, beheaded by sword on 4 May in the courtyard of the Bargello. Baroncelli, who had helped to murder Giuliano, succeeded in making his escape from Florentine territory and got as far as Constantinople; but there he was recognized and, following Lorenzo's official request to the Sultan, he was brought back in chains to Florence where he, too, was executed in the Bargello.

The disgrace of the Pazzi family was not permitted to end with their execution. Their names and their coat-of-arms were ordered to be suppressed in perpetuity by a public decree of the *Signoria*; their property was confiscated; their palace was given another name, as were all other places in Florence which formerly had borne it; orders were given for their family symbol – the dolphin – to be cut down or blotted out wherever it was to be found. No man who married a Pazzi was ever to be allowed to hold office in the Republic. All customs associated with the family were abolished, including the ancient ceremony of carrying the sacred flint to their palace on Easter Eve.[4] Representations of the Pazzi traitors, together with those of the other conspirators, were painted by Botticelli – for a fee of forty florins for each figure – on the wall of the Bargello as Florentine custom dictated. They were portrayed with ropes round their necks, representing the manner of their death, except in the case of Napoleone Francesi who was painted hanging by his ankle to indicate that he had escaped. Beneath each portrait was inscribed a suitable epitaph in verse composed by Lorenzo.

In contrast to these insulting representations, so Giorgio Vasari recorded,

Lorenzo's friends and relations ordered that, in thanksgiving to God for his preservation, images of him should be set up throughout the city. So [a skilled craftsman in wax] with the help and advice of Verrocchio, made three life-size wax figures with a wooden framework and a covering of waxed cloth, folded and arranged so well that the result was wonderfully attractive and lifelike. He then made the heads, hands and feet, using a coating of thicker wax, copying the features from life, and painting them in oils with the hair and other adornments. The results of this skilful work were so natural that the wax figures seemed real and alive, as can be seen today from the three figures themselves. One of them is in the church of the nuns of Chiarito, in Via di San Gallo, in front of the miraculous crucifix. This statue is dressed exactly as Lorenzo was when, bandaged and wounded at the throat, he stood at the windows of his house and showed himself to the people ... The second of the statues, dressed in the citizen's gown worn in Florence, is in the church of Santissima Annunziata above the lower door by the table where the candles are sold. And the third was sent to Santa Maria degli Angeli in Assisi and set up in front of the Madonna.

XI

THE SAVIOUR OF FLORENCE

*'That son of iniquity and foster-child
of perdition'*

O N ASCENSION Day 1478 Giuliano de' Medici was buried in
the old sacristy of San Lorenzo in the porphyry sarcophagus
which he and his brother had had made in memory of their
father and uncle. Twenty-five at the time of his murder, he had never
been married; but earlier that year his young mistress, Fioretta
Gorini, had borne him a son who was christened Giulio.[1] This boy,
whose mother soon afterwards died, was adopted by Lorenzo who
treated him as though he were his own child.

Of his own three sons, Lorenzo once said that the eldest was
foolish, the next clever, and the youngest good; but he loved them
all as he loved his daughters, and he delighted in playing games with
them, a habit upon which Machiavelli afterwards commented with
a hint of surprised reproach. Lorenzo wrote a little play for them,
San Giovanni e San Paolo, giving them each a part and reserving one
for himself. And he made it clear to them that however busy he was
with affairs of State and however busy they were with their lessons –
in which he took the deepest interest – he would always find time to
talk to them. 'If the wild beasts love their young,' he wrote, 'how
much greater should be our indulgence towards our children.'

When he was parted from them he missed their company as much
as they missed him. 'When will Lorenzo come?' they often asked
their tutors or their mother. 'When will Lorenzo come?' In the uncertain times following the Pazzi conspiracy, all the children were

The Ponte Santa Trinità was rebuilt by Bartolommeo Ammanati between 1567 and 1569.
ond it may be seen the Ponte Vecchio and the tower of the Palazzo della Signoria, by this time
wn as the Palazzo Vecchio.

20. The villa of Poggio a Caiano by Giusto Utens. It was converted by Giuliano da Sangallo for Lorenzo the Magnificent. The loggia and pediment were added in the time of his son, Pope Leo ⹁

Giovanni di Lorenzo de' Medici, Pope Leo X, portrayed by Raphael with the Pope's cousin, Giulio, future Pope Clement VII, on his right and Cardinal Luigi de' Rossi standing behind the chair.

22. Florence at the time of the siege of 1529–30 as depicted by Giorgio Vasari. The Prince of Orange's camp sprawls across the foreground. It was on Michelangelo's advice that the defences were extended circumvallate the hill of San Miniato on the right. The belfry of its church was protected from artillery fire by mattresses. Starved into surrender, the citizens were forced to accept the return of the Medici wh had fled from Florence after the Sack of Rome.

23. A joust in the Piazza Santa Croce where chariot races and games of *calcio* were also traditionally held. The church of Santa Croce in the background contains the tombs of Michelangelo and of several of Cosimo de' Medici's friends, including Leonardo Bruni. The present marble façade, though built to seventeenth-century design, was not added until 1863.

The Medici Palace as it appeared after its enlargement by the Riccardi family. The upper storeys
which can be seen facing the church and the overhanging cornice are as Michelozzo designed them.
The church on the left is San Giovannino degli Scolopi which was rebuilt between 1579 and 1661 by
Ammanati and Giulio and Alfonso Parigi.

25 (*above*). The Palazzo Vecchio (formerly known as the Palazzo della Signoria) and the Loggia dei Lanzi after the building of the Uffizi which can be seen behind the Palazzo.

26. The lily of the commune of Florence, surmounted by the granducal coronet, as represented in mosaic in the Cappella dei Principi.

FLORENTIAE·CIVITAS

sent away with their mother – and with Poliziano as tutor for the elder boys – to stay with their friends, the Panciaticchi, at Pistoia. Poliziano clearly did not enjoy his exile from Florence, though his letters to Lorenzo from Pistoia were uncomplaining. He gave him news of the children's activities, assured him that Andrea Panciaticchi had received them all with 'much kindness', that Clarice was very well but took little pleasure in anything except the scraps of good news that came occasionally from Florence. 'She rarely goes out. We want for nothing. Presents we refuse, save salad, figs, and a few flasks of wine, some *beccafichi* or things of that sort. These citizens would bring us water in their ears ... We keep good watch and have begun to put a guard at the gates. When you have time come and see your family who expect you with open arms.'

Lorenzo's family remained at Pistoia throughout the summer of 1478; but as winter approached they were moved to the greater security of the fortified villa at Cafaggiolo; and here, as the hard, cold weather set in, Poliziano became more and more miserable and unutterably bored. He continued to write to Lorenzo without complaining unduly about his situation; but to Lorenzo's mother, Lucrezia, he did not disguise his misery. It was so fearfully cold he had to spend most of his time sitting over the fire in his slippers and overcoat; it rained so constantly that the children could not go out and he had to invent games for them to play indoors. To make these games more interesting he had made the losers forfeit a course of their next meal, but this had not proved a good idea since, more often than not, the results were greeted with tears. It was all made far worse by the fact that he did not get on at all well with Clarice.

She, in her unimaginative, old-fashioned Roman way, was appalled to discover that little Giovanni was being taught to read Latin from classical texts instead of from the psalter. He, knowing that Lorenzo would approve his method of instruction, declined to alter it. Quarrels about this led to quarrels about other things until Clarice dismissed Poliziano from the villa. Lorenzo was obliged to condone his friend's dismissal, but in appointing in his place the less abrasive Martino da Comedia he let his wife know that he did not approve of her conduct. Clarice, in turn, upbraided him for allowing the objectionable Poliziano to live in Lorenzo's rooms at Fiesole, for making her a laughing-stock by so publicly displaying his forgiveness of a man she had had to send packing from her house. Lorenzo was then driven to write a sharp letter reproving her conduct. He reminded her that she had not sent on Poliziano's books as he had asked her to do, and demanded that they should be dispatched that very day.

Heated as it became, it was the one serious quarrel that Lorenzo and Clarice seem ever to have had. She was far from being an ideal wife for him. Despite that shyness and modesty, that willingness to please that his mother had noted in her as a young girl in Rome, Clarice had not been able to adapt herself to Florentine ways. She had remained a Roman at heart, a rather haughty, petulant creature, excessively proud of her ancient lineage, deeply troubled by her husband's quarrel with the Pope, ill at ease with his clever, witty, sardonic friends whose conversation she found it so difficult to understand.

Lorenzo was almost certainly not faithful to her. She may not have minded that too much, perhaps. After all, husbands were not given to fidelity then; and Lorenzo's affairs were not indiscreet. His attachment to Lucrezia Donati had been purely romantic. He had known her since she was a little girl; and though he wore her device in tournaments and wrote sonnets praising the beauty of her eyes and hands and the ever-changing expression of her lovely face, Clarice knew enough of Florentine society and of Lorenzo himself to be sure he would never disgrace the Medici by taking for a mistress the treasured daughter of such a family as the Donati. Besides, Clarice liked Lucrezia, who was already married when she met her, and was pleased for her to become godmother to her eldest son. Lorenzo's affairs with other women seem to have caused Clarice as little concern. Francesco Guicciardini said that when he was forty Lorenzo, who 'was licentious and very amorous', fell desperately in love with Bartolommea dei Nasi, the wife of Donato Benci, and spent night after night with her at her villa, returning to Florence just before dawn. But if this were so, the affair was either concealed from Clarice, meant little to her, or, perhaps, it did not begin until after her death. Certainly Lorenzo's relations with other women never seem to have disturbed his affection for his wife, nor her affection for him. That they were fond of each other cannot be doubted. She could share few of his interests; she knew little of art or literature, less of politics and philosophy. When she wrote letters to him she could think of nothing to relate other than the recommendation of some preacher whose sermon she had heard in church or an account of the health of the children. But she was affectionate in her way; and so was he. 'I have arrived safe and well,' he assured her in one characteristic letter.

This I think will please you better than any other news save that of my return, judging by my own longing for you and for home. Be good company to Piero, Mona Contessina [his ancient grandmother, who in accordance with the custom of the time lived in the family palace until her death in 1473] and Mona Lucrezia [who also lived with the family until she died in 1482]. Pray to God for me, and if you want anything from here [Milan] before I leave, let me know. Your Lorenzo.

To her children, especially to her daughter, Maddalena, Clarice was devoted. She had ten in all, three of whom died in infancy; and it was the death of the eleven-year-old Luigia that hastened her own. She was already ill with tuberculosis and had been so for some time. When she seemed a little better, Lorenzo, ill himself, left her to take a cure of the medicinal waters at Filetta. Nine days after his departure, Clarice died. Her husband heard the news with the utmost grief. 'The limit is passed,' he wrote. 'I can find no comfort or rest for my deep sorrow. I pray the Lord God to give me peace, and trust that in His goodness, He will spare me any more such trials as have visited me lately.'

Three days later the Ferrarese ambassador in Florence wrote home to tell the Duke that Clarice de' Medici was dead. He had not bothered to send the news before, he said, because he did not think it of much importance.

As Lorenzo had feared, the failure of the Pazzi conspiracy and the

Florentines' fierce reprisals against those who had been involved in it aroused the utmost fury in Rome. Followed by three hundred halberdiers, Girolamo Riario stormed off to the house of the Florentine ambassador, Donato Acciaiuoli, arrested him and would have thrown him into the dungeons of Sant' Angelo had not the Venetian and Milanese ambassadors strongly protested against this outrage of diplomatic immunity. Deprived of that chosen victim, Riario vehemently urged his uncle to use all the means at his disposal to avenge himself upon the Florentines in general and upon the Medici family in particular. The Pope, as angry as his nephew, needed little persuasion. He ordered the arrest of all the principal Florentine bankers and merchants in Rome, though he was compelled to release them when reminded that Cardinal Raffaele Riario was still held in Florence. He sequestrated the assets of the Medici bank and all Medici property he could lay his hands on; he repudiated the debts of the Apostolic Chamber to the bank; he dispatched a nuncio from Rome to demand that Lorenzo should be handed over to papal justice, and issued an enormously lengthy Bull of Excommunication against 'that son of iniquity and foster-child of perdition, Lorenzo dei Medici, and those other citizens of Florence, his accomplices and abettors'. These accomplices were deemed to include the *Gonfaloniere* and the entire *Signoria*, all the members of which were 'pronounced culpable, sacrilegious, excommunicate, anathematised, infamous, unworthy of trust and incapable of making a will'. 'All their property is to revert to the Church,' the document continued; 'their houses are to be levelled to the ground, their habitations made desolate so that none may dwell therein. Let everlasting ruin witness their everlasting disgrace.' If these sentences and punishments were not carried out within two months, the whole city of Florence was to be laid under interdict together with all its dependencies. Not content with this, the Pope declared war upon Florence and had no difficulty in persuading King Ferrante of Naples to do the same.

Eager to extend the dominion of the House of Aragon over Tuscany, King Ferrante's son, Alfonso, Duke of Calabria, promptly marched across the frontier and, having taken possession of the territory round Montepulciano, sent an envoy to Florence with grim warnings of the city's imminent destruction together with another fierce message from the Pope couched in even more virulent terms than the Bull of Excommunication.

To these and subsequent threats the *Signoria* issued defiant replies:

> You say that Lorenzo is a tyrant and command us to expel him. But most Florentines call him their defender ... Remember your high office as the Vicar of Christ. Remember that the Keys of St Peter were not given to you to abuse in such a way ... Florence will resolutely defend her liberties, trusting in Christ who knows the justice of her cause, and who does not desert those who believe in Him; trusting in her allies who regard her cause as their own; especially trusting in the most Christian King, Louis of France, who has ever been the patron and protector of the Florentine State.

Despite these protestations of trust, the Florentines had little cause to hope for much help from their allies. Admittedly, the French King had written a friendly letter of sympathy to Lorenzo and a protest to the Pope against his treatment of him; he had made vague threats of another General Council and of a renewal of Angevin claims to Naples; he had sent Philippe de Commines as a special envoy to Italy. But as Commines himself said, the citizens were, in fact, offered little more than sympathy: 'Louis's favourable inclination towards the Florentines was in some measure useful to them, but not so much as I wished, for I had no army with which to support them beyond my own retinue.'

In earlier years Florence might have expected military help from Milan; but ever since the murder of Galeazzo Maria Sforza, the feud between the widowed Duchess, guardian of their young son, Gian Galeazzo, and her brothers-in-law, his uncles, had prevented Milan from playing any effective part in Italian politics. A Milanese force under Gian Giacomo Trivulzio was eventually sent to Florence's help, but it was not large enough to be effective. Nor were the mercenary forces dispatched by the Medici's Orsini relatives in Rome; nor yet was the Bolognese force which was provided by Giovanni Bentivoglio, whom Lorenzo had visited years before as his father's representative and with whom he had ever since remained on terms of the closest friendship. Indeed, when all these disparate troops were placed under the overall command of Ercole d'Este, the tall, handsome, cunning and cautious Duke of Ferrara, there were few people – and the Duke himself was evidently not one of them – who believed that the Florentines could possibly withstand the onslaught which the Neapolitan army, advancing up the Chiana valley, was threatening to launch against them.

The Duke of Calabria's troops were not the only threat to Florence. By now, the Pope had induced Siena and Lucca to join forces with him and had entrusted the command of his own army to that formidable soldier, Federigo da Montefeltro, Duke of Urbino. Philippe de Commines, having seen the troops in the papal camp and compared them with the motley array that their enemies had so far assembled, was forced to conclude that the independence of the Florentine Republic was soon to be ended.

The Florentines themselves, far more optimistic than Commines, continued to reject all the demands the Pope made of them. The Tuscan bishops, reacting defiantly to the Bull of Excommunication, had unanimously decided at a meeting in the Cathedral in Florence that the actions which the *Signoria* had so far taken were completely justified. And, in accordance with this decision, they issued their own decree excommunicating the Pope. Copies of the excommunication were printed on the press set up in Florence the year before by Bernardo Cennini, and distributed throughout Europe under the imposing title, *Contrascommunica del clero Fiorentino fulminate contro il summo Pontifice Sisto IV*. Their attitude was wholeheartedly supported by their clergy, by their congregations and by Lorenzo himself.

By this time Lorenzo had established himself as the undisputed leader of the Florentine cause. He had called a meeting of the leading citizens and in his high-pitched, nasal voice had dramatically assured them that as he was himself the cause of the Pope's campaign against Florence he was willing to sacrifice himself and even his family if they thought that the exile or death of the Medici would prove the salvation of the city. Replying on their behalf, Jacopo dei Alessandri told him that it was their unanimous determination to stand by him to the end. They appointed a guard of twelve men to be responsible for his personal safety and elected him one of the Ten of War, the emergency committee set up to direct the campaign for the city's defence.

That this campaign did not end in the disaster for Florence which Commines expected was due far more to good fortune and to the peculiar traditions of fifteenth-century Italian warfare than to any notable competence in either the Florentine army or in its commander, the Duke of Ferrara, who appeared unwilling to test his strength against the Duke of Calabria, a skilful soldier who also happened to be his brother-in-law. Always careful to keep a good two days' march away from the enemy, the Duke of Ferrara took three weeks to cover the fifty miles between Pisa and Sarzana. When urged by the Florentines to move his men more quickly, he ridiculed such exhortation from 'mere mechanics who [knew] nothing of war'. 'The system of our Italian soldiers is this,' commented the Florentine apothecary, Luca Landucci. 'You turn your attention to plundering in that direction, and we will do the same in this. Getting too near each other is not our game.' By November 1478, no decisive battle having yet been fought, both armies retreated to their winter quarters.

The next year was less favourable for Florence. First of all, the uncles of the young Duke Gian Galleazo Sforza, worsted in their efforts to gain power in Milan, had gone to Naples where King Ferrante incited them to go back north with an army and seize the Duchy by force. The return of her brothers-in-law to Lombardy so alarmed the Duchess that she recalled the Milanese contingent from the defence of Florence to help defend her own government in Milan.

The Duchess was particularly alarmed by the return of Lodovico Sforza, known as il Moro, the Moor, because one of his Christian names was Mauro and he had a very dark skin. He was a rather effeminate-looking man with an extremely small mouth and neatly curled hair. He was vain, boastful and cowardly; yet he was undoubtedly clever. A bad judge of men, he knew a great deal about art and literature. He was cynical and amoral, but he was courteous and considerate. He had a definite talent for administration and diplomacy, and a remarkable memory. He was a man to be reckoned with.

By September he had come to terms with the Duchess, had established himself in power in Milan, and had made up his mind that the Florentine Republic, on the verge of collapse, was no longer a suitable ally for his Duchy. At the same time the Duke of Calabria's forces, rampaging about in the Val d'Elsa, captured the fortress of Poggio Imperiale and would have attacked Florence itself had not the small town of Colle, less than thirty miles south of Florence, offered so determined a resistance that he was held up there for two months. When at last Colle fell on 14 November – after the Duke's mortars, so Luca Landucci recorded in his diary, had been 'fired at it a thousand and twenty four times' – the winter was too far advanced for the Neapolitan army to continue its operations in the Val d'Elsa and the Duke of Calabria took his men away once more to hibernate in Siena. But though they had been given another breathing-space, the Florentines' situation was now more desperate than ever. The various *condottieri* in their service were perpetually quarrelling with each other; the Duke of Ferrara had wandered off in the wake of the Sforzas; gangs of brigands, pretending to be enemy raiding-parties, plundered the Tuscan countryside; plague had broken out in Florence; and its citizens were beginning to grumble about the heavy taxes which the war had forced the emergency committee to introduce. Moreover, the Florentine economy was in decline, partly due to the virtual cessation of imports of wool from England where manufacturers were now making their own cloth; while hundreds of workers were locked out of their factories by merchants with no work for them to do. Well aware that the Republic could not survive another season's campaigning and that his allies supported the general wish for peace, Lorenzo now took what appeared to the Florentines as an extraordinary and courageous decision: he made up his mind to go to Naples and to present himself at his enemy's court. Leaving the city in the care of the recently elected *Gonfaloniere*, Tommaso Soderini, he rode away to the sea. Before embarking he wrote to the *Signoria* from the town of San Miniato Tedesco on the road to Pisa:

In the dangerous circumstances in which our city is placed, the time for deliberation is past. Action must be taken ... I have decided, with your approval, to sail for Naples immediately, believing that as I am the person against whom the activities of our enemies are chiefly directed, I may, perhaps, by delivering myself into their hands, be the means of restoring peace to our fellow-citizens ... As I have had more honour and responsibility among you than any private citizen has had in our day, I am more bound than any other person to serve our country, even at the risk of my life. With this intention I now go. Perhaps God wills that this war, which began in the blood of my brother and of myself, should be ended by my means. My desire is that by my life or my death, my misfortune or my prosperity, I may contribute to the welfare of our city ... I go full of hope, praying to God to give me grace to perform what every citizen should at all times be ready to perform for his country. I commend myself humbly to your Excellencies of the *Signoria*. Laurentius de Medici.

When this emotional letter was read out to the *Signoria*, not a single one of the *Priori*, according to Filippo Valori, was able to restrain his tears. Profoundly distrusting King Ferrante, who was reported to preserve the bodies of his enemies embalmed in a private museum, they thought that they might never see Lorenzo again. Yet it was recognized that his offer of personal sacrifice was a gesture, perhaps the only gesture, that might save the Republic. The *Signoria*, therefore, gave Lorenzo their blessing, nominated him ambassador to Naples and wished him every success. The day after he received their reply he sailed from Vada, arriving in Naples just before Christmas 1479. He was twenty-nine years old.

Standing on the quay to meet him was King Ferrante's second son, Federigo, whom Lorenzo had met and grown to like as a boy. They greeted each other warmly. Lorenzo was welcomed with equal warmth by the Duke of Calabria's clever wife, Ippolita Sforza, whom he had also known well for years; and by Diomede Carafa, one of King Ferrante's principal advisers, an elderly author, connoisseur and collector of antiques for whom Lorenzo had done many favours in the past, by helping and entertaining his friends when they visited Florence, and to whom he had presented an exquisite bronze head of a horse which was one of the finest Roman antiquities in Carafa's collection. Indeed, it soon became clear to Lorenzo's suite that his mission was far less foolhardy than it had seemed and far less dramatic than he had been astute enough to present it in his letter to the *Signoria*.

Before writing that letter, he had for long been in secret communication with the Neapolitan court and had assured himself that his arrival there would not be unwelcome. The ship in which he had sailed, in fact, had been sent from Naples to fetch him. He knew that the Duke of Calabria, whose troops now controlled large tracts of land in southern Tuscany, was opposed to any peace settlement that did not recognize his conquests; but Lorenzo also knew that King Ferrante was extremely apprehensive about the King of France's continued threats of renewing Angevin claims to the throne of Naples and about the intentions of the Turks whose squadrons were sailing threateningly up and down the Italian shores of the southern Adriatic.

King Ferrante was not, however, a man with whom it was easy to come to terms. Shrewd and with much political ability, he was at the same time hard, vindictive and dissimulating. A sallow-faced man inclined to fat and to periods of moody silence, it was impossible to tell, so Commines commented, what he was really like or what he was thinking: 'no man knew when he was angry or pleased'. But he shared Lorenzo's love of country life, of falconry and hunting; he shared his taste for poetry, for the new learning and for the distant past. During his long talks with Ferrante, Lorenzo frequently alluded to those rulers in classical times who had achieved greatness by being men of peace, rather than of war, and to the ideal of a united Italy. In more practical terms, he argued that, although the Pope had been cultivating Naples of late, though he had created Ferrante's son, Giovanni, a cardinal, though his nephew had given a banquet of unparalleled magnificence for Ferrante's daughter, though he had waived the customary annual tribute due from Naples to the Pope, the Papacy could never prove so useful a friend to Naples as could Florence. Sixtus was merely trying to use Naples for his own selfish purposes.

But Ferrante seemed unconvinced; the talks dragged on; and

Lorenzo grew more and more depressed, walking gloomily round the gardens of the Duchess of Calabria's seaside villa. 'He seemed to be two men, not one,' an official in his suite commented.

During the day he appeared perfectly easy, graceful, cheerful and confident, but at night he grieved bitterly about his own ill fortune and that of Florence, saying repeatedly that he did not care a fig for his own life but that it distressed him beyond measure that he could not save his country from the dangers which beset her.

While doing his best to convince Ferrante by his arguments, Lorenzo succeeded in impressing the Neapolitans by his generosity. He had raised sixty thousand florins for his journey by mortgaging Cafaggiolo and his lands in the Mugello; and immediately upon his arrival he had bought the freedom of a hundred galley slaves to each of whom he had presented ten florins and a suit of smart clothes. He followed this up by providing handsome dowries for several poor girls and by donating generous sums to numerous charities. Valori said that he remembered hearing from Paolo Antonio Soderini the total amount that Lorenzo spent during his visit to Naples, but he dared not write so huge a figure down.

Yet still Ferrante declined to come to terms. Eventually, after nearly ten weeks in Naples, Lorenzo was driven to bring matters to a head by declaring that he was unable to wait any longer, that urgent matters required his immediate return to Florence. After hurried farewells, he rode out of the city and headed north. With equal haste, King Ferrante drew up a peace treaty and sent it after him.

The war was finally over. The terms of the peace were not very favourable to Florence. She had to agree to the payment of an indemnity to the Duke of Calabria and, at the Pope's insistence, to the release of the still imprisoned members of the Pazzi family; she had also to agree to various places in southern Tuscany remaining in alien hands. But at least peace had been secured; the Pope's ambitions had been thwarted; and Florence and Naples were friends and allies once more.

XII

THE NEEDLE OF
THE ITALIAN COMPASS

*'If Florence was to have a tyrant, she could never
have found a better or more delightful one'*

IN MARCH 1480 Lorenzo returned to Florence to be greeted by even
greater enthusiasm than had welcomed his grandfather on his
return from exile in 1434. During the war repeated efforts had been
made to ruin him. The Riario family had continued to plot his
destruction, and Girolamo Riario had twice attempted to have him
assassinated. Now, though there were complaints about the large
indemnity that had to be paid to the Duke of Calabria, his position
in Florence was virtually unassailable. And he made the most of his
opportunity to strengthen it.

Up till then, as the Milanese ambassador put it, he had been
'determined to follow his grandfather's example and use, as much as
possible, constitutional methods' in preserving his ascendancy. Indeed, he was still determined to do nothing that would antagonize
the Florentines' susceptibilities. But his long absence in Naples had
placed the Medicean regime under dangerous strain, and he considered it essential to provide it with a firmer base, to carry it to a
further stage in its development. Less than a month after his return
from Naples, the need to overcome the financial problems created by
the war was given as an excuse to create a new *Balìa*. The *Balìa* immediately created a Council of Seventy whose members were to
remain in office for five years. This new Council was to take over
from the *Accoppiatori* the right to elect the *Signoria*, which was not in

future to be permitted to initiate any important bills. The Council of Seventy was also empowered to elect from among its own members two new government agencies, the *Otto di Pratica*, which was to be responsible for foreign policy, and the *Dodici Procuratori* which was to have control of home affairs and finance. The authority of both the *Signoria* and the *Cento* was thus severely limited; and the Council of Seventy became, in effect, the government of Florence.

It was a government that even now Lorenzo did not fully control. Poliziano referred to him as Florence's *caput*; others would have liked to bestow upon him his grandfather's title of *Pater Patriae*. But the Council of Seventy, jealously guarding its independent authority, was not always willing to carry out his wishes. As he was to have cause to explain to some foreign envoys who failed to understand why he could not commit the State to a certain policy, he was 'not *Signore* of Florence but merely a citizen'. He had more authority than he deserved, he admitted, but even *he* 'had to be patient and to conform to the will of the majority'. Of course it often suited him for men to suppose that his influence was far less effective than it was. This enabled him not only to avoid granting inconvenient or expensive favours to friends – as his grandfather had done when asked to contribute to Pope Calixtus III's crusade – but also to disprove the charges of such enemies of his regime as Alamanno di Filippo Rinuccini that he was a dictator. In fact, his influence was extensive, persuasive and usually decisive. When he made it known to a council or an official what he wanted done, his wishes were normally carried out; when he suggested that a man should be elected to a certain office, the required election generally took place. He may never have held any official title as *Capo della Repubblica*, but when, after his death, an official document styled him *vir primarius nostrae civitatis*, no one could deny that he was, indeed, the first citizen of Florence. His enemies, of course, had no hesitation in labelling him a tyrant; but, as Francesco Guicciardini admitted, 'if Florence was to have a tyrant she could never have found a better or more delightful one'. This was a view which was certainly shared by most people in the city, particularly the poorer people. To them it did not matter whether he was a tyrant or not. Under his rule they had food, they had exciting public holidays and they had justice – or most of them had justice: 'On the fifteenth day of October 1480,' wrote Landucci in his diary of one poor fellow to whom justice was denied,

the said hermit [who was alleged to have attempted the assassination of Lorenzo] died in the hospital of Santa Maria Nuova because he was quite torn to pieces by various tortures. They said the soles were stripped from his feet, which were then put over the fire, and held over the logs till the fat ran. Then they stood him up and made him walk over coarse-crusted salt, so that he died of this. It was never really established whether he had sinned or not. Some said yes, and some said no.

Yet if Lorenzo's position in Florence was now secure, the fortunes of the Medici bank were fast declining. Lorenzo had none of his grandfather's taste or talent for business; he gave far too much scope to his branch managers and relied far too heavily upon the often ill-judged advice of his temporizing, ingratiating general manager, Francesco Sassetti. When other advisers warned him against Sassetti's policies he would brush their counsel aside while confessing that he 'did not understand such matters'. Mismanagement and excessive loans to King Edward IV during the Wars of the Roses put an end to the London branch; the Bruges branch also collapsed; so did the branch in Milan, where the premises which Francesco Sforza had given to Cosimo were sold to Lodovico il Moro. The branches in Lyons, Rome and Naples were all in difficulties, the result partly of managerial incompetence, partly of that general collapse in Florentine banking which was within twelve years to lead to its virtual eclipse.

Even before the Pazzi conspiracy, which had aimed not merely at bringing down the Medicean regime but also at destroying the Medici bank, the whole complex organization was tottering on the verge of bankruptcy. Indeed, it was mainly because he felt sure it would soon go bankrupt anyway, and that Lorenzo would tumble with it, that Renato de' Pazzi had declined to play a part in the plot. Now that the plot had failed, Lorenzo still faced financial ruin. Refusing as always to allow moral scruples to inhibit political or personal ambition, he did not hesitate to delay that ruin by dipping his hands into funds that did not belong to him. He helped himself to over 55,000 florins which was being held in trust for his two young cousins, the sons of Pierfrancesco de' Medici, whose guardian he had been appointed; and when these boys came of age in 1485 he could not pay them back. He was obliged to make over to them the villa of Cafaggiolo and other property in the Mugello, though they claimed that this did not fully compensate them for their loss. Lorenzo also helped himself to money from the public treasury. After his death his heirs were held responsible for the return of almost 75,000 florins which had been withdrawn 'without the sanction of any law and without authority, to the damage and prejudice of the Commune'.

Beset by financial worries, he was also troubled on his return to Florence by the continuing insecurity of the frontiers of the Republic. In his absence the Genoese had captured the fortress of Sarzana. Since then, Girolamo Riario had bought the town of Forlì, thus extending his possessions in the Romagna towards the borders of Tuscany; while the Duke of Calabria had taken advantage of an uprising in Siena to establish himself as its ruler. Worst of all, the Pope's venomous dislike of Lorenzo had been much increased by his having come to terms with Naples, an arrangement which prompted the Pope's other allies to forsake him. The Pope could not carry on the war by himself, yet he steadfastly refused to remove the interdict or to withdraw the Bull of Excommunication.

But then, in August 1480 – so conveniently for Lorenzo that it was afterwards suggested that it was he who had arranged the timing of the attack – a Turkish army of seven thousand men landed at Otranto and, having established a strong bridgehead in the heel of Italy, threatened to march across to Naples and from there north to Rome. This fearful calamity, dreaded for so long, brought the Duke of Calabria scurrying south from Siena, induced King Ferrante to hand back to Florence the towns that Neapolitan troops were still occupying in Tuscany, and persuaded the Pope that, with all Christendom in peril, this was no time for the Italian states to be quarrelling amongst themselves. So it was agreed that a deputation comprising members of leading Florentine families would go to

Rome, make vague apologies for the city's misbehaviour and, in return, receive His Holiness's forgiveness. The deputation arrived in Rome on 3 December and in St Peter's knelt before the Pope, who received them sitting on a canopied throne which had been specially erected in the nave for the occasion. Luigi Guicciardini, as leader of the deputation, mumbled their apology which could not be heard above the chatter of the onlookers. The Pope made a similarly inaudible speech of reproof, tapped them in turn on the shoulder with a penitent's staff, formally lifted his interdict, then gave them his blessing. The ambassadors, having promised to supply and equip fifteen galleys for service against the Turks, returned to Florence to report to Lorenzo that all had gone as planned. A few months later the Sultan, Mahomet the Conqueror, died suddenly at Gebze. His forces at Otranto were brought home, and peace in Italy seemed assured.

It was a peace that throughout the last ten years of his life Lorenzo did his utmost to maintain, endeavouring to thwart the Pope's attempts to embroil Italy in petty conflicts that might be turned to the advantage of his greedy family, and to create a united Italy powerful enough not only to keep the Turks at bay but also to frustrate the designs in Italy of France, Spain and the Empire. It was a policy which required patience and the most expert diplomacy, and was made all the more difficult to achieve by Girolamo Riario's unsatisfied ambitions to extend his dominions beyond the borders of the Romagna. Twice war broke out; and twice Lorenzo's personal intervention brought peace. On the second occasion, in August 1484, when the Pope's representative returned to Rome to report that the terms of the peace treaty denied his nephew the towns of Cervia and Ravenna for which the war had been fought, Sixtus, already excessively ill-tempered because of his gout, was at first so angry that he could not speak. Then he burst out furiously that he would never countenance such humiliating terms. The next day he collapsed, and within a few hours was dead.

His successor, Innocent VIII, was a far more easy-going and genial man, willing enough to advance his children, whom he complacently acknowledged as his own, but without that obsessive ambition which had dominated the policies of Sixtus IV. One of Lorenzo's agents referred to him as 'a rabbit', and there was certainly something undeniably rabbity about the slant of his rather doleful eyes and in his unassertive manner. Lorenzo, who had followed the course of the election with the greatest interest, had good cause to hope that in due course he might be able to exercise over him a profitable influence. For the moment, however, Innocent's chief adviser was a rough and bellicose cardinal, Sixtus IV's nephew, Giuliano della Rovere, whose influence in the Sacred College had been largely responsible for Pope Innocent's election. But, having pushed the Papacy into a costly and unrewarding war with Naples, the Cardinal began to lose favour. He was further discredited when a certain freebooter, Boccolino Guzzoni, made himself master of Osimo, a small town in the Papal States south of Ancona. The Cardinal was sent as Legate to drive Guzzoni out of the town. He failed to do so, and Lorenzo astutely took advantage of his discomfiture by buying Guzzoni off for a fraction of the cost of the ill-fated military expedition.

Lorenzo lost no opportunity of increasing the respect which Pope Innocent now felt for him and of gaining his friendship, if possible his affection. He took the trouble to discover the Pope's tastes and indulged them accordingly. He sent him regular consignments of ortolans; he sent him casks of his favourite wine; he sent him presents of fine Florentine cloth. He sent him courteous, flattering letters in which he assured him, when the Pope was ill, that he felt his sufferings as though they were his own, in which he encouraged him with such fortifying statements as 'a Pope is what he wills to be', and in which, as though incidentally, he included his views on the proper course of papal policies. Innocent was gratified by Lorenzo's attentions and convinced by his arguments; he recognized in Lorenzo a man whom he could trust. So completely, indeed, did he come to share his opinions that, as the disgruntled Ferrarese ambassador put it, 'the Pope sleeps with the eyes of the Magnificent Lorenzo'. The Florentine ambassador at Naples knew that this was so. 'It is recognized perfectly well all over Italy,' he assured Lorenzo, 'what influence you have with the Pope and that the Florentine ambassador *quodammodo* governs the policies of Rome.'

This influence was much increased after 1488 when Lorenzo's daughter, Maddalena, was married to one of the several sons which the Pope had had before his entry into the Church, Franceschetto Cibò. The bridegroom was almost forty, a portly, boring man, who drank too much and was reputed never to have made a single interesting remark in his entire life; and Maddalena, a rather plain, sharp-featured, round-shouldered girl of sixteen, did not look forward to the match with relish. Nor did her mother, who was so devoted to her that Lorenzo referred to the girl as her mother's *occhio del capo* – the eye within her head. But Maddalena was a dutiful child, and her mother was a dutiful wife: marriages were thus arranged in families such as theirs; besides, dull, sottish and addicted to gambling though he was, Franceschetto was said to be kind; and Lorenzo was generous. Since he was at the time in the midst of one of his recurrent financial crises, he found it difficult to pay Maddalena's dowry of four thousand ducats, there being, as he admitted to the Florentine ambassador in Rome, so many other 'holes to fill up'. But he did contrive to raise the money in the end. He also gave Franceschetto the Pazzi palace in Florence as well as the Pazzi villa at Montughi, and a fine estate at Spedaletto near Arezzo.

The Pope was delighted. Lorenzo's hold on him was confirmed and tightened, and it was now accepted throughout Europe that the policies of the Curia were in future to be directed by Florence, that, as in the time of Cosimo, a Medici was once again to be the virtual arbiter of Italian policy. European rulers sought his advice; Muslim potentates sent him lavish presents. Time and again he intervened to save the peace of Italy, restraining the Pope from venting his obstinate anti-Aragonese prejudices by attacking Naples, maintaining the precarious balance of power in the peninsula by coming forward to preserve the independence of smaller states. It is clear now that Lorenzo's reputation as a master of diplomacy was largely undeserved, that he was often rash and short-sighted, taking great risk for trivial gains, that Italy was not plunged into a general war rather by good luck than by good management and that foreign intervention would certainly have come earlier than it did had it suited the foreigners themselves. Yet in his own lifetime Lorenzo's high stand ing as a statesman was rarely questioned: he was 'the needle of the Italian compass'. In Florence he won immensely enhanced credit by finding plausible excuses to relieve the Genoese of the city of Pietrasanta and to retake from them the fortress of Sarzana, thus finally atoning for the humiliations suffered during the course of the War of the Pazzi Conspiracy. At both Pietrasanta and at Sarzana, though little-disposed to such activity, he appeared amongst the soldiers on the battlefield, encouraging them in the fight and supervising their entry through the breaches in the shattered walls.

After his triumphant return from Sarzana, the 'Republic of Florence', as Scipio Ammirato said,

remained free of all troubles, to the great reputation of Lorenzo. The Italian princes also enjoyed peace, so that, with everything quiet beyond her frontiers and with no disturbances at home, Florence altogether gave herself up to the arts and pleasures of peace, seeking to attract thither men of letters, to accumulate books, to adorn the city, to make the countryside fruitful. In short she devoted herself to all those arts and pursuits which caused men to esteem that age so happy.

XIII

LORENZO:
PATRON, COLLECTOR AND POET

*'He had a full understanding of such
and all other things'*

MORE THAN once during these years when he was repeatedly called upon to compose some tiresome quarrel between one Italian state and the next, Lorenzo was heard to observe that he longed for the opportunity of burying himself in some remote part of Tuscany where not even a rumour of the troubled affairs of the outside world could reach him. He longed to be able to spend more time with his friends, with that brilliant circle of scholars, writers and artists who gathered when they could at one or other of his country villas – at Fiesole, or at Careggi where every year on 7 November a banquet was given in honour of Plato's birth; at Poggio a Caiano, twelve miles north-west of Florence where an old villa was transformed by Giuliano da Sangallo;[1] or at the remote, fortress-like villa of Cafaggiolo in the valley of the Mugello on the road to Pistoia. Though occasionally overcast by petty quarrels and outburst of jealous pique among the members of his court, life at these villa was usually delightful and informal. At meal times guests sat down wherever they chose. They might find themselves next to Lorenzo himself, or his dearest friend, Angelo Poliziano, or to another poet the amusing, sardonic Luigi Pulci, known to their host as 'Gigi', or to Giovanni Pico, Count of Mirandola and Concordia, the clever earnest aristocrat whose influential works, one of which was dedicated

164

to Lorenzo, had been so strongly condemned by the Church. They might meet the entertaining bookseller, Vespasiano da Bisticci; or Marsilio Ficino, who dedicated his *Theologica platonica* to Lorenzo; or Gentile Becchi, Lorenzo's former tutor, now Bishop of Arezzo; or the great musician, Antonio Squarcialupi, the Cathedral organist, whom Lorenzo helped to find singers for his choir; or the artists, Filippino Lippi, Domenico Ghirlandaio and Sandro Botticelli, all of whom were at various times employed by Lorenzo on the decorations of the villa of Spedaletto; or Antonio Pollaiuolo, described by Lorenzo as 'the greatest master in the city'; or, during the last years of Lorenzo's life, the young Michelangelo Buonarroti.

The son of a poor Tuscan magistrate of aristocratic stock, Michelangelo had been sent at the age of seven or eight to Francesco Urbino's school in Florence, and then – much to the distress of his father who lamented his choice of so humble a trade – had been apprenticed to Domenico Ghirlandaio who ran a big painting studio in Florence. Soon after arriving there his precocious gifts had made a deep impression on his master who exclaimed, 'Why, this boy knows more than I do!' on seeing a drawing that the thirteen-year-old Michelangelo had done depicting his fellow apprentices at work in the Tornabuoni chapel at Santa Maria Novella. When Lorenzo asked Ghirlandaio to recommend some promising pupils for a new school that he had founded, Ghirlandaio had no hesitation in including Michelangelo among the list of names.

According to Giorgio Vasari, Lorenzo had founded his school with the purpose not only of providing boys with a training in particular crafts but also of giving them a far wider education than would otherwise have been available to them. He furnished a site, a garden between the Palazzo Medici and San Marco, employed a master, his old friend Bertoldo di Giovanni, a former pupil of Donatello, and lent the school numerous paintings, antique busts and statues to be set up in the studio and around the grounds.[2] It was while making a copy of one of these antiquities – the head of an old faun – that Michelangelo is said to have first come to Lorenzo's notice. 'Although this was the first time he had ever touched a chisel or worked in marble,' so Vasari recorded,

Michelangelo succeeded in copying the faun so well that Lorenzo was amazed. Then, when he saw that Michelangelo had departed a little from the model and followed his own fancy in hollowing out a mouth for the faun and giving it a tongue and all its teeth, Lorenzo laughed in his usual charming way and said, 'But don't you know old people never have all their teeth; there are always some missing.'

As soon as Lorenzo had gone away, Michelangelo broke off one of the faun's teeth

and dug into the gum so that it looked as if the tooth had fallen out; and he waited anxiously for Lorenzo to come back. And after he had seen the result of Michelangelo's simplicity and skill, Lorenzo laughed at the incident more than once and used to tell it for a marvel to his friends. He resolved that he would help and favour the young Michelangelo; and first he sent for his father, Lodovico, and asked whether he could have the boy, adding that he wanted to keep him as one of his own sons. Lodovico willingly agreed, and then Lorenzo arranged to have Michelangelo given a room of his own at the Palazzo Medici and looked after him as one of the Medici household. Michelangelo always ate at Lorenzo's table with the sons of the family and other distinguished and noble persons, and Lorenzo always treated him with great respect ... As salary and so that he could help his father, Michelangelo was paid five ducats a month; and to make him happy Lorenzo gave him a violet cloak and appointed his father to a post in the customs. As a matter of fact all the boys in the San Marco garden were paid salaries varying in amount through the generosity of the noble and magnificent Lorenzo who supported them as long as he lived.

Michelangelo remained at the Medici Palace for four years and during that time 'he showed the results of his labours to Lorenzo every day'.[3]

Far less rich than his father or grandfather, Lorenzo did not commission nearly as many sculptures or paintings; and many of those for which he was responsible have been destroyed, like the frescoes at Spedaletto, or lost. Several others, until recently supposed to have been commissioned by Lorenzo – such as Botticelli's two most famous works, *Primavera*[4] and the *Birth of Venus*,[5] are now known to have been painted for his namesake, his rich young cousin, Lorenzo di Pierfrancesco de' Medici, and to have been hung on the walls of the villa of Castello which the younger branch of the Medici family bought in 1477.[6] Botticelli's *Pallas and the Centaur* was also hung at Castello and was probably commissioned by Lorenzo di Pierfrancesco, although it seems to celebrate the elder Lorenzo's triumph over the Pazzi conspirators and the ending of the Florentine wars.[7]

But if Lorenzo did not himself commission much work from Botticelli, he went out of his way to ensure that he was well supplied with orders from other Florentine patrons and seems to have been responsible for his going to work in the Sistine Chapel in Rome. Lorenzo was equally active on behalf of Filippino Lippi whom he also sent to Rome, Antonio Pollaiuolo whom he sent to Milan, and Giuliano da Maiano whom he recommended to the Duke of Calabria. For Ghirlandaio he obtained work in Santa Maria Novella and in Santa Trinità,[8] and afterwards recommended him for employment in the Sistine Chapel. For Verrocchio, who, according to Vasari, 'never gave himself a moment's rest from painting or sculpture', Lorenzo obtained work all over Tuscany. He also commissioned – though the sculptor's brother claimed he never paid for – a bronze *David*[9] and a terracotta *Resurrection* for his own villa of Careggi.[10] And for the garden of his school he had Verrocchio restore and complete a badly broken red stone statue of the flayed body of Marsyas as a companion piece to a white marble *Marsyas* which Cosimo had bought in Rome. Verrocchio, so Vasari recorded,

made the missing legs, thighs and arms out of pieces of red marble so skilfully that Lorenzo was more than satisfied and was able to place it opposite the other statue, on the other side of the door. This antique torso, showing the flayed body of Marsyas, was made with such care and judgement that some slender white veins in the red stone were brought out by skilful carving in exactly the right places, appearing like the tiny sinews that are revealed when a human body is flayed.

When Verrocchio left Florence for Venice to work on his last masterpiece, the monument to the *condottiere*, Bartolommeo Colleoni, which stands in the Piazza di Santi Giovanni e Paolo, Lorenzo let him go with his blessing. He was equally amiable when Leonardo da Vinci decided to move to Milan. It is possible that Leonardo, like Michelangelo, had lived in Lorenzo's household for a time. It is certain that when, at the age of about twelve, this illegitimate boy from the Tuscan village of Vinci came to work in Verrocchio's workshop in Florence, Lorenzo took the greatest interest in his precocious genius; and that when Leonardo decided to spread the wings of his astonishing versatility in Milan, where Duke Lodovico Sforza was looking for an artist to make an equestrian statue of his father, Lorenzo, always alive to the political advantages of such generosity, recommended him to Lodovico by sending the Duke a silver lyre, made in the shape of a horse's head, which Leonardo had made.

Lorenzo certainly liked it to be known that he was a connoisseur of such things, just as he set great store by his reputation as an expert judge of architecture. It had, indeed, become common practice to consult him when important works were to be undertaken. His advice was sought, for instance, over a disputed design for the façade of Santo Spirito;[11] and Filippo Strozzi consulted him about the proportions of the Palazzo Strozzi.[12] Lorenzo was also asked to select the better of two models for the Forteguerri tomb at San Jacopo in Pistoia, the one submitted by Verrocchio, the other by Piero del Pollaiuolo, as he had 'full understanding of such and all other things'. And when a new altar panel for the church of Santo Spirito was commissioned from Ghirlandaio, one of the conditions was that it should be done 'according to the manner, standards and form' as would please Lorenzo.

Lorenzo himself submitted a design for the façade of the Cathedral which, in 1491, still remained without one. Since Verrocchio, Botticelli, Ghirlandaio and Filippino Lippi also took part in the competition, together with several other masters, the judges were naturally somewhat embarrassed. To escape their dilemma they asked Lorenzo to choose the design himself. But, having praised all the designs, Lorenzo told them that he could not make up his mind and advised that the matter should be adjourned.[13]

If Lorenzo spent far less on paintings and sculpture than his grandfather and left unfinished various buildings which Cosimo had begun

– such as the church of the Badia at Fiesole – he continued throughout his life to add to his magnificent collection of bronzes, medals, coins, ancient pottery, antique gems and Roman, Byzantine, Persian and Venetian vases, many of them carved in semi-precious stones and most of them inscribed with his name picked out in capitals: 'LAUR. MED'. He would, in fact, pay far more for a fine engraved gem, no doubt believing it to be a sounder investment, than he was prepared to pay for a big picture. Many of the gems in his collection were valued at over a thousand florins, while a Botticelli or a Pollaiuolo did not cost more than a hundred.

Lorenzo also continued to lavish money upon the patronage of writers and scholars and upon the purchase of books and manuscripts for the continually expanding Medici library. His agents were instructed to be perpetually on the watch for likely sources. Giovanni Lascaris – who was twice dispatched to the East at Lorenzo's expense to seek out manuscripts that might otherwise be lost – brought back to Florence from his second voyage over two hundred Greek works, the existence of almost half of which had not previously been known.

Although the art of printing from movable type had been invented in the middle of the century at Mainz, it had not at first made much headway in Italy where many scholars considered it a rather vulgar process, practised 'among the Barbarians in some German city', and many collectors, including Duke Federigo of Urbino, would have been ashamed to own a printed book'. Printing presses had been set up in Naples in 1465, in Rome in 1467, in Venice and Milan in 1469, in Verona, as well as in Paris and Nuremberg, in 1470. In 1476 William Caxton had set up his press at the Sign of the Red Pale in the shadow of Westminster Abbey. But it was not until 1477 that Bernardo Cennini had established his press in Florence. Before that – and, indeed for many years after, so strong was the tradition in the city – whole schools of scribes, illustrators and scriveners were employed by Lorenzo to make copies of his manuscripts so that their contents could be as widely diffused as possible and replicas presented to other libraries and institutions both within and beyond the frontiers of Tuscany, in particular to the libraries of Pisa.

Well aware that Pisa resented her subjection to Florence almost as

169

much as Volterra, Lorenzo had taken great pains to improve relations between the two cities and to gain credit for the Medici as benefactors of them both. He had developed the port of Pisa, bought land outside the city and a riverside house within the walls where he often took his family to stay, particularly in the colder winter months when the climate there was relatively mild and the wooded Apennines afforded shelter from the bitter east wind that, now unimpeded, blows down from the Romagna. Above all, Lorenzo had sought to reconcile the Pisans to Florence and the Medici by reviving Pisa's once renowned but now decayed university. In 1472 he had established it as the principal university in Tuscany, and he personally contributed more than twice the amount of the grant of six thousand florins a year that the foundation received from the State.

He also contributed handsomely to the funds of the University of Florence, which now had the reputation of being the only one in Europe where the Greek language was adequately taught. It employed as teachers and lecturers such scholars as Johannes Argyropoulos, Theodorus Gaza, and Demetrius Chalcondylas who, with Demetrius Cretensis, issued from Florence in 1488 the first printed edition of the works of Homer. Students from all over Europe came here to learn Greek. Thomas Linacre, who was to become physician to King Henry VIII and one of the founders of the Royal College of Physicians, spent a year in Florence in 1485–6 and was allowed to share the lessons given by Chalcondylas to Lorenzo's sons. Linacre's friend, William Grocyn, who was later one of the earliest scholars to teach Greek at Oxford, arrived in 1488. In 1489 there came another friend, William Latimer, who helped Grocyn and Linacre to translate Aristotle into Latin.

Lorenzo shared these scholars' enthusiasm for Greek philosopher and Latin poets, but he had no patience with those humanists who regarded the Italian language with disdain and caustically belittle the achievements of the Tuscan poets of the immediate past. When Lorenzo wrote poetry as a relaxation from the cares of business and private life, it was not so much the Latin poets whom he chose his exemplars but Dante and Boccaccio. It was not in Latin that he wanted to write but in that simple, beautiful language which he ha learned to speak as a child. Passionate in his devotion to Tuscan, he insisted – as Leon Battista Alberti had insisted – that it could be made far more subtle and pliable if only poets would endeavour to perfect their use of it, if only they could dismiss from their minds Niccolò Niccoli's absurd contention that Dante was a poet to be read only by common wool workers and bakers. Lorenzo himself wrote in Tuscan with a depth of feeling that might have transformed the mannered poetry of the *cinquecento* had he had more leisure to develop his remarkable gifts. As it was, he was a worthy successor to the accomplished poets of the late thirteenth century, the precursors of Petrarch.

Lorenzo's poetry was of a marvellous verve and diversity, sad and spirited, sometimes hopeful, more often disillusioned, moved by religious sentiment as well as by the desires of the flesh. He wrote devotional poems, as his mother had done, and blasphemous parodies which would have distressed her; he wrote hunting songs and loev songs, exuberant *canzoni a ballo*, carefree burlesques and libidinous *canti carnascialeschi*, like the 'Song of the Fir Cone Sellers', celebrating the delights of sexual passion and physical love. Above all, his feelings for the beauty of the Tuscan landscape, and for the pleasures and hardships of the life of country people, is expressed with an extraordinarily vivid intensity. He writes of flocks of bleating sheep migrating to upland pastures, the lambs trotting in their mothers' steps, the shepherds carrying lambs just born and lame sheep on their shoulders; and of these flocks at night, enclosed by lines of poles and nets, with the shepherds snoring in the darkness after their meal of bread and milk; of cranes flying towards the setting sun, and falcons swooping down upon their prey; of olive groves beside the sea, their leaves turning now grey now green as the breeze blows across the shore; of the sparks from a flint in dry autumn leaves lighting brushwood, of flames spreading to the forest trees, burning bushes and lairs from which terrified birds and animals flee in a clatter of wings and pounding hooves; of winter scenes of tall firs, black against the snow, frozen leaves crackling underfoot; of the hunted deer making its last desperate leap; the patient ox struggling with its burden of stones; and the exhausted bird falling into the sea, frightened to settle on the mast of a ship; of the river Ombrone in flood, its yellow waters cascading down the mountainside, carrying trunks and boughs of old ilex trees and the planks of a peasant's shed across the wide plain; and of the peasant's wife, her baby crying on her back, running with their cattle from the rising floods.

By the beginning of 1492 it was clear that Lorenzo, although only forty-three, was already a dying man. For years his intermittent attacks of gout had been increasingly painful and incapacitating; and now his general health was failing fast. He had made it a habit to take the waters each year, at Spedaletto or Porretta, at Vigone where St Catherine had scalded herself in the hot springs to prepare herself for Purgatory, or at Bagno a Morba, south of Volterra, an attractive spa which had been established by his mother. From each visit he returned protesting that he was now quite well again, but within a few months he had relapsed into his former debilitated state. He had to be carried in a litter to his favourite villa at Poggio a Caiano where he could do little but read, admire the frescoes which he had commissioned Andrea del Sarto to paint on the walls, supervise the farming of the surrounding land, or visit the menagerie where, with other exotic animals, was kept the beautiful giraffe – 'so gentle that it [would] take an apple from a child's hand' – which had been presented to him by the Sultan of Babylon.

In these last years his charm was overcast by outbursts of irritability. As his gout grew more and more painful he was often brusque and sometimes offensive. To a man who unfeelingly criticized the character of Squarcialupo, the musician, he said sharply, 'If you knew how hard it is to obtain perfection in any art, you would overlook such shortcomings.' To a Sienese who sympathized with him on his failing eyesight and commented that the air of Florence was said to be bad for the eyes, he retorted, 'And the air of Siena for the brain.' In reply to one of his cousins, a rather slovenly man, who spoke complacently of the unfailing water supply at his country villa, he replied, 'Then you could afford to wash your hands more often.'

In February 1492 it became known that he was no longer able to attend to business; he could neither walk nor even hold a pen. A slow fever had eaten away 'the whole man', Poliziano wrote, 'attacking not only the arteries and veins, but the limbs, intestines, nerves, bones and marrow'. At the beginning of the next month, having said goodbye to his younger son, Giovanni, who was going to live in Rome, he had to dispel rumours that he was on his deathbed by appearing at his bedroom window. A fortnight later he was taken to the villa of Careggi never to return to Florence.

He was accompanied to Careggi by Poliziano and some other friends who sat by his bedside talking to him, and, when he was too tired for conversation, taking it in turns to read aloud extracts from the works of the Tuscan poets he loved so well. He would devote the rest of his life to poetry and to study, he told Poliziano, leaving the government of Florence to his son, Piero. But Poliziano replied, 'The people won't let you.'

A few days after this Lorenzo heard that on the night of 5 April – following a day upon which two of Florence's lions were killed in a fight in their cage in the Via di Leone – lightning had struck the Cathedral lantern. One of the marble balls on its summit had crashed down into the piazza. On which side? Lorenzo wanted to know – and, on being told, said, 'I shall die, for that is the side nearest my house'. There were reports of other dreadful portents: she-wolves howled in the night; strange lights appeared in the sky; a woman in Santa Maria Novella was seized by madness during Mass and ran about, screaming warnings of a raging bull with flaming horns which was pulling the church down about her ears; Marsilio Ficino saw ghostly giants fighting in his garden and emitting fearful cries.

Lorenzo's own doctor, Piero Leoni, was joined by Lazaro di Pavia, a Lombard physician sent to Careggi by Lodovico Sforza. This man prescribed a concoction of pulverized pearls and precious stones which he noisily prepared himself in a room near Lorenzo's. 'Are you here, Angelo?' Lorenzo called out; and when Poliziano hurried to his bedside he asked him what on earth the doctor was doing. On being told, Lorenzo seemed for a moment to believe that the strange medicine might cure him and, taking both Poliziano's hands in his own, he gazed eagerly into his face. Poliziano looked away and, returning to his own room, burst into tears.

Later that day, when Pico della Mirandola came to see him, Lorenzo again acknowledged that he knew himself to be dying. His voice grew weaker as he spoke, but he was heard to say, 'I only wish that death had spared me so that I could finish helping you collect your library.'

Growing weaker under his doctors' ministrations, he sent for a priest to hear his confession and give him communion. For this, he insisted on getting out of bed and being dressed; but the effort was too much for him. He had to be carried back to bed where he fell back against the pillows.

From time to time Piero went into his father's room and whenever he did so Lorenzo 'put on a brave face', so Poliziano recorded, 'and so as not to increase his son's sadness by his own, held back his tears'.

On 8 April he lapsed into a kind of coma and was given up for dead until a Camaldolensian friar held the lenses of his spectacles to Lorenzo's mouth. When the story of Christ's Passion was read to him, though he could frame no words, he moved his lips to show that he understood them. His eyes were fixed on a silver crucifix which was held before his face and which occasionally he kissed, until finally his breathing stopped.

Piero Leoni had always supposed that Lorenzo's illness would not prove fatal. Disagreeing with the necromantic cures and potions of his colleagues, he had protested that all would be well provided the patient was kept warm and dry and protected from the night air, ate no pears and swallowed no grape pips. So distressed to have been proved wrong, and heartbroken by accusations of witchcraft and poisoning, Leoni left Careggi and threw himself down a well in the grounds of a villa at San Gervasio.

Lorenzo's body was taken to the monastery of San Marco, then to San Lorenzo where he was buried next to his brother, Giuliano, in the old sacristy.

PART THREE
1492-1537

⚜ XIV ⚜

PIERO DI LORENZO DE' MEDICI
AND THE FRIAR FROM
FERRARA

'Behold! It is the Lord God who is leading
on these armies'

At TWENTY-TWO Piero had little of his father's charm. Strong, healthy and athletic, with a mass of light brown hair which lay in a fringe on his forehead and fell to his shoulders, he was not unattractive; but his personality and manner were far from endearing. He had Lorenzo's ruthlessness without his tact; he was equally unforgiving towards his enemies but did not remain loyal to his friends. His early letters give the impression of an indulged and rather petulant child. 'Please send me some figs, for I like them,' he wrote to his grandmother when he was five. 'I mean those red ones, and some peaches with stones, and other things you know I like, sweets and cakes and little things like that.' He asked his father to send him 'the best sporting dog that can be had'; and when that arrived, he wanted a pony and grew impatient waiting for it. 'I haven't had that pony you promised me,' he complained. 'Everybody is laughing at me.'

As he grew older his temper became more violent and his manner more arrogant. And, either to avoid comparison with a father universally admired if often envied, or because he chose to believe that the Medicean regime had now acquired such permanence that he could behave without due regard for its supporters' opinions, he shied away from business and public affairs. Much of his time he spent out-of-doors or in writing poems in poor imitation of Lorenzo's vivid style, leaving the conduct of public affairs to his secretary, Piero Dovizi da Bibbiena, and the supervision of the disintegrating bank to his not very competent great-uncle, Giovanni Tornabuoni. His unpopularity with the Florentines was greatly increased by his wife, Alfonsina, whom he had married when he was seventeen. An Orsini girl, she made it only too plain in her haughty, narrow Orsini manner that she would have preferred to remain in Rome amongst the true *nobilità*, an attitude that the Florentines, provincials for the most part themselves, found peculiarly irritating.

Piero's reputation in Florence was also much damaged by his continual quarrels with his cousins, Lorenzo and Giovanni, the two sons of Pierfrancesco de' Medici, both of whom were older, and – despite their guardian's misappropriation of part of their inheritance – richer than Piero, and neither of whom took any trouble to hide either their animosity towards the senior branch of the family or their intention to abandon it to its enemies in any future struggle for power that might arise. This struggle was not long to be delayed. For years, indeed, it had been predicted by an eloquent, fiery, ascetic Dominican friar from Ferrara whose apocalyptic sermons had filled the congregations in the crowded Cathedral with shame, remorse and fear.

Girolamo Savonarola was born at Ferrara in 1452. His grandfather, who seems to have been responsible for his education, was a physician from Padua, an acknowledged authority on the curative properties of spa waters and an exponent of the beneficial effects of alcohol which he comfortingly maintained would, if taken in generous measure, help to ensure longevity. His views and reputation secured him a profitable appointment at the Ferrarese court as the Duke's physician; and, on his retirement, his son succeeded him. His grandson, however, had no taste for court life. After one visit to the Duke's castle he swore that he would never go there again. Girolamo was an introspective boy, gloomy, pale and withdrawn, given to composing melancholy verses, strumming plaintive, dirge-like strains upon the lute and studying the scriptures. It was later said of him that his demeanour became even more despondent after he had fallen in love with Laodamia Strozzi, the natural daughter of a Florentine exile, who loftily rejected his advances; but he himself maintained that he had never wanted to marry. Certainly his later life was marked by the most rigid austerity. He rarely even spoke to women except to sermonize them; he ate little and forbore to taste those strong liquors by which his grandfather had set such store; his clothes were worn and patched; he slept on a straw mattress laid on a wooden board.

One feast day in 1475, without telling anyone where he was going, he left his father's house to seek admittance as a novice in the monastery of San Domenico at Bologna, where he was to remain for seven years. 'You have more reason to thank God than to complain,' he wrote to his father, explaining his sudden departure.

For God has given you a son and has deemed him worthy to become His militant knight. Do you not think it a great grace to have a son who is a cavalier of Jesus Christ? ... I was unable any longer to endure the evil doing of the heedless people of Italy ... I too am made of flesh and blood, and as the instincts of the body are repugnant to reason I must fight with all my strength to stop the Devil from jumping onto my shoulders.

To help others fight the Devil, Savonarola was sent out by the Dominicans from Bologna to preach elsewhere in Italy, to Ferrara, to Brescia, to Genoa, and many other towns in Tuscany and Lombardy. In 1481 he came to Florence where he was appointed *lector* at San Marco and asked to give the Lent sermons at San Lorenzo. In 1489 he settled permanently in Florence at the Monastery of San Marco.

At first he was a far from effective preacher, as he himself well knew, confessing in the days when he could boast that 'all Italy' was moved by his preaching that in those early years he did not know 'how to move a hen'. 'His gestures and pronunciation pleased none, so that scarcely twenty-five women and children remained to hear him,' wrote Cinozzi, one of his first biographers. 'He was so discouraged that he seriously thought of giving up preaching altogether.' It was not only that his voice was hard and his gestures violent and uncouth; he was a far from prepossessing figure. Small, thin and ugly, with a huge hooked nose and thick, fleshy lips, it was only his eyes that gave any impression of his remarkable personality. Green, intense beneath heavy, black eyebrows, they 'sometimes gave forth red flashes'.

Although most people in Florence were inclined to prefer the more graceful, cultured and polished sermons of the Augustinian monk, Fra Mariano, for whose order Lorenzo de' Medici built a monastery outside the Porta San Gallo, the awkward Dominican gradually acquired a following of devoted supporters prepared to overlook all the faults of his delivery for the extraordinary content of his sermons and his passionate, urgent sincerity. By 1491 his congregations had increased so much that San Marco could no longer contain them; and his Lent sermons that year were delivered in the Cathedral.

They caused an uproar throughout Florence. Savonarola had convinced himself that he was gifted with foreknowledge of the future, that his words were divinely inspired and that to deny their truth was to deny the wisdom of God. 'It is not I who preach,' he said, 'but God who speaks through me.' After prolonged periods of fasting and meditation, visions of the future had been vouchsafed to him. He knew that the Church was to be scourged, then regenerated, and that 'these things would quickly come to pass'. He knew, too, that unless the people of Italy and, in particular, the people of Florence mended their ways they would be dreadfully punished. Only a return to the simplicity of the early Christian Church could save them. They must turn their back on Aristotle and Plato, who were now rotting in hell; they must abandon the luxuries and sensual pleasures that were destroying their souls, abolish gambling and card games, dissolute carnivals and *palio* races, fine clothes and scent, powder and paint; and they must give the money they saved to the poor. They must blot out all those pictures so wantonly painted that they made 'the Virgin Mary look like a harlot'. They must chastise prostitutes – those 'pieces of meat with eyes' – and burn sodomites alive. They must reform their political institutions. Cosimo de' Medici had been quite wrong to declare that states were not ruled by paternosters; they could be governed well in no other way. 'If you want to make good laws,' Savonarola pronounced from the Cathedral pulpit, 'first reconcile yourselves to the laws of God, since all good laws depend on the Eternal Law.' The Florentines had bartered their ancient liberties for the spectacles provided for them by a tyrant. They must frame a new constitution. 'I believe the best constitution is that of the Venetians,' he said. 'You should copy it; but leave out the worst features, such as the office of Doge.'

To such criticisms of the Medicean regime, Lorenzo had listened with patience and toleration. His friend Pico della Mirandola had assured him that Savonarola was a great and godly man; other friends of his, Poliziano and Botticelli amongst them, had spoken of him with similar respect and awe; Michelangelo as an old man was to say that he could still hear the friar's voice ringing in his ears. When the name of Savonarola had been put forward as Prior of San Marco, Lorenzo had raised no objection; nor had he shown any displeasure when Savonarola studiedly declined to acknowledge the Medici's special connection with the monastery to which they had contributed so much. Once, it seems, some senior supporters of the Medicean regime called on Savonarola and suggested that he 'should not preach such sermons'; but he had replied, 'Go and tell Lorenzo to repent of his sins, for God will punish him and his.' Yet Lorenzo on his deathbed had sent for Savonarola, as well as Fra Mariano, and, according to Poliziano, had been blessed by them both.

After Lorenzo's death, Savonarola's dire warnings of disaster and criticisms of the Medicean regime increased in intensity and became more explicit. In his sermons of 1492 he spoke of visions of the 'Sword of the Lord' hanging threateningly in a darkened sky over the city of Florence; of awful tempests, of plague and war, flood and famine; of a black cross, inscribed with the words 'The Cross of God's Anger', rising from Rome, its arms reaching across the whole earth on which storms raged tumultuously; and of another cross, a golden cross, reaching up to the sky from Jerusalem, bathed in sunlight.

'Repent, O Florence, while there is still time,' Savonarola called to a congregation that sat as though petrified by the horror of his vivid images. 'Clothe thyself in the white garments of purification. Wait no longer, for there may be no further time for repentance.' He made it clear to them what his visions foretold: unless they turned to the golden cross, disaster would befall them. There would, indeed, be pestilence and war; foreign enemies would pour across the Alps, like 'barbers armed with gigantic razors', bringing distress as bitter as a dish of borage and enforcing reforms as relentlessly 'as a mill grinding out the flour of wisdom'.

'The Lord has placed me here,' Savonarola declared, 'and He has said to me: "I have put you here as a watchman in the centre of Italy that you may hear my words and announce them to the people."' The people listened in fear. The Prior of San Marco had foretold the death of Lorenzo; and Lorenzo was dead. He had predicted the death of Pope Innocent VIII and of King Ferrante of Naples; they, too, were dead. He had prophesied that within the lifetime of many of his congregation, the Turks would be converted to Christianity; and though they were still Mohammedans, their conversion would surely now be effected as Savonarola said. So, also, would the Sword of the Lord fall upon Florence, and the armies of a foreign king would pour across the Alps.

On hearing of Lorenzo's death, Pope Innocent was said to have exclaimed, 'The peace of Italy is at an end!' The King of France, Louis XI, was also dead; and his death, too, caused men to think of war. For his successor, Charles VIII, was a young man of energy and ambition, who dreamed romantic dreams of rivalling the exploits of Roland and of gaining glory by brilliant use of that well-organized standing army which his father had raised to crush his enemies within the Kingdom of France. But Charles appeared ill cast for the role of knightly hero. Twenty years old when the Florentines were first warned of the coming of the 'Sword of God', he was very small, short-sighted and distressingly ugly with a nose even larger and more hooked than Savonarola's and with thick, fleshy lips constantly open though partially concealed by the wisps of a scattering, reddish beard. His head and hands twitched convulsively; the few words that ever escaped him were muttered rather than spoken; he walked with a crouch and a limp; his feet were so big that he was rumoured to have a sixth toe; he was notoriously gluttonous and lecherous; he was appallingly ill-educated. Yet there was something about his restlessness, his wayward, adventurous spirit that, for all his naïveté and uneasy affability, made men wary in his presence. His father, though he had enormously increased the area of France, had never been drawn into Italy to claim the Kingdom of Naples as inheritor by force of the rights of the House of Anjou; but it seemed more than probable that Charles would march across the Alps as soon as the opportunity was offered him. A young man who had paid court to the bright, good-looking Anne, Duchess of Britanny, when she was already engaged to Maximilian of Austria, and who had ridden off with her and married her, was not to be discounted.

Charles's opportunity to go to war was presented to him by Lodovico Sforza, il Moro, uncle of the Duke of Milan. The Duke, Gian Galeazzo, had come of age in 1490, but il Moro had subsequently shown no inclination to give up the powers of Regent which he had assumed. This did not much concern Gian Galeazzo himself, for he was a lazy young fellow, interested more in dogs, horses and food than in his Duchy and disinclined to assert his rights even had he dared to do so. His wife Isabella, however, was a far more positive character. Repeatedly she complained to her grandfather, King Ferrante of Naples, asking him to put her husband's uncle and his domineering wife in their proper places. King Ferrante at first seemed reluctant to do so, but eventually agreed to do what he could to help.

To forestall any trouble he might have with Naples and any move that might be made against him from elsewhere in Italy, il Moro decided to suggest to Charles VIII that he should reassert the Angevin claim to Naples and, when the claim was denied, lead an expeditionary force into Italy. The Duchy of Milan would lend him its support. Il Moro himself would raise in Italy any loan that might be required, and he did, in fact, succeed in borrowing 100,000 francs from a Genoese bank at fourteen per cent interest.

Charles needed little persuasion, and when King Ferrante died in January 1494 his mind was made up. Announcing his claim to the Kingdom of Naples, and to the Kingdom of Jerusalem which went with it, he prepared to invade Italy and to push Ferrante's successor, Alfonso II, off his throne. In September the invasion began. A huge army, over thirty thousand strong, marching behind white silk banners embroidered with the arms of France and the words 'Voluntas Dei', crossed the Alps and lumbered down into Lombardy where its vanguard was warmly welcomed by il Moro. King Charles then moved on to Pavia to pay his respects to his cousin, the ineffectual Duke Gian Galeazzo, whom he found ill in bed suffering from some mysterious disease which his doctors could not diagnose. The Duchess knelt tearfully at the French King's feet, begging him not to take his army on to Naples – but Charles had no mind to turn back now. Nor had Il Moro. As Charles left Pavia, marching south towards Piacenza, the Duke's illness took a sudden turn for the worse, a relapse which was naturally attributed to poison. A few days later, he was dead. Immediately his widow and their four children were arrested and imprisoned, and il Moro proclaimed himself Duke of Milan.

The immense French army and its straggling train of camp-followers, cooks, grooms, muleteers, farriers, musicians, sutlers, prostitutes and courtiers continued their ponderous advance un-opposed. No efforts to halt it were made in the Papal States; Venice announced her neutrality. Charles drew nearer to the Tuscan frontier, sending envoys on to Florence to ask Piero de' Medici to acknowledge the justice of the Angevin claim and to allow his army to march through Tuscany. After keeping the envoys waiting for his answer for five days, during which he promised the King of Naples his unqualified support, Piero declared that Florence would remain neutral. The French, however, would not allow Florence to remain neutral. They needed fortresses in Tuscany to give security to their rear while advancing further south. So, protesting grave displeasure at the discourteous way in which his envoys had been treated, Charles advanced on the Tuscan fortress of Fivizzano, sacked it and massacred the entire garrison with alarming brutality.

Suddenly displaying an energy that surprised his fellow citizens, Piero aroused himself to make what arrangements he could to prevent Charles advancing any further into Tuscany. Mercenaries were sent to the frontier forts; *condottieri* were summoned; Piero's brother-in-law, Paolo Orsini, was sent to Sarzana with reinforcements; Piero himself prepared to leave for Pietrasanta. His own energy was not matched, however, by any comparable determination on the part of most other leading citizens in Florence. While Savonarola gave vent to further prophecies, seeming to take a gloomy satisfaction in the verification of his predictions, a sense of fatality descended upon the city. 'A Dominican Friar has so terrified all the Florentines that they are wholly given up to piety,' the Mantuan envoy in Florence wrote to his master. 'Three days in the week they fast on bread and water, and two more on wine and bread. All the girls and many of the wives have taken refuge in convents so that only men and youths and old women are now to be seen in the streets.'

'Behold!' cried Savonarola,

the Sword has descended; the scourge has fallen; the prophecies are being fulfilled. Behold, it is the Lord God who is leading on these armies ... Behold, I shall unloose waters over the earth ... It is not I but God who foretold it. Now it is coming. It has come!

Listening to his voice in the Cathedral, Pico della Mirandola felt a cold shiver run through him and his hair stand on end. Lorenzo Lenzi, the rich diplomat, soon to be appointed ambassador to France, was equally alarmed. When Piero de' Medici asked for more money for the defence of Florence, Lenzi protested that the city would be ruined; resistance was useless. Piero's cousins thought so too; and, anxious to dissociate themselves from his anticipated defeat, Lorenzo and Giovanni di Pierfrancesco de' Medici dispatched messages to the French camp assuring King Charles that, far from supporting Piero's actions, they were completely in sympathy with the French invasion. They would lend their influence to promote a sympathetic attitude towards it in Florence and would, if required, advance money to support it. Their message being intercepted, the brothers were arrested and confined in Medici villas – Lorenzo at Cafaggiolo and Giovanni at Castello. Both, however, soon escaped and joined Charles's headquarters at Vigetano where they assured him that if Piero were to be disposed of, the Florentines would readily join the French against the Neapolitans.

By the end of October Piero, deserted by most of the Medicean party, had himself accepted the hopelessness of his position. No help was to be expected from the Pope or from Venice or from Naples, part of whose army had already been routed in the Romagna by the left wing of the invading forces under the Duc de Montpensier. The French right wing, having bypassed Sarzana, were within a few miles of Pisa; and Pisa, like Florence, was powerless to resist attack. So, without troubling to consult the *Signoria*, Piero left for King Charles's camp at San Stefano, believing his only chance of saving Florence lay in endeavouring to win his friendship by offering his humble submission. No doubt he hoped to score the same sort of diplomatic triumph that his father had achieved in Naples during the Pazzi war. He sent back to Florence a letter modelled on that which his father had written on the road to Pisa.

Charles greeted him disdainfully, demanding an enormous loan and the right to occupy the fortresses of Sarzana, Pietrasanta, Sarzanello and Librafratta, as well as the towns of Pisa and Leghorn, until what he called his 'enterprise' was successfully concluded. To the obvious astonishment of the French staff, who later told Philippe de Commines 'with smiles and laughter' how absurdly anxious he was to give way on every point, Piero immediately acceded to Charles's terms and, on 8 November, returned to Florence to tell the *Signoria* what he had done.

Early the next morning, a sword at his side and surrounded by an armed guard, he went to the Palazzo della Signoria to make his report. Already aware of the terms of his capitulation, the *Priori* had the main gate slammed in his face, professing outrage at so abject a surrender yet thankful to have found so convenient a scapegoat for their own helplessness. They sent a message saying that he might enter the palace through a side door, provided the guard remained in the piazza. When Piero did not move, a group of *Priori* and officials came out of the building to remonstrate with him, but failing to persuade him to dismiss his guard, they returned inside the building, slamming the gate shut once more. Soon afterwards the *Vacca* began to toll, and crowds of people hurried towards the square. Piero stood there, sword in hand now, as the crowds shouted insults at him, hissed at him and threw stones. He did not seem afraid but he was certainly hesitant, not sure what to do until some of his companions persuaded him to go back to the Medici Palace. His brother, Giovanni, who had been vainly trying to rally support for the family by riding up and down shouting '*Palle! Palle! Palle!*', met him in the Via Larga, and together they returned to the palace where Luca Landucci later saw Giovanni kneeling at a window in prayer.

At nightfall Piero, with his wife, their two young children and his cousin Giulio fled the city by the Porta San Gallo and made for Venice by way of Bologna, taking with them as many of the most valuable small items from the family collections as they could carry. Giovanni disguised himself as a Dominican monk in order to convey some of the treasures of the Medici library from the palace to San Marco; then he, too, fled from Florence. Following their departure, the *Signoria* decreed that the family should be banished from the State for ever, and that a reward of four thousand florins should be offered for Piero's head and two thousand florins for Giovanni's. Their cousins, the sons of Pierfrancesco, hastily changed their name to Popolano and took down the Medici arms from the walls of their palace.

Apartments at the Medici Palace had been prepared for the French King on the orders of Piero; but as soon as it became known that the Medici had flown from Florence, the French nobleman placed in charge of the apartments 'fell to rifling the palace upon pretence that the Medici bank at Lyons owed him a considerable sum of money', so Philippe de Commines reported. 'And among other things he seized upon a whole unicorn's horn [highly prized both for detecting poison and as an aphrodisiac] besides two great pieces of another; and other people followed his example. The best of the Medici furniture had been conveyed to another house in the city, but the mob plundered it. The *Signoria* got some of Piero's richest jewels, twenty thousand ducats in ready money from his bank in the city, several fine agate vases, besides an incredible number of cameos admirably well cut, three thousand medals of gold and silver, weighing almost forty pounds' and many pictures and statues.[1]

While the plunderers were at work, the French army was marching into Pisa, which Charles VIII immediately declared free from the tyranny of the Republic. To make some sort of protest against the

French action and to obtain what modification they could in the terms agreed to by Piero de' Medici, a delegation of four ambassadors left Florence to wait upon King Charles at Pisa. One of the ambassadors was Savonarola who, far from delivering any kind of protest, greeted the French King as an instrument of the divine will. 'And so at last, O King, thou hast come,' he is reported to have said to him.

Thou hast come as the Minister of God, the Minister of Justice. We receive thee with joyful hearts and a glad countenance ... We hope that by thee Jehovah will abase the pride of the proud, will exalt the humility of the humble, will crush vice, exalt virtue, make straight all that is crooked, renew the old and reform all that is deformed. Come then, glad, secure, triumphant, since He who sent you forth triumphed upon the Cross for our salvation.

Savonarola went on to beg mercy for God's chosen city of Florence and to ask the King to pardon those who had attempted to resist his advance; for they had offended in all innocence, not realizing that Charles was 'sent by God'. Impressed by these assurances, Charles agreed to treat Florence with leniency. He remained determined, however, to enter the city with an enormous, intimidating army.

XV

THE EXCOMMUNICANT

'Someone has his seat in Hell already'

K ING CHARLES VIII entered Florence through the Porta San
Freliano, on 17 November 1494, as though he were a conquering hero. He was wearing gilt armour, a cloak of cloth-of-gold
and a crown, and he carried his lance at rest as commanders then did
when entering a vanquished city. He rode under a splendid canopy
held over his head by four knights, his generals on either side of him.
Behind him followed the hundred-strong, magnificently clothed
royal bodyguard; then came two hundred knights on foot. These
were followed by the King's Swiss guards, the men armed with steel
halberds, the officers in helmets surmounted by thick plumes. Five
thousand Gascon infantry and five thousand Swiss infantry marched
in front of three thousand cavalry in engraved armour with brocade
mantles and velvet banners embroidered with gold. Behind these
came four thousand Breton archers and two thousand crossbowmen.
The artillery was drawn by horses not by oxen or mules, a sight no
Florentine had ever seen before.

The cuirassiers presented a hideous appearance, with their horses looking
like monsters because their ears and tails were cut quite short. Then came
the archers, extraordinary tall men from Scotland and other northern
countries, and they looked more like wild beasts than men.

As the sun was setting Charles arrived in the Piazza del Duomo
and dismounted from his immense black war-horse. The people in
the streets had been cheering up till then, persuaded to follow Savonarola's lead in welcoming him as a liberator; but the cheers subsided

as they noticed with a shock of surprise how very small he was, how jerky his movements. It was a brief interruption, though, observers said. Soon the acclamations rose again as loud as ever. And while his soldiers billeted themselves upon those apprehensive citizens of Florence – whose houses had been marked with chalk by the French quartermasters – Charles, after attending Mass, rode off to the Medici Palace with shouts of '*Viva Francia!*' ringing in his ears.

The alarm felt by their unwilling hosts at sight of those northern soldiers proved unjustified. During the eleven days that the twelve thousand troops of the French army remained in Florence there were only a few disturbances and no more than ten men killed. In general it was a surprisingly quiet time; and it was not until afterwards, when the army had moved off, declining to pay for most of the cost of their occupation of the city, that any widespread resentment was felt.

It was also a dispute over money which caused the one serious quarrel between Charles himself and the *Signoria*. He had agreed with them that they should grant him the use of the fortresses which his troops had occupied, that he should also for the moment retain Pisa, which would be handed back when his 'enterprise' was success-fully concluded, and that he should be paid 150,000 ducats towards the cost of the expedition. But when he met the city's representatives on 25 November and a herald read out the terms of the treaty, he heard that the sum inserted into the document was only 120,000 ducats. Standing up, he angrily interrupted the herald. The figure of 150,000 must be restored, otherwise he would order his trumpeters to call out his men who would thereupon sack the city without mercy. Infuriated by such a threat from the unprepossessing youth whom he had known when Charles was a puny child, Piero di Gino Capponi, once Florentine ambassador in France, snatched the treaty out of the herald's hands and tore it up, scattering the pieces on the floor. Defiantly, and in a voice which Guicciardini described as 'quivering with agitation', he shouted the words which were to become a Florentine proverb: 'If you sound your trumpets, we will ring our bells.'

Unwilling to risk the city being called to arms for the sake of so relatively small a sum, Charles gave way, making a feeble joke: 'Ah!

Capponi, Capponi,' he said, 'You are a fine capon indeed.' Then, having signed the treaty, he headed south for Rome.

Two days after his departure, a *Parlamento* was summoned in the Piazza della Signoria, and by popular vote a *Balìa* was established. This was followed by the appointment of twenty *Accoppiatori* who, having abolished the Medicean councils, were in future to be responsible for selecting the members of the *Signoria*. Whatever constitutional changes were effected, however, Savonarola's supporters were anxious to make it known that the real power in Florence now lay with the Prior of San Marco, that a theocratic government was to be established and the State would, indeed, be ruled by paternosters.

Savonarola made this clear enough himself. 'The Lord has driven my ship into the open sea,' he declared in a sermon on 21 December.

The wind drives me forward. The Lord forbids my return. I spoke last night with the Lord and said, 'Pity me, O Lord. Lead me back to my haven.' 'It is impossible,' said the Lord. 'See you not that the wind is contrary?' 'I will preach, if so I must, but why need I meddle with the government of Florence?' 'If you would make Florence a holy city, you must establish her on firm foundations and give her a government which favours virtue.'

It was a divine call which Savonarola was not reluctant to obey. In sermons of irresistible force he pointed the way and the citizens followed it. With crucifix in hand he urged the people to put to death all those who advocated the restoration of the Medici. God had called him to reform the city and the Church, and God's will would be done. There must be continual fasting; the gold ornaments and illuminated books, the silver chalices and candlesticks and jewelled crucifixes must be removed from the convents and monasteries. 'Blessed bands' of children, their hair cut short, must march through the streets, singing hymns, collecting alms for the poor, and seeking out those rouge pots and looking-glasses, those lascivious pictures and immoral books, all those 'vanities' which were the Devil's invitations to vice. These children must shame their elders into abandoning the gambling table for the confessional box; they must report to the authorities all infractions of the law, all examples of unbecoming or ostentatious dress, all other children who threw stones.

In future, carnivals must be religious pageants to the glory of God in whose name 'vanities' must be destroyed in sacrificial bonfires. And so they were. During one well-remembered carnival, processions of white-robed children marched through the streets, carrying olive branches and red crosses, singing hymns and dancing, 'so that it seemed' to Cinozzi that 'the angels had come down to earth to rejoice with the children of men'. A statue by Donatello of Jesus as a boy, holding the crown of thorns in his hands, was carried from church to church. Later an enormous scaffold in the shape of a pyramid was erected opposite the Palazzo della Signoria. Around the base of the pyramid was arranged a garish collection of expensive dresses and fancy costumes once worn for masquerades, looking-glasses, velvet caps, wigs, masks, false beards, scent bottles and pomade pots, jars of rouge, beads, fans, necklaces, bracelets and trinkets of every kind. On top of these were piled profane books and drawings that might engender lascivious thoughts, chessboards and diceboxes, packs of cards and manuals of magic, busts and portraits of celebrated beauties; sensual pictures by Lorenzo di Credi, Botticelli and Fra Bartolommeo sacrificed by the now reformed artists themselves. At the very summit was an effigy of a Venetian merchant who had offered 20,000 *scudi* for the works of art now about to be consigned to the flames. The huge pile was surrounded by guards, and while the *Signoria* looked down from a balcony the whole was set alight. The flames rose to the chanting of a choir, the blowing of trumpets and the ringing of countless bells.

Naturally there were those who objected to such demonstrations of piety, who condemned Savonarola's dedicated adherents as *masticapaternostri* (prayer mumblers) or *piagnoni* (snivellers). They beat drums and made 'all sorts of noise' to drown his voice when he was preaching, and they encouraged urchins to throw stones at his followers. But there were many more who saw Savonarola as a great reformer; who shared his dream of a world, simple and pure, in which all men would turn to Christ; who agreed with Cinozzi that

Florence was then 'a glorious place'; who, like Luca Landucci, were proud to have children among those 'blessed bands and held in such reverence that everyone abstained from scandalous vice'; who, like Giorgio Vespucci, uncle of the navigator, and the Strozzi brothers, hoped one day to see Florence made 'a new Jerusalem'.

King Charles VIII met little opposition on his march south. Rome fell without a struggle; and Ferrante's son, King Alfonso II, terrified by weird dreams and portents, haunted by the ghostly victims of his brutality, and hearing the stones beneath his feet cry out '*Francia! Francia!*', abdicated and fled to a Sicilian monastery. The French army crossed the Neapolitan frontier, massacring the people of Monte di San Giovanni and setting fire to the town as a warning of the dreadful fate that awaited all opponents. They filled the whole kingdom with the greatest terror, so Guicciardini said, by a way of making war that 'had not been practised in Italy for many centuries'. Choosing to regard him as their deliverer from the House of Aragon, the Neapolitans gave Charles as enthusiastic a welcome as he had enjoyed in Florence. Indeed, the welcome of the people and the delights of their city were so beguiling that all thoughts of going on to Jerusalem as Charles had originally intended were now abandoned. The King settled down to enjoy the pleasures of his new domain and a succession of pretty mistresses, whose portraits he had bound together in a big book. But, as he languished beneath the Neapolitan sun, his rivals to the north were busily plotting his downfall.

None of these rivals was more active than the new Pope, Roderigo Borgia, Alexander VI. He was fat and bald, plain and flamboyant, yet it was not only his riches and his influence that made him attractive to women. He had an undeniable charm, an invigorating energy, a kind of childlike eagerness in his profligacy that endeared him to numerous mistresses. Like so many of his predecessors, he was determined to use his office for the benefit of his family, in particular for the advancement of his six sons of whom the sinisterly beguiling Cesare Borgia was the most talented and the most ambitious. But the Pope recognized that before these ambitions could be fully realized, an attempt must be made to unite Italy against the foreign invader. Accordingly he set about forming what he liked to term a Holy League, dedicated to the expulsion of the French.

It was an alliance that Lodovico Sforza was only too anxious to join. For Il Moro was now deeply regretting the consequences of having enticed the French into Italy where the Duke of Orleans, jealous of Charles VIII's success in Naples, was making claims upon the Duchy of Milan. As well as Milan, Venice joined the Pope's Holy League, so did the Emperor Maximilian, so did Ferdinand King of Aragon and Castile. Despite this threat to their position in Naples, the French army did not withdraw from the city immediately. It was not, in fact, until seven weeks after the Holy League had been established that Charles, leaving a large garrison behind him to hold the kingdom in his name, led his army north again.

It was a long, slow march. May passed and the whole of June, 1495. July began and still the French army, accompanied by a mule loaded with treasure to every two men, had not crossed the Appenines. By now the Holy League had managed to bring a strong army together under command of the fierce-looking, bulging-eyed Francesco Gonzaga, Marquis of Mantua. Slowly the two armies drew closer together; and this time there would be no deft avoidance as in the earlier fashion of Renaissance warfare. As Francesco Guicciardini observed, the French invasion had for ever ended those prolonged, choreographic campaigns so beloved by the old *condottieri* who had protracted their wars – as one of them, Jacopo Piccinino, himself admitted – in order to increase their pay, who had safeguarded their men by spending 'most of their time retreating to the security of river banks and ditches', who, when they had fought at all, had fought for prisoners rather than to kill. The picture of Italian warfare before the French invasion as a bloodless parade has, of course, been exaggerated. In the battle of Anghiari in 1440, for instance, about nine hundred men were killed, not 'one man' as Machiavelli claimed But all the same, it was not unusual for engagements, in which thousands of men took part, to end without a single casualty and with congratulatory handshakes exchanged between the rival commanders The Italian soldier fought bravely when he had to fight; but most o the time his commanders made sure that he occupied himself in plundering rather than in conflict, in driving cattle with his lance rather than in shooting at the enemy with his cross-bow. Troops of infantry pass through the pages of contemporary chronicles, wearing smart jerkins and parti-coloured tights, marching along to the music of drum and fife, occasionally shouting the name of the prince who paid them, looking more like strolling players than men of war. In sharp contrast, the soldiers of Charles VIII's army were experienced, professional, trained to kill. 'They would face the enemy like a wall without ever breaking rank.' Above all, as Guicciardini said, they had brought with them

a great quantity of artillery of a sort never before seen in Italy [which] rendered ridiculous all former weapons of attack … These were called cannon and they used iron cannon balls instead of stone as before, and this new shot was incomparably larger and heavier than that which had previously been employed. Furthermore, they were hauled on carriages drawn not by oxen as was the custom in Italy but by horses … and were led right up to the walls and set in position there with incredible speed. And they used this diabolical weapon not only in besieging cities but also in the field.

When the French and Italian armies finally clashed by the banks of the river Taro in July 1495, the mercenary troops of the Holy League were no match for King Charles's artillerymen and cavalry. The battle was short and ferocious, more savage and bloody, indeed, than any battle fought in Italy since the end of the thirteenth century. Italian losses were enormous; and, as the greatly outnumbered French army continued its northward march, hundreds of French camp-followers ran on to the field with knives and axes to hack apart the screaming, wounded Italians. Since he retained possession of the battle-ground and had captured the French baggage train – which included a sword and helmet said to have belonged to Charlemagne, jewels and plate, the royal seals, a piece of the Holy Cross, a sacred horn, a vest of the Blessed Virgin, a limb of St Denis and a book depicting naked women 'painted at various times and places . . . sketches of intercourse and lasciviousness in each city' – the Marquis of Mantua claimed the victory. But by the end of August Charles and his army, still a powerful force, though mauled and weary, were across the Alps and safely home in France, leaving the Italians shocked by the realization that for all their virtues, talents, wealth, past glory and experience, for all their skill as military engineers, they had been utterly unable to withstand the advance of the ruthless men from the north.

In this traumatic campaign Florence had played no part. Firm in his allegiance to 'God's instrument', Savonarola had declined to have anything to do with the Holy League. Amazed that an obscure Dominican should wield such influence, and annoyed not only by his sermons in support of the invader but also by his claims to be God's chosen mouthpiece, the Pope asked Savonarola to come to Rome to explain himself. Savonarola replied that Florence could not spare him, that he was not well enough to travel, and that, in any case, it was contrary to God's will that he should do so. Thus had begun a correspondence which, growing increasingly less restrained, had ended with the Pope's forbidding Savonarola to deliver any further sermons. For a time Savonarola had obeyed the Pope's commands, his place in the pulpit being taken by his devoted disciple, Fra Domenico da Pescia; but in February 1496, choosing to suppose that the Pope's ban was no longer in force, Savonarola began a course of sermons which were given every day in the Cathedral until 3 April.

The Pope used every means at his disposal to bring Savonarola to heel. He gave instructions that the Tuscan Dominicans, who had been granted independence, should revert to Roman control since this would enable him to send Savonarola to another monastery far from Florence. Savonarola declined to accept the Pope's jurisdiction in the matter. Alexander even offered him a cardinal's hat if he would give up preaching his sermons. Savonarola replied that another sort of red hat would suit him better, 'one red with blood'.

At length, in June 1497, the Pope took the final step and excommunicated him. For six months Savonarola pondered his dilemma, fasting and praying, until God guided him to the decision that it was his duty to defy the Pope. On Christmas Day he did so publicly by celebrating High Mass in the Cathedral. Alexander responded by demanding of the *Signoria* that they either dispatch 'that son of iniquity, Fra Hieronymo Savonarola' to Rome or lock him up in Florence. If they did not do so, he would lay the entire city under an interdict.

'You have not listened to my expositions,' Savonarola replied to the Pope.

I can no longer place any faith in your Holiness, but must trust myself wholly to Him who chooses the weak things of this world to confound the strong. Your Holiness is well advised to make immediate provisions for your own salvation.

With the *Signoria*, whom he considered to have been far too mild in their response to the Pope's threats, Savonarola was even more harshly admonitory. 'Tell those who are seeking to make themselves great and exalted that their seats are prepared for them – in Hell . . . Tell them that the rod has come. Someone has his seat in Hell already.'

But the Pope had timed his threat well. Savonarola's supporters were losing ground in Florence where, indeed, they had been only partly responsible for the impermanent changes which had taken place in the government of the city. There had been poor harvests that year in Tuscany; starving people had fallen down and died in the streets; there had also been an outbreak of plague. Savonarola's hero, King Charles, had not returned Pisa to Florence as he had promised to do, but had handed it over instead to its inhabitants who had taken up arms to defend their independence. And the subsequent war, fought as usual by ill-paid mercenaries, dragged on indeterminately. Making much of these calamities, Savonarola's opponents had been more and more outspoken in their criticisms of his regime. A party of high-spirited young men known as *Compagnacci*, mostly sons of rich families, had gone so far as to smear the Cathedral pulpit with grease, hanging round it the putrid skin of an ass, and to contrive the fall of a heavy chest which came crashing down to the stone floor of the nave, sending the panic-stricken congregation rushing out of the Cathedral in the middle of the Prior's sermon.

It was one of the last sermons which Savonarola was to deliver; for it had been decided in Florence that, in view of the Pope's

197

warnings, he must be asked to preach no more. He agreed to desist on condition that he be allowed the opportunity of vindicating himself. He attempted to do so on 18 March in a sermon in which he insisted on his right to resist unlawful authority, made reference to the fulfilment of his prophecies and castigated the Church as a Satanic institution for the promotion of whoredom and vice. He had not preached because he wanted to but because he had been compelled to by a raging fire within the very marrow of his bones: 'I feel myself all burning, all inflamed with the spirit of the Lord. Oh, spirit within! You rouse the waves of the sea, as the wind does. You stir the tempest as you pass. I can do no other.'

After this final sermon the Franciscans, who had long challenged the Dominicans' claims to a special relationship with God, renewed their request that Savonarola should produce some evidence of His peculiar favour. Fra Francesco da Puglia, a Franciscan monk, in particular insisted that Savonarola's claims to divine inspiration were false, and that he could not prove they were otherwise. He offered to walk through fire in company with Savonarola to satisfy the world that the Dominican was not under God's protection. Savonarola declined to take part in the ordeal, protesting that he was reserved for higher work; but he agreed that his passionately devoted supporter, Fra Domenico da Pescia, might represent him. Fra Domenico eagerly accepted the challenge. Fra Francesco, however, refused to match himself with anyone other than Savonarola; so another Franciscan, Fra Giuliano Rondinelli, was found to take his place.

Most members of the *Signoria* were horrified by this suggested reversion to the barbarism of past ages. One suggested that their ancestors would be ashamed of them if they could hear them even so much as discussing the propriety of the proposed ordeal. Another put forward the idea that walking across the Arno without getting wet would be 'just as good a miracle' to settle the dispute. Yet it was felt that the populace had by now become so excited by the prospect of an ordeal by fire that it might prove dangerous to disappoint them. It was settled that if the Dominican, Fra Domenico, died then Savonarola would be banished from Florence; if the Franciscan, Fra Giuliano perished – as, indeed, he expected to do – but the Dominican did not then Fra Francesco da Puglia would be banished. It was also settled that the ordeal should take place in the Piazza della Signoria on Saturday 7 April 1498 between ten o'clock in the morning and two in the afternoon, that on the appointed day all strangers must leave the city, the streets be barricaded, and the approaches to the Piazza held by armed guards.

An avenue thirty yards long and ten yards across was constructed in front of the Loggia dei Lanzi. Each side of the avenue was lined with piles of sticks soaked in oil leaving a passage in the middle about three feet broad through which the monks had to pass. The Loggia dei Lanzi was divided into two for the accommodation of the rival supporters.

The Franciscans were the first to enter the arena, where they were kept waiting for the arrival of the Dominicans, who marched towards the Loggia in pairs behind a crucifix, chanting an appropriate psalm. At the end of the procession walked Fra Domenico next to Savonarola in 'whose excommunicated hands' the Franciscans were appalled to see the Host. There was further consternation when it became apparent that Fra Domenico intended to take a crucifix with him into the flames. He eventually agreed that he would not do this, but he could not be persuaded to be parted from the consecrated Host. The arguments continued until a heavy thunderstorm broke above their heads, and it was announced that no ordeal would take place that day after all.

This was too much for the people to bear. The next day, Palm Sunday, an angry mob attacked a congregation who had assembled in the Cathedral to hear a sermon by one of Savonarola's disciples. The congregation fled from the Cathedral and, pursued by sticks and stones and the execrations of the *Compagnacci*, ran for the shelter of San Marco. Here, unknown to Savonarola who urged them to seek protection only in prayer, the monks had assembled a small store of weapons and were prepared to withstand a siege. Some of them loosened a pinnacle at the top of the monastery church and sent it hurtling down on the heads of the mob in the square below; others struck out with lances at men trying to set fire to the monastery walls. Several rioters and monks were killed before the assailants managed to clamber over the walls and down into the choir. Savonarola took refuge in the library where, soon afterwards, a guard arrived from the *Signoria* with orders for his arrest. He was escorted through the streets, hooted and jeered at by the mob, and cast into the Alberghettino in the tower of the Palazzo della Signoria where Cosimo de' Medici had been imprisoned sixty-five years before.

Orders were given for Savonarola to be tortured. Suffering the exquisite agonies inflicted by the *strappado*, he made all such confessions as were required of him, retracting the confessions when the ropes were removed from his body, and then being tortured again. Together with Fra Domenico and another of his most faithful disciples Fra Silvestro, he was found guilty of heresy and schism and condemned to death. A scaffold, surrounded by tinder, was erected in the Piazza della Signoria and on this Savonarola and his two companions were hanged in chains and burned. As the flames leapt towards the early summer sky, a voice called out derisively, 'O prophet, now is the time for a miracle! Prophet save thyself.'

'In a few hours the victims were burned, their legs and arms gradually dropping off,' Landucci recorded in his diary.

Part of their bodies remaining hanging to the chains, a quantity of stones were thrown to make them fall, as there was a fear of the people getting hold of them; and then the hangman and those whose business it was, hacked down the post and burned it on the ground, bringing a lot of brushwood, and stirring the fire up over the dead bodies so that the very last piece was consumed. Then they fetched carts, and accompanied by the mace-bearers, carried the last bit of dust to the Arno near the Ponte Vecchio in order that no remains should be found.

✺ XVI ✺

RETURN OF THE MEDICI

*'The town of Prato was sacked, not without
some bloodshed'*

THEIR TREASURES lost, their palaces and villas forfeited, the
Medici wandered over Europe like the members of an out-
cast tribe. Piero remained in Italy, occasionally pawning a
gem or a cameo, offering his services to the Republic's enemies,
making repeated attempts to reinstate himself in Florence by force,
joining forces with Cesare Borgia, who was creating an empire for
himself in the Romagna and who hoped that by re-establishing the
Medici in Florence he would make a valuable ally for himself in
Tuscany. Once Piero actually appeared at the Porta Romana with a
band of men-at-arms, who trotted away to Siena when it became
clear that the Florentines were not in the least disposed to favour a
Medicean restoration under Piero's leadership. Eventually Piero
decided to offer his services to the French in return for some vague,
unfulfilled promises of their support in yet another attempt to regain
Florence.

King Charles VIII was now dead, having struck his head violently
against a beam at his château at Amboise; but his successor, Louis XII,
reasserted the family's right to the throne of Naples. He also claimed
the Duchy of Milan on the grounds that his grandfather had married
Valentina Visconti. Both these claims were, however, strongly contested by King Ferdinand of Spain; and although in 1500 Ferdinand
made an agreement with Louis to share Naples with him, he and the
French, quarrelling over their prospective spoils, were soon at war again.

In December 1503, the French were defeated by the Spaniards under the spirited command of Gonsalvo de Córdoba. Attempting to escape across the Garigliano to Gaeta, Piero de' Medici, who had been serving in the French army, was drowned in the swollen waters of the river when his boat capsized. His body was later recovered and buried in the abbey of Monte Cassino.[1] He left two children, a daughter, Clarice, and a son, Lorenzo, who was eleven. Their uncle, Giovanni, who became head of the family on Piero's death, was already recognized as a most remarkable man.

Born in the Medici Palace on 11 December 1475, Giovanni was now twenty-eight. From his earliest years his parents had entertained great hopes for him. The night before his birth his mother had had a strange and alarmingly vivid dream. She had seen herself in the Cathedral, writhing in agony and about to be delivered; but the baby when it came was not a human child. It was an immense lion.

As though encouraged by this vision to believe that the House of Medici would derive great profit from a son being made a prince of the Church, Lorenzo determined to launch Giovanni on an ecclesiastical career. As soon as the boy displayed sufficient promise to merit early preferment, orders were given to the manager of the Lyons branch of the bank to keep a sharp look out for vacancies, French benefices being easier to obtain than Italian. Early preferment Giovanni certainly achieved. Having received the tonsure at the age of eight he was presented with the abbey of Fontdouce by the King of France who would also have made him Archbishop of Aix in Provence had it not been discovered just in time that the present Archbishop was still alive. To compensate him for this disappointment, Giovanni was given the priory of Saint-Gemme near Chartres, made a canon of every cathedral in Tuscany, and presented with the abbeys of Passignano and Monte Cassino as well as with over twenty other honourable and profitable offices. After the death of Sixtus IV and the election of Giovanni Battista Cibò as Innocent VIII, the way lay open to even higher preferment. Fearing that the new Pope might die before his hopes were fully realized, Lorenzo did all he could to persuade him to create Giovanni a cardinal at the earliest possibl date. And after the marriage of his daughter, Maddalena, to the Pope's son, Franceschetto Cibò, he instructed the Florentine ambassador in Rome to miss no opportunity of pressing Giovanni's claim. He enlisted the help of two cardinals, Roderigo Borgia and Ascanio Sforza, both of whom had great influence at the Curia; and he wrote letter after personal letter reminding the Pope of his 'chief desire'. In March 1489 Innocent gave way, making the appointment conditional, however, upon Giovanni's leaving Florence to study canon law at Pisa and upon his elevation remaining secret for three years. Lorenzo had no objection to the first condition, but, constantly apprehensive that Innocent might die within the stipulated period and that a new Pope would declare his predecessor's unusual appointment invalid, he tried to have his son's elevation made public immediately. He was unsuccessful. The old Pope, his health declining slowly month by month, refused to give way. Lorenzo afterwards confessed that scarcely a day passed when he did not expect to receive the dreaded news from Rome. Innocent died on 25 July 1492, but he had lived just long enough for Lorenzo's ambitions to be fulfilled. Three months before the Pope's death and three weeks before his father's in March 1492, Giovanni had entered the ancient Badia at Fiesole and there the insignia of his rank had been blessed before the High Altar and the papal brief had been read out.

Emerging from the church wearing his mantle, scarlet hat and sapphire ring, the sixteen-year-old boy had not presented a prepossessing appearance. He was tall enough and looked both good-natured and intelligent; but his face was pasty and flabby, his body already extremely fat, and his eyesight evidently failing. His nose was markedly snubbed and he kept his mouth half open. Nor did his appearance belie his nature. He was intelligent, his tutors all agreed; he was of a happy and generous disposition; but they had due cause to complain of his laziness, his precocious and excessive predilection for good food, good drink and pleasure. In Rome he had ample opportunity to indulge these tastes, and he did not stint himself. 'He *will* not get out of bed in the morning,' one of his tutors reported. 'And he *will* sit up late at night. I am most concerned, since these irregular habits are likely to injure his health.'

Well aware of these faults, his father had thought it as well to write him a long letter of advice in the hope that he might be persuaded to lead a life more befitting his exalted rank:

The first thing that I want to impress upon you is that you ought to be grateful to God, remembering always that it is not through *your* merits, or *your* wisdom that you have gained this dignity, but through *His* favour. Show your thankfulness by a holy, exemplary, and chaste life ... During the past year I have been much comforted to see that, without being told to do so, you have often of your own accord gone to confession and to Holy Communion. I do not think there is a better way of keeping in God's grace than to make this a regular practice. I know only too well that in going to live in Rome, which is a sink of iniquity, you will find it hard to follow this advice because there will be many there who will try to corrupt you and incite you to vice, and because your promotion to the cardinalate at your early age arouses much envy ... You must, therefore, oppose temptation all the more firmly ... It is at the same time necessary that you should not incur a reputation for hypocrisy, and in conversation not to affect either austerity or undue seriousness. You will understand all this better when you are older ... You are well aware how important is the example you ought to show to others as a cardinal, and that the world would be a better place if all cardinals were what they ought to be, because if they were so there would always be a good Pope and consequently a more peaceful world ...

You are the youngest cardinal, not only in the Sacred College of today but at any time in the past. Therefore, when you are in assembly with other cardinals, you must be the most unassuming, and the most humble ... Try to live with regularity ... Silk and jewels are seldom suitable to those in your station. Much better to collect antiquities and beautiful books, and to maintain a learned and well regulated household rather than a grand one. Invite others to your house more often than you accept invitations to theirs; but not too often. Eat plain food and take plenty of exercise ... Confide in others too little rather than too much. One rule above all others I urge you to observe most rigorously: *Rise early in the morning.* This not only for your health's sake, but also so that you can arrange and expedite all the day's business ...

With regard to your speaking in the Consistory, I think it would be best for the present while you are still so young, to refer whatever is proposed to you to His Holiness, giving as your reason your youth and inexperience. You will find that you will be asked to intercede with the Pope for many small objects. Try at first to do this as seldom as you can, and not to worry him unduly in this way. For it is the Pope's nature to pay the most attention to those who bother him least ... Farewell.

Lorenzo's reference to Rome as a sink of iniquity was not unjust. There were reckoned to be almost seven thousand prostitutes in a population of less than 50,000, most of them working in brothels licensed by the papal authorities and many of them suffering from syphilis, 'a kind of illness very common among priests', according to Benvenuto Cellini, who caught the disease himself. There were almost as many professional criminals as prostitutes, many if not most of whom avoided punishment by paying bribes. There were alleged to be an average of fourteen murders a day; and although the stench from the rows of rotting corpses of executed men hanging from the battlements of the Castel Sant' Angelo made it an ordeal to cross the bridge beneath, most murderers, if caught, were soon released. Roderigo Borgia, one of the richest cardinals, explained when asked why so many malefactors escaped execution, 'The Lord requires not the death of a sinner, but rather that he may pay and live.' It was this Roderigo Borgia who, on the death of Innocent VIII, secured his own succession as Alexander VI by disbursing the most lavish gifts to all his rivals and potential supporters. Five asses laden with gold were believed to have entered the courtyard of the one cardinal, Ascanio Sforza, whose own riches and influence might have defeated him.

The young cardinal Giovanni de' Medici seems to have enjoyed his early years in Rome to the full; but once a price had been placed on his head by the government of Florence he thought it advisable to go abroad for a time. So, having obtained permission from Alexander to travel beyond the Alps, he left for Venice en route for Bavaria in company with his cousin Giulio, who had been studying at the university at Pisa. From Bavaria they went to Brussels, then travelled up to the Flemish coast with the intention of sailing for England. Changing their minds, they rode south for Rouen instead, then to Marseilles whence they took boat for Genoa to stay with Giovanni's sister Maddalena. From Genoa, they returned at last to

Rome where Alexander VI, having himself by then quarrelled with Florence, greeted them kindly.

They settled down in a palace in the city where, disregarding the meagreness of his resources, Giovanni determined to enjoy life to the full, surrounding himself with genial friends and a constant stream of guests.[2] As well as his cousin Giulio, there lived in the palace Bernardo Dovizi da Bibbiena, brother to Piero Dovizi, a brilliant, amusing and wily man, five years older than Giovanni, formerly his tutor and soon to become his secretary. Often to be seen there also was Giovanni's younger brother, Giuliano, a well-mannered, kind, rather feckless though not unambitious young man whose cheerful good nature had endeared him to the families of the Duke of Urbino and the Marquis of Mantua, his hosts during his years of exile. Another frequent guest was the Pope's favourite nephew, Cardinal Galeotto Franciotto, whom Giovanni had at first chosen to cultivate for selfish reasons but whom he grew to love so much that, after Franciotto's early death, he could not hear his name mentioned without tears starting to his eyes.

With Franciotto on one side and Dovizi on the other, with Giuliano and Giulio, with various cardinals and visitors from Florence whose good opinion he was anxious to cultivate, and with numerous artists by whom the name of Medici was still revered, Giovanni played the part of host with such lavish generosity that he was frequently in debt. His guests became used to the constant disappearance and reappearance of his most valuable pieces of silver, which made their way between his dining-room and the shops of the Roman pawnbrokers.

Yet although he spent long evenings at the dining-table, long mornings discussing the several arts in which he took a lively interest, and long afternoons hunting and hawking in the Campagna – explaining that such exercise, incongruous though it might be for a cardinal, was a necessary duty for one so corpulent – Giovanni was far from content to devote all his life to the pleasures he so obviously enjoyed. He seemed always to have one pale, short-sighted eye turned in the direction of the thin, bearded, restless figure of the newly elected Pope.

Julius II, who after the twenty-six-day Papacy of Alexander VI's successor, the decrepit Pius III, had been elected Pope in November 1503, was the grandson of a fisherman, a tall, handsome, rough, talkative, syphilitic, irascible man. He was much given to boasting of his poor childhood – when he had sailed with cargoes of onions down the Ligurian coast – of his lack of scholarship and of his taste for the life of a soldier. 'I am no schoolman,' he said once when asked to suggest a suitable emblem for a statue of him being made by Michelangelo. 'Put a sword in my hand, not a book.'

Julius delighted in the sword. Not long after his elevation he set off, with twenty-four cardinals in unwilling attendance, to reduce the rebel cities of Perugia and Bologna whose obedience to the Church he was determined to compel. Shaken by the news of his approach, Gian-Paolo Baglioni, the ruler of Perugia, surrendered the city into his hands, kneeling before him and begging for mercy. The Pope forgave him but added, 'Do it again and I'll hang you.' Then, leaving his cardinals no time for rest, he marched them through the marshes of the Romagna to Bologna. The city having been deserted by Giovanni Bentivoglio, they entered it on 11 November 1506, exhausted and peevish, their hands and faces red and lumpy with mosquito bites.

Having regained Bologna and Perugia for the Church, Julius now determined also to recover Rimini, Faenza and Ravenna, which had fallen into the hands of Venice. To do so he called into existence the League of Cambrai, allying himself not only with Louis of France and Ferdinand of Spain but also with the Emperor Maximilian who were all to take a share of the Venetian dominions. The combination was far too powerful for Venice whose troops were routed at Aguadello near Cremona on 14 May 1509. Yet the Pope, having so successfully extended the dominions of the Church, could not but regret that this had entailed foreign powers gaining footholds in Lombardy. He determined to drive them out, repeatedly declaring, 'I will not have these barbarians taking over Italy.' He called upon all Italy to drive them back once more across the Alps, beginning with the French. 'Let's see,' he said riding off to turn a French garrison out of Mirandola, 'Let's see who has the bigger balls, the

King of France or I.' Inspired by his relentless determination his troops captured Mirandola, through whose shattered walls he scrambled by means of a wooden scaling ladder. But it was to be many months before he was able to achieve a more significant success, for most Italian states, including Florence, showed little inclination to respond to his call.

France was the Florentines' traditional friend. The friendship had, admittedly, been placed under severe strain by Charles VIII, but the war with Pisa which the French had provoked was now over. The Pisans had been forced to sue for peace after the defeat of their supporters, the Venetians, at Aguadello. The Florentines, therefore, decided to remain neutral – 'a bad example', the Pope declared angrily; but it was one which other Italian states thought it prudent to follow. So Julius, unable to rouse Italians by his call for a crusade against the French, turned to the Spaniards, now in firm possession of Naples. With them he formed a new Holy League whose forces marched north to Bologna which, having been retaken with French help by Alfonso d'Este, Duke of Ferrara, had been returned to Bentivoglio. At the same time, Julius announced that once Bologna had been recaptured his Legate there would be Cardinal Giovanni de' Medici. Julius had been much impressed by Giovanni's good-natured acceptance of the discomforts of campaigning and had already rewarded him with the see of Amalfi and the promise of further preferment. In Florence, the *Signoria* heard of Giovanni's ascendance with alarm.

The forces of the Holy League, however, were far from successful. They had failed to take Bologna; and, on Easter Saturday 1512, they were stopped in their tracks on the banks of the Ronco on their way to the relief of Ravenna. In the ensuing savage battle – in which the Spanish and French cannon, roaring ceaselessly in the smoke, sent their balls bouncing and ploughing through whole rows and columns of men-at-arms – the losses on both sides were so enormous that scarcely ever before in the history of Europe had so many men been left dead upon the field. Almost ten thousand soldiers of the Holy League are said to have been killed, and nearly as many men in the French army.

Cardinal Giovanni, who had ridden along the Spanish ranks on a white palfrey before the battle began, exhorting the troops to fight well and praying to God for victory, had been captured as he gave comfort to the dying amidst the littered corpses of the dead. He was escorted to Bologna where his stout figure in scarlet robes and his sweating face beneath the broad-brimmed tasselled hat were exposed to the taunts of the populace. The Bentivogli, however, treated him with kindness. He was also treated well upon his removal to Modena where Bianca Rangone sold her jewels to provide him with food and clothing. At his eventual destination, Milan, he was provided with comfortable lodgings in the house of Cardinal Federigo Sanseverino.

The French, so Giovanni then believed, had gained an undoubted victory outside Ravenna from which they had forced the cruelly mauled forces of the Holy League to withdraw. The Florentines thought so, too, and lit huge bonfires to celebrate the Pope's defeat as they had done to celebrate the rout of the Venetians at Aguadello. But it proved to be an immensely costly victory from which the winning side could reap no advantage. In the closing stages of the battle, the talented young French commander, Gaston de Foix, had been knocked from his horse by a stray shot and, spattered with blood and brains, had been hacked to death by Spanish infantrymen. Moreover, a large Swiss army had marched down towards French-occupied Lombardy to take advantage of the confusion, while France itself was threatened with invasion by both England and Spain. The French forces, running short of provisions, were obliged to withdraw from Ravenna and Bologna, then from Milan, and finally from Lombardy altogether.

Cardinal Giovanni, far too valuable a hostage to leave behind, was compelled to go with them. But determined to decamp long before he reached the Alps, he feigned illness at a village on the banks of the Po, where a priest who was accompanying him managed to slip away from the French guard and to enlist the help of two local landowners in a plan of escape. As the cardinal was about to step into a barge at the river bank the following morning, a band of armed peasants from the landowners' estates burst out of the reeds and, in the ensuing uproar, hustled the captive away. Improbably disguised as a soldier,

Giovanni was then taken to a pigeon-house in the courtyard of a castle belonging to one of the landowners' kinsmen, then to Voghiera, then to Mantua where he learned that preparations were already far advanced to use the army of the Holy League, now free of the French, to enforce a change of government in Florence. His arrival in Mantua ensured that there could be no doubt what form that new government would take.

Since the execution of Savonarola, Florence, no longer an important power, had failed to regain the vitality and gaiety of the golden age it had enjoyed during the last years of Lorenzo the Magnificent. A series of financial crises had brought several guilds almost to the verge of ruin. The long, exhausting, humiliating war against Pisa, incompetently conducted by treacherous *condottieri*, had drained the *Signoria*'s resources. The French King's representative in Tuscany, Robert de Balzac Entragues, had sold Sarzana to Genoa and Pietrasanta to Lucca. Gloom descended over the city, a gloom which was reflected in the final paintings of Botticelli, a prematurely old man now, limping through the streets, 'unable to stand upright and moving about with the help of crutches'.[2]

Four years after the death of Savonarola, an attempt had been made to strengthen the government of the city by appointing a *Gonfaloniere* for life. The man chosen for this appointment was Piero Soderini, an honest, hard-working but unremarkable administrator whose fame has been eclipsed by that of the relatively minor official in the government whom he came to consult on all matters of importance, Niccolò Machiavelli.

Machiavelli was a thin, neat, pale man whose sparse black hair was brushed straight back from a high and bony forehead. In the only portrait of him that survives he returns the spectator's gaze with a look at once amused, questioning and sardonic. The son of a lawyer from an old Tuscan family, he had been appointed to his present post at the age of thirty following the execution of Savonarola, whose ideas and methods he had disdained. One of the concerns of Machiavelli's department was war; and it was his strongly held view, as it had been of other Florentines before him, including Leonardo Bruni, that the Republic's traditional system of hiring troops to fight its battles would have to be abandoned in favour of a national militia. It had been found so often in the past that *condottieri* were utterly untrustworthy: sometimes they declined to fight alongside other bands hired to co-operate with them; at other times they refused to fight against *condottieri* with whom they were on friendly terms; occasionally they accepted money from both sides; always they were unwilling to risk the lives of their men and thus waste their assets. Soderini agreed to have the formation of a national militia approved by the *Signoria* and he entrusted Machiavelli with the task of organizing it. Machiavelli began to do so with energy and enthusiasm, and by February 1506 he was able to hold a parade in the Piazza della Signoria of the first recruits. They were mostly peasants from the outlying country who were, so Landucci recorded,

each given a white waistcoat, a pair of stocking, half red and half white, a white cap, shoes, and an iron breastplate. Most also had lances; some of them had arquebuses. They were soldiers but lived in their own homes, being obliged to appear when needed, and it was ordered that many should be equipped in this way throughout the country, so that we should not need any foreigners. This was thought the finest thing that had ever been arranged for Florence.

Landucci's confidence in the militia was not dispelled when the Spanish forces of the Holy League began to march for the Florentine frontier from Bologna under command of Raymond de Cadorna. Even when the Spaniards, repeatedly demanding a change of government in Florence, reached Barberino and advanced on Campi and frightened peasants ran in from the hills to seek shelter behind the walls of the city, it seemed to Landucci as to all 'intelligent people' that there was 'no need of fear. On the contrary it was rather for the enemy to fear, because if they came down into these plains, they would fare badly. Many battalions of militia had been levied, and all the men-at-arms were eager to encounter the enemy'.

Although Machiavelli, who had been busy organizing the defences of the Mugello, took a more realistic view of the situation,

Soderini in Florence shared Landucci's confidence. He had nine thousand men under arms; he knew that the Spanish army was much smaller, and that, although the Medicean party in Florence were growing stronger as the Spaniards advanced on the city, their hopes of a revolution in Florence were ill-founded.

Cadorna himself was not at all sure that his army was large enough to reduce Florence if threats proved not enough to gain the ends of the League. He had been reluctant to advance into Tuscany at all. The Pope's nephew, the hot-tempered Duke of Urbino, had also disapproved of the expedition. But Cardinal Giovanni de' Medici was insistent. When the Duke of Urbino declined to supply Cadorna with artillery, Giovanni offered the money to buy two cannon himself. When Cadorna complained of a lack of provisions, he paid for these also himself. And when a Florentine delegation approached the Spanish army with an offer of reasonable terms, it was Giovanni who insisted that no terms could be accepted which did not provide for the restoration of the Medici. The Cardinal was already in touch with sympathizers in Florence, sending messages to them by means of a peasant who deposited them in the wall of a cemetery in Santa Maria Novella. His cousin, Giulio, had arranged a secret meeting at a country villa with Antonfrancesco degli Albizzi, one of their most influential supporters, who assured him that, while Soderini would put on an act of defiance, the spirit of his supporters would collapse as soon as they heard the roar of the Spaniards' cannon.

Faced with the cardinal's demand that he should deliver up the city, Soderini gave orders for the imprisonment of all known supporters of the Medici; and in an eloquent speech before the assembled citizens in the Piazza della Signoria he gravely warned of the dangers of allowing the Medici to return to Florence even though they professed themselves anxious to do so only as private citizens. After all that had happened, they could not possibly remain private citizens; they would certainly set themselves up as tyrants. It was true, Soderini continued, that Lorenzo di Piero had never made an ostentatious display of power but had covered his real prerogative with a mantle of private equality; but his son had never done so; and his young grandson, Lorenzo, whom Cardinal Giovanni represented,

could remember nothing of the traditions of the family. 'It is therefore for you to decide whether I am to resign my office (which I shall
cheerfully do at your bidding) or whether I am to attend vigorously
to the defence of our country if you want me to remain.' The people
loudly voiced their support of Soderini; and preparations for the
defence of Florence were continued with renewed vigour.

While Machiavelli's militia manned the city's strong-points, the
Spanish army approached the gates of Prato, twelve miles north-
west of Florence, where, so the hungry troops had been promised,
they would find food enough to spare. When Giovanni himself had
entered Prato twenty years before a triumphal arch created to welcome him had crashed down into the street killing two children
dressed as angels in his honour. This tragic event was remembered
now when, at the cardinal's second coming, even more dreadful
events were foretold by the old men standing beneath the city's high,
brown, crumbling walls.

A hole in these walls was soon torn out by Cadorna's cannon. It
was scarcely bigger than a window, Jacopo Nardi recorded. Behind
it was a high monastery wall, and behind that again were pikemen
and bowmen who could perfectly well have covered the breach. But
at the approach of the Spanish infantry, they all 'ran away, scandal-
ously throwing their arms to the ground, as though the enemy had
suddenly jumped on their backs'. 'The Spaniards, amazed that
military men as well as humble inexpert civilians should show such
cowardice and so little skill,' Guicciardini recorded,

broke through the wall with scarcely any opposition, and began to race
through the town, where there was no longer any resistance but only cries,
flight, violence, sack, blood and killing, the terrified Florentine foot
soldiers casting away their weapons and surrendering to the victors.

For two days the Spaniards raged through the city, raping, killing
priests at their altars, ransacking churches, burning monasteries,
breaking into convents. The inhabitants were tortured to disclose the
hiding places of their treasure chests; they were then killed, stripped
of their clothes, and their naked bodies flung into ditches or wells
already choked with severed limbs. 'Nothing would have been

spared the avarice, lust and cruelty of the invaders,' Guicciardini added, 'had not the Cardinal de' Medici placed guards at the main church and saved the honour of the women who had taken refuge there. More than two thousand men died, not fighting (for no one fought) but fleeing or crying for mercy.'

As yet unaware of the worst of what Machiavelli was later to describe as 'an appalling spectacle of horrors' and afterwards unable to prevent them, the Cardinal wrote blandly to the Pope on 29 August 1512:

> This day, at four o'clock in the afternoon, the town of Prato was sacked, not without some bloodshed such as could not be avoided ... The capture of Prato, so speedily and cruelly achieved, although it has given me pain, will at least have the good effect of serving as an example and a deterrent to the others.

Certainly it had this effect. Even as the reports of the sack of Prato were still coming into Florence, a party of Medici supporters marched to the Palazzo della Signoria demand that Soderini should resign. He was fully prepared to do so, and thought it as well to escape while he still could. So, having sent Machiavelli to ask for a safe passage for him, he was escorted from the city on his way into exile on the Dalmatian coast.

Later the Florentines were required to agree to the return of the Medici, to join the Holy League and to elect a new *Gonfaloniere*. The militia was abolished; and in the purge of Soderini's officials, Machiavelli was replaced by a Medicean. Soon afterwards, denied the opportunity of serving the Medici which he would have welcomed, Machiavelli left Florence for his country house at Sant' Andrea in Percussina where, the following year, he wrote *The Prince*.

 XVII

'PAPA LEONE!'

*'God has given us the papacy.
Let us enjoy it!'*

ON THE day that Soderini left Florence – 1 September 1512 –
Cardinal Giovanni's younger brother, Giuliano de' Medici,
entered it. Having shaved off the beard he had grown in
exile and dressed himself in an inconspicuous *lucco*, he walked un-
attended through the streets. Workmen were already busy removing
the crimson cross of the Florentine citizens which had replaced the
Medici *palle* on various buildings in the city, and, to the cheers of a
crowd of onlookers in the Via Larga, painters and masons were hard
at work restoring the Medici emblems on the family palace. But
Giuliano did not go to the palace. He went instead to the house of
Antonfrancesco degli Albizzi, seeming anxious by the modesty of
his demeanour to demonstrate his willingness to be accepted as a
private citizen of Florence with little interest in the control of its
government.

This was an attitude quite contrary to his elder brother's plans.
The Cardinal had not gone to all this trouble just to find the Medici a
home. He himself returned to Florence with 1,500 troops, and entered
his former palace in the full panoply of his rank with the air of a man
who had returned to his native city in order to rule it.

He seemed at first content to allow the republican institutions of
the State to remain outwardly unchanged. But two days after his
ceremonial entry into the city a demonstration was organized in the
Piazza della Signoria which was filled with people shouting '*Palle!*

215

Palle! Palle!' and demanding a *Parlamento*. The request was granted; a *Parlamento* was called; and power was handed to a *Balìa* of forty members, nearly all of them members of the Medicean party.

Yet although the Florentines were to be left in no doubt that they now had a master, Cardinal Giovanni appeared ready to reassure them that his rule would not be severe, nor would their burdens be heavy. The significance of his personal device – an ox-yoke – was unmistakable; but the motto beneath it was *'Jugum enim meum suave est'* – 'Truly my yoke is easy'. Indeed, from the beginning, the Cardinal was careful to persuade the Florentines that the restoration of the Medici would lead to a return to the happy days of his father, not to the dismal interregnum of Savonarola. Entertainments and pageants were to be encouraged; the carnival songs, which Lorenzo had so much enjoyed and which Savonarola had so rigorously denounced, were now once more to be heard in the streets; and the presence in the city of the Cardinal's kindly brother, Giuliano de' Medici, was to be a pledge that the government would be understanding and humane.

Less than six months after his family had been returned to power in Florence, the Cardinal was informed that his benefactor, Pope Julius II, was dying. Giovanni, now aged thirty-seven, was himself ill; but in order to attend the enclave he gave orders that he should be carried south to Rome in a litter.

Exhausted by the journey, in great pain from a stomach ulcer and troubled by an anal fistula, he arrived in Rome on 6 March 1513. Weeping women, mourning the death of their patriotic Pope, were kissing the pontifical feet which had been left protruding from the grille of the mortuary chapel. The Cardinal had missed the opening ceremonies of the conclave, including the Mass of the Holy Spirit which, since St Peter's was being reconstructed, was sung in the chapel of St Andrew, where the wind had howled through the cracks in the walls repeatedly extinguishing the candles on the altar. For several days Giovanni was too ill to get out of bed, submitting gloomily to the painful ministrations of his doctor, while the other cardinals, in little groups, argued and plotted. After a week, in order to force them to a decision, their daily meal was reduced to a single unappetising dish which, combined with the stale air of the building whose doors were locked and whose windows were sealed as custom directed, soon led to a decision.

In the early discussions the name of Cardinal Giovanni de' Medici had been little mentioned but as time went by he was admitted to be notably *papabile*. He was amiable and well liked, tactful, gregarious and approachable. He was relatively young, but had been a cardinal for nearly twenty-five years and so was not inexperienced. He took his religious duties seriously and fasted twice a week. He was evidently prepared to be ruthless when the interests of his family were threatened; but how many popes were not? Moreover, he was not in good health, so if his election proved ill-considered his Papacy might well be of no lengthy duration. The younger cardinals from ruling families such as Ippolito d'Este of Ferrara, Ghismondo Gonzaga of Mantua and Alfonso Petrucci of Siena were all anxious for the election of a man like themselves, rather than another rough peasant like Julius II who might march them off again on some tiresome campaign. Cardinal Francesco Soderini, Piero's brother, naturally did not favour him; but Giovanni's secretary, Bernardo Dovizi, gradually won Cardinal Soderini over by suggesting the possibility of a marriage between the Medici Cardinal's nephew, Lorenzo, and some young lady from the Soderini palace. So, on 11 March, when the votes were taken out of the urn and counted by Cardinal Giovanni de' Medici himself as Senior Deacon, he was able to announce his own nomination. He did so with becoming modesty, announcing that he would, if the Sacred College approved the choice, be known as Leo X.

The news of the election of a Medici pope was greeted by the *Palleschi* in Florence with the wildest excitement. For four days the celebrations continued to the constant clanging of bells, the explosion of fireworks and crackers, the boom of cannon fired from the surrounding hills, the lighting of bonfires fuelled with the furniture of former *Piagnoni*, the repeated drunken shouts of 'Palle! Palle! Papa Leone! Palle! Palle!' 'In the Mercato Nuovo youths tore boards and planks from the establishments of the silk-merchants and the bankers, so that by next morning every single roof belonging to them was burned. If the authorities had not intervened, no doors or roofs in the whole area would have remained.' On the *ringhiera* of the Palazzo della Signoria the citizens were offered sweet white wine from rows of gilded barrels; and in front of the Medici Palace trestle tables were piled with food to welcome a procession bearing the miraculous statue of the Virgin, arrayed in cloth of gold, from Impruneta.[1]

In Rome the celebrations were more controlled, though the *Sacro Possesso*, the formal entry into the Vatican, was as splendid an occasion as the new Pope, who delighted in pageantry, could possibly have hoped for. It had to be admitted that Leo himself did not cut a very imposing figure. As he rode in the procession sitting side-saddle on a white Arab horse, it was noticed how his face, almost purple with the heat, ran with sweat despite the canopy of embroidered silk which was held over his head by eight Romans of distinguished birth. It was noticed, too, how corpulent he was, how vast his paunch, how fleshy his short neck, how fat the rolls beneath his chin, how bulging his weak eyes. Those whose duties brought them close to him were also distatesfully aware of the smell that now and again was emitted from the huge bottom on the saddle. Yet there was something endearing about the pleasure he so obviously took in the pageant; the nods of satisfaction he gave when his attendants read out to him the inscriptions on the triumphal columns which his own eyes did not enable him to see; the amiable expression with which he regarded the cheering onlookers to whom his chamberlains flung coins from their money-bags; the friendly smiles bestowed upon them when he gave them his papal benediction, raising the plump yet shapely white hands of which he was so proud though they were now encased in perfumed gloves sewn with pearls. His contentment was so transparent as to be infectious. The days of exile and poverty were over and he was about to enjoy the benefits of power and riches. 'God has given us the Papacy,' he is reported to have said to his brother, Giuliano. 'Let us enjoy it.'

Pope Leo's determination to enjoy the Papacy did not, however, interfere with his equally determined ambition not only to make the House of Medici once more a dominating influence in Italian politics but also to drive the foreigner from Italian soil. To achieve the first of these aims he intended to form central Italy into a single strong state by uniting the duchies of Ferrara and Urbino, and by joining to them the cities of Parma, Modena and Piacenza. This new unified state was intended eventually to be placed under the rule of the Medici, perhaps under that of the Pope's nephew, Lorenzo, Piero's son, an ambitious, good-looking, energetic young man, who was now at the age of twenty sent to Florence as Leo's representative in company with a secretary whose orders were to send daily reports to Rome upon his youthful master's progress. At the same time, by diplomacy rather than by war, the Spaniards, who had helped the family to regain power in Florence, were to be driven out of Milan and the Kingdom of Naples. It might even be that the Kingdom of Naples would subsequently be given to Giuliano de' Medici who, after his brother's election as Pope, had been recalled from Florence to be created *Gonfaloniere* of the Church and who seemed prepared to embark on greater enterprises.

It appeared to the Pope a promising augury for his intended policies when on the first day of 1515 Louis XII died, exhausted by the demands and antics of his energetic young English bride, Princess Mary, daughter of Henry VII. Louis was succeeded by Francis I, a youth whom Leo had high hopes of bringing under his influence, particularly after a marriage was arranged between Francis's aunt, Princess Philiberte of Savoy, a sister of the widowed Duchess of Orleans, and the Pope's charming brother Giuliano.

The new French King, however, proved to be a far less pliable young man than the Pope had hoped. Tall, handsome and restless, Francis I was both intelligent and attractive, with a fixed determination to regain for France that influence in Italy which she had held for so short a time in the days of Charles VIII. Deeply perturbed by reports of Francis's independence and of his ambitions in Italy, the Pope consulted his advisers, who in turn sought the advice of others, including Machiavelli. It was Machiavelli's well-reasoned opinion that they should throw in their lot with the French; but the Pope hesitated to do so, and ultimately decided to ally himself with King Ferdinand of Spain, the Emperor and the Swiss.

Undeterred by this alliance, of which he professed himself contemptuous, King Francis crossed the Alps and marched down into Piedmont with an army of nearly 100,000 men. Hastily the allies assembled their forces, a motley collection of Spaniards under Cadorna, Swiss mercenaries commanded by Matthew Schinner, the fierce Cardinal of Sion, and Florentines under the leadership of Lorenzo de' Medici as Captain General and of Cardinal Giulio as Papal Legate. The Italians were not in the least anxious to fight; and after both Lorenzo and Giulio had entered into negotiations with Francis, his army brushed their troops aside and then defeated the Swiss with heavy loss of life at Marignano. Having disposed of his unworthy opponents, Francis despatched troops to occupy Milan and marched on to Bologna, where a conference was to be held with the Pope.

The Pope left for Bologna by way of Florence. Here his nephew, Lorenzo, had now consolidated the Medici power. A few months before, Lorenzo had paid a visit to Rome, leaving Florence in the hands of his uncles, Jacopo Salviati and Piero Ridolfi. In Rome he had been authorized to adopt the title of Captain General of the Florentine Republic which the *Signoria* had obediently bestowed upon him on his return. Thereafter he had become increasingly authoritarian, requiring councils to meet in the Medici Palace rather than in the public places of government, rejecting the advice of the more moderate and experienced citizens while surrounding himself with young dandies as subservient as courtiers.

A splendid reception for the Pope was prepared in Florence under the direction of Lorenzo and of Piero Ridolfi, who had been elected *Gonfaloniere* for the occasion. Two thousand men were put to work making decorations, obelisks, trophies and emblems, statues of classical gods and triumphal arches ornamented with classical quotations, at a total cost, so it was said, of 70,000 florins. Supervised by Jacopo Sansovino, Baccio Bandinelli and Andrea del Sarto, churches were turned into workshops, and houses were demolished to open up fresh vistas. The Piazza Santa Trinità was overshadowed by a huge castle resting on twenty-two columns, and the Mercato Nuovo by a painted obelisk fifty feet high. The Cathedral was given a temporary façade which

made everybody marvel, with so many pictures and ornaments; and it was said that it was done as a model for the building of a permanent façade because it pleased everybody, so proud and lovely did it appear.

Indeed, such transformations were being effected in Florence that when the Pope arrived rather earlier than expected he was asked not to enter the city straight away but to wait for a few days at the Gianfigliazzi villa at Marignolle until the preparations had been completed.[2] Never a man either to disappoint his admirers or to decline an invitation to play an honoured role in a pageant, Leo readily agreed to the suggestion and left for Marignolle to wait until the last triumphal arch had been erected, the final screen had been painted and decorated with allegorical figures, and the beautiful façade of wood and plaster, painted by Andrea del Sarto and designed by Jacopo Sansovino, had been placed against the Cathedral's western front.

When all was ready, on St Andrew's Day, 30 November 1515, the Pope, wearing a jewelled tiara and a dazzling cope, entered Florence through the Porta Romana accompanied by a huge train of attendants, men-at-arms and cardinals. At the sight of a bust of his father which had been erected on a screen by the church of San Felice and beneath which, through his spy-glass, he discerned the words, 'This is my beloved Son', the tears came to his eyes. He was also thinking, no doubt, of his sister Contessina who had recently died, a bereavement which gave her husband, the *Gonfaloniere*, an excuse to appear among the scarlet robes in a 'black satin cloak lined with sable, not minding that in such an office and on such a day mourning should be suspended'. By the time he had proceeded down the Via Maggio, across the bridge of Santa Trinità and into the Piazza della Signoria, the Pope was smiling once more, raising his hands in benediction and nodding complacently as his attendants tossed silver coins towards the cheering crowds. Now and again he would halt the cavalcade to admire the decorations. In the Cathedral, where a raised platform had been erected in the nave so that the congregation could get a better view of him, he stood still in his white brocade rochet, crimson cape and skull cap, then turned from side to side before offering up his prayers.

The Pope's reception in Bologna was in sad contrast to this glorious day in Florence. He proceeded through the streets in a silence broken only by an occasional shout in support of the recently expelled Bentivogli, and waited at the Palazzo Pubblico for the arrival of the French King. When Francis arrived, very late, he curtly informed Giulio de' Medici, who had been sent to meet him at the city gates, that he 'cared not a jot for processions' and wished to get down to the negotiations without delay. He greeted the Pope courteously enough, but it was soon plain that he had not come to bargain. He insisted on the surrender of the cities of Parma and Piacenza, which he claimed by right as conqueror of Milan. He also insisted that Reggio and Modena, which the Pope had recently acquired from the Emperor, should be handed back to France's ally, Alfonso, Duke of Ferrara. Faced by the King's uncompromising attitude, the Pope declined to abandon his known intention of ejecting Francesco Maria della Rovere from Urbino, and refused, for the moment, to lend any support to Francis's plans for assuming power in Naples, protesting that this would be out of the question while King Ferdinand of Spain was still alive.

It was not in the Pope's nature, though, to provoke a quarrel. Eventually he undertook to restore Reggio and Modena to the Duke of Ferrara, though without any intention of abiding by the agreement; and he indicated that he might change his mind – as indeed he did change his mind – about ultimately helping Francis in his claim to Naples. He graciously created the King's tutor a cardinal, and expressed profound satisfaction when, in return, Francis created Giuliano de' Medici Duke of Nemours. He even smiled agreeably when Francis made the astonishingly importunate request that the Pope should present to him the marble group of Laocoön which, recently discovered in Rome, was one of the most prized treasures of the papal collection.[3]

Outwardly complacent but, according to one of his companions, inwardly disgruntled by his unsatisfactory dealings with the French King, the Pope returned to Florence to find that the Arno was in flood, that the citizens were sullenly enduring a food shortage and that his brother was seriously ill with consumption at the Medici Palace. He had Giuliano moved to Fiesole, though there was little hope of his recovery there. He appeared 'utterly shrunken and spent like an expiring candle'. The Pope visited him often, but their meetings were small comfort to Giuliano who, knowing of his brother's intentions to oust Francesco Maria della Rovere from Urbino, begged him not to do so. Giuliano was fond of Della Rovere and his wife, Elisabetta, who had always been kind to him during the days of his exile. The Pope brushed his pleas aside. 'Do not bother yourself with politics, dear Giuliano,' he would say to him. 'You must concentrate on getting well.'

Giuliano grew rapidly worse, and on 17 March he died. He had no children by his wife, Philiberte of Savoy; but, like his uncle and namesake, he left an illegitimate child, Ippolito.

A month before Giuliano's death, the Pope had left Florence never to return. He had been recalled to Rome by the death of King Ferdinand of Spain, and the accession to power in Spain and Naples of the Archduke Charles. This supremely important event, which brought an end to the series of wars initiated by the League of Cambrai, gave Lorenzo and the Pope their opportunity to deal with the Duke of Urbino, which they had been reluctant to do while Ferdinand and Giuliano were both still alive.

First of all a dreadful, half-forgotten scandal was raked up: five years before, the savage-tempered Duke had attacked and killed in a street in Ravenna his arch-enemy, Cardinal Francesco Alidosi. At the time a court of inquiry, of which the Pope himself had been a member, had decided that the Duke's provocation by the unpleasant Alidosi – supposedly Julius II's catamite – had been virtually irresistible. The Duke was now informed, however, that the murder, whether pardonable or not, made it impossible for him to hold Urbino any longer in the name of the Church. At the same time he was reminded of his refusal to comply with Pope Julius II's request to assist in the restoration of the Medici to Florence and of his subsequent refusal to help to defend Italy against the invading army of King Francis I. He was summoned to Rome to explain his disgraceful conduct.

When he declined to go, the Pope excommunicated him and Lorenzo de' Medici marched out of Florence to take Urbino from him. Lorenzo experienced little trouble in doing so. The Duke was forced to flee from Mantua, and Lorenzo entered Urbino in May. Less than a year later, however, the dispossessed Duke returned with Spanish troops to take his Duchy back. The short but arduous campaigns in the mountainous districts of Urbino cost the Florentines and the Pope a great deal of money. They aroused lasting resentments and resulted in Lorenzo's being so badly wounded by an arquebus that he was gradually to waste away both in body and in will. The Pope, however, was for the moment well satisfied. Lorenzo was proclaimed Duke of Urbino and Lord of Pesaro, and seemed well on the way to becoming master of that large, unified, Medici-dominated state in central Italy which Leo dreamed of creating.

With Italy at peace and his family established in Urbino, Leo settled down happily to enjoy the pleasures of the Vatican. His expenditure was prodigious. It has been claimed that within a year he had got through not only all the savings of his parsimonious predecessor, but the entire revenues of himself and his successor. He 'could no more save a thousand ducats', Machiavelli's friend, Francesco Vettori, remarked, 'than a stone could fly through the air.' Soon deeply in debt to almost every banking house in Rome, some of which were charging him interest at forty per cent, Pope Leo made not the slightest attempt either to reduce the enormous number of his household or to curtail the extravagance of his almost constant entertainments and banquets.

The cardinals followed his example. 'Yesterday,' the Marquis of Mantua was informed by his wife's secretary,

Cardinal Riario gave us a dinner so extraordinarily sumptuous that it might well have sufficed for all the queens in the world. We sat for four full hours at table, laughing and chatting with those most reverend cardinals.

'The meal was exquisite,' wrote the Venetian ambassador, describing another dinner at the palace of Cardinal Cornaro.

There was an endless succession of dishes, for we had sixty-five courses, each course consisting of three different dishes, all of which were placed on the table with marvellous speed. Scarcely had we finished one delicacy than a fresh plate was set before us, and yet everything was served on the finest of silver of which his Eminence has an abundant supply. At the end of the meal we rose from the table both gorged with rich food and deafened by the continual concert, carried on both within and without the hall and proceeding from every instrument that Rome could produce – fifes, harpsichords and four-stringed lutes as well as the voices of a choir.

Cardinals and Roman patricians alike vied with each other to provide entertainments of unparalleled splendour. The immensely rich Sienese banker, Agostino Chigi, whose bathroom fixtures were all of solid silver, once invited the Pope to dinner in a magnificent room hung with the most exquisite tapestries. The sumptuous meal was served to the guests on plate specially engraved with their individual crests. When the last course had been served the Pope congratulated Chigi on the excellence of the meal and the beauty of his new dining-hall. 'Your Holiness, this is not my dining-hall,' replied Chigi giving a signal to his servants to pull down the tapestries which concealed rows of mangers. 'It is merely my stable.' On another occasion Chigi invited the entire Sacred College to dinner and placed before each of the assembled cardinals food specially brought from his own district or country. Chigi had even been known to order his servants to toss his silver into the Tiber after every course to show that he had so much he never had to use the same piece twice – though afterwards other servants were seen pulling up nets in which the discarded dishes had been caught.

The Pope's own dinners were noted for their rare delicacies, such as peacocks' tongues, of which he himself, however, ate but sparingly. They were also noted for their jocularity, for such surprises as nightingales flying out of pies or little, naked children emerging from puddings. Dwarfs, buffoons and jesters were nearly always to be found at his table where the guests were encouraged to laugh at their antics and at the cruel jokes which were played upon them – as when, for instance, some half-witted, hungry dwarf was seen guzzling a plate of carrion covered in a strong sauce under the impression that he was being privileged to consume the finest fare. The Pope himself derived a peculiar pleasure from watching his favourite jester, Fra Mariano Fetti, a Dominican friar who had once been a barber and was eventually appointed to the office of Keeper of the Papal Seals. Quick-witted, shrewd and outrageously coarse, Fra Mariano could make the Pope laugh more heartily than any other member of his court, not merely by the wit of his vulgarity, but also by his celebrated capacity to eat forty eggs or twenty chickens at a sitting and by the apparent relish with which he savoured pies specially prepared for him at his master's instigation containing ravens cooked complete with beaks and feathers.

No practical joke in Leo's entire pontificate seems to have afforded him more amusement than that played upon poor Baraballo, an elderly priest from Gaeta, who seems to have persuaded himself that his feeble and even ludicrous attempts at verse were the products of commanding genius. It was suggested to him that he ought to press his rightful claim to a public coronation on the Roman Capitol, an honour once accorded to Petrarch. The Pope eagerly entered into the spirit of the enterprise, assuring Baraballo that his verses undeniably merited such a mark of distinction and offering to make available to him His Holiness's beloved elephant, Hanno, which had recently arrived in Rome as a present from King Manuel I of Portugal and which was housed in the Belvedere. On this creature, suitably caparisoned, Baraballo was to make his stately progress from the Vatican to the Capitol, clothed in a scarlet toga fringed with gold. 'I could never have believed in such an incident if I had not seen it myself and actually laughed at it,' wrote the Pope's first biographer, Paolo Giovio: 'the spectacle of an old man of sixty bearing an honoured name, stately and venerable in appearance, white haired, riding upon an elephant to the sound of trumpets.'

But the resounding fanfares, combined with the shouts and cheers of the spectators, so frightened the elephant that he stood trumpeting loudly before the bridge of Sant' Angelo, refusing to cross it.

Baraballo had to climb down from his ornately decorated saddle and the joke was over, much to the evident mortification of Leo who had been sitting on a nearby balcony happily watching the proceedings through his spy-glass.

Although this kind of display could not often be arranged, the Pope was able to indulge himself more frequently in his palace with a succession of those dramatic performances, plays, masques, ballets, mummings and *moresche*, in which he took a far deeper delight. Two of the earliest blank verse historical tragedies, Giovanni Rucellai's *Rosmunda* and Gian-Giorgio Trissino's *Sophonisba*, were both performed in his presence. But apparently he preferred the broad comedies and more or less indecent farces of Ariosto, Machiavelli and Cardinal Bernardo Dovizi da Bibbiena. He witnessed with evident pleasure the performances of Ariosto's *Cassaria* and *Suppositi*; Machiavelli's *Mandragola* was performed for him in 1519; and his favourite piece of all appears to have been Dovizi's *Calandria*, whose plot, involving a stupid young man in love with a girl who changes clothes with her twin brother to play a trick upon her paramour, presented the kind of situation which made a strong appeal to Pope Leo's taste.

He would happily spend hour after hour watching these performances, or sitting at the gambling table playing *primiero* – an undemanding card game rather like beggar-my-neighbour – losing money without complaint or throwing his winnings over his shoulder. Whole days at the time of the Carnival were spent attending bull-fights, sitting through endless banquets, watching cardinals and their ladies dancing at masked balls, or contemplating the Romans enjoying their favourite sports, their regattas and processions, their orange-throwing contests, and the violent, dangerous game of rolling barrels down the grass slopes of Monte Testaccio, at the bottom of which crowds of peasants risked broken limbs to seize the pigs inside.

Yet Leo's life was not entirely given over to frivolity. If he spent vast sums on entertainments, on French hounds and Cretan falcons, on furs and gold chains, and on his ever growing household, he lavished money, too, on the improvement and development of

Rome. He built the Via Ripetta so as to provide a new outlet from the congested old town up towards the Piazza del Popolo; he restored the church of Santa Maria in Domnica and provided it with its splendid porticoed façade; above all, he enthusiastically continued the reconstruction of the Vatican Palace and the rebuilding of St Peter's, retaining Julius II's architect, Donato d'Angelo Lazzari, known as Bramante, who had begun work on the new church in 1505. Pope Leo also conceived an ambitious plan to drain the Pontine Marshes and asked Leonardo da Vinci to devise an appropriate method.

Determined to make Rome the most cultured city in Europe, he offered numerous inducements to attract the most accomplished artists, writers and scholars to live there, making freely available to them his extensive library to which he was constantly adding valuable new manuscripts. He loved books himself, both the reading and possessing of them, and could quote long passages from his favourite authors. Even when his finances were peculiarly strained he always contrived in some way – often selling benefices or cardinals' hats – to help those writers and scholars, poets and dramatists, who came to him for help. He gave his support to the Roman Academy; he helped to reorganize the University, increasing the range of facilities and the number of professors; he encouraged the use and study of the Latin language and made money available to Latin prose writers and poets; he brought Lascaris to Rome and suggested that he should edit and print the Greek manuscripts in his possession.

It had to be admitted, though, that his own taste was far from impeccable. Those few of his writings that have survived display none of his father's talent. His attempts at musical composition were even less successful; and, although he engaged the best European choristers for the Sistine Chapel, the music that he liked to listen to best, humming to himself and waving his plump, white hands in the air, was considered trivial. So, too, was his taste in the literature of his own times. Apart from their comedies, he did not esteem Machiavelli or Ariosto highly; nor did he admire Guicciardini. Indeed, those who profited most from his lavish patronage were far inferior writers such as Bernardo Accolti, whose work Leo professed to admire almost as highly as did Accolti himself.

The Pope's neglect of Michelangelo, however, seems to have been due less to his failure to appreciate his greatness than to his lack of patience with the artist's abrasive temperament. Michelangelo, who had been encouraged to come to Rome by Julius II, was gloomy, touchy, independent and self-absorbed, choosing to work in a locked room, quite unwilling to follow unquestioningly any patron's brief or to undertake to finish a work in any given period. The Pope professed to feel a deep affection for him and would relate 'almost with tears in his eyes' how they had been brought up together as boys; but they never really got on well together. The Pope encouraged Michelangelo to become an architect and urged him to leave Rome and return to Florence in order to provide a new façade for Brunelleschi's San Lorenzo.[4] Leo far preferred to deal with the younger, more complaisant, unobtrusive and polite Raffaello Sanzio.

Raphael, a native of Urbino, had already been set to work on the decoration of the official apartments of the apostolic palace by Julius II to whose notice he had been recommended by Bramante. Pope Leo asked Raphael to continue with the work; and under their combined direction the Loggie di Raffaello and the lovely halls known as the Stanze di Raffaello were completed.[5]

XVIII

THE MARCH ON ROME

*'To teach the Pope a lesson he would
never forget'*

A
S OFTEN as he could Pope Leo rode out of Rome to the Villa
Magliana, his country house on the road to Porto. Here,
continuing to use the advice of the court physicians as his
excuse for a flagrant breach of canon law, he indulged to the full his
passion for hunting, hawking and ferreting. Huge tracts of land around
the villa were reserved for his use. In the grounds an immense netted
enclosure was filled with the doves, jays and herons which provided
the hawks with their prey, and there was also a *conigliare* well stocked
with rabbits for the ferrets.

At the Villa Magliana, where the Pope would remain for six weeks
at a time, he abandoned his stole and rochet, and to the consternation
of the papal master of ceremonies actually put on 'long riding boots,
which is most improper, seeing that the people consequently cannot
kiss the Pope's feet'. His poor eyesight did not permit him to participate in the early stages of the hunt, so he rode out on his favourite
white horse to watch the killing through his spy-glass from a high
mound or specially constructed platform.

The ground to be hunted had already been sealed off by tall strips
of tough sail-cloth attached to poles. To prevent any animals inside
the pen escaping into nearby thickets or marshes, soldiers of the
Swiss guard and mounted gamekeepers assisted by peasants were
drawn up in ranks around it. When the grooms holding the greyhounds and mastiffs in leash were ready, and the cardinals, gentlemen

of the papal court and all their friends had also taken up their positions, the Pope raised a white handkerchief as a signal for the horn to be sounded. Then the under-keepers, shouting, blowing trumpets and exploding charges of gunpowder, entered the pen and began to drive the game towards a gap in the canvas screen. Soon a torrent of animals came rushing out into the open, stags and boars, hares and rabbits, wolves, goats and porcupines. The waiting sportsmen would then eagerly fall upon their chosen target with spear or sword, axe or halberd, or gallop away after the greyhounds in pursuit of any animal that might have escaped their swinging blades.

The Pope would watch these scenes of slaughter through his glass, laughing at the antics of Fra Mariano, who would usually contrive to get into some sort of ludicrous difficulty, or admiring the strength of the enormous Cardinal Sanseverino who, on these occasions, habitually wore a lion skin across his shoulders. If an animal became entangled in a net or rope, the Pope would then proceed closer and, holding his glass to his left eye and taking up a spear, he would kill the struggling creature, cheerfully acknowledging the congratulations of his attendants.

The Pope especially enjoyed one day, according to the poet Guido Silvester. It was a day of many accidents. First a member of the papal court killed a hound in mistake for a wolf, which appears to have much amused the Pope when shown the result of the man's stupidity. Then there was a fight over the carcass of a boar in which one of the disputants lost an eye. Finally one of Cardinal Cornaro's kennel-men, notorious for his drunkenness, made a lunge with his spear at a wounded boar running for safety into the woods, missed his aim, killed his favourite hound, and, infuriated, threw himself onto the back of the boar which he tried to throttle. The boar shook the drunkard from his back and gored him to death. His companion carried the body back to Cardinal Cornaro who ordered the face to be washed with the best old wine while he composed an epitaph to commemorate his servant's fate. As the Pope rode back, followed by the carcasses slain, he was heard to observe, 'What a glorious day!'

To his description of these violent events, Guido Silvester adds the comment that after such a day's hunting, the Pope would invariably be in so good a mood that he would happily agree to anything that was proposed to him, sign documents with contented smiles, grant requests with genial words; whereas a bad day's hunting would produce only growls and complaints. A courtier or churchman with some special favour to ask would accordingly wait until the Pope's return from a successful hunt in the Campagna, or from a happy day's fishing in the artificial salt-water lake he had had constructed near Ostia, or from a visit to Cardinal Farnese's estate at Viterbo where pheasants, partridges and quails could be bagged in their thousands and flocks of ortolans, thrushes, larks and goldfinches could be snared in the cardinal's *uccellari*.

Well liked as the Pope was by those country people upon whom he extravagantly bestowed his largesse when riding out to hunt or fish, and by those churchmen and members of his court to whom he had granted some ambitious request, there were cardinals in Rome who had cause to feel dissatisfied with his behaviour. The costly war with Urbino was not the only Medicean cause which was straining the resources of the papal treasury; nor, when it became plain that Leo was attempting to arrange a marriage between his nephew, Lorenzo, and a French princess, was Francesco Soderini the only cardinal who felt outraged by a broken promise.

Cardinal Raffaele Riario had never forgiven the Pope for driving his kinsman Francesco Maria della Rovere from Urbino to provide a duchy for the wretched Lorenzo; nor had Cardinal Alfonso Petrucci overcome the anger that had swept over him when Leo had helped to remove his brother Borghese Petrucci from the governorship of Siena. They and many other cardinals had been further offended when Leo raised to the cardinalate various intimate friends and relations, ignoring the claims of more worthy members of their own families. Within months of his election he gave Bernardo Dovizi a scarlet hat; he also gave one to another Tuscan friend, Lorenzo Pucci; a third went to his nephew, Lorenzo Cibò. And, so as to do equal honour to Giulio de' Medici, whom he had already appointed Archbishop of Florence, he established a commission to inquire into the circumstances of his cousin's birth, making it clear enough to its members that he wished them to find – as dutifully they did find – that his uncle, Giuliano, had been secretly married to Simonetta Gorini and that Giulio was their legitimate son. This might not have been so objectionable had Giulio been better liked; but as Francesco Guicciardini observed

he was rather morose and disagreeable, disinclined to grant a favour, reputedly avaricious and very grave and cautious in all his actions. Perfectly self-controlled, he would have been highly capable had not timidity made him shrink from what he should have done.

By no one in the Sacred College was Giulio more disliked than by Alfonso Petrucci, the handsome, arrogant, dissolute, twenty-two-year-old cardinal whom the Pope had so deeply offended by interfering in his family's affairs at Siena. His outspoken attacks on Leo, whom he had helped to elect, met with a good deal of sympathy in Rome, particularly from Cardinals Riario and Soderini, from Petrucci's rich young friend, Cardinal Sauli, and from Cardinal Adrian of Corneto, formerly Bishop of Bath and Wells. Adrian had no family grudge against the Pope, but he was said to have taken so seriously the prophecies of a soothsayer, who foretold that the next pope would be 'Adrian, a learned man of humble birth', that he had conceived it his sacred duty to do all he could to bring about the prophecy's fulfilment as soon as possible.

It was at first decided that the easiest way to dispose of the present Pope would be to pay an assassin to stab him while he was out hunting. But then a more subtle plan was devised: His Holiness would be dispatched by means of poisoned bandages which a quack doctor from Vercelli, aided by Petrucci's secretary and a Sienese friend of his, would in some way find reason to apply to the Pope's anal fistula. Having satisfied himself of the likely efficacy of this complicated plot, Petrucci left to discuss its consequences with Francesco Maria della Rovere, the deposed Duke of Urbino. In his absence the conspiracy was uncovered through the indiscretions of a page; and the quack, Petrucci's secretary and his Sienese friend were all handed over to the attentions of the papal rack-master.

Soon afterwards Petrucci was asked to return to Rome to discuss certain matters with the Pope who at the same time sent him promise of safe conduct. Either trusting in this guarantee, or supposing that the Pope had repented of his previous conduct to his family, the ingenuous Petrucci returned immediately to Rome where, in company with Cardinal Sauli, he presented himself at the Vatican. Both men were promptly arrested and thrown into 'the most horrible dungeon' of Sant' Angelo, Petrucci cursing the treacherous Leo at the top of his voice, Sauli furiously tearing his rochet to pieces. Like their minions, they, too, were tortured on the rack. Their confessions having been duly elicited, orders were given for the arrest of Cardinal Riario, who was discovered in a state of such abject terror that he had to be carried to his place of confinement in a litter.

Rather than arrest the other sympathizers with Petrucci's plot, the Pope now convoked the consistory, before whom he appeared in so unaccustomed a rage that some of his audience believed him to be playing a part in order to intimidate them. His obese body trembling and his voice so loud that it could be heard ringing round the adjoining corridors, he demanded the names of the other guilty men. Cardinal Soderini and Cardinal Adrian both confessed their knowledge of the conspiracy, and knelt in humble submission at the Pope's feet.

Adrian managed to escape from Rome and disappeared into oblivion. Soderini, having paid a vast fine which helped to settle some of Leo's more pressing debts, thought it best to follow Adrian's example. Riario was relieved of a sum even greater than that taken from Soderini and went to live in Naples. Sauli, who had powerful friends in France as well as in Italy, was allowed to leave his dungeon and to live under house arrest at Monte Rotondo, where he died in mysterious circumstances the next year. Petrucci was executed in his dungeon by the Pope's Muslim hangman who either strangled him or cut off his head. The Vercelli quack, Petrucci's secretary and his friend, were dragged by horses through the Roman streets; gouts of flesh having been nipped from their bodies with red-hot pincers, they were then gibbeted on the parapet of the bridge of Sant' Angelo.

Although his finances had been much improved by the huge fines imposed on Riario and Soderini, the Pope still felt it necessary to bring in further sums of money to his treasury by creating numerous new cardinals to fill up the vacant places in the Sacred College, and by requiring the richer of those elected to make suitable contributions. Money, however, was not Leo's only reason for the creation of thirty-one new cardinals. He hoped to create a far more reliable College than its predecessor, and one that would raise no objections to the advancement of Medicean interests. So, while there were several worthy men on the Pope's list, there were also those who had been selected for more selfish reasons. Among these were young princes of the royal houses of France and Portugal; Ercole Rangone, the son of Bianca Rangone of Modena, Leo's former benefactress; Pompeio Colonna, whose unruliness it was hoped a scarlet hat might serve to moderate; two Florentine nephews, Niccolò Ridolfi and Giovanni Salviati; and a third Florentine relation, Luigi Rossi.

With the Sacred College thus conveniently packed with Medici friends and relations and those who had cause to be grateful to the Medici, the Pope felt that the time was now propitious for the marriage of his nephew Lorenzo, Duke of Urbino, to Madeleine de la Tour Auvergne, cousin of Francis I, King of France. Accordingly, in March the next year, 1518, Lorenzo was sent north across the Alps with an immense train of crimson-clad attendants and his uncle's lavish presents, amongst which were to be found thirty-six horses and an astonishing nuptial bed made of tortoise-shell inlaid with mother-of-pearl and enriched by precious stones.

Much as they were impressed by the evident riches of his family, the denizens of the French court were far from struck with the Duke of Urbino himself, whose arrogant nature they found objectionable and whose physique at the age of twenty-five was now pitiable. After a few months of marriage, indeed, it became evident that the Duke did not have much longer to live. Nor, as it happened, did his wife. She died at the end of April 1519 soon after the birth of a daughter, who was christened Caterina and was one day to be Queen of France. Her husband died a few days later of tuberculosis aggravated by syphilis. Even in the villas of Careggi and Poggio a Caiano, where he had spent the last months of his life in the company of a Pistoian secretary and another male companion of sinister reputation, there was little evidence of grief.

Ever since Lorenzo had returned from France, the Florentines had been grumbling about his increasingly lordly manner, his political ambitions that enfeebled health had in no way diminished, his mis-management of the city's finances and the influence of his haughty, greedy and domineering mother, Alfonsina, whose interests were wholly bound up in her son and whose death in Rome eight months after his was received with as little sorrow.

Well aware of Florence's discontent, Cardinal Giulio de' Medici, who had hurriedly left Rome to secure the family's hold upon the city, was careful to give no offence. He arrived just before the news of Lorenzo's death became generally known, and was able to ensure that there was no unrest and that the people were prepared to leave the administration of the Republic to him, and to those leading citizens whose advice he tactfully sought, until the Pope's future plans for Florence were settled.

It was fortunate for the Medici party in Florence that Giulio's conduct of affairs was so conciliatory and astute, and that under his conscientious administration of its financial affairs the city enjoyed a period of prosperity. For the Pope seemed far from decided what to do about either Florence or Urbino now that the Medici heir was a half-French baby girl and the only boys on his side of the family were both bastards – Ippolito, the son of Giuliano, Duke of Nemours, by a sensuous lady from Pesaro; and Alessandro, presented as the son of Lorenzo, Duke of Urbino, but rumoured to be Cardinal Giulio's son either by a Moorish slave from Naples or by a peasant woman from the Roman Campagna.

The Pope eventually decided to create Caterina de' Medici Duchess of Urbino and to annexe her Duchy to the states of the Church, calling upon the Florentines to contribute a large part of the money which had been expended on driving out della Rovere, while com-pensating the Republic with the fortress of San Leo and the conquered district of Montefeltro. There still remained, however, the problem of what to do about the government of Florence, a problem which was complicated at the beginning of 1519 by the long-awaited death of the Emperor Maximilian and by the subsequent election as his successor of Charles V.

Both the King of France and the Pope did their utmost to prevent this election of a young ambitious man who was not only the King of Spain and Naples, but master of the Netherlands and an Austrian Grand Duke. But having failed to prevent the election, Leo decided, after many tergiversations and vacillations, to abandon the French and to enter into secret negotiations with Charles V whose help he needed to settle a matter which could no longer be ignored, the matter of that tiresome Augustinian friar, Martin Luther.

For years the Pope had been endeavouring to dismiss from his mind all thoughts of Luther and of German demands for reform in the Church, hoping that the problems would eventually resolve themselves in the pettifogging arguments of German monks. But Luther would not go away; and the Pope had been driven to excommunicate him. He now hoped that Charles V as a good Catholic would finally settle the matter for him by having the heretic tried and executed. The Emperor had no particular objections to doing so; but the German princes, who listened with some sympathy to Luther's impassioned declarations, were of a different mind. Charles could overrule them, of course; and, so the Pope was informed, he *would* overrule them. There was, however, to be a *quid pro quo*: in exchange for the condemnation of Luther, the Emperor would require the Pope's support in his intended attack upon France's remaining possessions in Italy, including Milan. Leo agreed to this on condition that once the French had been divested of the occupied territories, the Papacy could not only take back from them the towns of Parma and Piacenza, which Francis I had declined to return at the conference at Bologna in 1515, but also receive Charles's help in taking Ferrara. So the bargain was struck and the Emperor's army prepared to march.

A dispatch from Cardinal Giulio with news of the Emperor's victory over Francis I, the fall of Milan, and the flight of the French army towards the Alps was awaiting the Pope at Villa Magliana where, despite a recent operation on his anal fistula, he had gone for a day's hunting. The day had been humid; the night was cold and windy; and as Leo sat in his bedroom in front of a blazing fire, with his back to an open window to which he moved from time to time to watch a celebratory bonfire blazing in the courtyard below, he caught a severe and feverish cold. Two days later he was carried back to Rome where he was told of the capture of Piacenza and Parma.

On Sunday, the first day of the month of December [1521] at about the seventh hour, Pope Leo expired of a violent chill without anyone warning him that his sickness was mortal, since the physicians all protested that he was but slightly indisposed owing to the cold he had taken at the Magliana.

Immediately on receipt of the news of the Pope's sudden death, Cardinal Giulio hurried back for the conclave, which began on 28 December, evidently hoping to succeed his cousin. But Cardinal Francesco Soderini had also made haste for Rome and, having arrived first, had already succeeded, with the help of Cardinal Pompeio Colonna, in forming so strong an opposition to Giulio's election that he decided to support the candidature of Charles V's former tutor, an obscure, virtuous and ascetic Flemish cardinal, Adrian Dedel, of whom many members of the Sacred College had scarcely even heard. The subsequent election of this modest scholar, which had been engineered to thwart the ambitions of more powerful candidates such as Alessandro Farnese and Thomas Wolsey, caused no one more surprise and consternation than the new Pope himself, who received the news with horror. Choosing the title of Adrian VI – tardily to fulfil the prophecy of the soothsayer whose prognostications had so excited the English Cardinal Adrian of Corneto – the Pope reluctantly left for Rome where he contrived to live, spending a ducat a day, upon frugal meals served to him by an old Flemish harridan of whom he seemed unaccountably fond. The failure of his forlorn attempts to reform the Church, the struggle to make stringent economies in the papal household and the deep enmity of those whose previously

238

enjoyable lives were transformed by his parsimony, all proved too much for him. He contracted a kidney disease, and this, combined, so it was inevitably said, with poison, resulted in his death in just over a year. The thankful citizens of Rome, who never since have been required to put up with a Pope who was not Italian, laid festive garlands at the door of his doctor, naming him their liberator.

Satisfied that Florence – where the bastards, Ippolito and Alessandro, as well as Caterina de' Medici were all now living – was securely in the hands of the Medici party, Cardinal Giulio had set up house in Rome in the fine palace which had been wrested from Cardinal Riario for condoning the plot against the life of Leo X. Without undue ostentation he had lived there as a generous Medici was expected to live, a patron of artists and musicians, a protector of the poor, a lavish host. Neither his cold manner nor his saturnine appearance fitted him for such a part; but it was as well that he had played it, for in the tedious conclave which followed the death of Adrian VI he needed all the friends he could muster. At first it seemed impossible that he could win the election. The French were strongly opposed to him, and his other enemies were many and implacable, none more determined to thwart him than the powerful Cardinal Pompeio Colonna, who hoped to secure the election himself. Weeks passed; a month went by, two months; there were demonstrations and riots in Rome. There had never been a longer conclave in living memory. Then at last, after many bribes had changed hands, when many secret promises had been made, when Cardinal Colonna removed his objections for fear that in the impasse his rival, Cardinal Orsini, might be chosen, and when it was known that a Medici election was acceptable to both Charles V and to Henry VIII as well as to Francis I – who thought it unlikely that the Medici would remain loyal to the Emperor – Cardinal Giulio emerged from the conclave, after sixty days' incarceration as Pope Clement VII. He was twenty-five years old. Few of his opponents in the conclave had been converted to friendship, but there were many in Rome who wished him well and 'trusted to behold again a flourishing court, a liberal Pontiff and a revival of the arts and letters which had been banished under the late barbarian rule of Adrian'.

Certainly Pope Clement did prove himself both a generous and a discriminating patron. He was not open-handed by nature, and far from convivial or gregarious: he preferred to spend his time listening to music or discussing theological and philosophical questions to the more ebullient pursuits of Leo X. But he understood the value and rewards of liberality. He was as munificent in his almsgiving as Leo, and quite as bountiful a patron. He continued his family's patronage of Raphael, asking him to submit designs for a villa to be built on the cypress-covered slopes of Monte Mario.[1] He gave several commissions to that most versatile, most quarrelsome and most boastful of Florentines, Benvenuto Cellini. He gave his encouragement to the Polish astronomer, Nicolaus Koppernigk, known as Copernicus. He put Giulio Romano and Gian Francesco Penni to work in the Vatican, where he had already arranged for Leonardo da Vinci to be provided with his own apartments. And he confirmed the commission which Leo X had already given to Michelangelo to design a chapel at San Lorenzo in Florence to house the tombs of their fathers, Giuliano and Lorenzo, and of their two cousins, Lorenzo Duke of Urbino, and Giuliano, Duke of Nemours.[2] Michelangelo was also asked to design a library at San Lorenzo to which the family's collection of books could one day be returned.[3]

As Francis I had foreseen when withdrawing his objections to his election, Pope Clement soon proved himself a far from faithful ally of the Emperor; and towards the end of 1524, after many tortuous turns of policy, he had allied the Papacy once more with France, whose army was again on the march. No sooner had this decision been taken than Clement, more indecisive and irresolute with each passing month, began to regret it. He had due cause to do so, for in February 1525 news reached Rome that the Emperor, in alliance with the Duke of Milan, had defeated the French army at Pavia and that Francis I had been taken prisoner. The Pope, now virtually a prisoner

The Grand Duke Cosimo I, 1519–1574, by Bronzino.

28 (*top left*). The Grand Duke Cosimo I as portrayed by Cellini whom he treated with the 'greatest affection' on Cellini's return to Florence.

29 (*top right*). Cosimo I's son, the Grand Duke Ferdinando I, 1549–1609, by Pulzone.

30. The Pitti Palace was bought by Cosimo I's wife, Eleonora of Toledo, in 1549 and thereafter becam the residence of the Grand Dukes of Tuscany.

nd 32. Two views of Florence from the Arno. In the lower picture the Palazzo Vecchio,
nelleschi's dome and Giotto's campanile are all easily identified.

(*opposite*). The *studiolo* of the Grand Duke Francesco I in the Palazzo Vecchio built for him by Vasari
filled with Florentine late Mannerist paintings. The circular portrait in the lunette is of Francesco's
ther, Eleonora of Toledo, by Bronzino.

(*top left*). The Grand Duke Cosimo II, 1590–1621, by Bronzino.

(*top right*). The Grand Duchess Vittoria della Rovere, by Dolci. She was the wife of Ferdinando II and
ther of Cosimo III.

The festival of the *Omaggi* on St John the Baptist's Day when the Grand Duke 'received homage
n such as hold territories, forts and castles of him, within his dominions . . . which was performed by
r passing one by one before him, lowering the banner they carried'. It was celebrated every year on
une until 1808.

opposite). The Grand Duke Ferdinando II, 1610–1670, by Sustermans.

nd 39. The spectacular performance of *Il Mondo Festeggiante* was given in the Boboli gardens before
ut 20,000 people to celebrate the wedding of the Grand Prince Cosimo and Princess Marguerite-
ise (see page 289). A gigantic Atlas appeared bearing the world on his shoulders and moved around
arena ingeniously propelled by hidden contrivances. After his awesome announcement that
cules had descended from the sky for Cosimo's wedding, the sphere on his shoulders suddenly
:e, discharged its contents and transformed him into the Atlas mountain with four girls sitting
d the summit. The metamorphosed giant is shown in the lower picture where horse-drawn
iots are also to be seen bearing Apollo, the sun-god, and Cynthia, goddess of the moon.

40 (*top left*). The Grand Prince Cosimo, later Cosimo III, 1642–1723, by Sustermans.

41 (*top right*). The Grand Prince Ferdinando, 1663–1713, by Bernini.

42 (*above left*). The Grand Duke Gian Gastone, 1671–1737.

43. Princess Anna Maria de' Medici, Electress Palatine, 1667–1743, by Douven.

of Charles himself, endeavoured to extricate himself from his unfortunate position not by openly coming to terms with the Emperor, as sensible men expected him to do, but by entering into secret negotiations with Francis who, released from imprisonment, determined to cross the Alps once more.

These negotiations, secret as the papal agents endeavoured to keep them, did not long remain hidden from the Emperor, who well understood what the Pope was trying to do and took appropriate measures to forestall the formation of an anti-imperial alliance. In September 1526, abetted by Don Ugodi Moncada, the Emperor's envoy, Cardinal Pompeio Colonna with a strong force of retainers and hired men-at-arms fell upon Rome, occupied the suburbs around St Peter's, and pillaged the apostolic palace from which the Pope was forced to flee to the greater safety of Castel Sant' Angelo. There he was constrained to sign a treaty by which he undertook to abandon the league against the Emperor and to pardon Colonna for his insulting attack.

It was a treaty which Clement had no intention of keeping. A few weeks after signing it, papal troops were dispatched to the Colonna estates with orders to destroy their strongholds and castles, to intimidate their tenants, and to serve notice upon the family that they were to be declared outlaws and deprived of all their titles. In a rage so furious that he was seen to tremble at the very mention of Pope Clement's name, Cardinal Colonna offered his services and that of all the men he could muster to Charles de Lannoy, Charles V's Viceroy at Naples, who now landed at Gaeta with a strong army dispatched to 'teach the Pope a lesson he would never forget'.

Even more alarming threats had already come from Germany where the old warrior, George von Frundsberg, had assembled an immense army of *Landsknechte,* mostly Lutherans from Bavaria and Franconia, fired with a missionary zeal to have their revenge upon the Roman Anti-Christ and with a more practical but no less intense desire to relieve him of his valuable possessions. This intimidating force, undeterred by torrential rains and Alpine snowstorms, descended into Lombardy. And although the Pope's other enemies, Colonna and Lannoy, were checked in their advance on Rome at

Frosinone, nothing seemed capable of halting the further progress of von Frundsberg's tough Germans.

The courageous warrior, Giovanni delle Bande Nere, who had married Lorenzo il Magnifico's granddaughter, made a brief attempt to halt their relentless advance; but he was hit in the right leg by a ball from a falconet as he was trying unsuccessfully to prevent them crossing the Po. He held up a torch so that a surgeon could amputate the smashed limb. The surgeon wielded his saw so incompetently, however, that the wound proved fatal, and Giovanni delle Bande Nere died on 30 November. Francesco Guicciardini, who had been appointed the Pope's Lieutenant-General, had repeatedly warned Giovanni not to take so many risks and had urged the Pope to give the same advice. 'His person is of too great value,' Guicciardini had written to Clement, 'and it is clear the enemy seek his life with great determination. If we lose him we shall be losing too much.' Now Guicciardini bitterly regretted that the warnings had gone unheeded. 'It has pleased God,' he lamented, 'to extinguish so much courage at the time when we needed it most.'

Soon after the death of Giovanni delle Bande Nere, von Frundsberg – who had already accepted the help of a young adventurer in the Emperor's service, Philibert, Prince of Orange – was joined by a large army of Spanish soldiers from Milan. The combined forces which now marched south towards Bologna numbered over 30,000 men.

Recognizing at last the true measure of his dreadful plight, the Pope endeavoured to secure a truce to which the commanders of the advancing host seemed disposed to agree. But the *Landsknechte* had not come so far to be turned away empty-handed now. Shouting their determination to pillage Rome or to be well paid for not doing so, they rounded upon von Frundsberg, whose fat and ancient frame had not well withstood the rigours of the campaign, and reduced him to apoplexy. As he was carried away rigid to Ferrara, the march continued under the uncertain leadership of Charles, Duke of Bourbon, the Germans having made it clear that they were prepared to obey the orders of the new commander no longer than it pleased them.

A far more forthright leader than the Duke of Bourbon would have found it difficult to control the motley force that now hurried on to Rome. Almost starving, their clothes ragged, their filthy bodies washed by the pouring rain and the roaring mountain streams through which they stumbled, holding hands to keep their balance, they reached Isola Farnese, seven miles from Rome, on 4 May. From here, Bourbon sent messengers into Rome offering to spare it for a ransom sufficiently generous to satisfy his men.

The Pope declined to treat with him, turning his attention to long-postponed measures for the city's defence. Many prelates and nobles, with a keener awareness of their danger, had long since fled. Others had hidden their treasures, stoutly fortified their palaces, and employed men to defend them. Yet Clement himself had appeared to be 'struck by a kind of paralysis'. It was not until 26 April that he had asked the Commune for a gift towards the cost of Rome's defence; it was not until 3 May that, after repeated urgings, he himself raised 200,000 ducats by agreeing to create six rich men cardinals – 'suffering', so Guicciardini said, more scruples over this 'than over ruining the Papacy and the whole world'. And it was not until 4 May that he at last summoned the Great Council of Rome and urged the people to defend the city under the leadership of Renzo da Ceri.

The people, however, were not much inclined to do so. They preferred to believe that if the approaching army did make themselves masters of Rome, they 'would prosper and have the same advantages as they had had under the dominion of priests'. They prevented Renzo da Ceri from blowing up the bridges over the Tiber; and had Renzo not stopped them, they would have sent out their own envoys to make a separate peace with the Duke of Bourbon. Few of them turned out of their homes at the sound of the great bell of the Capitol ringing the tocsin. In all Renzo had scarcely more than eight thousand men, including two thousand Swiss Guards and two thousand former members of Giovanni de' Medici's Black Bands, with which to defend the long expanse of the city wall.

XIX

SIEGE AND MURDER

'Mild measures are useless'

THE FIRST attack, launched at dawn on 6 May 1527, was
repulsed by the papal gunners; but soon afterwards a thick mist
rose from the Tiber and, unobserved beneath its cover, the
Duke of Bourbon's men were able to mount scaling ladders made
from vine-poles against the city walls. Bourbon himself was hit by a
stray shot from an arquebus and carried away to a nearby chapel by
the Prince of Orange. By the time of his death, the assaulting troops,
followed by vengeful men from the Colonna estates and other
pillagers, had forced their way through breaches in the wall and were
threatening to break into the centre of the city. The defenders fought
bravely but were no match for the far greater numbers of the imperial
army. Soon a vast mass of people were rushing headlong for the
drawbridge of Castel Sant' Angelo until the bridges spanning the
river were so blocked by those struggling to get across that scores of
bodies were trampled underfoot.

The Pope was also running for the Castle. The Bishop of Nocera
had found him in an agony of indecision in his oratory and had induced him to make use of the stone corridor that linked the apostolic
palace to the Castle. The Bishop held up the Pope's skirts to enable
him to run the faster, and flung his purple cloak over his head and
shoulders 'lest some barbarian villain in the crowds below might
recognize [him] by his white rochet, as he was passing a window, and
take a shot at his flying form'.

Some Spanish troops did fire at him; but he reached the Castle in
safety. So did some three thousand other fugitives, including thirteen

cardinals, one of whom was dragged aloft in a basket. But when the drawbridge was pulled up all the remaining inhabitants of Rome, except those in well-fortified palaces, were left to the mercy of the invaders. Scant mercy was shown to anyone. The army spent most of the rest of that day in securing food and a comfortable place to spend the night, but the next morning, 7 May, the town was sacked and its inhabitants murdered and mutilated with appalling ferocity. The doors of churches and convents were smashed, their contents hurled out into the streets, their bells and clocks, chalices and candlesticks beaten into fragments, their sacred treasures defaced, their holy relics used as targets by arquebusiers, and their ancient manuscripts as litter for horses. Priceless vestments were tossed over the shoulders of drunken whores, and nuns changed hands on the throw of a dice. The name of Martin Luther was carved with a pike on one of Raphael's frescoes in the Stanze. Shops and houses were so thoroughly plundered that even the hinges were wrenched from the shutters and the handles from the gates. The rich were held as hostages for ransom, the poor being tortured or slaughtered out of hand. Priests were stripped naked and obliged to take part in profane travesties of the Mass and to utter blasphemies on pain of death; orgies and gambling games were held round altars splashed with blood and wine; crucifixes were hurled about the streets. Fingers were cut off for the sake of rings; arms were lopped off for bracelets, ears for pendants. A merchant who could not pay the ransom demanded of him was tied to a tree and each day one of his finger nails was pulled off; eventually he died. It has been estimated that on the first day alone 8,000 people were killed.

Inside the Castel Sant' Angelo, according to his own lurid and vainglorious account, Benvenuto Cellini was a tireless, brilliant and inspiring gunner. 'So there I was in the castle,' he recalled.

I went up to some guns that were in charge of a bombardier [who] was staring out over the battlements to where his poor house was being sacked and his wife and children outraged. He dared not fire in case he harmed his own family, and flinging his fuse on the ground he started tearing at his face and sobbing bitterly. Other bombardiers were doing the same. When I saw this I seized one of the fuses, got help from some of the men who were not in such a sorry state, and lined up some heavy pieces of artillery and falconets, firing them where I saw the need. In this way I slaughtered a great number of the enemy ... I continued firing, with an accompaniment of blessings and cheers from a number of cardinals and noblemen. Inspired by this I forced myself to try to do the impossible. Anyway, all I need say is that it was through me that the castle was saved ... I carried on with the work all day until evening approached.

Throughout the ensuing days Cellini applied himself 'with unimaginable energy and zeal', to helping 'a great Roman nobleman called Antonio Santa Croce, whom Pope Clement had put in charge of all the bombardiers'. Not everyone appreciated Cellini. He 'made bitter enemies' of two particular cardinals whom he ordered off the high platform where the guns were ranged as their 'nasty red birettas could be seen a long way off'; and he nearly killed two other cardinals when the blast from one of his cannonades dislodged a barrel of stones which crashed on to the terrace at their feet. But the Pope himself, so Cellini said, had nothing but praise for him. 'Not a day passed without [his] achieving some outstanding success'; and as a result, his 'stock with the Pope went up and up'. When Cellini asked the Pope to absolve him of all the killing he had done

while serving the Church in the castle, the Pope raised his hand, carefully made a great sign of the cross above [his] head, and said that he gave [him] his blessing, that he forgave [him] all the homicides [he] had ever committed and all those [he] ever would commit in the service of the Apostolic Church.

Cellini continued,

After I left him, I climbed back to the tower and spent all my time firing away at the enemy, hardly ever wasting a shot ... If I told in detail all the great things I did in that cruel inferno I should astonish the world ... I shall skip a good deal and come to the time when Pope Clement, in his anxiety to save the tiaras and mass of wonderful jewels belonging to the Apostolic Camera, sentf or me ... and ordered me to remove them from their gold settings. I did as I was told; and then, after I had wrapped them up in pieces of paper, we sewed them into the linings of the Pope's clothes [and into those of his faithful servant, Cavalierino]. When this was done they gave me all the gold – which came to about two hundred pounds – and told me to melt it down as secretly as I could.

Every morning when it was light the Pope looked north hoping to catch sight of the army which was supposed to be advancing to Rome's relief. But he looked in vain. At the beginning of June, after more than a month's incarceration in the Castle, he was forced to surrender to the Emperor's envoy. His fellow refugees were dying of hunger and disease around him; and the army, which he had hoped would come to rescue him, was retreating towards Viterbo. He was obliged to deliver up Civitavecchia, Ostia and Modena as well as Parma and Piacenza to the imperial forces. He was also required to find a huge ransom, to restore the Colonna to their possessions and to hand over seven important men as hostages, including Jacopo Salviati and Lorenzo Ridolfi.

Yet although he had surrendered he was not permitted to leave Castel Sant' Angelo, which had now become his prison, until the ransom demanded from him had been paid. The summer passed and the autumn, and still he was detained there. The imperial army was driven from Rome by plague and hunger, but two thousand troops were left behind to guard the city and to make sure that the prisoner remained where he was. Then, at the beginning of December, after German and Spanish troops, having plundered the surrounding countryside, had returned to Rome threatening to hang their captains and cut the Pope to pieces if they did not receive the arrears of pay that were due to them, the captive was told that his guards would look the other way if he made his escape. Early on the morning of 7 December he did so, wearing the clothes of his major-domo. With a few companions, he got away to Orvieto where, in the remote fastness of the episcopal palace which could be reached only by a mule track from the valley of the Paglia, he endeavoured to rebuild his shattered power and reputation.

It was at Orvieto, in this 'ruinous and decayed old palace' with the 'roofs fallen down and thirty persons, riff-raff and others, standing in the chambers for a garnishment', that an embassy from England sought him out in order to obtain his authority for Henry VIII's divorce from Catherine of Aragon. Clement would have welcomed the opportunity of obtaining Henry's friendship, but Catherine was Charles V's aunt and the now penniless Pope could do no more than make vague promises that he would grant the King's request once he was free to move back to Rome again. In fact, the Pope's mind was occupied by other matters that seemed to him more important. None of these appears to have concerned him more than the problem of Florence, where the sack of Rome and his own subsequent imprisonment had had the most unfortunate repercussions.

The Florentines had deeply resented the presence in the Medici Palace of the Pope's representative, the ill-mannered and avaricious foreigner, Cardinal Silvio Passerini, who had been followed to Florence by two other papal representatives, Cardinals Innocenzo Cibò and Niccolò Ridolfi. Nor had the Florentines taken kindly to Passerini's charges, the two young Medici bastards, in particular to the unprepossessing Alessandro. Both these boys had been upbraided in public by Piero di Lorenzo's daughter, Clarice Strozzi, who had indignantly attacked them for being utterly unworthy of their great name, adding that Clement himself no more deserved to be Pope than Passerini deserved to be his representative.

'I have seen in the short time I have been here a thousand things like it,' wrote Francesco Guicciardini to the Pope, reporting on a riot in the Piazza della Signoria,

and all derive from the ignorance of this eunuch [Passerini] who spends the whole day in idle chatter and neglects important things … He does his best to fill himself and everyone else with suspicion; he makes everyone despair; and has no idea himself what he is doing.

His two charges, Guicciardini considered, were equally reprehensible.

There was no doubt that the Florentines agreed with Guicciardini. When the news from Rome reached the city, they marched through the streets shouting slogans and singing songs of thanksgiving. And as soon as Passerini and his two pupils had scurried away, they threw the Pope's effigy out of the church of the Annunziata, tore it to pieces in the square, and loudly declared their approval of a new republican constitution, the re-establishment of the Grand Council as well as the militia, and the election of anti-Medicean *Gonfaloniere*, Niccolò

Capponi, to hold office for a year. On the façade of the Medici Palace – which was, however, protected by a strong guard from mobs of would-be looters – a descendant of Ghiberti painted a picture of the Pope climbing up a ladder to the gallows.

The Pope determined to tolerate the situation no longer than his present powerlessness and bankruptcy obliged him to do. He could hope for no more help from the French whose forces, having yet again invaded Italy and advanced as far as Naples, were ravaged by the plague and obliged to surrender once more to the Spaniards. So he came to terms at last with the Emperor. On the understanding that the Pope would recognize his position in Italy and would crown him on his proposed arrival there, Charles undertook, by a treaty signed at Barcelona on 29 June 1529, to return the Medici to Florence – if necessary by force.

Thinking that they in turn would be well advised to come to an agreement with the Pope, whose conduct of the city's government in the past had not been exceptionable, a few of the older and more cautious citizens of Florence now proposed the formulation of some sort of compromise. The younger citizens, however, refused to listen to such pusillanimous proposals and in their patriotic enthusiasm they carried the majority of the people with them. They called out the militia, voted money for mercenaries, pulled down villas beyond the walls which might have afforded cover to the Imperialists, built new strong-points, and improved the city's fortifications. The military command they gave to a Perugian *condottiere*, Malatesta Baglioni, whose father had fought against the Medici and whose services to Florence would, he hoped, be rewarded by his returning to power in his native city. At the same time the ingenious Michelangelo, whose colossal and inspiring statue of David now stood in the Piazza della Signoria, was appointed to supervise the works of defence.[1]

Having proposed that the defences should be extended to circumvallate the hill of San Miniato and that the belfry of its church should be protected from artillery fire by mattresses, Michelangelo waited to see the works almost completed, then lost his nerve and fled from the city. A few days later he returned, and though not reinstated in his former responsible position, his behaviour was attributed to his artistic temperament and he was forgiven.

By then the Pope had enlisted the help of the Prince of Orange, the adventurer who had commanded the imperial troops during the Sack of Rome and who now agreed to lead an almost equally unruly, mostly Spanish force against Florence. In the early autumn of 1529 this force appeared on the hills above the city, calling out, so it was said, 'Get out your brocades, Florence, for we are coming to measure them with our pikestaffs'. But although the army was nearly 40,000 strong, the Prince did not consider it either large or manageable enough for a direct assault and decided to starve the city into surrender.

Owing largely to the heroic activities of the gifted and ruthless Florentine commander, Francesco Ferrucci,[2] who repeatedly led out fighting patrols to keep the supply routes open, the city held out for no less than ten months. On 3 August 1530, however, Ferrucci was surrounded in the village of Gavinana in the mountains above Pistoia by a troop of Spanish soldiers who hacked him to pieces; and with his death Florentine resistance collapsed. For weeks past, indeed, surrender had seemed inevitable. Malatesta Baglioni, though he marched about the streets with the word *'Libertas'* emblazoned on his hat, had already entered into secret negotiations with the enemy. The population was starving and plague-ridden; mobs marched forlornly through the streets shouting for bread and for the return of the Medici as the only means of getting it. 'Everyone was beside himself with fright and bewilderment,' Benedetto Varchi recorded.

No one knew what to say any more, what to do or where to go. Some tried to escape, some to hide, some to seek refuge in the Palazzo della Signoria or in the churches. Most of them merely entrusted themselves to God and awaited resignedly, from one hour to the next, not just death but death amidst the most horrid cruelties imaginable.

A week after Francesco Ferrucci's death a deputation of Florentine citizens agreed to the terms of surrender demanded by the representatives of the Emperor and the Pope. They were forced to hand over fifty hostages as pledges for a huge indemnity, to give up the fortresses still held by Florence to the imperial army, and to release all

Medici supporters who had been imprisoned. In return, the liberties of the city were to be guaranteed, and an undertaking was given that pardons would be available for 'injuries received from all citizens', whom His Holiness would treat with that 'affection and clemency he had always shown them'. But neither side expected the Pope to consider himself bound by these promises, as, in fact, he did not.

A week after the Emperor's representatives had entered the city, those citizens prepared to vote for the creation of a *Balìa* were admitted to a *Parlamento* in the Piazza della Signoria. A Medicean *Balìa* was accordingly established. A faithful supporter of the Pope was appointed *Gonfaloniere*, and Francesco Guicciardini, who had left the city at the approach of the Imperial forces, was sent back to supervise further measures of 'reform' – and of revenge.

When Guicciardini arrived on 24 September he found

the people and their resources exhausted, all the houses around Florence destroyed for many miles, and in many towns of the Florentine dominion the peasant population immeasurably decreased, the common folk disappeared almost entirely.

His own villas were in ruins. He decided immediately that, if the State were to be put on 'a proper footing again, mild measures [were] useless'. Mild measures were certainly not employed. Francesco Capponi, the leader of the extreme anti-papal party known as the *Arrabbiati* (the Angry Ones), was tortured and executed. So were several of his supporters. Raffaele Girolami, the newly elected *Gonfaloniere*, was also condemned to death, though eventually sentenced to perpetual imprisonment. Scores of other leading citizens were banished from Florence for ever.

To replace them in the government of the city, the Pope dispatched the dark, frizzy-haired, now nineteen-year-old youth, Alessandro de' Medici, for whom he had bought the Dukedom of Penne from Charles V and to whom he hoped to marry the Emperor's natural daughter, Margaret.

Having thus roughly and decisively settled the future of Florence, to which he himself never again returned – and having created Ippolito a cardinal, an honour to which that cheerful, gregarious, extravagant and sensual young man in no way aspired – the Pope now concentrated his attentions upon the family's one remaining asset, the little Caterina de' Medici, a pale, thin, rather plain but strong-willed girl of twelve. He had high hopes for her. Indeed, there were some who said he had made Ippolito a cardinal merely to remove him as a possible suitor, for she had shown signs of being unduly fond of the boy, and Clement had no mind to let her make a marriage so unprofitable both to the Medici and to himself as Pope. He wanted, in fact, to arrange for her a marriage with a son of the King of France.

So ambitious a project needed extremely tactful handling. He must not appear too eager; nor must he act without the consent of the Emperor. He played his part extremely well. The Venetian ambassador, for one, was not at all convinced that the Pope had made up his mind about the match; while the Emperor evidently thought it so unlikely that the French court would agree to it that, when the Pope travelled to Bologna to seek his permission, Charles gave way as though it were a matter of not very much importance. To the Emperor's surprise, however, the French were not at all averse to the match. And so it was that on 28 October 1533, the Pope himself conducting the ceremony in Marseilles, the fourteen-year-old Caterina de' Medici, Duchess of Urbino, was married to Henri de Valois, Duke of Orleans, second son of Francis I.

It was Clement's last triumph. Already ill when he began his journey to Marseilles, accompanied by those lavish wedding gifts for which the taxpayers of Rome and Florence had yet to pay, he returned to the Vatican a dying man. He was pitiably thin and shrunken; he was almost blind in his right eye, which had always had a slight squint; his liver was diseased and his skin was consequently pale and yellowish. Exasperating problems faced him on every side: there was the quarrel with England over the supremacy of the Holy See; there was the growing enmity of the Emperor who, irritated by the recent Medici marriage, was making renewed demands for a General Council of the Church; there were – vexatious above all – the persistent quarrels between Ippolito and Alessandro and the danger that between them they would be responsible for their family losing Florence once again.

When Benvenuto Cellini went to see the Pope on 22 September 1534 to show him some models he had designed for him, he found him in bed and failing fast.

He ordered his spectacles and a candle to be brought, but nevertheless he could discern nothing of my workmanship. So he set to examine the models by the touch of his fingers, but after feeling thus for some length of time he fetched a deep sigh, and told one of the courtiers that he was sorry for me, but if it pleased God to restore his health, he would make me a satisfactory payment. Three days later he died.

Cellini confessed that the tears filled his eyes as he kissed the dead Pope's feet; but there was no one else to mourn for him. On the contrary, Rome rejoiced. As Francesco Vettori said of him, he had gone 'to a great deal of trouble to develop from a great and respected cardinal into a small and little respected Pope'. Night after night St Peter's was broken into; the corpse was transfixed by a sword; the temporary tomb was smeared with dirt; and the inscription beneath it, '*Clemens Pontifex Maximus*', was obliterated and in its place were written the words, '*Inclemens Pontifex Minimus*'.[3]

The news from Rome was received in Florence with glum foreboding. It was felt that, following the death of the Pope whom many supposed to be his father, Alessandro de' Medici would impatiently throw off all restraint and institute that tyrannical government to which his own tastes seemed naturally inclined. So far he had behaved quite circumspectly. Nine months after his ceremonial entry into the city, he had been proclaimed hereditary Duke; but, so as to allay the outrage to republican susceptibilities which this proclamation caused, he was at the same time required to consult various councils of Florentine citizens and to heed their advice. For a time he had done so; the people had been gradually reassured; and it was grudgingly allowed that, ill-favoured and rude as he was, there might, when he grew older, be discovered some good in Alessandro after all.

The Pope's death brought all the old fears back, and before that winter was over they were seen to be justified. Even the pretence of consultation with the elected councils was abandoned as Alessandro indulged his young fancy for authoritarian rule and became ever more blatant in his sexual escapades. He outraged the citizens by having the great bell in the Palazzo della Signoria – which had been smashed in the Piazza to symbolize the death of the Republic – melted down and recast into medals glorifying his family; by having his coat-of-arms carved over the gateway of the recently enlarged fort at the Porta alla Giustizia;[4] by impounding all weapons, even those hung as votive offerings in the churches; and by building a huge new fortress, the Fortezza da Basso,[5] 'a thing totally inappropriate to a free city, as the examples of Venice, Siena, Lucca and Genoa clearly show'. There was murmured talk of tyrannicide; but the memory of the recent long siege was still fresh in men's minds, and the dissidents hung back from so violent a solution to their plight which might bring another imperial army to the gates of the city. For a time it was hoped that the jealous Ippolito might settle the Florentines' problems for them; and Ippolito did, indeed, agree to present a case against Alessandro at Charles V's court; but before he was able to do so he died on 10 August 1535 at Itri, either of malaria or of poisoning. His body was carried back to Rome by the handsome athletes – Moors, Tartars, Turks, Negro wrestlers and Indian divers – with whom it had been his extravagant fancy to go out upon his travels.

The leading Florentine exiles then presented themselves to the Emperor with a long list of complaints against Alessandro. Their spokesman, Jacopo Nardi the historian, gave a horrifying account of the Duke's misdeeds and of the miseries of Florence now being overawed by a 'great fortress, built with the blood of her unhappy people as a prison and slaughter-house for the unhappy citizens'. But although the Emperor promised 'to do what was just', he preferred to set less store by Nardi's charges than by the extremely cunning and wholly inaccurate rebuttal of them by Alessandro's chief adviser, Francesco Guicciardini, who went so far as to conclude his peroration with the words, 'One cannot reply in detail to the charges about women, rape and similar calumnies uttered in general; but His Excellency's virtue, his fame, the opinion of him held throughout the city, of his prudence, of his virtuous habits, are a sufficient reply.'

Thus assured of the excellent qualities of his prospective son-in-law, the Emperor declined to accept the exiles' charges. Alessandro's marriage to the fourteen-year-old Margaret accordingly took place, and the Duke returned to Florence in firmer control of the city than ever and evidently anxious to make the most of his good fortune. Within a few months, though, he was dead.

There had arrived in Florence a thin, plain, sad-faced young man of eccentric habits and unwholesome reputation, Lorenzaccio de' Medici, son of Pierfrancesco and cousin of Giovanni delle Bande Nere. He had spent much of the past few years in Rome, but his habit of slashing off the heads of antique statues when drunk had led to his being asked to leave and to his coming to Florence where he had become a constant companion of his kinsman, Alessandro, who was just three years older. Together they went out drinking and whoring; they indulged a mutual taste for disguising themselves as women; they galloped through the streets on the same horse, shouting insults at the passers-by; sometimes they shared the same bed. Alessandro was obviously fond of Lorenzaccio, though he seems not to have known what to make of him. Intrigued by his mysterious smile and subtle, ambivalent remarks, he nicknamed him 'the philosopher'. But it was equally clear that Lorenzaccio did not really like Alessandro, that he resented his power and rank, that he fancied himself in the role of hero, in any role, in fact, that would bring him fame or even notoriety. The role in which he eventually decided to cast himself was that of tyrannicide.

He evolved a complicated plan. He had a good-looking cousin, Caterina Soderini Ginori, a rather supercilious woman who was celebrated for her virtuous demeanour and her affection for an elderly, boring husband. Lorenzaccio suggested to Alessandro that anyone who could get Caterina to bed was a seducer of uncommon distinction: if Alessandro wanted to try his luck he would arrange to bring her to him one night and leave them alone together. He suggested a Saturday evening, the night of Epiphany, a public holiday, when everyone in Florence would be out enjoying themselves, and when no one would take much notice of either Caterina or Alessandro entering Lorenzaccio's house. Alessandro eagerly agreed and on the appointed evening went to Lorenzaccio's house. Having left his body-guard outside the door, he unbuckled his sword, took off his clothes and lay waiting for Caterina on a bed. He was almost asleep when the door of the bedroom opened to admit not Caterina but Lorenzaccio and a hired murderer, Scoroncolo. Lorenzaccio approached the bed and, murmuring 'Are you asleep?', lunged with all his power at Alessandro's naked stomach. As Lorenzaccio pushed his hand over Alessandro's screaming mouth, Alessandro bit one of his fingers to the bone. Scoroncolo stabbed Alessandro through the throat. Spattered with his blood, his bleeding, savagely bitten hand encased in a glove, Lorenzaccio ran out into the street and galloped off to Bologna by way of Scarperia, leaving the citizens of Florence to make what use of the assassination they could when the body was found.

He had taken care to ensure that the body would not be found until he was safely across the frontier by taking the key of his room with him. He had also made it impossible for opponents of the government to take immediate advantage of the murder by keeping his plans dark from them. It was Benedetto Varchi's belief that if a single man had come forward immediately to lead a revolution, the Medicean party might well have been overthrown. Realizing this, 'Guicciardini, who without any doubt was the leader of the *Palleschi*, Cardinal Cibò and all Alessandro's former courtiers trembled with fright . . . as the populace was most hostile and they themselves were without arms' – the captain of the Duke's guard, Alessandro Vitelli, together with several of his men, being away at Città di Castello.

Cardinal Cibò was first made aware of his danger when, on Sunday morning, Alessandro's bodyguard asked how long they were expected to stand on duty outside Lorenzaccio's house. Cibò told them to stay there until further notice, ordering them not to breathe a word to anyone about their reason for being there. Then, having made sure that Alessandro had not returned to his own house, he gave it out that the Duke had had a particularly exhausting night and was now in bed resting. It was not until evening that he had the door of Lorenzaccio's bedroom broken open to reveal Alessandro's body.

And it was not until the following day that the news of his murder became known to the opponents of the regime. By then it was too late for successful action. Vitelli had returned, and the *Palleschi* were in command of the situation. A group of would-be revolutionaries approached Francesco Vettori, the most prominent of those distinguished citizens supposed to be anti-Medicean. Vettori, however, while making some vague promises of support, recognized that the time for an uprising was now past. He immediately went to Guicciardini and threw in his lot with the *Palleschi*.

The *Palleschi* met on Monday morning to discuss the succession at the Palazzo della Signoria, now renamed the Palazzo Vecchio. Cardinal Cibò suggested that Alessandro's illegitimate son, Giulio, then four years old, should be created Duke with himself as Regent. But this suggestion was rejected by the others who proposed calling upon Cosimo de' Medici. Cosimo was the son of the great Giovanni delle Bande Nere and of Maria Salviati, granddaughter of Lorenzo il Magnifico, a young man, politically inexperienced and morally unexceptionable, in no way compromised by the evils of Alessandro's rule. In fact, Guicciardini, who had hopes not only of using Cosimo to win the government for himself but also of arranging a marriage between him and one of his daughters, had already sent an invitation to the seventeen-year-old boy to come to Florence without delay from his villa of Il Trebbio in the Mugello.

When the Council was asked to approve this solution the following day, however, not all its members agreed to do so. One of them, Palla Rucellai, bravely announced that he 'wanted neither Dukes nor Lords nor Princes in the Republic', and, picking up a white bean to toss into the urn on the table, added, 'Here is my vote and here is my head!'

Giucciardini riposted by declaring that he, 'for one, would not endure that a mob of *ciompi* should ever again govern Florence'. He was not proposing that Cosimo should be created Duke but merely elected head of the Republic and subject to constitutional limitations as well as to what were to be known as 'magnificent counsellors'. The discussion continued for hours and would have continued longer had not Vitelli, the captain of the guard, who had been promised the lordship of Borgo San Sepolcro for his support of Cosimo's nomination, intervened decisively. Tiring of the wrangle in the council chamber, he contrived a noisy scuffle between his soldiers under its windows. There were shouts that 'Cosimo, son of the great Giovanni, *must* be Duke of Florence! Cosimo! Cosimo! Cosimo!' And an authoritive voice cried out, 'Hurry up. The soldiers can't be held any longer!'

This settled the matter. Cosimo's nomination was approved, and Guicciardini looked forward to the exercise of power in his name. Yet those who knew Cosimo took leave to doubt that Guicciardini would be able to control him in the manner he intended. As Benvenuto Cellini commented:

They have mounted a young man on a splendid horse – then told him you must not ride beyond certain boundaries. Now tell me who is going to restrain him when he wants to ride beyond them? You can't impose laws on a man who is your master.

PART FOUR

1537-1743

XX

DUKE COSIMO I

*'There is little joy to be discerned
in the faces of the people'*

COSIMO HAD been born in Florence, in the large and gloomy Palazzo Salviati, the family home of his mother, Maria, daughter of Giacomo Salviati who had married Leo X's sister, Lucrezia. Leo X had stood as his godfather and had suggested that the baby should be christened Cosimo, 'to revive', so he had said, 'the memory of the wisest, the bravest and most prudent man yet born to the house of Medici'.

The mother had been fond of her uncle, the Pope, to whom she bore a strong resemblance. Her eyes were big and dark, her face pudsy and her skin unnaturally pale, the result of drastic cosmetic treatment she had undergone in order to render herself more attractive to her husband, whose unconcealed preference for other women at first distressed and finally embittered her. She had rarely seen him, for he had so often been away at the wars and his visits home to Florence had never been prolonged. On one of these brief visits, so a characteristic story of him went, he had come clattering down the Corso on his charger and, looking up to the windows of the Palazzo Salviati, had caught sight of his son in the arms of a nurse. 'Throw him down!' he had called out. The nurse had naturally been reluctant to obey. 'Thrown him down,' Giovanni had shouted again. 'Throw him *down*. I order you to do so.' The nurse had held out her arms, shut her eyes and let go. Giovanni had caught the boy and kissed him, and, delighted by the calm, uncomplaining way in which Cosimo accepted both the fall and the embrace, had declared, 'Aye, you'll be a prince! It's your destiny.'

Seeing little of his father, Cosimo seems never to have developed much affection for him. When he was told that Giovanni had been mortally wounded trying to prevent the Germans crossing the river near Mantua, he 'did not weep much', according to his tutor, but said merely, 'In truth I had guessed it.' He was seven years old then, a healthy, good-looking boy, tall for his age, with chestnut hair cut short as he was always to keep it. He was living in Venice, having left Florence in the uncertain times that had followed the arrival there of Alessandro and Ippolito as protégés of Clement VII. From Venice he went to Bologna, from Bologna to Giovanni's villa of Il Trebbio, and from there back to Bologna where his grandfather, Jacopo Salviati, was to supervise his disrupted education. After a time he left Bologna for Genoa, from there went back to Florence once more, and then for a time to Naples.

This constant travelling was not good for him, so one of his tutors implied: it unsettled him, made it difficult for him to concentrate on his work, and led him to yearn to leave his books for the pleasures of the countryside and the excitement of the soldiers' camp. It was his ambition, indeed, to become a soldier. At the age of fourteen, so Pope Clement was informed, he already 'went about clad like a cavalier and seeming such in his actions'. He was also reported to be surrounded by officers formerly in his father's service. Disturbed by these reports, the Pope sent orders for him to abandon his 'foreign dress' and to wear instead the ordinary Florentine *lucco*. He obeyed the command with a sulky ill grace.

Yet Cosimo was neither an uneducated nor an uncouth young man. Graceful in his movements, reserved in his manner, he was shrewd and silent. If there were gaps in his knowledge, he was prepared to fill them; and once filled they were filled for ever, for his memory was astonishingly retentive. There were those who already noticed a certain secretiveness about him which was later to become notorious; there were those who were repelled by an undoubted coldness in his nature which was to leave him unmoved by cruelty; and there were those who had good cause to fear that he would make

a stern, tyrannical ruler. The general opinion, however, as Benedetto
Varchi put it, was that Cosimo,

with the twelve thousand ducats granted him as his private income, would
devote himself to enjoyment and employ himself in hunting, fowling and
fishing (sports wherein he greatly delighted) whilst Guicciardini and a few
others would govern and, as the saying goes, suck the State dry. But it is
no good reckoning without your host; and Cosimo, who had been considered slow witted, though of sober judgement, now showed himself so
admirably endowed with understanding that people went about telling
each other that as well as having the State bestowed upon him, he had also
wisdom given to him by God.

Trusting no one, neither Cardinal Cibò nor Alessandro Vitelli nor
Guicciardini, all of whom, he felt, wanted to make use of him for
their own purposes, Cosimo was determined to be his own master.
He listened to the advice of his gifted secretary, Francesco Campana,
and to his mother who could tell him all he needed to know about
the ruling families of Florence; yet he kept his feelings and opinions
hidden even from them and made up his mind alone.

His opponents were far less resolute. With the support of the lower
classes who had gained nothing from their masters in the days of the
recent Republic, of those who would have rallied to the help of any
son of Giovanni delle Bande Nere, of the reconstituted militia and of
several of Florence's most patrician families, Cosimo gradually over-
whelmed his enemies. First, with Spanish help, he rid himself of
danger from the *Fuorusciti*, exiles from Florence plotting his overthrow, whose forces were routed at Montemurio near Prato in July
1537. Throughout the city after this battle were heard cries of '*Palle!
Palle!* Victory! Victory!' reported a Sienese observer. 'There is great
rejoicing, and from two windows on the ground floor of the Signor
Cosimo's palace much bread hath been thrown and is still being
thrown, and from two wooden pipes they are continually pouring
out streams of wine.'

The free entertainment was well advised, for the rejoicing was far
less spontaneous than the Sienese supposed and far from universal.
The exiles' army had included young men from several of Florence's
most distinguished families and had been led by Piero Strozzi, son of

the great Filippo. Piero had escaped but scores of others had been taken prisoner and, after being ignominiously paraded through the the streets of Florence, were savagely punished. Sixteen were condemned to death; many more died in prison; others were tracked down and assassinated in the foreign cities where they had sought refuge.

Having dealt with the exiles and executed their captured leaders, four of whom were beheaded each morning on four consecutive days in the Piazza della Signoria, Cosimo turned his attention to the Spaniards whose garrisons he now wished to remove from the Tuscan fortresses. At first the Emperor declined to comply with Cosimo's requests. He was prepared to recognize Cosimo as Duke of Florence, but he insisted that the Duchy must be considered an Imperial fief. He would not order the withdrawal of Spanish troops; nor would he consent to Cosimo's marriage with Alessandro's young widow, Margaret, who was given instead to Ottavio Farnese, grandson of Pope Paul III, Clement VII's successor, since the Emperor considered it more important to oblige the Papacy than Florence. Yet Cosimo did manage to obtain for himself a politically useful bride in Eleonora, daughter of Don Pedro de Toledo, the extremely rich Spanish Viceroy at Naples.[1] And not long after his marriage to Eleonora had taken place, the Emperor, who had fallen out with the Pope and had come to recognize that the Duke of Florence was in a position to render him important services, agreed to the withdrawal of Spanish troops from Tuscany.

Free from foreign occupation, Cosimo had also by now freed himself from interference in his government by any of his ministers. Although the *Signoria* and the office of *Gonfaloniere* were abolished by decree, there were still councils and magistracies in existence; but the Duke, as president of all of them, was easily able to ensure that they came to no decisions of which he disapproved; and as time went by he troubled himself less and less even to consult them. Guicciardini and Vettori were both 'put aside'; so was Cardinal Cibò and, according to Luigi Alberto Ferrai, 'in so dexterous a way that he was alienated and offended as little as possible'.

Cosimo was not, however, a tactful man by nature. On the contrary he was brusque to the point of asperity, often so ungracious as to appear gratuitously insulting; and in ridding himself of his opponents he displayed a harshness quite untempered by compunction or remorse. He had no qualms about throwing real or imagined enemies into the dreadful dungeons of Volterra, or about hiring assassins to dispose of troublesome dissidents and dangerous rivals. After surviving as an outlaw for ten years, during which he published his *Apologia* in celebration of tyrannicide as a selfless act of the greatest merit, Lorenzaccio was eventually caught in Venice, where he was stabbed to death with a poisoned dagger near the Ponte San Toma. Likewise, wishing to rid himself of the Dominicans of San Marco, Cosimo accused them of having made 'public professions of dissent', and had no hesitation in expelling them from their monastery. To their nervous protestations he curtly replied, 'Tell me, my fathers, who built this monastery? Was it you?'

'No.'

'Who put you in this monastery then?'

'Our ancient Florentines and Cosimo the Elder of blessed memory.'

'Right. Well, it's the modern Florentines and Cosimo the Duke who are kicking you out.'

Master of Florence, Cosimo, after a long and cruel war, became master of Siena too. The war began in 1554, but it was not until 1557 that the cession of the city to Cosimo, to be held by him and his descendants as a Spanish fief, was at last ratified. By then the Sienese, whose population had been reduced from 14,000 to 6,000, had undergone unspeakable sufferings; and their surrounding territory had been ravaged without mercy. Their traditional dislike of the Florentines was fixed for generations to come, while Cosimo's enemies at home were able to point with derision and disgust to the folly of expending so many lives and such huge sums of money on acquiring lordship over a devastated territory yielding less than 50,000 ducats a year.

Certainly Cosimo himself was far from satisfied with his new acquisition. He wanted much more than Siena. He wanted to be recognized as Grand Duke, a title for the assumption of which papal authority was required. So determined, indeed, was he to gratify this ambition that to achieve it he sought the necessary authority with a relentless persistence which on occasions seemed to assume the compulsion of a mania. And at last he had his way. Pope Pius V bestowed the title of Grand Duke upon him in 1569.

But when, in December that year, all the bells in Florence rang, bonfires raged and cannon roared in celebration of the Duke's new title, there was, so an observer noticed, 'little real joy to be discerned in the faces of the people'. Two years later, however, when once again the bells were tolled and celebratory fires were lit, when the Cathedral and churches of Florence rang with heartfelt Te Deums, the rejoicing was spontaneous and sincere; it was universally agreed that his Excellency, the Grand Duke, now addressed as *Altezza* and *Serenissimo*, had good reason this time to take upon himself some personal credit. For at the battle of Lepanto where the Turkish fleet was once and for all swept from the eastern Mediterranean, Florentine galleys had played an important part. And it was Cosimo who – intent upon protecting his shores from the raids of Turkish marauders and from Barbary pirates, as well as making himself and Tuscany appear more formidable in the eyes of Spain – had been responsible for the creation of Florence's victorious navy.

'A man is not powerful,' he had said years before to the Venetian ambassador, 'unless he is as powerful by sea as he is by land.' And in pursuit of this power he had ordered galleys to be built, discussed designs with naval architects, superintended the enlistment of sailors and the purchase of foreign slaves, written out instructions for voyages, made lists of necessary armaments. He had created a new order of military knights, the Knights of Santo Stefano – admittedly in later years a less crusading than piratical order – in which were enrolled his two illegitimate sons, Cosimo and Lorenzo, and Duke Alessandro's illegitimate son, Giulio. He had established a new naval base on the island of Elba, which had been ceded to him by the Duke of Piombino, and had fortified the capital to which he had given the name Cosmopolis.[2] 'I have devoted all my attention to naval matters,' he assured the Venetian ambassador without undue exaggeration. 'I have galleys finished and others being built. And so I shall continue and keep all my ships fully equipped with every-thing that is needed.'

He was true to his word. The first two galleys to be launched, *La Saetta* and *La Pisana*, set out on their maiden voyages in 1550; the *San Giovanni* soon followed them. By 1565 there were several more galleys available for the expedition to relieve the besieged Knights of St John on Malta; and by 1571, the year of Lepanto, Pope Pius V had good reason to be grateful for the Grand Duke's now considerable fleet and for the huge sum of 60,000 *scudi* which his treasury con-tributed to the great Christian enterprise.[3]

Cosimo, though prone to sea-sickness, took great pleasure in sail-ing with his fleet himself. He would set out from Lerici and to the 'blowing of trumpets, the firing of guns and the shouts of the people' he would be rowed up to Sestri or down the coast to Leghorn where he would disembark for a day's fishing or fowling or hunting.

For none of these pleasures did he ever lose his taste. Whenever he could spare the time he would leave Florence for his villa of Il Trebbio, or for Poggio a Caiano, Castello or Cafaggiolo, or for one or other of his smaller country houses, Cerreto, Lecceto or Monte-lupo; and in red breeches, high boots of Spanish leather, doeskin jerkin and black velvet jewelled cap, he would ride out with his huntsmen, falconers, pages, courtiers and couriers into the surround-ing woods and valleys. They chased wild boars and roebuck, they galloped after greyhounds, coursing hares; they took out falcons and setters; they bagged pheasants and partridges. And 'in the little stream of the Sieve, which flows into the valley of the Mugello,' recorded Cabriana,

the Duke would catch various fish, such as trout, and would divide his haul among his courtiers and watch them with great delight as they ate the fish which they had cooked in the neighbouring meadows, he himself lying on the grass.

For his courtiers the days did not always pass so pleasantly. The Duke was an exacting master, critical of the slightest fault, insistent upon uniformity in all matters of procedure and dress, requiring, for example, all his pages unfailingly to wear red caps in winter, purple caps in summer. He was also as exasperatingly secretive in his private life as he was in his dealings with his ministers. His attendants never knew how many days they would be away from home or where they would be taken. As one of them reported, voicing a typical complaint, 'We have never known one day what there would be to do the next, his Excellency being more than ever secret in the matter of whither he is riding.' Another of his courtiers found his penchant for practical jokes quite as irritating as his secretiveness. 'This morning,' he grumbled, 'the Duke went to see the nets spread for the birds, and took several and made one of them peck me, which it did really painfully. It was my right hand too. The others say it was a great favour; but to me it is great pain.'

It would all have been more bearable had the Duke been less capriciously unpredictable; but his moodiness was, in fact, notorious. On occasion he seemed to welcome friendliness, even to tolerate familiarity; at other times he would rebuff the slightest hint of disrespect. Sometimes 'he lays aside all authority and dignity and with the utmost intimacy makes jokes with everyone and appears to want everyone to use this freedom towards him', a Venetian envoy recorded.

But once the time for amusement is past, he recognizes no one and it is as if he had never known them. If anyone is bold enough to make the least sign of familiarity, he at once withdraws into his accustomed severity, so much so that it is said of him in Florence that he doffs and dons the Duke whenever he pleases.

Similar complaints were made about his wife.

The Duchess, Eleonora da Toledo, was quite as exacting as her husband. The letters of her attendants are replete with anxious requests for the immediate dispatch of some commodity which has not arrived on time or for the replacement of some unsatisfactory article – to 'forward instantly the salted fish from Spain such as the Duchess likes, the present consignment being all stale and broken', to 'send without delay his Excellency's cloak and doublet', to 'have made for his Excellency two pair of leather hose, but not miserably short and tight like the others'.

Yet however demanding, capricious and arrogant her servants and attendants found her, Eleonora was a good wife to Cosimo, who loved her as much as it was in his nature to love anyone. Soon after their marriage they moved from the Medici Palace to the Palazzo Vecchio which was transformed into the ducal palace with apartments for the Duchess on the upper floors, for the Duke on the lower, and for his mother on the floor between. Neither the Duke nor the Duchess got on very well with his mother, who had never been easy to love and who became increasingly irritating and increasingly untidy as she grew older. On one occasion at least she and her son had a blazing row when he was ill in bed and her fussy interference exasperated him even more than his doctors' incompetence. He lost his temper with her; she left the room in tears; and the next day they declined to speak to each other. With his wife, however, Cosimo seems always to have remained on excellent terms, allowing her without complaint to indulge her passion for gambling, and never showing irritation at her exasperating changes of mind. She, for her part, put up complaisantly with his secretiveness, his outbursts of ill temper and his long periods of gloomy silence. They seem to have had differences only over the upbringing of their children.

There were five sons – Francesco, the heir; Giovanni, who became a cardinal at seventeen and died of a 'malignant fever' two years later; Ferdinando, who also became a cardinal and later Grand Duke of Tuscany; Garzia, who died at the age of seventeen, a fortnight after Giovanni; and Pietro, who was born in 1554. There were also three girls, Maria, Isabella and Lucrezia. All the girls were brought up strictly in the Spanish way, being rarely allowed outside the palace except to go to Mass, seeing few men other than priests, doctors and tutors. Both Maria and Lucrezia died when young, Maria when she was seventeen, Lucrezia at sixteen, less than a year after her marriage to Alfonso d'Este, Duke of Ferrara. Isabella, who was married to Paolo Giordano Orsini and went to live in the Medici Palace, survived only to be murdered by her husband. Cosimo did not live to hear of this tragedy; but on learning of the death of Maria, who succumbed to malaria while they were staying at the castle at Leghorn, he went out onto the bastion alone so that no one should see him give way to his grief. 'Her constitution was like mine,' he said forlornly. 'She ought to have been allowed more fresh air.' On his return to Florence he continued to mourn for her, and spent hours by himself in his room where her portrait hung on the wall.

But he was never, even in less distressing times, a man who seemed to take much pleasure in life, except in hunting. He was rarely seen to smile; he had a poor appetite, contenting himself with the plainest food and in his later years with one simple meal a day; he had no taste for wine; he usually wore a black velvet robe indoors and used to say he would have preferred to wear a plain Florentine *lucco*. His apartments in the Palazzo Vecchio were richly decorated, but he chose to sleep in a sombre room whose walls were hung with dark green and blue gold-stamped leather. He would have been just as satisfied, so it was felt, with rooms of monastic simplicity such as those used by his secretaries who had to make do with 'three desks, two brass lamps, two benches and four large stone inkstands'.

These secretaries worked inordinately long hours, as he did himself. He was up and dressed at dawn, reading and answering the correspondence which he allowed no one else to see, marking documents, compiling reports, writing instructions for his secretaries to copy, impatient to be out-of-doors, complaining when heavy rain kept him at his desk, 'I am sitting here like a falcon on its perch.' His paperwork finished, he would go to Mass, usually in the Cathedral, sometimes in the church of the Santissima Annunziata; and afterwards he would play tennis or go out for a walk or a ride in the town, not for pleasure but for exercise. If on foot he always walked fast, wearing a coat of mail under his jerkin, a sword and a dagger hanging from his belt, and with 'numerous small *stiletti*, with very sharp points, almost as fine as needles, stuck into the lining of his scabbard as into a needle-case'. He was invariably accompanied by a Swiss bodyguard.

Cosimo had good reason to fear assassination. Several attempts were made on his life; and the savage punishments inflicted on the would-be assassins did not deter others from trying to murder him. One Giuliano Buonnaccorsi, who had planned to shoot him from a window, was tortured with red-hot pincers, dragged round the streets by his ankles, disembowelled and tossed into the Arno. Yet soon afterwards Cosimo's agents discovered another plot to kill him by submerging a *chevaux de frise* of swords and spikes beneath the waters of the Arno at the place where he used to dive in for a swim during the summer months.

Ever since 1546 Cosimo had been thinking of bringing all the scattered judicial and administrative offices of Florence, as well as the city's major guilds, under one roof near the Palazzo Vecchio and hence under his own closer, more personal and efficient control. He appointed Giorgio Vasari his architect, and work on the huge new building, the Uffizi, began in 1559.[4] A year later the Duke and his family moved from the Palazzo Vecchio across the Arno to the Palazzo Pitti, the vast palace which Luca Pitti had begun to build a hundred years before. The Duchess had bought the palace from the Pitti family for 9,000 florins in 1549, and instructions had been given to Bartolommeo Ammanati to enlarge and embellish it.[5] Work was still being carried out on the great courtyard and on the new 'kneeling windows' on the ground floor of the façade when the family moved in, as the Duchess had refused to consider delaying her departure from the Palazzo Vecchio. She had been impatient to enjoy the more spacious splendour of the Pitti Palace, to be able to walk in lovely gardens with magnificent views instead of up and down the small enclosed terrace at the Palazzo Vecchio which was all the space she had there for her rare plants and flowers.

Behind the Pitti Palace, or the Ducal Palace as it was now officially known, were acres of land stretching south to the heights of San Giorgio and west almost as far as the Porta Romana. These had been bought from a variety of families including the Bogoli, and it was by a corrupt form of their name, Boboli, that the gardens laid out there were subsequently known. For ten years up to his death in 1550 the landscaping had been in the hands of Niccolò Pericoli Tribolo, who had designed the big amphitheatre and the pond behind it to be known as the Neptune Pond. Since then the work had been in the hands of Buontalenti, Giulio and Alfonso Parigi, and of Baccio

Bandinelli, who had designed an elaborate rustic grotto at the Duchess's suggestion.[6]

The Duchess's impatience to move to the new palace was aggravated by her failing health. She was now 'always indisposed', the Venetian ambassador reported, suffering from a chronic cough and 'every morning bringing up her food'. She feared she did not have long to live, and her fears were justified. Within less than two years of leaving the Palazzo Vecchio, a fortnight after the death of her favourite son, Garzia, she too died, 'grieving and despairing, refusing to be guided by physicians as was her wont'. Cosimo was with her at the end, holding her in his arms. As when Maria died he refused to be comforted, shutting himself away from everyone to grieve alone, instructing his eldest son, Francesco, not to attempt to console him for that would only make his loss all the more unbearable. He never fully recovered from it, and in June 1564 he delegated most of his duties to his heir.

There were rumours that in his prolonged grief he sought distraction by 'indulging in a thousand follies, little suited to his rank and still less to his years [43] ... making love to many women, and especially to one of the leading ladies of Florence'. Certainly, he took as mistress a beautiful young woman, Eleonora degli Albizzi, whom it was believed he might marry, and by whom he had a son. One of the Duke's favourite servants, Sforza Almeni, warned Francesco that his master was considering getting married again, which led first to a row between father and son and then to another between Cosimo and the servant. 'Sforza,' he said to him, 'Get out of my sight. Get out now. And never count on me for anything whatsoever again.'

Supposing that the Duke would soon overcome his anger and forgive him, Almeni did not leave Florence. He even went so far as to return to the Pitti Palace where, at sight of him, Cosimo lost control of himself, and shouting, '*Traditore! Traditore!*' lunged at him with a hunting spear which he drove clean through his body. Afterwards his one regret was that he had degraded himself by stooping so low as to kill a man 'so mean'.

Yet Almeni was right. The Duke *was* to get married again – not to Eleonora degli Albizzi but to another young mistress, Camilla

Martelli, who had also born him a child. She was tall, grasping, selfish and ill-tempered, and she wore her husband out. To escape from her he took to shutting himself up with scholars who were required to read to him, or to spending his evenings with his daughter, Isabella Orsini, at the Medici Palace. It was here one evening that he was seized by an apoplectic fit; a second attack cost him the use of his arms and legs and eventually his voice. After this he spent most of his time dozing in a chair, sometimes mumbling incoherently. One evening after dinner he suddenly took it into his head to get into his coach and go to watch a *calcio* match. It was a cold day and it was raining. For two hours Cosimo sat at a window occasionally looking down at the players, but mostly in a kind of faint. For two months he lingered on, unconscious for days on end, until at last, on 21 April 1574, at the age of fifty-five, he died. His body was laid out in the great hall of the Pitti Palace in the full grand-ducal regalia, while the church bells tolled. The next day 'all the shops were closed ... and wherever one went, the palace was hung all over with black, and black hangings reached all the way across the Piazza dei Pitti'.

Yet Cosimo's death was not generally regretted. He had been rather less unpopular of late, able to ride around the city, so the Venetian ambassador noticed, 'alone in his coach with but a single lackey'. He was known to have been an active member of the fraternity of San Martino who were pledged to give anonymous help to the poor, and he was given some small credit for having encouraged and patronized the traditional popular entertainments of the Florentines, the pageants, the horse-races and the games of *calcio*, and for having added to their number by inaugurating chariot races in the Piazza Santa Maria Novella where posts still mark the limits of the course. He was given rather more credit for having released Florence from her former dependence on Spain, for having provided her with a small but efficient fleet, and for having extended so far the boundaries of the State. But although the government was stable, justice impartial if severe and finances sound, Cosimo was more widely blamed for having denied Florence her former freedom than he was praised for having given her stability. People were far more ready to point accusing fingers at his spies and prisons, his heavy taxes and unscrupulous use of monopolies in private trading than they were to give him credit for the improvements he instigated in the farming, draining and irrigation of Tuscany, for building canals and promoting olive plantations and silver mines, for the development of Pisa and Leghorn, or for having achieved some sort of political unity between these and other Tuscan towns. If someone mentioned his encouragement of Bartolommeo Ammanati who, after the devastating floods of 1557, built the lovely Ponte Santa Trinità[7] and rebuilt the Ponte alla Carraia;[8] or his patronage of Giorgio Vasari, who decorated so much of the Palazzo Vecchio, and of the Flemings known in Florence as Giovanni Rosso and Niccolò Fiamingo, who set up a tapestry factory in the city under his auspices; or his payments for portraits, murals and allegorical paintings by Agnolo Bronzino; or his patience with Benvenuto Cellini whose fine *Perseus*, commissioned by the Duke, was set up in the Loggia dei Lanzi in 1554;[9] there was sure to be someone else to grumble about the cost of the alterations to the Pitti Palace, and of the private corridor between the Pitti and the Palazzo Vecchio (in the hasty construction of which five men were killed), the expensive adornment of the Boboli Gardens, the grandiose scheme for the huge baroque mausoleum at San Lorenzo where the later Medici were to be buried in such gloomy pomp,[10] Pontormo's decoration of the villa of Castello and Tribolo's fountains in its ornate gardens,[11] the lavish expenditure on the park at Poggio a Caiano, and on the wall round the huge wood known as the Pineta. If an admirer were to speak approvingly of his promotion of Pisa University and the Studio Fiorentino, of his invitation to such gifted men as Benedetto Varchi to come back to live in Florence, of his encouragement of Italian music, of scientists and botanists and of Etruscan archaeology, of his improvement of Florence's herb gardens, his foundation of Pisa's School of Botany, and his introduction into Tuscany of medicinal plants from America and of farm crops from the Orient, of his connoisseurship of antiques, medals and Etruscan workmanship, a detractor would undoubtedly contrast the golden age of the Republic under Lorenzo il Magnifico with the dark times now sure to follow under the new Grand Duke Francesco.

XXI

THE HEIRS OF COSIMO

*'Such entertainments have never
been seen before'*

FRANCESCO HAD neither his father's taste for business nor his industry. Irresponsible, taciturn, wayward yet withdrawn, he was 'of low stature', the Venetian ambassador reported disapprovingly, 'thin, dark complexioned and of a melancholy disposition'. 'He shows little grace in his dress,' another ambassador wrote, 'and he is quite as graceless in his bearing.' He was 'a man of quiet thoughts' who spoke with 'care and circumspection'. 'Much absorbed by the love of women', he set 'little store by virtue'.

His wife, the Archduchess Joanna of Austria, who was as pale, thin and charmless as Francesco, was miserably homesick living in Tuscany. Ill and unhappy, ignored by her husband, and condemned by the Florentines for her Austrian hauteur, she never felt at home in Florence. Her father-in-law was kind to her in his way. He had the courtyard of the Palazzo Vecchio specially decorated for her: the lunettes were painted with murals of Austrian towns by pupils of Vasari, and Verrocchio's gay fountain of the little urchin with a spouting fish was brought down from the Careggi villa where it had been set up in the garden by Lorenzo il Magnifico.[1] But Joanna was not to be comforted. She died in 1578 at the age of thirty, a year after the birth of her one sickly son Filippo, who was also to die soon afterwards. Apparently unmoved by her death, Francesco resolved to marry his mistress, Bianca Capello.

Bianca was an attractive, well-educated Venetian noblewoman

who, to the dismay of her family, had secretly married a clerk in a Florentine company. Obliged to leave Venice she had come with her husband to Florence where Francesco, catching sight of her one day as he rode beneath her window, had fallen in love with her. A meeting had been arranged; she had become his mistress; her husband had been placated with a lucrative appointment in Francesco's household and had been given a palazzo conveniently situated near the Pitti Palace for the regular visits his master made to his wife.[2] Francesco also built a country villa for Bianca, the charming Villa Pratolino whose amazing garden so much impressed Montaigne, a guest there in 1581.[3] As well as bronzes by Giambologna and fountains by Ammanati, there were grottoes with movable scenery by the ingenious Bernardo Buontalenti. There were organs, musical waterfalls and all manner of mechanical figures. There were promenades of ilex and cypress, mazes of box-hedges cut into fantastic shapes and arcades formed by jets of water which, rising above the head, fell into little streams on either side of the path. In one corner, passing an aviary and a labyrinth, the visitor came upon Vulcan and his family, standing in a grotto, the walls of which were covered with coral and shells and 'copper and marble figures with the hunting of several beasts, moving by the force of water'. In another corner, near a lawn from whose surface water spouted from unseen sources, a shepherdess walked out of a niche in a wall to fill her bucket with water from a well to the accompaniment of a bagpipe played by a satyr.

The Florentines detested Francesco's mistress, Bianca Capello, for whom this Villa Pratolino had been built, maintaining that she was a witch, that she possessed the evil eye, that she had poisoned the wretched Joanna of Austria. When – her husband having been disposed of – Francesco married her at a wedding which was alleged to have cost no less than 30,000 florins, the people's indignation was unbounded.

Yet outraged as they were by Francesco's behaviour, there were other members of his family whose shameful conduct disgusted them even more. The most iniquitous of all was his younger brother, Pietro, who at the time of Francesco's succession was twenty years old. An emotionally unstable parasite and profligate, Pietro not merely neglected his wife, Eleonora, but openly insulted her. She consoled herself with various lovers, including Bernardino Antinori, who was first imprisoned in his palace for killing one of his rivals in a duel and then exiled to Elba after his mistress had been seen walking up and down the street beneath his windows in the hope of catching sight of him.[4] He was later brought back to Florence to face trial and execution by strangulation in his cell in the Bargello. The distracted grief displayed by Eleonora on learning of her lover's fate so infuriated Pietro that he summoned her to Cafaggiolo where he strangled her, with the evident approval of the Grand Duke.

It was not the only murder in Francesco's family. His sister, Isabella, was quite as unhappy in her marriage as her brothers had been and took for a lover her husband's cousin, Troilo Orsini. Her husband, Paolo Giordano Orsini, a violent, vindictive man, had himself fallen desperately in love with Vittoria, the young and passionate wife of Francesco Accoramboni. They had taken it into their unbalanced minds to rid themselves of both Isabella and Accoramboni and then to marry each other. First Vittoria had her husband killed by professional murderers at the Villa Negroni. Then Orsini, having paid other assassins to kill his cousin, Troilo, murdered his wife at their villa of Ceretto Guidi near Empoli.[5] He did so in a peculiarly macabre way: having waited until they had finished dinner, he signalled for four accomplices in the room above to let down a rope through a hole in the ceiling. Pretending to kiss her, he strangled his wife with the rope which the accomplices then pulled back into the room above. Announcing that Isabella had died of a sudden apoplectic seizure, Orsini soon afterwards married Vittoria, ignoring a papal ban imposed upon the marriage by Gregory XIII, and took her off to his castle at Bracciano. The horrifying affair might there have ended had not Gregory XIII died and been succeeded by Sixtus V. The new Pope was not only a relentlessly severe pontiff, determined to repress the disorders and lawlessness which had become so scandalous in the times of his predecessor, but was also the murdered Francesco Accoramboni's uncle. Rather than attempt to defend himself at Bracciano against the Pope's troops, Orsini fled to Venice where he died. He left a will bequeathing his great wealth to Vittoria who was consequently stabbed to death in Padua by her husband's aggrieved brother who had hoped to be his heir.

His reputation sinking ever lower in a sea of scandal, the Grand Duke Francesco retreated from the world into the isolated privacy of Pratolino where he fed his goldfish and his Swedish reindeer, planted the rare shrubs that were sent to him from India and talked of cosmography, chemistry and the secrets of nature. Whole days were spent in his garden house at Pratolino and in the laboratory which Vasari built for him at the Palazzo Vecchio where, towards the end of his life, he even held meetings with his Ministers, unwilling to leave the chemical and other scientific experiments which so absorbed him. He had other interests, too, which kept his mind from business: on the third floor of the Uffizi, which had been completed by Bernardo Buontalenti and Alfonso Parigi after Vasari's death in 1574, he created an art gallery and established studios for young artists. In 1583, he also established the Accademia della Crusca (the Chaff), an academy for ridding the Tuscan language of its impurities, and, indeed, for maintaining the supremacy of Florence as the only worthy arbiter of Italian literary taste – a function the *Accademia* performed so vigorously that it had the playwright, Girolamo Gigli, expelled from the Duchy for the unpardonable affront of declaring that Saint Catherine of Siena was a better writer than that great Florentine of blessed memory, Giovanni Boccaccio.[6] But it was chemistry and alchemy, smelting and glass-blowing, gem-setting and crystal-cutting that occupied most of Francesco's time. He became, indeed, an acknowledged expert: he was adept at making vases from molten rock crystal and precious metals; he invented a new way of cutting rock crystal and a revolutionary method of making porcelain which enabled Tuscan potters to produce exquisite wares comparable to those imported from China.[7] He also developed ingenious methods of manufacturing fireworks and imitation jewellery. Yet even his scientific experiments brought him vilification rather than credit: locked up there in that noisome laboratory he was manufacturing poison to be used by that witch, Bianca. The notion seemed only too credible when in October 1587 they both suddenly died – in fact, of malarial fever – on the same day.

Francesco's brother and successor, Ferdinando I, who assured his people that the deaths had been due to natural causes, had spent most of his life in Rome. He had gone there in 1563 as a fifteen-year-old cardinal, and within ten years had become an influential member of the Sacred College. Though he had little taste for religious life he founded the missionary society of the Propaganda Fide and proved himself a capable administrator. He also found ample opportunity to indulge his enthusiasm for classical statues of which he assembled a large collection, mostly Roman copies of Greek originals, including the Venus de' Medici. He bought a villa on the Pincio in which to display them,[8] and on his brother's death brought many of them back with him to Florence where six statues of Roman women, restored by Carradori, were placed inside the Loggia dei Lanzi.

Ferdinando was thirty-eight years old at the time of his accession, a far more genial man than his brother whom he had never liked. Though extravagant and ostentatious, he immediately displayed a sincere concern for the well-being of Florence, and showed himself determined to maintain her independent position – if necessary, by force – in contrast with Francesco's policy which had been to avoid trouble at any price. Under Ferdinando's relatively benign yet efficient rule the government became less corrupt, the finances more stable, while trade and farming flourished. Hospitals were built in Florence and a college for scholars was founded at Pisa. The fleet, originated by his father, became more powerful; and Leghorn – 'the masterpiece of the Medicean dynasty', as Montesquieu called it – was further developed and populated with new citizens from all over Europe who were drawn to it by the Grand Duke's promise of religious toleration, a promise that attracted not only persecuted Protestants but so many Jews that there is still today a higher proportion of Jews in Leghorn than in any other Italian city. By numerous acts of kindness and magnanimity the Grand Duke Ferdinando endeared himself to the people. He inaugurated, for example, a new and enjoyable ceremony at San Lorenzo where every year he distributed dowries to poor girls who might otherwise have found it difficult to find suitable husbands; and in the winter of 1589, when the Arno in full flood caused havoc in Florence and the surrounding countryside, he personally distributed baskets of food to the victims of the disaster and then made a perilous journey in a small boat to promise help to stricken villages.

Although he preferred to hoard money rather than to invest it – and instructed Bernardo Buontalenti to make an impregnable safe for him at Forte di Belvedere, the forbidding fortress overlooking the city, which was built to Buontalenti's designs on the heights of San Giorgio between 1590 and 1595[9] Ferdinando I did not hesitate to be lavish when the occasion seemed to demand it. He bought Petraia, a medieval castle, from the Salutati family and instructed Buontalenti to transform it into a magnificent villa with an appropriately splendid garden.[10] He built an equally splendid hunting lodge at Artimino, the Villa Ferdinanda, which was also designed for him by Buontalenti.[11] He continued to pour money into the Pitti Palace and the Boboli Gardens; he enlarged the Uffizi gallery and built the Tribuna; he bought numerous rare manuscripts from Persia and Egypt for the Medici library. He spent a thousand ducats on a colossal and highly intricate gilded sphere, the most complicated construction of its kind ever made, to prove that Ptolemy was right in contending that the moon, sun and stars revolve in circles round the earth and that Copernicus had been wrong to deny it.[12] To Giambologna he gave the Palazzo Bellini,[13] commissioning him to construct in a foundry there a gigantic equestrian statue of the Grand Duke Cosimo for the Piazza della Signoria.[14] On the occasion of his marriage to Caterina de' Medici's agreeable granddaughter, Christine of Lorraine, he spent an enormous amount of money as though determined to demonstrate that the House of Medici had lost none of its grandeur, and that the reversal of his brother's pro-Spanish policy was worthy of a celebration of unparalleled splendour.[15]

Christine entered the city through a series of magnificent triumphal arches dedicated to Florence, to the glorious history of the Medici and the House of Lorraine. For weeks past scores of architects, painters and sculptors had been working on the construction and decoration of these arches, while hundreds of other artists and craftsmen, cooks and carpenters, mechanics and ropemakers, musicians and singers, soldiers and actors, gardeners and pyrotechnists had been busy preparing as original and elaborate a sequence of parades, receptions, banquets, pageants, plays, musical entertainments and *intermezzi* as Florence, or indeed, Europe had ever seen. The highlight of these extraordinary wedding celebrations, which marked a vital stage in the development of theatrical production, of ballet and the new *dramma per musica*, was a musical performance at the Pitti Palace, during which all manner of ingenious scenic devices, from exploding volcanoes to fire-eating dragons, astonished the spectators, and at the climax of which the courtyard was flooded to a depth of five feet so that eighteen galleys manned by heroic Christians could storm a Turkish fort.

Entertainments such as this, the inspiration of many a fête performed at Versailles for the pleasure of Louis XIV, were Ferdinando's speciality; and he lost no opportunity in using them to exalt the Medici and his own policies in the eyes of Florence and of the world. The finest of all his court festivals were those over which he presided on the occasion of the marriage of his niece, Maria, to Henry of Navarre, whose triumph over the Catholic League and accession to the French throne owed much to Medici money. As well as the familiar horse races and tournaments, processions and pageants, firework displays and water fêtes, there were marvellously inventive performances at the Uffizi of Giulio Caccini's *Il Rapimento di Cefalo* with settings by Buontalenti and of *L'Euridice* by Jacopo Peri, whose now lost *Daphne*, which has been called the first opera, was also performed at the Uffizi under Ferdinando's auspices. And on 5 October 1600, when Maria de' Medici and King Henry IV of France were married by proxy in the Cathedral, a stupendous banquet was given in the Palazzo Vecchio where each extravagantly shaped and decorated dish formed part of a fantastic allegory upon the martial brilliance of the French King and the outstanding virtues of the House of Medici into which he had so wisely married.

After Ferdinando's death in 1609, his nineteen-year-old son, Grand Duke Cosimo II, increased the family's reputation for lavish entertainments. When he was married to the Emperor Ferdinand II's sister, the Archduchess Maria Maddalena, there was so spectacular a display on the Arno that observers claimed nothing like it had ever before been seen. The stage was the whole stretch of river between the Ponte alla Carraia and the Ponte Santa Trinità, which was embellished with statues for the occasion. The audience, sitting in immense grandstands erected on the Lungarni, were treated to a performance of the *Argonautica* in which Jason, avoiding the hazards presented by gigantic dolphins, lobsters and fire-spitting hydra, sailed round an artificial island, captured the Golden Fleece and presented the Archduchess Maria Maddalena with six red apples symbolic of the Medicean *palle*.

Cosimo II also shared his father's taste for building. He extended the Palazzo Pitti, and reconstructed yet another villa for his family, the villa of Poggio Imperiale near Arcetri.[16] Here he set up a telescope which Galileo Galilei had brought with him to Florence and here Galileo himself was offered sanctuary.

Galileo was born at Pisa in 1564 the son of a poor descendant of a Florentine noble family. He had wanted to be a painter, but his father had discouraged him and he had studied medicine instead. Turning to mathematics and physics, he had exasperated his tutors at the University of Pisa by his constant questioning of their assertions, his maddening presumption and quick temper. He had been offered a chair, but his colleagues, unable to tolerate his sarcasm and independence, had made it clear to him that his resignation would be welcome. He had gone to the University of Padua where he had remained for eighteen years until Cosimo II, who had once been a pupil of his, invited him to come to Florence where he could continue his studies and experiments in peace, free from the interference of his detractors and the accusations of the Church. Galileo accepted the offer and spent the last years of his life under the protection of the Medici. The satellites of Jupiter, whose discovery he had made known to the world in a book published in 1610, he called *Medicea Sidera*.[17] He long outlived his indolent patron, Cosimo II, who died at the early age of thirty, having achieved very little worthy of record; but when Galileo himself died in 1642 and the Church forbade any monument to be erected to his memory, Cosimo's son, Ferdinando II, had him buried in the Novices' Chapel at Santa Croce.[18]

XXII

FERDINANDO II AND THE FRENCH PRINCESS

*'It is her usual conceit to say that she
has married beneath her'*

TEN YEARS old when his father died, Ferdinando II was an easy-going, agreeable boy who gave as little trouble to his tutors as grounds for hope that he would be much credit to them. At the age of seventeen he went abroad on a continental tour, leaving Florence in the care of his mother and grandmother, neither of whom, perpetually quarrelling with each other and their council, appears to have either regretted his absence or to have welcomed his return. The people of Florence, however, grew more kindly disposed towards him the better they got to know him. In 1630, when he was twenty, he and his brothers stayed in Florence throughout an out-break of the plague, doing all they could to help the stricken people, while most others who could afford to do so fled from the city. He did not look like a hero: in his portraits by the court painter, Justus Sustermans, he is seen adopting a commanding patrician pose which contrasts almost absurdly with the bulbous nose, the fleshily jutting Habsburg mouth and the black moustache whose thick ends rise up-wards, like arrow-heads, towards the soft and heavy-lidded eyes. He was rather fat and extremely good-natured, more attracted to hand-some young men than to women, fond of hunting and fishing and of playing games like bowls, provided he was allowed to win – some-times losing his temper when he did not win, a spectacle all the more disconcerting on account of his usual placidity and courtesy.

283

His style of life was entirely without ostentation – wicker-covered bottles hung over the gate of the Pitti Palace indicating that wine could be bought there in the same way as from other lesser palaces in the city – yet Ferdinando was never mean. He spent as much on pageants, masques and spectacles as any of his predecessors; and, encouraged by his brother Leopoldo, he was a generous patron of scientists and men of letters. In 1657 the justly celebrated academy, Del Cimento (the Test) – whose motto was *'Provando e Riprovando'* and whose emblem was a furnace with three crucibles – began to meet at the Pitti Palace; and although it was to survive for only ten years, dissolving in a welter of recrimination, jealousy and discord, its publications made important contributions to scientific knowledge. Ferdinando and Leopoldo, both disciples of Galileo, took a real interest in its proceedings, composing its quarrels, signing its correspondence, following closely the work of Evangelista Torricelli da Modigliana, inventor of the barometer, experimenting themselves with telescopic lenses and all manner of scientific instruments, and commissioning those thermometers, astrolabes, quadrants, hygrometers, calorimeters and other ingenious mechanical devices which visitors to the Pitti Palace saw displayed in such profusion.

Fascinated as they were by these devices, their interests ranged over a much wider field. Leopoldo, indeed, was a true polymath. He spent four hours each day 'up to his neck in books'. He read everything that came to hand, 'books of criticism, gallantry, satire and curiosities ... manuscript reports on the geography, customs, and inhabitants of countries ... in every part of the world'. The secretary of the Cimento wrote to an agent commissioned to buy books for Leopoldo:

You may forward documents of natural history like that [description] of a fish I sent you, or that [account] of a strange pregnancy ... or like that skeleton so similar to a human one that [was] found at Castel Gandolfo; information about medals, newly-discovered statues, cameos and other ancient relics, architectural designs, stories with a bit of spice – anything will do.

For 'like a little boy with a piece of bread', Leopoldo always kept 'a book in his pocket to chew on whenever he [had] a moment to spare'.

Ferdinando was both more selective and more practical, his main interest, apart from the experiments conducted by the Cimento, being the development of the Florentine craft of creating mosaics in *pietra dura*. Scores of craftsmen were kept busily at work in this intricate manufacture, assembling ornaments and bas-reliefs and elaborately decorating furniture in marble, ivory, crystal, gold, brightly coloured minerals and semi-precious stones.[1] To contain these works, and the family's ever increasing collection of paintings and sculpture, Ferdinando was obliged to make extensive alterations to the Pitti Palace and to provide it with suitable galleries which he had adorned with murals by some of the most accomplished artists of his time – Cirro Ferri, Francesco Furini, Pietro da Cortona who painted the fine Baroque murals in the Sala della Stufa, and Giovanni da San Giovanni who worked in the Museo degli Argenti sitting in a tub suspended from the ceiling, his gouty legs swathed in bandages.[2] In the galleries thus beautifully decorated, visitors were able to inspect the latest additions to the Grand Ducal collections.[3]

As a ruler, Ferdinando's policies were largely governed by a desire to avoid all trouble and unpleasantness. He was drawn into a brief war with the Pope's tiresome Barberini relatives, but otherwise contrived to face every threat to Florence's peace and security with mollifying complaisance. Rather than offend the Pope he declined to advance his claim to Urbino on the abdication of the childless Duke, Francesco Maria II, allowing the Duchy to become a part of the Papal States. Similarly he gave way to the Pope by agreeing that the officials of the Board of Health should kneel in submissive apology for having obliged various monks and priests to abide by the laws of quarantine during an outbreak of plague. He adopted the same placatory attitude towards the highly censurable activities of various members of his unruly family. He had no trouble with the good-natured, accommodating Leopoldo, who, on the dissolution of the scientific academy, Del Cimento, left for Rome to become a cardinal. Nor did Ferdinando have any difficulty with his other brother, Mattias, who served with some credit as a general in the Thirty

Years' War during which he assembled that remarkable collection of ivory ornaments which is one of the minor marvels of the Pitti collection,[4] and after which he formed an equally extraordinary collection of human deformities including a hideous dwarf with 'thinly scattered tusks for teeth' and an appetite so enormous that he could gobble up forty cucumbers, thirty figs and a water melon as *hors d'œuvres* before a massive dinner. Ferdinando did, however, have trouble with his brother, Gian Carlo, a cardinal like Leopoldo, but a man of far less disciplined instincts.

Gian Carlo was not without taste. He invited Salvator Rosa, whom he had met in Rome, to come to Florence where he was paid an annual income to paint for the Court while remaining free to accept commissions from other patrons. Gian Carlo also provided funds for a company of actors to build a theatre in the Via della Pergola;[5] and for another company he rented a palazzo in the Via del Cocomero for which Ferdinando Tacca was asked to design sets and scenery.[6] But Gian Carlo's true interests were not so much painting and the theatre as food, which he consumed in immense quantities, and women, whom he pursued with the insatiable lust of a satyr. Expelled from Rome for refusing to be accompanied by older and less libidinous cardinals on his visits to Queen Christina of Sweden, he returned to Florence still young, rich and good-looking, exquisitely dressed, his hair long and curly, determined to devote himself to pleasure. He moved into a beautiful villa built in the middle of an entrancing and exotic garden off the Via della Scala.[7] Here he made love to a succession of mistresses – often, it was said, to several at once – and had at least one tiresome rival drowned in a carp pond. He once ordered the release of a notorious murderer, whose wife he had immediately taken to bed when she had come to him on her husband's behalf, and threatened to cut off the Sheriff's head if his order was not obeyed. The Sheriff appealed to the Grand Duke who stood in silence for a few moments before resignedly declaring, 'Obey the Cardinal, since he is my brother.' Everyone knew that Ferdinando was frightened of Gian Carlo, and when the news was brought that he had died of apoplexy, Ferdinando received it with evident relief, rather than sorrow.

The Grand Duke found his wife, Vittoria della Rovere, hardly less troublesome than Gian Carlo. She was a prim and interfering woman, plain and fat, who early on in her married life developed a double chin far more uncompromising than her husband's. She found it extremely difficult to bear him an heir: her first child, a boy, survived for less than a day, her second for only a few minutes. It was not until 14 August 1642 that she finally gave birth to a baby strong enough to live. This was the future Cosimo III, but his advent did not improve the uneasy relationship between his parents. Soon after his birth his mother came upon her husband fondling a handsome page, and for weeks she declined to speak to him. When she decided to try to come to terms with him, he declined to be reconciled, and it was almost twenty years before their quarrel was properly made up. A second son, Francesco Maria, was born in 1660; yet the marriage remained an unhappy one.

One principal cause of disagreement was the upbringing of their son, Cosimo. The Grand Duke wanted him to be given a modern education with due attention paid to the scientific discoveries which he himself found so deeply interesting. But the Grand Duchess would have none of that. She insisted that their son be educated by priests in the old-fashioned way. And so he was. He was taught to suppose that the scientific experiments of the Cimento were not only impious but beneath a prince's notice. He accepted the teaching and soon developed a priggish intolerance that was to mar his character for life. When he was sixteen he was already exhibiting 'symptoms of a singular piety', the Lucchese ambassador reported.

He is dominated by melancholy to an extraordinary degree, quite unlike his father. The Grand Duke is affable with everyone, as ready with a laugh as with a joke, whereas the Prince is never seen to smile. The people attribute this to an imperious and reserved disposition.

Cosimo did not like music, except church music; he did not like dancing; he preferred to go to Mass rather than to the theatre; he would rather talk to monks than to girls or courtiers; he went out shooting, but when a bird flew over his head he would murmur, 'Poverino' and lower his gun – though afterwards he would eat with relish the birds that others had shot. His father decided that the sooner he was married the better, and that the ideal bride for him would be Marguerite-Louise, daughter of Gaston d'Orléans, Louis XIV's uncle. This was a match that was also favoured in Paris, where Cardinal Mazarin entertained hopes of becoming Pope and was anxious to obtain the support of the Medici. The prospect, however, of being married to a gloomy, plump Italian with thick lips and droopy eyes, the heir to an impoverished duchy, was not at all pleasing to Marguerite-Louise herself. She was a high-spirited girl, quick, energetic, playful and capricious. Besides, she was in love with her cousin, Prince Charles of Lorraine. She begged her other cousin, King Louis XIV, not to send her to Florence. She knelt before him at the Louvre, imploring him to spare her such a dreadful fate; but he helped her to her feet and told her that it was now too late to break her word. So she was married to Cosimo by proxy in Paris on 17 April 1661. She was fifteen years old. Cosimo, who was in bed with measles at the Pitti Palace, was eighteen.

The bride left for Florence, 'crying aloud for everyone to hear', delaying her departure from every town where they stopped for the night, reaching Marseilles in the pouring rain, pretending to be too ill to leave her cabin in the flower-bedecked galley in which she was rowed to Leghorn. The bridegroom was waiting to meet her at the Villa Ambrogiana, near Empoli.[8] He displayed no pleasure when he saw her for the first time, declining to kiss her; while she, for her part, did not attempt to disguise her relief when her doctor said that, although she had already had measles and the Prince was no longer infectious, she ought not yet to share his bed.

When they did go to bed together, after a magnificent ceremony in the Cathedral, the Prince was not enthusiastic, and was soon asleep. He would be stronger, the bride was assured, when he had fully recovered from his recent illness; but Marguerite-Louise seemed not to care whether he ever got better or not. According to Princess Sophia of Hanover, he never really did recover properly. 'He sleeps with his wife but once a week,' she reported years later, 'and then under supervision of a doctor who has him taken out of bed lest he should impair his health by staying there overlong.' Marguerite-

Louise thoroughly disliked him; even his politeness seemed to her a kind of insult.

On the second night of her marriage she asked him to give her the crown jewels. He replied that they were not his to give, whereupon she lost her temper with him, declaring that she would rather live in the most squalid hut in France than in a palace in Tuscany. The next day she helped herself to several of the jewels anyway and gave them to her French attendants from whom they were only recovered with difficulty. After that she rarely spoke to her husband. By the end of their first month together, so the Bishop of Béziers reported, the Prince had only 'couched with her three times'. 'Every time he does not go,' the Bishop continued, 'he sends a valet to tell her not to wait up for him. The French ladies ... are much embarrassed because she is always sad ... She finds the life here very strange.'

It was hoped that the splendid entertainments which were staged in Florence that summer would dispel her gloom. There were banquets in the Palazzo Vecchio, balls at the Pitti Palace, firework displays over the bridge of Santa Trinità, horse races in the Via Maggio, chariot races in the Piazza Santa Maria Novella, processions through the carpeted streets. On St John the Baptist's Day, the *Festa degli Omaggi* was held as usual in the Piazza della Signoria. A week later, before an audience of almost twenty thousand people in the amphitheatre in the Boboli gardens, a performance was given of *Il Mondo Festeggiante*, a fantastic and spectacular combination of masque, *tableaux vivants*, costume parade, ballet on horseback, musical pageant and phantasmagoria in which Cosimo himself appeared in jewelled armour as Hercules. Ten days after this there was a presentation of Jacopo Melani's *Hercules in Thebes* at the theatre in the Via della Pergola. Thereafter Marguerite-Louise was taken on a tour of the villas and gardens of the Medici, from Poggio Imperiale to Poggio a Caiano, from Artimino to Castello and Pratolino. Yet still the Princess only occasionally displayed traces of her former high spirits. Most of the time she was homesick, unhappy, bored and crotchety, finding fault with everything Tuscan because it was not French, rarely going out in public and then always masked. When someone asked her if she liked Florence, she grumpily replied that she would have liked it much better had it been near Paris. She was also extravagant, spending such sums of money on her clothes and her table that the frugal Grand Duke was horrified. Worse than this, she was indiscreet. When Prince Charles of Lorraine visited Florence she made no secret of her love for him, writing passionate letters to him after his departure. His replies were intercepted and there was another row. In August 1663 she gave birth to a son, Ferdinando, and afterwards fell ill with a tumour on her breast. During her convalescence she refused to see anyone other than her French attendants. Blaming them for her petulant behaviour, Cosimo replaced twenty-eight of them with Italians as a result of which Marguerite-Louise became more rebellious than ever.

'She is deaf to protests,' the Venetian ambassador wrote. 'She attaches importance to no one. It is her usual conceit to say that she has married beneath her, into a family vastly inferior to her proper merit; and this pricks the family at the most delicate point of their sensibilities.' She took the most extreme measures to avoid her husband, moving from room to room in the palace so as not to be near him, asking her father-in-law to allow her to live by herself in a country villa. The Grand Duke Ferdinando had been patient, understanding and tolerant for a long time, but eventually he was driven to firmness. He replied that he would have her sent not to a villa but to a convent if she went on behaving like this. Pertly she replied that he would be sorry if he did, for she would soon have all the nuns skipping about like monkeys. She took a malicious delight in piquing Cosimo, in spreading stories of his inadequacy, telling him in public that he would not even make a good groom, let alone a proper husband. The Grand Duke retaliated by having her moved to his brother Mattias's villa of Lappeggi when the rest of the Court drove off to Artimino for the shooting, and by having her closely watched by attendants who were instructed to follow her wherever she went and to ensure that she received no unauthorized letters. She took her revenge by pretending that the Medici were trying to poison her, and that it was necessary for a steward to taste all her dishes which must be prepared by French cooks. She gave it out that the marriage had been forced upon her, and that she was not therefore legally married to Cosimo. She was living as a concubine; her husband was a fornicator. She would *have* to enter a convent now – a French convent, of course. When this solution to her problem was put to Louis XIV, he replied that if she returned to France at all it would certainly not be to a convent but to the Bastille, and he followed up this threat by sending an envoy to Tuscany with a letter of remonstrance sternly condemning her 'capricious' behaviour and her 'invincible obstinacy'.

She refused to mend her ways. Hearing that she was ill, Cosimo went to see her at Poggio a Caiano, whither she had been taken from Lappeggi; but she picked up a bottle from her bedside table, threatening to break his head with it unless he left her alone. On her recovery she resumed her practice of walking very fast up the mountain paths behind the villa, taking pot shots at birds on the way and leaving her exhausted attendants trailing far behind her.

Suddenly in October 1665, bored with her monotonous, secluded country life, she presented herself at the Pitti Palace requesting the Grand Duke's permission to return to Court. Ferdinando quickly assured her that he would like nothing better. Cosimo kissed her. Everyone seemed delighted to welcome her back since she was evidently quite prepared to behave more circumspectly. And, for a time, all went well: she was gracious; she was pretty; she danced; she laughed; she made love with Cosimo; and she became pregnant again. Then the troubles began once more. She refused to stop galloping about on her horse; she continued to walk as far and as fast as ever; she resumed her complaints that the Medici were robbing her of her freedom, holding her a prisoner. Despite her violent exercise and an attack of influenza, for which her physicians bled her profusely, she gave birth to a healthy daughter, Anna Maria Luisa, on 11 August 1667. But after that, the abscess on her breast broke out again and she contracted smallpox. As a cure, the doctors not only bled her drastically, but also cut off her hair. In her misery and pain, she railed against Cosimo more virulently than ever. The Grand Duke thought it advisable to send him abroad for a time, first to Germany and the Netherlands and then, since Marguerite-Louise remained unappeasable on his return, to Spain and England.

✤ XXIII ✤

COSIMO III AND THE
GRAND PRINCE FERDINANDO

'Eighteen years is enough. It will
serve out my time'

COSIMO, AT twenty-six, was just as gloomy as ever but far
more self-confident than at the time of his wedding. An
inveterate trencherman, he was now excessively fat; but he
had a certain charm of manner, and though he was unduly fond of
pious interjections, his conversation was wide-ranging and not un-
interesting. In England, where he was well received in academic
circles owing to his family's protection of Galileo, he was seen
coming out of the Queen's Chapel by Pepys who described him as
a 'comely, black, fat man, in a morning suit . . . a *very jolly and good*
comely man'. At the French Court he created a similarly favourable
impression. The King wrote to Marguerite-Louise, 'Consideration
for you alone would have obliged me to give my cousin all the
favourable treatment he has received from me. But from what I
perceived of his personal qualities, I could not have refused them to
his peculiar merit.' In the less reliable words of Mademoiselle, 'He
spoke admirably on every topic. His physique was rather plump for
a man of his age. He had a fine head, black and curly hair, a large red
mouth, good teeth, a healthy ruddy complexion, abundance of wit,
and was agreeable in conversation.'

Cosimo returned to Florence much taken with the countries of the
north. 'I hope for nothing in this world so ardently as once again to
see [that] paradise called England,' he said soon after his return. 'I

long to embrace again all my old friends there.' He was equally enthusiastic about France, and evidently prepared to make more allowances for the wayward behaviour of his French wife who, he was pleased to note when he got home, was now on good terms both with his mother and his father. His father, however, was failing fast with dropsy and apoplexy, and suffering agonies from the treatment of his doctors; towards the end, not content with bleeding him, they placed a cauterizing iron on his head and forced *polvere capitale* up his nose; they also applied to his forehead four live pigeons whose stomachs had been ripped open for the purpose. The Grand Duke Ferdinando II died on 27 May 1670 and was buried with his father and grandfather in the great baroque mausoleum at San Lorenzo.

Cosimo III entered upon his inheritance with the deepest apprehension. In spite of his father's personal economy and his rigid and extensive system of taxation, there had been no recent improvement in the finances of Tuscany whose trade was rapidly declining and whose population was being constantly decreased by malaria, plague and food shortages due to a backward agriculture. At first, Cosimo endeavoured to deal effectively with the problems that beset him; but soon, recognizing that they were utterly beyond his ability to control, he withdrew more and more into the soothing darkness of his chapel, leaving his mother and her friends to deal with most affairs of state and even deputing his brother, who was not yet twelve, to receive foreign ambassadors. This pleased his bossy mother well enough, but it certainly did not please his wife who angrily complained about a mere della Rovere presuming to take precedence over a daughter of the royal house of France.

In the summer of 1671, after Marguerite-Louise had given birth to a second son, christened Gian Gastone after his grandfather, Gaston d'Orléans, relations between Cosimo and his wife deteriorated rapidly. Believing that she had cancer of the breast she asked Louis XIV to send her a French doctor. Louis agreed to do so; but when the doctor arrived, he discovered that the little bump on her bosom was 'nowise malignant'. However, sympathizing with her urgent desire to return to France, he did suggest to the Grand Duke that her general health might be improved by taking the medicinal waters at Sainte-Reine in Burgundy. Cosimo took leave to disagree, and naturally his objections led to heated protests from his wife. There were further quarrels over the quality of various jewels he gave her, over her extravagance, over her servants, and particularly over a male cook with whom she behaved outrageously in order to punish Cosimo for having dismissed two German grooms and a French dancing-master. 'Now this cook,' so it was recorded,

either dreaded, or pretended to dread, being tickled, and the Duchess, aware of his weakness, delighted in tickling him ... He defended himself, shouting and running from one side of the room to the other, which made her laugh excessively.

When tired of this she would beat the cook over the head with a pillow, and the cook would take shelter under her bed where she went on beating him until, tired out with her exertions, she sank into a chair. As she did so her band of musicians started once more to play the tune they had abandoned when the romp had begun. One night the cook, being very drunk, made so much noise while the Grand Duchess was belabouring him with her pillow that he aroused the Grand Duke who, coming down to see what was happening, 'instantly condemned the cook to the galleys' – though he later reprieved him. Eventually the Grand Duchess decided to settle the matter once and for all. She wrote to inform Cosimo that she could bear her situation not a moment longer:

So I have made a resolution which will not surprise you when you reflect on your base usage of me for nearly twelve years ... I am the source of your unhappiness, as you are of mine. I beg you to consent to a separation to set my conscience and yours at rest. I shall send my confessor to discuss it with you.

The Grand Duke replied,

I do not know if your unhappiness could have exceeded mine. Although everybody else has done justice to the many signs of respect, consideration and love which I have never tired of showing you for nearly twelve years, you have regarded them with the utmost indifference ... I await the father confessor you are sending to learn what he has to say on your behalf ...

Meanwhile I am giving orders that besides proper attendants and conveniences Your Highness will receive [at Poggio a Caiano] all the respect which is your due.

Hearing that the marriage had reached this sad pass, Louis XIV sent yet another envoy to Tuscany, this time the Bishop of Marseilles. The Bishop found the Grand Duchess established at Poggio a Caiano with an extremely large household numbering over a hundred and fifty servants and attendants. Her conduct and movements were closely regulated – she was followed everywhere and nobody could visit her without the Grand Duke's express permission – but, as the Bishop discovered, although full of complaints about her husband, she was far from downcast. Indeed, she was 'lively and brilliant, bold and enterprising . . . playful and merry'. It seemed not at all surprising to the Bishop that the Grand Duke, so 'melancholy and sombre' himself, should be so continually at variance with her. Yet the Bishop hoped that some sort of reconciliation could nevertheless be patched up. Between the dancing and the dinners, the music and comedies with which the tireless Grand Duchess regaled him, he managed to find out what her principal grievances were. But when the Grand Duke promised to redress them, she was still not satisfied. 'Having tried in vain for twelve long years to change her feelings, she could not alter them now.' Besides, she could not continue to live with him 'without offending God' for she had been married to him under duress so was not really his wife at all. At length the Bishop was forced to conclude that his mission was hopeless, and in May 1673 he returned to France to report to the King.

Louis and Cosimo both thought that, if a formal separation had to be approved, Marguerite-Louise ought to remain in Tuscany for the sake of appearances. But the Grand Duchess was determined to go home to France, and on 26 December 1674 permission was at last given her to do so. She was to retire to the convent at Montmartre. She saw to it that she did not go empty-handed. As well as a generous pension and lavish expenses for her journey, she was to be allowed to take hangings and beds as well as 10,000 crowns' worth of silver. In fact, she took a great deal more. She removed several valuable articles from Poggio a Caiano, and gave away so much money before she left that she had to ask for more in case she found herself 'penniless on the highway'.

As might be expected, she did not remain long in seclusion at Montmartre. At first she behaved with due piety and resignation, but soon she was off to Versailles, with Louis XIV's permission. Letters from her demanding more money arrived in Florence by regular posts. She took to gambling, to wearing double layers of patches, thick rouge and a yellow wig. She was as talkative and restless as ever. She was rumoured to be having an affair with the Comte de Louvigny, with an adjutant in the Maréchal de Luxembourg's guards, as well as with a guardsman in the same regiment. Later she took a fancy to her groom who cracked nuts for her with his teeth, was allowed to win money from her at cards and who helped her to take a bath. She got deeper and deeper in debt, demanding another 20,000 crowns from Cosimo, who exasperated her by the inordinately long time he took in replying to her urgent letters. She created uproar at Montmartre by furiously chasing a young, newly appointed abbess through the convent for having dared to criticize her conduct, brandishing a hatchet in one hand and a pistol in the other. After this escapade she obtained permission to leave Montmartre for the smaller community of Saint-Mandé where she soon took another lover, this time a renegade monk.

But she was now forty-seven and beginning to show signs of becoming less unruly. She professed herself shocked by the goings-on at Saint-Mandé where the nuns climbed over the walls at night and the Mother Superior, dressed as a man, disappeared for months on end. Impressed by her reformist zeal, the Archbishop appointed her Mother Superior in place of the absconding transvestite. Four years later she inherited a handsome fortune from her sister, and so had no further need to bother Cosimo for money. She lived to the age of seventy-six, endlessly talking about her past, yet protesting that she never regretted having left Tuscany. 'Ah!' she would say. 'I care little about that so long as I never have to set eyes on the Grand Duke again.'

The Grand Duke, for his part, had marked the departure of his tiresome wife by loading his tables with the most exotic foods and his guests with the most splendid presents as if anxious to show that he was far from being as mean as the Grand Duchess's supporters had suggested, and that he was still as rich as the Medici had always been supposed to be, though in fact no longer were. His banquets were supervised by foreign servants in their national costumes; his capons, weighed in front of him, were sent back to the kitchen if they did not turn the scales at twenty pounds; his pastries and jellies were presented to him in the form of castles and heraldic beasts; his wines were cooled in snow. He himself consumed gargantuan platefuls of the richest delicacies, becoming fatter than ever with a complexion not so much ruddy as inflamed.

In other ways he was less indulgent. His Christianity became more and more narrow. Sexual intercourse between Jews and Christians was strictly forbidden, and any Christian prostitute who leased her body to a Jew was whipped before being sent to prison, while the Jew who hired her was heavily fined. Fines were also imposed on Christians who worked as servants or shop assistants for Jewish masters. If they could not pay the fine they were stretched on the rack when fit enough to bear the torture or, when not, imprisoned. In obedience to the wishes of the Inquisition, scientists and philosophers were no longer afforded the protection they had been accustomed to receive from the Medici. The staff at the University of Pisa were expressly forbidden by the Grand Duke's personal command 'to read or teach, in public or in private, by writing or lecturing the philo-sophy of Democritus', expounder of the atomic theory of the universe. And, for fear lest they should be contaminated by contact with such theories at other universities, Tuscan students were not permitted to attend any academic institutions beyond the borders of the Grand Duchy.

In his determination to stamp out immorality as well as heresies, Cosimo banned the May Day festival of the *Calendimaggio* on account of its supposedly pagan origins. Girls who persisted in singing the songs of May in the streets were liable to be whipped. At the same time an edict was issued forbidding young men and girls to dally at doors and windows by night, a practice condemned as 'a great incentive to rapes, abortions and infanticides'. Men could be, and were, tortured on the rack for making love to girls with whom they were officially forbidden to consort, and beheading was the punishment for sodomy as well as for all manner of crimes against property. Public executions became so common, in fact, that in one year well over two thousand were carried out in the city. Murderers were not merely executed but afterwards quartered, and Cosimo would have have had one particular murderer tortured with red-hot pincers had not the magistrate advised him against it 'because of the disgust that it would give the city'.

Yet Cosimo constantly did disgust the city by his burdensome taxes and other financial exactions. Scarcely a month passed without the imposition of some new tax, while the existing rates were perpetually being increased. The clergy were largely exempt, just as they usually escaped punishment for criminal offences, except in the case of particularly notorious crimes like those of the priest who persuaded numerous young women of his congregation that, with his help, they might give birth to the Holy Spirit whose appearance in human shape was imminent. But if little money was exacted from the clergy, prostitutes were a lucrative source of revenue. They were compelled to buy licences to perambulate the streets at night, and they were fined if they did so without a lighted torch. They had to pay six crowns a year for immunity from arbitrary arrest by agents of the Office of Public Decency who might otherwise pounce on them for some such trivial breach of the regulations governing their conduct as not wearing the prescribed yellow ribbon in their hat or hair. Women thus caught were then marched off to prison from which the public executioner would whip them to the old market place with a placard reading 'For Whoredom' hung over their breasts.

Cosimo also raised large sums of money by selling merchants the exclusive right to deal in certain essential commodities such as flour or salt – and then, for a fee, issuing tradesmen with special licences enabling them to evade the monopoly. Savage punishments were devised for those who attempted to side-step the regulations: bakers caught trying to avoid the flour monopoly were threatened with the galleys; and extracting salt from fish brine was declared a capital offence. Occasionally the money raised by taxation and the sale of monopolies was used for some worthwhile purpose, the purchase of books for the Grand Ducal library or miniatures to add to the collection formed by Cardinal Leopoldo. More often it would be lavished on expensive gifts of gloves or scent, on cases of Chianti to some person Cosimo had met in England, on holy relics of dubious provenance, or on some new extravagance at Court.

No member of that Court was more extravagant than the Grand Duke's younger brother, Francesco Maria, the latest cardinal in the family. Cheerful, carefree and immensely fat, Francesco Maria had moved to Lappeggi on his uncle Mattias's death, but the villa was not nearly grand enough for his taste. He asked the architect, Antonio Ferri, to make various suggestions for its embellishment. Of the designs submitted he unerringly picked the most imposing and asked what it would cost. Ferri named a sum which was more than the Cardinal had at his disposal. 'And if I spend no more than thirty thousand crowns, but still have the work carried out to this design, how long would it last?' Ferri reckoned he could guarantee it would stand for eighteen years. 'In that case carry on,' the Cardinal instructed him. 'Eighteen years is enough; it will serve out my time.'[1]

The work was soon finished. The gardens were laid out to rival those at Pratolino, and Francesco Maria settled down to indulge himself for his appointed span. He had an infinite capacity for self-indulgence. He loved scent, and so one of the rooms at Lappeggi was turned into a perfumery. He loved the company of young men, so he filled the villa with them, inviting them to gamble at his expense and to wait on him at table, dressed as girls. He had a passion for eating, so dosed himself with emetics to make room for a second dinner after his first. He enjoyed practical jokes, so he lavished money on those who could devise amusing ones and help him perpetrate them. He lavished money, too on his servants and would throw packets of coins from the villa windows onto the lawn where they wrestled for them both with each other and with the peasants of the neighbourhood. His servants cheated him at every opportunity, but he affected not to care and even to encourage them in their pilfering. At Easter he would have them brought before him to confess, and would then give them absolution, announcing that he willingly presented them with all they had taken. In constant need of more money he pursued new benefices and stipends with unremitting assiduity, and, if he obtained them, handed over the work involved to a secretary.

It naturally distressed Cosimo deeply that this lazy, insanely extravagant brother of his should have so much influence over his heir, the Grand Prince Ferdinando. Ferdinando had grown into a good looking young man, sprightly and amusing, intelligent, artistic and independent, with far more in common with his French mother than with his lugubrious father. By the age of fifteen he had already mastered the difficult art of ivory-turning and produced pieces of which any collector would have been proud. He was also a gifted musician, an excellent performer on the harpsichord and a singer of unusual skill and charm. In later years he had a theatre built on the third floor of the Villa Pratolino and – unlike his uncle Francesco Maria who instructed the actors at Lappeggi to gabble through their parts in case he went to sleep in the middle of the performance – Ferdinando was responsible for the production at Pratolino of some remarkable works, including five operas by Alessandro Scarlatti with whom he conducted a long correspondence. He also corresponded with Jacopo Peri, Bernardo Pasquini and Handel, all of whom were invited to Florence to collaborate with him and his designers on various productions which gained high credit in musical circles all over Europe. Ferdinando was also a master impresario of pageants and was responsible for that memorable joust in the Piazza Santa Croce on Shrove Tuesday 1689 when a huge audience in wooden stands erected all round the square were regaled with a tournament between magnificently apparelled teams of European and Asian knights. Above all, as a patron and collector, he was both discriminating and eclectic, as good a judge of ceramics as of painting. He bought pictures by Raphael and Andrea del Sarto; he purchased Parmigianino's unfinished *Madonna dal Collo Lungo*; he employed Sebastiano Ricci and Giuseppe Maria Crespi at the Pitti Palace when they were both almost unknown; he saved altarpieces from neglect in Florentine churches – amongst others, Raphael's *Madonna del*

Baldacchino and Fra Bartolommeo's *San Marco* – and paid for copies to replace them. On St Luke's Day 1701, in the cloister of Santissima Annunziata he organized the first formal exhibition of paintings to be held in Florence, lent several pictures from his own collection and prepared the catalogue.

Yet, for all his talents and panache, Ferdinando was a disappointment to his father. Apart from anything else, there was his unfortunate passion for handsome singers, first for one Petrillo, who was found one day by the Prince's tutor hugging and kissing him; and subsequently for a conceited Venetian *castrato*, Cecchino, who, having insinuated himself into his household, was to wield great influence over him. The Grand Duke decided that the sooner Ferdinando was married the better. He needed a wife to remove him from the bad influence of Cecchino and Cardinal Francesco Maria. The dynasty also needed an heir. Moreover, the obligations of marriage might awaken Ferdinando to the responsibilities of government for which at present he showed so little aptitude. Unfortunately the bride selected for him was scarcely likely to interest Ferdinando in the least.

Princess Violante Beatrice of Bavaria was a plain young woman, timid and impressionable. She adored her husband from the first moment she saw him, but he made no secret of the fact that he was marrying her only because his father had told him to. The marriage took place on a day so cold that two soldiers on guard at the Porta San Gallo froze to death, and the sixteen-year-old bride buried her face in her muff on the way from the Cathedral to the Pitti Palace. She had never been so cold, she said miserably. But she rarely complained again. She bored her husband and was sensible enough to realize that grumbling would merely turn boredom into dislike. He virtually ignored her. And anyway, she turned out to be barren. One day he left for Venice, where he contracted syphilis from a lady of noble family. And then, to the horror of the domineering Cecchino and to his patient wife's distress, he added insult to injury by returning to Florence with a young mistress.

XXIV

THE LAST OF THE MEDICI

*'Florence is much sunk from
what it was'*

SINCE NO heir could be expected from Ferdinando, the Grand Duke
Cosimo turned his attention to his second son, Gian Gastone.
Previously he had not given much thought to him, and Gian
Gastone was certainly not a young man who commanded much attention. Introspective, lonely, unhappy, he spent most of his time by himself, shunning the noisy, extravagant circles in which his brother and
uncle lived, preferring to spend his time in botanical or antiquarian
studies or in learning foreign languages, including English. He was a
pleasant-looking man, gentle and considerate, but he had no close friends
of either sex and evidently no ambitions. He certainly had no ambition
to be a husband, and he contemplated the prospect of marriage to the
bride selected for him with the deepest apprehension. The apprehension turned to horror when he saw her, for Anna Maria Francesca,
daughter of the Duke of Saxe-Lauenberg and widow of the Count
Palantine, Philip of Neuberg, was a woman of truly exceptional
ugliness. She was also stupid and quarrelsome, 'of enormous weight,
immense self-will and no personal attractions'. She had few interests
other than the more strenuous outdoor sports, and seemed quite
content to spend the rest of her life in her dank, ugly castle in the
gloomy, dispiriting village of Reichstadt near Prague to which she
took her reluctant husband after their marriage in the chapel of the
Elector's palace in July 1697. Both the place and the woman disgusted
him. Of stronger homosexual tendencies than his brother, he com-

forted himself with a sly but pretty groom, Giuliano Dami, and thought of little but escape from the slough of hovels and sedgebeds that was his prison.

In the spring of the next year he went unaccompanied and incognito to Paris, to the fury of his father who upbraided him for demeaning the Medici by a visit conducted in such poor style. Soon after his return he left for Prague, taking his paramour, the groom, with him. There, he tried to forget the misery of his life at Reichstadt by gambling, making love with impoverished students and streetboys, and getting drunk in low taverns where he 'grew accustomed to wallow and debauch, smoking tobacco and chewing long peppers with bread and cummin-seed in order to drink more heavily in the German fashion'. After a time he braced himself to return to his wife at Reichstadt where he was more miserable than ever. He spent hours on end alone in his room, gazing out of the window at the doleful view, bursting into tears, rarely able to bring himself to answer letters or even to sign documents written for him by his secretary. Occasionally he roused himself from his torpor, drinking to excess and gambling with his Italian attendants – to whom he lost so much money that he was driven to pawn his wife's jewels for less than half their value. He begged his wife, who spent most of the day 'holding conversations in the stables', to come with him to Florence where they could be miserable in less depressing surroundings. She refused, however, to leave Reichstadt for which she had an unaccountable attachment. In any case, so her confessor warned her, she would undoubtedly be murdered in Florence, a fate that sooner or later overtook all wives of the Medici.

In Florence, Cosimo grew old in worry and disappointment. Years of over-eating and lack of exercise had led to a breakdown in his health, an 'overflow of bile' which he had been advised to counteract by 'a severe Pythagorean regimen', a plain diet of fruit and vegetables, and vigorous hunting and riding. He had followed the advice, but an improvement in his health had not been matched by any elevation of his spirits. He had been much disheartened by the difficulties he had encountered in finding a husband for his favourite child, his daughter, Anna Maria, a tall, dark-haired, rather gauche girl with a masculine voice and a loud laugh. She had been turned down not only by Spain and Portugal, but also by the Duke of Savoy and the Dauphin. Eventually she was accepted by William, the Elector Palatine, who married her at Innsbrück and soon afterwards infected her with a venereal disease which was held responsible for the miscarriages that marred her early life.

Despairing of ever seeing an heir produced by any of his children, Cosimo turned to his brother, Francesco Maria. The Cardinal was horrified. He had never felt the need of a wife, and he certainly did not want one now. To marry would entail foregoing most of the pleasures of Lappeggi; it would also mean giving up his cardinal's hat. He was forty-eight, set in his ways, and he had not been feeling very well lately. In the end, though, he had to give way. But the bride that was found for him, the twenty-year-old Princess Eleonora, daughter of the Duke of Guastalla and Sabbioneta, was as reluctant to marry him as he was to marry her. She was reminded of the great honour which was being bestowed upon her family, but she was not so much concerned with honour as with the prospect of having to go to bed with a gouty, fat, blotchy-faced man who was known to prefer pretty boys. For the first few weeks of the marriage, indeed, she could not be persuaded to go to bed with him at all; and when she did, induced at last by her husband's kindness and patience, she was unable to hide her distaste. Francesco Maria seems to have found the experience painful as well as debilitating. It was, in fact, altogether too much for him, and within two years he was dead.

His nephew, Ferdinando, whose marriage to Princess Violante had been quite as disastrous, did not long survive him. Ferdinando had never been properly cured of the disease he had contracted in Venice. At the time of Francesco Maria's marriage his memory had gone, and he spent most of the day in a kind of stupor broken by epileptic fits. He died at the end of October 1713. Less than three years later his brother-in-law, the Elector Palatine, also died; and the Elector Palatine's widow, Anna Maria, prepared to go home to Florence.

Her brother, Gian Gastone, was already there. Leaving his wife in her grim valley, Gian Gastone had returned to Florence in 1708, at the age of thirty-seven. Since then he had been living in seclusion, talking to few people other than Giuliano Dami, frequently so drunk that he was unable to keep a seat on his horse, spending every evening in an alcoholic daze, suffering from asthma, so apathetic that he declined to open any letters to avoid having to answer them. 'Some fear that he will predecease his father which would not be surprising,' wrote a French visitor to Florence, 'because the Grand Duke has a robust constitution and takes great care of his health, whereas his son seems merely to accelerate his death.'

Cosimo had long since dismissed Gian Gastone from his affections, and in the problem of the Tuscan succession had been anxious only to protect the interests of his daughter, Anna Maria. At one time he had been inclined to follow the advice of his Council and decree that the sovereignty of the State should revert to its citizens as in the days of the early Republic. But then he had decided that if Anna Maria survived her brothers, she ought to be Grand Duchess before the Republic was revived. This led to a diplomatic squabble which went on for years: the Emperor, Charles VI, put in a claim to the succession; the House of Este also came forward as claimants; so did Philip V of Spain and Elizabeth Farnese. Worried and harassed by the apparently intractable problem, Cosimo endeavoured to escape from it into the comfort of his religion.

Some years before he had made a pilgrimage to Rome where he had fulfilled a lifetime's ambition by being appointed a canon of St John in Lateran which accorded him the right to touch the *Volto Santo*, the handkerchief that Christ had used on his way to Calvary; and ever since that day when he had held in his hands this sanctified cloth he had become, so it was said, more pious than ever. Having presented the Pope with a painting of the Annunciation worth 200,000 crowns, he had returned to Florence with boxes full of relics, a sacred collection to which he soon afterwards added a piece of St Francis Xavier's intestines. He would show these relics to privileged visitors with the utmost reverence, and would humbly fall on his knees before them. An English tourist was assured that he had a machine in his own apartment whereon were fix'd little images in silver of every saint in the calendar. The machine was made to turn so as to present in front the saint of the day, before which he continually perform'd his offices ... He visited five or six churches every day.

His zeal for gaining converts to the Catholic faith was boundless. He spent hours on end teaching the Christian doctrine with infinite patience to three cheeky little Cossack boys who had been presented to him by the Bishop of Cracow, and he provided handsome pensions to foreign Protestants who abandoned their faith for his own. He was equally zealous in ridding Florence of works of art which he thought might give rise to lascivious thoughts. He had Baccio Bandinelli's marble statue of Adam and Eve removed from the Cathedral, and he even considered having the nude statues on display in the Uffizi hidden from view when told by priests that some people found them disturbingly erotic. His own life was ascetic in its self-restraint: he ate only the plainest food, and nearly always alone; he drank nothing but water; he went to bed very early and rose soon after dawn; he never went near a fire. He had outgrown most of his faults, except bigotry; yet few people had ever learned to love him. Now that he was over eighty he was treated with a kind of wary respect. No longer did the mob gather threateningly beneath his windows, shouting for bread, plastering insulting placards onto the palace walls. But on those rare occasions when he left the palace in a slow-moving, two-horse carriage, surrounded by Swiss guards with halberds, footmen and pages, though men bowed to him, there was no cheering. And when at last he died, on 31 October 1723, there was little grief.

Florence had other causes for sorrow. The city was a sad place now, poor, gloomy and disconsolate. Tourists reported it as being full of beggars, vagabonds and monks, passing in dreary procession beneath dark buildings with windows of torn oiled paper. A generation before, Gilbert Burnet, Bishop of Salisbury, lamented the pitiable condition into which it had fallen. 'Florence is much sunk from what it was,' he wrote, 'for they do not reckon there are above fifty thousand souls in it . . . As one goes over Tuscany, it appears so dispeopled that one cannot but wonder to find a country that hath been a scene of so much action now so forsaken and so poor.'

THE LAST OF THE MEDICI

Subsequent travellers were similarly dismayed. 'The declining state of this city is very visible,' reported one of them,

a great deal of the ground within the walls being unbuilt, and many of the houses ill-inhabited, so that it is not very populous; nor are the inhabitants useful, the clergy making up the bulk of the people ... I counted above four thousand monks and friars in one procession.

Despite the burdensome taxation imposed upon the people by Cosimo who had authorized a new form of income-tax on his death-bed, the State was almost bankrupt. So were many of the noble families whose ancestors had been so rich and so hospitable. Now guests were rarely invited to anything more exciting than a card party or a *conversazione*, at which nothing except lemonade, coffee or tea would be served with an occasional ice-cream – the nobles finding it difficult enough to pay for their own food, which was often brought in from some nearby cook-shop, let alone for the numerous servants who hung about their gateways in the hope of better times.

Better times could hardly be expected under Cosimo's successor, Gian Gastone, fifty-two was not expected to overcome his indolence, his alcoholism or his taste for slovenly lubricity. He began his rule well enough, displaying a genuine concern for the welfare of the people and disdaining to spend money in the flamboyant manner of most of his relations. He reduced the intolerable level of taxation and lowered the price of corn; he discontinued public executions and provided the city's beggars with a decent workhouse; he freed the government from the stranglehold of the Church which under Cosimo III had gripped it so tightly; he restored to scientists and scholars the freedom that had lately been denied them; and he rescinded the laws which had been passed against the Jews. But soon his constitutional sloth overcame him and he took to spending most of his time in bed; the crafty Giuliano Dami kept unwanted visitors at bay, and dealt with the craftsmen and antiquaries who relied on the Grand Duke's lazy good nature to sell him objects that no dis-criminating collector would ever wish to possess.

Giuliano Dami also provided Gian Gastone with that motley troupe of young companions, male and female, but mostly rowdy boys, who were collectively known as *Ruspanti* after the coins – the *ruspi* – with which they were paid for their services. These *Ruspanti*, often handsome youths from the poorest Florentine families, were required to entertain the Grand Duke by rollicking about in his room, shouting insults and obscenities, and, when his fancy ran that way, drawing him into their horse-play. Sometimes he would give a splendid dinner, calling them by the names of his ministers or other leading citizens of Florence, proposing toasts to these suddenly trans-mogrified celebrities. Then, after the meal was over, he would persuade them for his pleasure to make love to each other. Every month the number of *Ruspanti* grew until by the end of 1731 there were nearly four hundred of them. As they grew in numbers, so also they grew more troublesome and violent, raising riots in the Boboli gardens, and raiding the cookshops and the stalls in the market when their wages were in arrears.

Gian Gastone's sister-in-law, Violante, who had chosen to remain in Italy after the death of Prince Ferdinando, tried to interest the Grand Duke in less degrading pleasures than the *Ruspanti* afforded him. She organized banquets to which she invited the most amusing and accomplished people to entertain him. He merely got incapably drunk, swearing and belching as he ate his food, making occasional comments of indescribable lewdness. At one peculiarly embarrassing dinner, after vomiting into his napkin, he took off his wig and wiped his mouth with it.

Most of his meals, however, were eaten in bed; dinner at five o'clock in the afternoon, supper at two in the morning. Before dinner he would receive those few official visitors to whom he accorded admittance. Propped against pillows, surrounded by freshly picked roses to give sweetness to the fusty air of the bedroom, he wore a shirt covered with snuff, a long cravat and a nightcap. Rarely did he emerge from the room and then only to disprove rumours that he was dead. Thus, he appeared on St John the Baptist's Day in 1729. Having got drunk beforehand to make the ordeal more tolerable, he lolled about in his carriage, poking his head from the window from time to time in order to be sick into the street. At the Porta al Prato he stumbled out to watch the horse races during which he shouted obscenities at his pages and the ladies around him; then, having fallen asleep, he was conveyed back to the Pitti Palace in a litter. Thereafter he scarcely ever left it. Once he was carried in a sedan-chair to the notorious baths at San Sperandino; and once, wearing a straw hat and a dressing-gown, he was taken in a litter to the villa of Poggio Imperiale. But most of his days he spent in bed where, in June 1737, he was found dying by the Prince de Craon, representative of Maria Theresa's husband Francis, Duke of Lorraine, whom the European powers – without bothering to consult Gian Gastone – had decided should be his heir. 'The Grand Duke is in a pitiable condition,' the Prince de Craon reported to the Duke of Lorraine. 'He could not get out of bed; he had a long beard; his sheets were very dirty, his eyesight weak, his voice low and muffled. Altogether he had the air of a man who had not a month to live.' The Prince was right. The Grand Duke Gian Gastone died on 9 July 1737 at the age of sixty-five.

The six thousand Austrian troops of the new regime had already crossed the frontier, and all important appointments in the government had been assigned to foreigners. Tuscany was to become a mere appendage of the Austrian empire, while the Medici's last representative, Anna Maria, the Electress Palatine, was permitted to live out her days in her apartments at the Pitti Palace.

A tall, dignified, rather haughty and stiff-backed old lady, she had strongly disapproved of her younger brother's conduct and had, after many painful interviews and insulting dismissals, prevailed upon him to accept the ministrations of the Church before he died. She was profoundly religious herself, and on the rare occasions when she drove out of the Palace courtyard, 'with guards and eight horses to her coach', observers could be fairly sure that she was either going to Mass, to donate money to one of her favourite charities, or to inspect progress on the family mausoleum at San Lorenzo, work on which had been abandoned but was now resumed again at her expense. She received few visitors, and when she did so, as the poet Thomas Gray discovered, she remained standing and unsmiling beneath a black canopy in a comfortless room full of silver furniture. She was always very conscious of the fact that she was the last of the Medici.

So were the people of Florence. Resentful and humiliated to be once again ruled by foreigners whose cannon in the city's fortresses were turned against them, they looked back to the great days of the Medici with pride and a sense of loss. They watched with deep regret as the Medici balls were taken down from public buildings and replaced with shields emblazoned with fleurs-de-lis, an eagle and the cross of Lorraine. They were outraged when they heard that the celebrations of the birthday of Cosimo *Pater Patriae*, of the elevation of Pope Clement VII, of the election of Duke Cosimo I, and all the public holidays connected with the Medici were to be abolished. They would have given two-thirds of all they possessed to have the Medici back, the French scholar Charles de Brosses decided, after a visit to Tuscany at this time; 'and they would give the other third to get rid of the Lorrainers . . . They hate them.' When Anna Maria died in February 1743, at the age of seventy-five, all the town was in tears for the loss of her, the British envoy's assistant reported:

The common people are convinced she went off in a hurricane of wind; a most violent one began this morning and lasted for about two hours, and now the sun shines as bright as ever – this is proof. Besides, for a stronger, just the same thing happened when John Gaston went off. Nothing can destroy this opinion which people think they have been eye-witnesses to ... On the Monday morning her Confessor by a stratagem was carried to her, for she would not have him sent for and ... he was bid to tell her she must soon die, to which she answered by asking him with some emotion, 'Who told you so?' He replied: 'Her physicians.'

'Very well, then let us do what there is to be done; and do it quickly.' So they brought her the Communion ... She was sensible to the last, but she did not speak for about an hour and a half before she died ... She has lain in state in the great hall of the palace since Thursday morning, and is to be buried tonight ... [So] the poor remains of the Medici is soon to join her ancestors.

The family mausoleum at San Lorenzo is not, however, her true memorial. In her will she bequeathed to the new Grand Duke and his successors all the property of the Medici, their palaces and villas, their pictures and statues, their jewels and furniture, their books and manuscripts – all the vast store of works of art assembled by her ancestors, generation after generation. She made one condition: nothing should ever be removed from Florence where the treasures of the Medici should always be available for the pleasure and benefit of the people of the whole world.[1]

NOTES ON BUILDINGS AND
WORKS OF ART

CHAPTER I (pages 19–29)

1. The PALAZZO DELLA SIGNORIA, or Palazzo Vecchio, the seat of the city's government, was begun in 1299 and enlarged and altered at various times up till the end of the sixteenth century. The courtyard was rebuilt by Michelozzo Michelozzi in the 1440s. The Sala del Maggior Consiglio was formed to accommodate the Grand Council in the time of Savonarola. During the reign of Duke Cosimo I, who moved here from the Medici Palace in 1540, the palace was remodelled and redecorated by Giorgio Vasari. When Duke Cosimo took up residence in the Pitti Palace, he handed over the Palazzo della Signoria to his son, Francesco, for whose bride, the Archduchess Joanna of Austria, the courtyard was specially decorated.

2. There has been a bridge where the PONTE VECCHIO now stands since Roman times. The present structure, which replaced a twelfth century bridge destroyed by the floods of 1333, was built in 1345. At that time most of the shops on the bridge were occupied by tanners and pursemakers. The butchers who succeeded them were replaced by goldsmiths and jewellers at the end of the sixteenth century on the orders of Grand Duke Ferdinando I.

3. ORSANMICHELE derives its name from the ancient oratory of San Michele in Orto which originally occupied the site. The present building, started in 1336, was designed for use as a communal granary as well as a chapel. The statues in the niches along the outside walls were commissioned by the city's guilds. The original of Donatello's marble *St George* which was made for the Armourers' Guild, and a copy of which stands in the most westerly niche on the northern wall, is now in the Bargello.

4. The MERCATO VECCHIO was demolished at the end of the nineteenth century to make way for the present Piazza della Repubblica.

5. VIA CALIMALA which literally means Street of Ill Fame is perhaps a corruption of the Roman Callis Major.

6. The church and convent of SANTA CROCE in the Piazza Santa Croce was built between 1228 and 1385. In 1863, the distinctive marble façade was added to a seventeenth-century design. The tombs of Michelangelo and of Cosimo de'

Medici's friends Leonardo Bruni, Carlo Marsuppini and Vespasiano da Bisticci are all here; as also are the chapels of several of the leading families of Florence, including those of the Bardi family into which Cosimo married. The Novices' Chapel was built for Cosimo by Michelozzo in about 1445.

7. The BARGELLO known as the Palazzo del Podestà in the fifteenth century was originally built as the city hall in 1254–5. It was reconstructed in the middle of the fourteenth century when the stairway in the courtyard was built. In 1574 it became the residence of the Chief of Police. It is now the Museo Nazionale and contains many busts and statues of the Medici family as well as works of art commissioned by them.

8. The Alberti family palace in the Via de' Benci (no. 6) is now the MUSEO HORNE. The Alberti were responsible for the chancel in Santa Croce.

9. The PALAZZO RUCELLAI, which was finished in the 1450s, is in the Via della Vigna Nuova (no. 18). It was built by Bernardo Rossellino after a design by Leon Battista Alberti. Alberti was also commissioned by Giovanni Rucellai to design the façade of the Dominican church of Santa Maria Novella which contains the Rucellai chapel. Part of the restored Rucellai gardens, the ORTI ORICELLARI, can be seen between the railway station and the Porta al Prato.

10. Niccolò da Uzzano lived in the Via de' Bardi in the palace now known as the PALAZZO CAPPONI (no: 36).

CHAPTER II (pages 30–41)

1. The number of *palle* (or balls) on the MEDICI EMBLEM was never fixed. Originally there were twelve; but there were usually seven in Cosimo de' Medici's time – as on the shield on the south-east corner of the Medici palace – though there are only six at the corners of Verrocchio's roundel in the chancel at San Lorenzo. There are eight on the ceiling of the old sacristy at San Lorenzo, five on Duke Cosimo's tomb in the Capella dei Principi and six on the Grand Duke Ferdinando's arms on the entrance to the Forte di Belvedere.

2. Work on the Cathedral of SANTA MARIA DEL FIORE, known as the DUOMO, was begun towards the end of the thirteenth century to a design by Arnolfo di Cambio. Brunelleschi's dome was not finished until 1436 and the exterior was still not completed when he died ten years later. The neo-Gothic façade is late-nineteenth-century (see note 13 to Chapter XIII).

3. The Via Porta Rossa was then dominated by the PALAZZO DAVANZATI (no: 9). At that time it was owned by the Davizzi who had built it in about 1330. It is now a museum.

4. The MERCATO NUOVO, now known as the Straw Market, was built by Giovanni Battista del Tasso in 1547–59.

5. The FLORENTINE LILY appears less frequently on the buildings of Florence

than the *palle* of the Medici. One example is on the fifteenth-century doorway of the old Mint behind the Loggia dei Lanzi.

6. The Dominican church and monastery of SANTA MARIA NOVELLA was begun in the middle of the thirteenth century and finished in the sixteenth. The apartments which were built for Pope Martin V overlook the Chiostro Grande. The interior of the church was redecorated by Vasari in the 1560s. The Rucellai, Bardi and Strozzi all built chapels here. A chapel in the Chiostro Grande was redecorated for the visit of Giovanni di Lorenzo de' Medici, Pope Leo X, by Jacopo Carrucci Pontormo and Ridolfo Ghirlandaio in 1515.

7. The grim, late-thirteenth-century palace of the Spini family, now the PALAZZO SPINI-FERRONI is on the corner of Via Tornabuoni and Lungarno Acciaiuoli by the Ponte Santa Trinità. The next palazzo downstream is the fourteenth-century Palazzo Gianfigliazzi (see note 2 to chapter XVII). A few doors further down (Lungarno Corsini, 10) is the seventeenth-century PALAZZO CORSINI whose picture gallery is open to the public.

8. The monastery of Santa Maria degli Angeli has now been absorbed by the Hospital of Santa Maria Nuova. The octagonal chapel known as the ROTONDA DI SANTA MARIA ANGELI in the Via degli Alfani was started in 1434 to designs by Brunelleschi.

9. Tournaments were traditionally held in the PIAZZA SANTA CROCE where chariot races and the football game known as *calcio* were also played. A plaque dated 10 February 1565 marks the centre of the *calcio* field.

10. It was Palla Strozzi who commissioned Gentile da Fabriano to paint the altarpiece, the *Adoration of the Magi*, for the chapel of Palla's father, the CHAPEL OF ONOFRIO STROZZI in the church of Santa Trinità. The altarpiece, which contains portraits of various members of the Strozzi family, is now in the Uffizi. The STROZZI CHAPEL in the Dominican church of Santa Maria Novella has an altarpiece by Andrea Orcagna and murals by Nardo di Cione. The Strozzi family villa of Poggio a Caiano was later acquired by Lorenzo il Magnifico.

11. The VIA DE' BARDI was almost entirely redeveloped by the Bardi family. Before they built their palace (which no longer exists) the street was a slum known as the Borgo Pigiglioso (the Fleapit). The fourteenth-century BARDI CHAPEL in the church of Santa Croce contains murals by Giotto and his assistants.

12. Carlo di Cosimo de' Medici was also a collector in a modest way. Roger van der Weyden's *Entombment*, now in the Uffizi, was one of his pictures.

CHAPTER III (pages 42–53)

1. The medieval tower house of the ALBIZZI is in the Borgo degli Albizzi. The palazzo built by Rinaldo degli Albizzi no longer exists. PALAZZO ALTOVITI stands on its site at no. 88.

2. Domenico Veneziano's *Saints Francis and John the Baptist* from the Cavalcanti chapel is in the MUSEO DELL' OPERA DI SANTA CROCE. The Cavalcanti *Annunciation* by Donatello is in the church of Santa Croce.

3. The Studio Fiorentino has developed into the UNIVERSITÀ DEGLI STUDI. The present building near the Piazza San Marco was converted from the stables of the Grand Dukes of Tuscany. The botanical gardens to the north, the GIARDINO DEI SEMPLICI, which face onto the Via Lamarmora, were laid out on Cosimo I's instructions in the middle of the sixteenth century.

4. IL TREBBIO stands at the top of a hill about a mile from Cafaggiolo where the Medici had owned property for generations. According to Vasari the original medieval fortress was altered for Cosimo by Michelozzo who made it less bleak by rebuilding the courtyard, adding the loggia and the covered passage round the ramparts and tower. It was sold by the Medici to Giuliano Serragli in 1644. In 1864 it passed into the hands of Prince Marcantonio Borghese and was later bought by Dott. Enrico Scaretti who restored it in the 1930s. His widow, Lord Gladwyn's sister, is still living there at the time of writing.

5. The PALAZZO GUADAGNI in Piazza Santo Spirito (nos. 7–9) was built for the Dei family in the early sixteenth century. Donato Guadagni bought it in 1684.

6. The sixteenth-century PALAZZO PUCCI is in Via de' Pucci (nos. 2–4). The coat of-arms on the corner of Via de' Servi is that of Giovanni di Lorenzo de' Medici, Pope Leo X. The Pucci paid for the loggia in Santissima Annunziata which was designed by Caccini and finished in 1601. The Pucci Chapel flanks the eastern wall of the Chiostrino dei Voti in Santissima Annunziata where Verrocchio's now lost effigy of Lorenzo il Magnifico was displayed after his escape from assassination by the Pazzi. According to Vasari, Botticelli's tondo, the *Adoration of the Magi*, now in the National Gallery, London, was commissioned by the Pucci.

CHAPTER IV (pages 54–63)

1. The library at San Giorgio Maggiore in Venice has been destroyed; but the dormitory may have been begun by Michelozzo whose influence is apparent in the design.

2. The Acciaiuoli had several houses in the Borgo Santi Apostoli, including the PALAZZO DEGLI ACCIAIUOLI (nos. 3–10). Their palace on the Arno was destroyed in 1944 when the retreating Germans blew up the nearby bridge.

3. The PALAZZO GUICCIARDINI is in the Via Guicciardini. Francesco Guicciardini wrote his *History of Italy* in the Villa Ravia in the Via di Santa Margherita a Montici (no. 75).

4. The houses and palaces of the Peruzzi family were in the PIAZZA PERUZZI where several buildings bear the family emblem – pears. The PERUZZI CHAPEL in Santa Croce contains murals by Giotto and his assistants.

5. The CAPPONI CHAPEL in the church of Santa Felicità was built for the Barbadori who made over their rights in it to the Capponi in 1525.
6. The church of San Pier Scheraggio was pulled down to make way for the Uffizi.
7. The MARTELLI CHAPEL is in the Basilica of San Lorenzo. It has an altarpiece by Fra Filippo Lippi.
8. The VILLA OF CAREGGI was purchased in 1417 by Cosimo de' Medici's brother, Lorenzo. Michelozzo enlarged it for Cosimo, and Giuliano da Sangallo added the loggias on the south side for Lorenzo il Magnifico. It was looted and damaged by fire after the flight from Florence of Lorenzo's son, Piero. Verrocchio's David, his terracotta Resurrection (both now at the Bargello) and his fountain of a little boy holding a spouting fish (now at the Palazzo della Signoria) were all commissioned by the Medici for this villa. Restored by the Grand Duke Cosimo I, it subsequently fell into disrepair and was sold by the Medici's successors to Count Vincenzo Orsi. It is now a hostel for staff of the Ospedale di Careggi.

CHAPTER V (pages 64–78)

1. Ficino's villa is now known as LE FONTANELLE.
2. Cosimo kept the MEDICI LIBRARY first at Careggi and later at the Medici Palace. Confiscated by the Signoria in 1494, when fines of as much as fifty florins were imposed on borrowers who did not return books immediately, it was transferred to San Marco at the suggestion of Savonarola. The library was bought back in 1508 by Pope Leo X who removed it to Rome. Returned to Florence by Clement VII, it was – in 1532 – placed in the building in the cloisters of San Lorenzo where it remains.
3. Long supposed to have once been a Roman temple, the octagonal black-and-white BAPTISTERY OF ST JOHN was probably built in the twelfth century. The portal surround to Pisano's bronze doors on the southern front are by Vittorio Ghiberti, Lorenzo's son.
4. Lorenzo Ghilberti's BRONZE DOORS on the northern front show scenes from the life of Christ with the four Evangelists and four Church Fathers.
5. The HOSPITAL OF SANTA MARIA NUOVA was founded in 1286 by Folco Portinari, the father of Dante's Beatrice.
6. Lorenzo Ghiberti's GILDED BRONZE DOORS on the eastern front contain a self-portrait of the artist whose bald head can be seen poking out of a round aperture.
7. The TOMB OF POPE JOHN XXIII in the Baptistery was designed by Donatello and, apart from the bronze effigy, made by Michelozzo.
8. In the building of the OSPEDALE DEGLI INNOCENTI, which faces onto the Piazza Santissima Annunziata, Brunelleschi was helped by his assistant

Francesco della Luna. The middle nine arches are theirs; the others were added in the sixteenth and seventeenth centuries. The medallions of swaddled babies were made by Andrea della Robbia.

9. The fourth-century basilica of SAN LORENZO had been replaced by another in the eleventh century. Brunelleschi's early Renaissance masterpiece was begun in 1421. The old sacristy, where Giovanni di Bicci de' Medici was buried, was completed in 1429. Brunelleschi did not live to finish the work; and his death in 1446 led to outbursts of violent quarrelling between various Florentine craftsmen who wanted to take over its direction and who appealed to Cosimo to support their conflicting claims. Giovanni di Domenico and Antonio Manetti, under Cosimo's personal direction, seem to have been largely responsible for finishing it.

10. Brunelleschi's carefully guarded secret was to provide a double cupola for the DOME OF SANTA MARIA DEL FIORE, the biggest in Europe, one dome inside another, each resting on a drum and bound together, the stones carefully dovetailing one into the next so that they were almost self-supporting.

11. Ghiberti's ST MATTHEW at Orsanmichele, which was made between 1419 and 1422, occupies the most northerly niche in the western wall. The bronze St *John the Baptist* and *St Stephen* are also by Ghiberti.

12. The NOVICES' CHAPEL was built about 1445 by Michelozzo. The glazed terracotta altarpiece is from Andrea della Robbia's studio. The Grand Duke Ferdinando II arranged for Galileo to be buried here in 1642.

13. Also know as the Rotonda, the CHOIR OF SANTISSIMA ANNUNZIATA was started by Michelozzo in 1451 and finished by Alberti in the 1470s.

14. The BADIA FIESOLANA at San Domenico di Fiesole was the cathedral of Fiesole until 1018. Rebuilding continued between 1456 and 1469 at Medici expense.

15. Michelozzo was working at SAN MARCO for Cosimo from 1437 to 1444 when his library was finished. The double-chambered cell at the end of the corridor by the library is the one used by Cosimo. Savonarola's cell is at the end of the western corridor.

16. The Via Larga is now known as the Via Cavour. The church of SAN GIOVAN-NINO DEGLI SCOLOPI was rebuilt in the sixteenth and seventeenth centuries by Bartolommeo Ammanati and by Giulio and Alfonso Parigi.

17. The MEDICI PALACE was built between 1444 and 1460. The 'kneeling windows' on the Via de' Gori front were subsequently replaced by flat, square bars of a more austere design. The iron rungs to be found on either side of these windows were intended for holding the staffs of banners or flambeaux and for tying up horses. The stone benches beneath them were provided not only for servants of visitors to the palace, but also for the convenience of any passers-by who might care to accept this modest offer of Medicean hospitality. According to the unreliable evidence of Giovanni Avogrado, the original palace had a polychrome

façade of red, white and green. The building narrowly escaped destruction in 1527 when the Medici were forced to flee from Florence after the sack of Rome. Michelangelo, an enthusiastic republican, proposed that it should be razed and that a piazza, known as the Square of the Mules in allusion to the illegitimate birth of the Medici Pope, Clement VII, should be built on the site. It survived, however, to be taken over by the State for the Trustees of Minors until reverting to Medici possession on their return to Florence in 1550. It remained in the possession of the Medici until 1659 when the Grand Duke Ferdinando II sold it to Marchese Gabrielle Riccardi. (The palace was much enlarged by the Riccardi who added another seven to the ten windows of the upper floors.) Purchased by the government of the Grand Duchy in 1814, it is now known as the Palazzo Medici-Riccardi and serves as the Prefecture.

18. Permission to attach these large spiked lamps to the walls of a palace had to be obtained from the government. Niccolò Grosso was given his nickname because he always insisted on payment in advance. *Caparra* means pledge.

19. CAFAGGIOLO was more like a fortress than a villa. Vasari described it as having 'all the requisites of a distinguished country house' with a pleasant garden, groves and fountains. But its high towers and battlemented arches were surrounded by a moat crossed by a drawbridge. It was bought, together with Il Trebbio, by Prince Borghese who had the central tower pulled down and the moat filled in. It now presents a rather desolate appearance and the garden has been taken over by dandelions and chickens.

20. The VILLA MEDICI – formerly BELCANTO – originally belonged to the Bardi. The reconstruction carried out for Giovanni de' Medici was finished in 1461. Sold by the Grand Duke Cosimo III in 1671, it was renovated in the 1770s for Horace Walpole's sister-in-law, the Countess of Orford; and in the nineteenth century was bought by the English painter and collector, William Blundell Spence, when it became known as the Villa Spence. More recently it belonged to Lady Sybil Cutting whose daughter, Marchesa Iris Origo, was brought up there.

CHAPTER VII (pages 90–98)

1. DONATELLO's *David* (c. 1430) is now in the Bargello. On its confiscation by the Grand Council after the expulsion of Piero de Medici in 1494 orders were given for it to be erected on a column in the courtyard of the Palazzo della Signoria.

2. DONATELLO's *Judith Slaying Holofernes* (c. 1460) was removed from the Medici Palace by order of the *Signoria* after the flight of the Medici in 1494. It was set up on the *ringhiera* at the Palazzo della Signoria – it now stands in front of the Palazzo – with an inscription on its base to the effect that it had been placed there as a warning to all tyrants: '*Exemplum.Sal[utis].Pub[licae].Cives.Pos[uere]*.

MCCCCXCV'. The original inscription read: 'Kingdoms fall through luxury. Cities rise through virtue. Behold the head of pride severed by humility. Piero di Cosimo de' Medici dedicates the statue of this woman to the liberty and fortitude bestowed on the Republic by the invincible and constant spirit of its citizens.'

3. Most of SANTA MARIA DEL CARMINE was destroyed by fire in the eighteenth century when it was rebuilt by Giuseppe Ruggieri and Giulio Mannaioni. The Brancacci chapel was, however, spared by the fire. The cycle of murals by Masaccio and Masolino was completed by Fra Filippo Lippi's son, Filippino Lippi.

4. FILIPPO LIPPI's *Coronation of the Virgins* is now in the Museo dell' Accademia (Via Ricasoli, 52).

5. FRA ANGELICO's *Crucifixion* is in the Chapter Room at San Marco on the opposite side of the cloister from the San Marco Museum which contains the high altar of San Marco with Cosimo's patron saints, Cosmas and Damian, shown kneeling on a carpet.

6. All the CELLS AT SAN MARCO are decorated by Fra Angelico and his assistants. Fra Angelico's *Annunciation* is at the top of the stairs to the dormitory corridor.

7. Giovanni di Bicci de' Medici's sarcophagus in the OLD SACRISTY AT SAN LORENZO is by Andrea Cavalcanti Buggiano. It is placed beneath a marble table on which are the seven red balls of the Medici emblem.

8. COSIMO'S MARBLE MEMORIAL in the chancel at San Lorenzo, the only memorial ever to be placed here, was designed by Verrocchio. The inscription reads:

Cosmus Medices
Hic situs est
Decreto Publico
Pater Patriae
Vixit
Annos LXXV Menses III Dies XX

CHAPTER VIII (pages 101–12)

1. In GHIRLANDAIO'S MURALS in the Cappella Maggiore at Santa Maria Novella, Lucrezia Tornabuoni, sister of the donor, Giovanni Tornabuoni, is represented as the third female figure on the right in the *Birth of the Baptist*.

2. The TABERNACLE OF THE CRUCIFIX in San Miniato al Monte was built for the crucifix of San Giovanni Gualberto, whose chapel, designed by Caccini, is in Santa Trinità. The Guild of the *Calimala*, which was responsible for the maintenance and ornamentation of San Miniato al Monte, gave permission for the tabernacle to be built provided that the guild's coat-of-arms was the only

one displayed on it. Piero de' Medici, however, insisted that his own arms – a falcon holding the Medici diamond ring with the motto 'semper' and three feathers – should also be displayed; and so they were.

3. The TABERNACLE OF SANTISSIMA ANNUNZIATA was made in about 1450. Like the tabernacle in San Miniato al Monte it was designed for Piero de' Medici, probably by Michelozzo.

4. LUCA DELLA ROBBIA'S SINGING-GALLERY is now in the Museo dell' Opera del Duomo (Piazza del Duomo, 9). Donatello's gallery is also here. They were both removed from the Cathedral in 1688 to make room for more singers at the wedding of Prince Ferdinand to Princess Violante Beatrice.

5. Work on the CAMPANILE began in the 1330s when Giotto was Capomaestro of the Cathedral works. Luca della Robbia's reliefs were done in the 1430s.

6. Part of LUCA DELLA ROBBIA'S GLAZED TERRACOTTA decorations made for Piero de' Medici's study are now in the Victoria and Albert Museum, London.

7. The three panels of UCCELLO's Rout of San Romano have been dispersed. One is in the Uffizi, another in the Louvre, the third in the National Gallery, London. The Florentine commander pictured in the National Gallery panel is Niccolò da Tolentino, the subject of the marvellous cenotaph memorial by Andrea del Castagno in the Duomo. The cenotaph next to it in the Duomo, a memorial to the English condottiere, John Hawkwood, is by Uccello.

8. POLLAIUOLO's Labours of Hercules are in the Uffizi. His Hercules and Antaeus is in the Bargello.

9. BOTTICELLI's Madonna of the Magnificat is in the Uffizi.

10. BOTTICELLI's Adoration of the Magi was painted as an altarpiece for Santa Maria Novella and is now in the Uffizi. According to Giorgio Vasari, the King holding out his hands towards the Holy Child's feet is Cosimo; the kneeling figure in the white robe is Giuliano, Lorenzo's brother; and the man behind him, 'shown gratefully adoring the child', is Cosimo's second son, Giovanni. The man on his knees in the centre foreground has been identified as Piero de' Medici; and the man on the extreme right in the saffron gown as Botticelli himself. The figure in the black gown with a red stripe down the shoulder may be an idealized portrait of Lorenzo il Magnifico.

11. BOTTICELLI's Fortitude is in the Uffizi.

12. FILIPPO LIPPI's The Virgin Adoring the Child was removed from the Medici Chapel in 1814 and is now in Berlin. The painting at present in the chapel is a copy by Neri di Bicci.

13. GENTILE DA FABRIANO's Adoration of the Magi is now in the Uffizi.

14. The pretty young man in blue near the front of the procession riding a prancing horse on which also sits a leopard is usually identified as Giuliano de' Medici, though it has been suggested that Gozzoli may have intended by way of a pleasant joke to represent the fearsome and cruel Castruccio Castracani degli Antelminelli, lord of Lucca, Florence's most powerful enemy in the

fourteenth century. The leopard was the symbol of the Castracani. In accordance with the custom of his time Gozzoli, of course, made little attempt to portray accurate likenesses being content to represent the people in his pictures by symbols and details immediately recognizable by their contemporaries.

15. VERROCCHIO'S TOMB FOR PIERO AND GIOVANNI in the old sacristy at San Lorenzo, a magnificent structure of serpentine, bronze, porphyry and marble, was finished in 1473.

CHAPTER IX (pages 113-27)

1. The RIDOLFI were shortly to build the palazzo on the corner of Via Maggio – now known as the Via Maggiore – and Via Mazzetta. It is now known as the Casa Guidi. This is where Elizabeth Barrett Browning died in 1861.

2. The fourteenth-century PALAZZO SALVIATI is on the corner of the Via della Vigna Vecchia and the Via Palmiere.

3. The BORGO SAN PIERO is now the Borgo degli Albizi.

4. The Abbey of CAMALDOLI, mother house of the Camaldolensians, was founded at the beginning of the eleventh century by St Romualdo. Its name derived from Campus Maldoli, the three-thousand-acre forest site presented to the order by one Maldolus, a rich merchant from Arezzo. The pharmacy is sixteenth-century, other buildings are mostly seventeenth-and eighteenth-century.

CHAPTER X (pages 128-43)

1. The family palace, now known as the PALAZZO PAZZI-QUARATESI, was built in the last quarter of the fifteenth century possibly to the designs of Giuliano da Sangallo, and is in the Via Proconsolo (no. 10). After the Pazzi conspiracy it passed into the hands of the Medici, then into those of Cibò and Strozzi.

2. The CHURCH OF SANT' APOSTOLI was built at about the same time as the Baptistery. The early-sixteenth-century main portal is by Benedetto da Rovezzano. The painted wooden roof is early-fourteenth-century.

3. After Brunelleschi's death the PAZZI CHAPEL was completed by Giuliano da Maiano who made the wooden doors. The terracotta decorations are by Luca della Robbia. The stained-glass window of St Andrew is a copy of the original now kept, with many other treasures, in the Museo dell' Opera di Santa Croce, which is approached from the cloisters.

4. The SCOPPIO DEL CARRO has been resumed. It used to take place at Midnight Mass on Easter Saturday. Now the ceremony is performed at noon on Easter Day. The flints are collected from the church of Sant' Apostoli and, at the appointed hour, in front of the High Altar of the Cathedral, they are used to

strike sparks which ignite a rocket, shaped like a dove. The dove shoots along a wire out of the Cathedral and into the Piazza where, it is earnestly hoped, it will reach a cart full of fireworks, set the fireworks ablaze and then fall back down the wire into the Cathedral. The operation successfully performed gives promise of a good harvest.

CHAPTER XI (pages 144–55)

1. The severe and unflattering *Portrait of a Young Woman* by BOTTICELLI in the Pitti Palace has been identified as Clarice Orsini and – less probably – as Simonetta Vespucci. A more likely identification seems to be Fioretta Gorini.

CHAPTER XIII (pages 164–74)

1. Lorenzo bought the VILLA OF POGGIO A CAIANO in 1479. Giuliano da Sangallo began converting it to a purely Renaissance design the next year, but it was not until the following century that the pediment and gabled loggia were added. The outside staircases were built in the seventeenth century. The mural inside the loggia is by Filippino Lippi. The walls of the *salone*, the courtyard of the original building, are decorated with paintings by Francesco di Cristofano Franciabigio, Alessandro Allori, Andrea del Sarto, and Jacopo Carrucci Pontormo. Apart from this room, the interior of the building has been much changed. It now belongs to the State and is being restored as a museum.

2. According to Vasari, the site of Lorenzo's school was a garden near the Piazza San Marco which had once belonged to the Badia Fiesolana and had formed part of Clarice Orsini's dowry. Contemporary records do not mention it and its precise location is unknown.

3. Various examples of Michelangelo's earliest work may be seen at the CASA BUONARROTI (Via Ghibellina, 70) which was built by his nephew on the site of property long owned by his family. The *Madonna of the Stairs* was done in about 1490, the *Battle of the Centaurs* about 1492.

4. BOTTICELLI's *Primavera* (now in the Uffizi), replete as it is with classical and literary allusion, has been the subject of the most complicated explanations. It has pleased some writers to recognize in both Venus and Flora the features of Simonetta Vespucci whose kinsman, Amerigo Vespucci, the navigator, was to give his name to America. The figure of Mercury on the left of the picture does certainly bear a resemblance to Botticelli's *Portrait of Giuliano de' Medici* (in the Crespi Collection, Milan) which was painted two or three years earlier – about 1475.

5. It has also been suggested that the model for Venus in BOTTICELLI's *Birth of Venus* was Simonetta Vespucci. The picture (now in the Uffizi) was painted in about 1485.

6. BOTTICELLI's *Primavera, Birth of Venus* and *Pallas and the Centaur* all once hung in the Medici VILLA OF CASTELLO. The villa was bought in 1477 by Lorenzo di Pierfrancesco de' Medici. The gardens were laid out in the time of Duke Cosimo I by Niccolò Pericoli Tribolo and his successor, Bernardo Buontalenti. Various stone and bronze statues in the ponds and grottoes are by Tribolo, Ammanati, Giambologna and Pierino da Vinci. Others of Giambologna's bronze animals have now been transferred to the Bargello. The villa, which was remodelled and redecorated for the House of Savoy, is now being restored as the headquarters of the Accademia della Crusca.

7. It has been claimed that BOTTICELLI's *Pallas and the Centaur* (in the Uffizi), painted in about 1482, is a celebration of Lorenzo's successful negotations with King Ferrante. The bay in the background has been identified as the Bay of Naples. Undoubtedly Pallas's dress is embroidered with the Medici device of interlocking diamond rings.

8. On Lorenzo's recommendation, Ghirlandaio was commissioned in 1485 to decorate the CAPPELLA MAGGIORE in Santa Maria Novella. The murals, which were finished by his assistants, are his work; so is the stained-glass window. His altarpiece was broken up at the beginning of the nineteenth century and transported to Germany. Lorenzo also helped Ghirlandaio to obtain the commission to paint the murals and the altarpiece in the SASSETTI CHAPEL at Santa Trinità. Francesco Sassetti was general manager of the Medici Bank. He and his four sons are all depicted in the mural behind the altar. Standing next to Filippo is Lorenzo himself. Lorenzo's sons can be seen walking up the steps with their tutors, Luigi Pulci and Agnolo Poliziano.

9. VERROCCHIO's *David*, made in about 1474, is now in the Bargello.

10. VERROCCHIO's *Resurrection*, made in about 1479, is also in the Bargello.

11. The medieval monastery of SANTO SPIRITO – all final remains of which, apart from the refectory, were destroyed by fire in 1471 – was rebuilt to the designs of Brunelleschi between 1434 and 1487, the monks having given up one of their daily meals for half a century to help to pay for it. After Brunelleschi's death there was a dispute about his plans for the façade of the church, which, despite the protestations of Giuliano da Sangallo, other craftsmen wished to alter. Lorenzo's help was sought, but the façade was never finished. Giuliano da Sangallo made a model for the sacristy at Lorenzo's instigation.

12. The huge PALAZZO STROZZI on the corner of Via Tornabuoni and Via Strozzi was built for Filippo Strozzi towards the end of the fifteenth century and the beginning of the sixteenth. The original design may have been by Giuliano da Sangallo but most of the work was supervised by Benedetto da Maiano, Giuliano's brother and Simone del Pollaiuolo.

Filippo Strozzi's son told the story that his father overcame any opposition there might have been to his building so magnificent a palace by making it appear that he had done so on Lorenzo's advice. At first he rejected the plans of the various architects and craftsmen he employed on the grounds that their suggestions were too grandiose: he wanted a more modest palace altogether. But on being told that Lorenzo desired the city to be adorned and exalted in every way, he allowed himself to be persuaded to consult him. So Lorenzo was invited to look at the plans; and, having done so, he gave his approval to one of the most imposing. Still Strozzi feigned modesty, yet at the same time flattered Lorenzo by praising his taste. He wondered if such a grand building was really suitable for a man in his position; he had to admit, though, that Lorenzo understood these matters of space and style far better than he did. Eventually Strozzi built the palace he had always wanted. The foundation stone, as was usual at the time, was laid on a day deemed propitious by his astrologers – 6 August 1489.

13. The CATHEDRAL FAÇADE was accordingly left unfinished. A temporary façade was erected in 1515 for the occasion of the entry of Leo X as described in Chapter 17. In the time of the Grand Duke Ferdinando I another attempt was made to find a suitable design. Buontalenti, Giambologna and Lodovico Cardi all submitted models. So did Cosimo I's gifted illegitimate son, Don Giovanni de' Medici who helped also with the designs for the church of San Gaetano, the Cappella dei Principi at San Lorenzo and the Forte di Belvedere. Nothing came of the new proposals for the Cathedral façade, however, and eventually it was covered by a canvas curtain. When the wind tore this curtain down in the 1680s, Duke Cosimo III sent to Bologna for craftsmen to cover the brown stone with frescoes. These frescoes slowly crumbled away and were replaced in the late nineteenth century by the marble and mosaics which are there now.

CHAPTER XIV (pages 177–88)

1. Although the Medici collections, the richest ever assembled in Renaissance Italy, were widely dispersed, some of the treasures were later recovered. For example, four exquisite vases, two of jasper, one of agate and one crystal, all on gold or silver stands, with precious stones and bearing Lorenzo's name engraved on their bases, were examined in 1502 by Leonardo da Vinci on behalf of Isabella d'Este who had heard they were for sale. For some reasons, perhaps because of the high price demanded, she did not buy them; and they were afterwards acquired once more for the family by Duke Cosimo I. Various statues found their way to the Rucellai gardens, the Orti Oricellari.

CHAPTER XVI (pages 201–14)

1. THE TOMB OF PIERO DI LORENZO DE' MEDICI in the abbey of Monte

Cassino was designed by Antonio and Francesco da Sangallo. It was in the choir of the old church.

2. In particular BOTTICELLI expressed Florence's tragedy in the *Derelitta* (now in the Pallavicini collection at Rome), the *Story of Virginia* (in the Galleria dell' Accademia Carrara at Bergamo) and in *The Tragedy of Lucrezia* (in the Isabella Stewart Gardner Museum, Boston). The two latter were probably painted for the Vespucci, who lived in the Via de' Servi.

CHAPTER XVII (pages 215–29)

1. The miraculous image of the Madonna is in the church of SANTA MARIA DEL IMPRUNETA. The church which was originally built in the thirteenth century was rebuilt in the fifteenth and after being severely damaged in the war, has now been restored. The marble predella of the Madonna is by a follower of Donatello.

2. Filippo Strozzi's second wife was Selvaggia de' Gianfigliazzi. The family chapel of the Gianfigliazzi is in Santa Trinità. The PALAZZO GIANFIGLIAZZI is in Lungarno Corsini (no. 2). This is where the Countess of Albany, wife of the Young Pretender, lived and where Byron and Stendhal both stayed. Sir Horace Mann's house was nearby. On the opposite bank of the Arno, in Lungarno Guicciardini, was Charles Hadfield's famous inn where in the middle of the eighteenth century hundreds of Englishmen stayed while visiting Florence on the Grand Tour. Many of them were painted here by Thomas Patch, who lived in Florence from 1755 until his death in 1782.

3. Orders were immediately given to the Florentine sculptor, Baccio Bandinelli, to prepare with all speed a copy of the marble group of Laocoön which might pass for the original. The original had been discovered by a man digging in his vineyard near the Baths of Trajan in January 1506. Pope Julius II bought it for 4,140 ducats and had it transported to the Vatican along roads strewn with flowers.

4. Michelangelo had competed against Giuliano da Sangallo, Jacopo Sansovino and Baccio d'Agnolo, but his winning design was never realized. After he had spent the best part of two years at the Carrara quarries, contending with all sorts of technical difficulties, the project for a new façade at San Lorenzo was abandoned.

5. Various complimentary allusions to Pope Leo X and the Medici were made in the STANZE DI RAFFAELLO. In the Stanza of Heliodorus, for example, Raphael was induced to change the meeting of Attila and St Leo into an allegory of the Battle of Ravenna, and to show the Pope, in the character of St Leo, riding the white palfrey which had been his mount on that momentous occasion. The features of Leo X are also to be seen in the Stanza dell' Incendio which was painted by Raphael's assistants as the Pope's diningroom in 1514–

17. The pictures here represent scenes from the lives of two popes of the eighth and ninth centuries, Leo III and Leo IV. The fresco on the wall opposite the window shows the great fire of 847 which threatened St Peter's with destruction and which was halted, so it was said, when Pope Leo IV made the sign of the cross into the flames. Like St Leo in the Stanza of Heliodorus, Leo IV is here represented as Leo X.

CHAPTER XVIII (pages 230–243)

1. The villa which Raphael designed for Clement VII on the Monte Mario above the bend of the Tiber at the Ponte Molle was blown up, before it was finished, by the Pope's enemy, Cardinal Colonna, during the sack of Rome in 1527. It was rebuilt for Margaret of Austria and became known as the VILLA MADAMA.

2. The NEW SACRISTY AT SAN LORENZO, known as the Medici Chapel, was completed by Michelangelo in 1534. Lorenzo and Giuliano are buried by the *Madonna and Child* near the entrance door. The sarcophagus of Giuliano, Duke of Nemours, is ˀn the right. The Duke is portrayed as an officer in the service of the Church with a male statue of Day and a sleeping female Night reclining at his feet. On the left is the tomb of Lorenzo, Duke of Urbino, the dedicatee of Machiavelli's *The Prince*, portrayed as a soldier, his eyes cast down in thought. Below him are statues of Dawn and Dusk. The decoration of the chapel was not finished when Michelangelo left Florence in 1534. Plans for tombs for Lorenzo il Magnifico and Giuliano, as well as for Pope Leo X, were never realized. In the seventeenth century the Prince of Denmark came to Florence to see this chapel which he described as being 'one of the most magnificent pieces of art in the world'.

3. Michelangelo's superb entrance and staircase to the BIBLIOTECA LAUREN-ZIANA were largely finished by the time the artist left Florence. They were completed by Bartolommeo Ammanati and Giorgio Vasari in accordance with plans and instructions which Michelangelo left behind. The library was opened to the public in 1571.

CHAPTER XIX (pages 244–58)

1. MICHELANGELO's *David*, which was finished in 1504, had been commissioned soon after Piero Soderini became *Gonfaloniere* in 1501. Although Botticelli wanted it placed in the Loggia dei Lanzi, and others proposed the steps of the Cathedral as a more suitable position, it was eventually placed in front of the Palazzo della Signoria where one of the arms was broken in a riot in 1527. The statue continued to stand in front of the Palazzo until 1873 when it was replaced by the copy which stands there now. The original – the gilding of the hair and the band across the chest long since worn away by sun, wind and rain – is in the MUSEO DELL' ACCADEMIA (Via Ricasoli, 52).

The heraldic lion, the *Marzocco*, to the left of the copy of Michelangelo's *David* (next to DONATELLO's *Judith and Holofernes*) is also a copy of the original made by Donatello in 1418–20. The original is in the Bargello. After their removal from the Piazza San Giovanni in the fourteenth century, the city's lions were brought to the Piazza della Signoria; but in the sixteenth century, when Duke Cosimo I occupied the Palace, he had the lions moved because of their smell. The VIA DEI LEONI marks the site of their pen. *Hercules and Cacus* to the right of the *David* was finished by Baccio Bandinelli in 1534. The original commission for a Hercules had been given to Michelangelo; but, evidently supposing that Michelangelo might use this opportunity to hint at the virtues of the crushed Republic, Pope Leo X ordered that the marble block should be given instead to Bandinelli. The order was confirmed by Clement VII who wanted to keep Michelangelo fully occupied on work for the Medici.

2. Francesco Ferrucci's birthplace was at VIA SANTO SPIRITO, 32. As in the case of many other Florentine heroes, a wreath is placed here every year in his honour.

3. Clement VII was ultimately buried, in a fine porphyry urn taken from the Pantheon, in the Corsini chapel at the Basilica of St John in Lateran.

4. The Porta alla Giustizia is now the PIAZZA PIAVE.

5. The forbidding symbol of despotism, the FORTEZZA DA BASSO, covered an area of almost 120,000 square metres and is the biggest historical monument in Florence. The foundation stone was laid on 15 July 1534, a date deemed appropriate by the skilful astrologers of Bologna. The convent of San Giovanni Evangelista was demolished in order to clear the site.

CHAPTER XX (pages 261–74)

1. The Viceroy of Naples conducted his daughter to Florence where he and his suite were lodged in the monastery of Santa Maria Novella. Thereafter the former chapter house in the Green Cloister, which was built and decorated in the middle of the fourteenth century, was known as the SPANISH CHAPEL and became the chapel of the Spanish colony in Florence.

2. Cosmopolis became Portoferraio rather more than a century later. The Casa del Duca at the foot of Colle Reciso is said to be the place from which Cosimo and his architect watched the building in progress. Cellini's bust of Cosimo, which stood above the entrance to Forte Stella, is now in the Bargello.

3. The great NEPTUNE FOUNTAIN in the Piazza della Signoria was intended to symbolize Duke Cosimo's naval achievements. The design of the fountain was originally entrusted to Bandinelli who died before he could begin it. After a competition had been held, the commission was given to Ammanati. The fountain was finished in 1575. The Piazza, now renamed the Piazza del Granduca, had been repaved in 1543.

4. The UFFIZI PALACE was paid for by the various government offices which

originally occupied it. Their names or mottoes still appear over the big doors under the colonnade. After Vasari's death in 1574 work on the Uffizi was continued by Bernardo Buontalenti and Alfonso Parigi. It has been one of the great art galleries of Europe for three centuries. Many of the finest pieces of the Medici collection were housed in the Tribuna in which Zoffany portrayed numerous well-known English connoisseurs, diplomats and collectors in the painting he did under the patronage of Queen Charlotte between 1772 and 1778. Sir Horace Mann is shown standing beneath the VENUS DE' MEDICI, a Roman copy of a Greek original found at Hadrian's villa at Tivoli, brought to Florence in the time of the Grand Duke Cosimo III and still in the Tribuna today. Other works of art shown in Zoffany's picture, like Titian's *Venus of Urbino* were brought in from other rooms in the Uffizi or from the Pitti Palace for the painter's purpose.

5. The original PITTI PALACE was built in the 1450s and 1460s by Luca Pitti who received 20,000 florins from Cosimo as a contribution towards its cost as a reward for his political services to the Medicean party. It was probably designed by Luca Fancelli. After Ammanati had finished his alterations for Duke Cosimo I and Eleonora of Toledo – the courtyard was completed in 1562 – the façade was again widened by Giulio and Alfonso Parigi in the seventeenth century and two new wings were added by Giuseppe Ruggieri in the eighteenth century. At that time it was known as the Grand Ducal Palace. After the Risorgimento, the Pitti was made over to the House of Savoy and was presented to the nation by King Victor Emmanuel III. It now houses five museums. The Museo degli Argenti on the ground floor contains many of the treasures collected by the Medici.

6. The BOBOLI GARDENS still contain works by all these artists as well as by Giambologna, Fancelli, Cioli, Pietro Tacca, Caccini and Romolo del Tadda. The amphitheatre, shaped on a Roman model, was the site of the performance of *Il Mondo Festeggiante* given to celebrate the marriage of the Grand Duke Cosimo III. The Giardino del Cavaliere is laid out on the site of a bastion built by Michelangelo during the siege of 1529. The terrace beneath was built for Cardinal Leopoldo de' Medici.

7. The original PONTE SANTA TRINITÀ was built in the thirteenth century. The statues on Ammanati's bridge, *Spring* and *Autumn* (by Giovanni Caccini), *Summer* (by Pietro Francavilla) and *Winter* (by Taddeo Landini) were made for the Grand Duke Cosimo's marriage in 1608. The bridge was blown up in 1944. It was rebuilt after the war exactly as it had been before, the masons using copies of sixteenth-century tools to ensure its authenticity. The façade of the CHURCH OF SANTA TRINITÀ was commissioned by the Grand Duke Ferdinando I from Buontalenti and completed in 1594.

8. The PONTE ALLA CARRAIA, first built at the beginning of the thirteenth century, was three times destroyed by floods, and once, in 1304, collapsed

under the weight of spectators watching a river festival. It was re-built for the fifth time by Ammanati in 1559. The present bridge was built after the last war, its predecessor having been blown up in 1944.

9. The LOGGIA DEI LANZI was originally known as the Loggia dei Signori. It was built towards the end of the fourteenth century to plans drawn by Simone Talenti as a covered area for public ceremonies. Its present name is derived from Duke Cosimo I's Swiss soldiers, the *Landsknechte*, who were quartered in barracks nearby. In Duke Cosimo's time, it became the open-air sculpture gallery that it still is. Cellini's *Perseus* was placed there in 1554. Giambologna's *Rape of the Sabines* came in 1583 when Donatello's *Judith and Holofernes*, which had formerly been placed on the *ringhiera* of the Palazzo della Signoria, was returned to the Piazza. Behind these two pieces are another Giambologna, a Roman copy of a Greek statue of *Menelaus supporting the body of Patroclus* and Pio Fedi's *Rape of Polixena*. Six Roman statues which the Grand Duke Ferdinando I brought from the Villa Medici in Rome are in the back row.

10. Although work began in 1605, under the direction of Ferdinando I, to realize Cosimo I's conception of a huge CAPPELLA DEI PRINCIPI, the structure was not finished until 1737, and the decoration of the cupola not completed until 1836. Until ready to receive them in the reign of Cosimo III, the bodies of the Grand Dukes and their wives and sons were temporarily buried in the new and old sacristies. Generations of craftsmen in *pietra dura* were kept intermittently at work on the elaborate tombs of the three Cosimos, the two Ferdinandos and the Grand Duke Francesco which surround the walls.

The sixteen coats-of-arms inlaid in the floor in marble, coral, jasper, agate, mother-of-pearl and lapis-lazuli are of the cities subject to the Grand Duchy. All the Grand Dukes were buried in the crypt below the mausoleum with their jewelled crowns still upon their heads and their sceptres in their hands. All the Grand Duchesses were also buried here with the one exception of Francesco I's widow Bianca Capello. When Buontalenti asked Ferdinando I where his sister-in-law should be buried, the Grand Duke, who had detested her, replied 'Wherever you like, we will not have her amongst *us.*' The site of her grave is unknown.

11. The complicated and inventive plans for the GARDEN OF THE VILLA OF CASTELLO (see note 6 to chapter XIII) were drawn up by Benedetto Varchi for Duke Cosimo I and put in hand by Tribolo, Ammanati and Buontalenti. But they were never fully realized. Works by Tribolo, Ammanati and Giambologna can all still be seen in the gardens, though Giambologna's *Fountain of Venus Wringing out her Hair* has been removed to Petraia and his bronze animals from the grotto are in the Bargello.

CHAPTER XXI (pages 275–82)

1. The putto on the fountain at present in the COURTYARD OF THE PALAZZO
   VECCHIO is a copy of the original by Verrocchio, which is kept in one of the
   rooms off the Sala dei Gigli. The murals are by Marco da Fienza, Giovanni
   Lombardi and Cesare Baglioni.

2. BIANCA CAPELLO'S HOUSE is in the Via Maggio (nos. 24–6).

3. VILLA PRATOLINO – designed by Buontalenti and fifteen years in the making
   – was demolished in 1822 on the grounds that it was too expensive to maintain.
   Fifty years later the estate was purchased by Prince Paul Demidoff. The Villa
   Demidoff which replaced Pratolino passed into the hands of Prince Paul of
   Yugoslavia who restored it and has now sold it. Giambologna's huge statue,
   L'APPENINO, remains in the grounds. Other statues were taken to the Boboli
   Gardens, like *Perseus and the Dragon*, which was intended as an allegorical
   portrait of the Grand Duke Cosimo I.

4. The PALAZZO ANTINORI at the junction of the Via Tornabuoni and the Via
   Rondinelli was built for the Boni family.

5. The VILLA OF CERETO GUIDI originally belonged to the Guidi. Buontalenti
   renovated it and built the immense double ramps leading up to it for the Grand
   Duke Cosimo I in the 1560s.

6. The headquarters of the ACCADEMIA DELLA CRUSCA, which will soon be
   transferred to the Villa Castello, are at present in the Palazzo dei Giudici.

7. The porcelain made in Florence in the time of the Grand Duke Francesco was
   the first to be made in Europe, and is now the rarest, there being only about
   seventy pieces in existence. One of these – a small, misshapen bowl – was sold
   in New York in 1973 for £180,000, the highest recorded price paid at an
   auction for European porcelain. Other pieces are in the Louvre, the Musée de
   Sèvres, the Metropolitan Museum in New York and the Victoria and Albert
   Museum, London.

8. The VILLA MEDICI in Rome, designed by Annibale Lippi for Cardinal Ricci
   in 1544, was purchased by Cardinal Ferdinando de' Medici in 1577. He was
   the first of several Medici cardinals to live there. The façade and the ground
   plan of the garden remain unchanged. The figure of MERCURY (c. 1565), now
   at the Bargello, once formed part of a fountain in the villa grounds. The fountain
   now in front of the villa originally had a Florentine lily in the centre. This was
   replaced by the existing stone cannon-ball after Queen Christina, being given
   permission to experiment with one of the Castel Sant' Angelo cannon, had
   fired at random down into the town instead of up into the air. Her shot struck
   the Villa Medici. Napoleon bought the villa in 1803. It now houses the French
   Academy.

9. The FORTE DI BELVEDERE, also known as the Fortezza di San Giorgio, now
   houses numerous murals removed from various buildings in other parts of the

city, including those from the Chiostro degli Aranci at the Badia Fiesolana, from the Chiostro Verde at Santa Maria Novella, from the Loggia of the Bigallo in Piazza San Giovanni (by Ambrogio di Baldese and Rosello di Jacopo Franchi) and from Via Pietrapiana (No. 7) by Mino da Fiesole whose house this was. Also stored here is Botticelli's *Annunciation* from the church of San Martino in Via della Scala.

10. The VILLA PETRAIA was brought by Cardinal Francesco de' Medici from the widow of Filippo Salutati in 1595. The courtyard is decorated with frescoes celebrating the history of the Medici family by Baldassare Franceschini, 'il Volterrano', who painted them for the Grand Duke Ferdinando I's son, Don Lorenzo de' Medici. After the *Risorgimento* the villa passed into the hands of the House of Savoy and was altered and redecorated by King Victor Emmanuel II.

11. The VILLA FERDINANDA at Artimino, which is about four miles south-west of Poggio a Caiano, was built in 1594-5. It was sold to Marchese Lorenzo Bartolommei in 1781 and, though restored in the early years of this century, now lies empty.

12. This sphere is now in the MUSEO NAZIONALE DI STORIA DELLA SCIENZE in the Palazzo dei Giudici overlooking the Arno, next to the Uffizi. The palazzo formerly belonged to the Castellani family whose chapel is in Santa Croce. It takes its present name from the Consiglio di Giustizia which was established here in the time of the Grand Duke Ferdinando I. The museum contains numerous terrestial globes, astrolabes, clocks and maps as well as Michelangelo's compasses and Galileo's telescopes.

13. The PALAZZO BELLINI is in Borgo Pinti (no. 26). The Grand Duke Ferdinando I's bust is over the door.

14. The STATUE OF DUKE COSIMO in the Piazza della Signoria was made by Giambologna in the Palazzo Bellini between 1587 and 1599. The equestrian STATUE OF GRAND DUKE FERDINANDO I in the Piazza Santissima Annunziata was begun by Giambologna in the last year of his long life and finished in 1608 by Pietro Tacca who moved into the Palazzo Bellini on his master's death.

15. Although he decided that the Medici emblem, the *palle*, was too commercial in its associations and had it replaced by a bee (the ancient symbol of the autarch whose life is busily devoted to his people's welfare). Ferdinando I nevertheless sought to honour the great founders of the Medici fortunes. At the base of the immense granite COLUMN OF JUSTICE which had been set up in the Piazza Santa Trinità in 1565 to mark the place where a messenger had given Cosimo I news of the victory of Montemurlo, Ferdinando erected four stucco statues. One was a representation of Augustus; another was of Charlemagne; the third was of Cosimo I; and the fourth was of Cosimo the Elder, *Pater Patriae*. The column came from the Baths of Caracalla and was presented to Duke Cosimo I by Pope Pius IV. It was hauled from Rome to Civitavecchia

on rollers, and transported from Pisa to Florence on barges. The porphyry statue, which was placed on it in 1581, is believed to be by Romolo del Tadda.

16. The VILLA OF POGGIO IMPERIALE had once belonged to the Baroncelli and then to the Salviati. It derives its present name from the Grand Duchess Maria Maddalena of Austria who bought it in 1619. It was afterwards the home of Napoleon's sister, Elisa Baciocchi, and is now a girls' school.

17. Three hundred volumes of Galileo's papers are now housed in the BIBLIOTECA NAZIONALE in the Corso dei Tintori where collections of Poliziano's, Michelangelo's and Machiavelli's papers are also kept. Many of the manuscripts and books are from the Grand Ducal Library, the Palatina, formed by Ferdinando II and his brothers, Gian Carlo and Leopoldo.

18. Galileo's body was removed from the Novices' Chapel in Santa Croce in 1737 and reburied on the north side of the west door.

CHAPTER XXII (pages 283–291)

1. The ORIFICIO DELLE PIETRE DURE was moved from the Uffizi in 1796 and is now in the Via degli Alfani (no. 78) where craftsmen still work and are trained.

2. The work of GIOVANNI DA SAN GIOVANNI may be seen on the east wall of Room IV at the Pitti Palace. Assisted by Baldassare Franceschini, il Volterrano, he also painted the *Allegory of the Union of the Houses of Medici and Della Rovere* in the vault. *Lorenzo and the Platonic Academy at Careggi* and the *Allegory of Lorenzo's death* on the north wall are by Francesco Furini. *Lorenzo the Magnificent Receives Apollo* on the south wall is by Cecco Bravo. *Lorenzo surrounded by Artists*, between the windows, is by Ottavio Vannini.

3. Among these latest acquisitions were numerous beautiful pieces of sculpture including the *Hermaphrodite*, the head of Cicero, and the *Idolino*. Ruben's *Consequences of War* was bought by Ferdinando II. Veronese's *Daniele Barbaro*, *Portrait of a Man* and *Holy Family with Santa Barbara* were in Cardinal Leopoldo's collection. Raphael's portrait of Pope Julius II, Titian's *Recumbent Venus*, *Magdalena*, *La Bella* and *Portrait of a Grey-eyed Nobleman*, together with Piero della Francesca's famous portrait of Federigo da Montefeltro, Duke of Urbino, and his wife Battista Sforza, were all acquired in 1634 on Ferdinando's marriage to Vittoria della Rovere.

4. Most of these turned-ivory ornaments were brought back to Florence by Prince Mattias de' Medici from the Castle of Coburg. They are in Room X.

5. The TEATRO DELLA PERGOLA (Via della Pergola, 12) was built by Ferdinando Tacca in 1656. The present building, designed by Bartolommeo Silvestri, is early-nineteenth-century.

6. The Via del Cocomero is now the Via Ricasoli.

7. Gian Carlo's garden in the Via della Scala, where the members of the Platonic Academy had sometimes held their debates, has now been built over.

8. The enormous, forbidding VILLA AMBROGIANA was originally built as a hunting lodge. The Grand Duke Cosimo III hung its walls with pictures of rare animals and flowers. It is now a mental hospital.

CHAPTER XXIII (pages 292–301)

1. The VILLA LAPPEGGI stood for longer than eighteen years, though after the Cardinal's death the second storey had to be removed for fear that the walls supporting it would fall down into the garden. Its shaky structure was badly damaged by an earthquake in 1895 and will soon, by all appearances, collapse altogether.

CHAPTER XXIV (pages 302–311)

1. It was left to the despised Lorrainers and the ministers of the Grand Duke Francesco's energetic son, Pietro Leopoldo, to reform the exhausted and oppressed State, the chaotic legislation and the exploited countryside of Florence which were the social and economic legacy of the later Medici. The splendour of their artistic and cultural legacy – the exuberance and elaborate craftsmanship of Florentine baroque art as triumphantly exemplified by such masters as Cosimo III's sculptor, Giovanni Battista Foggini – has only recently been recognized. The exhibition held in Detroit and at the Pitti Palace in 1974, 'The Twilight of the Medici' – which would have made scant appeal to Bernard Berenson – was the first of its kind.

THE PRINCIPAL MEDICI
PORTRAITS, BUSTS AND STATUES
IN FLORENCE

Subject	Work	Artist	Location
Giovanni di Bicci	Posthumous painting	Bronzino	Medici-Riccardi Palace
Giovanni di Bicci	Painting	Zanobi Strozzi	Medici-Riccardi Palace
Cosimo *Pater Patriae*	Posthumous painting	Pontormo	Uffizi
Cosimo *Pater Patriae*	Painting (being presented with model of San Lorenzo by Brunelleschi)	Vasari	Palazzo della Signoria
Lorenzo di Giovanni	Posthumous painting	Bronzino	Uffizi
Piero di Cosimo	Bust	Mino da Fiesole	Bargello
Giovanni di Cosimo	Bust	Mino da Fiesole	Bargello
Lorenzo il Magnifico	Posthumous painting	Vasari	Uffizi
Lorenzo il Magnifico	Fresco (with members of the Sassetti family)	Ghirlandaio	Sassetti Chapel, Santa Trinità
Lorenzo il Magnifico	Fresco (seated before Cardinal Giovanni)	Vasari	Palazzo della Signoria
Lorenzo il Magnifico	Painting	Florentine school, early fifteenth century	Medici-Riccardi Palace
Lorenzo il Magnifico	Death mask		Medici-Riccardi Palace
Piero Francesco di Lorenzo	Painting	Vasari	Palazzo della Signoria

334

Subject	Work	Artist	Location
Piero di Lorenzo	Painting	Bronzino	Medici–Riccardi Palace
Piero di Lorenzo	Bust	Verrocchio	Bargello
Giuliano di Lorenzo	Fresco (as boy with tutor, Poliziano)	Ghirlandaio	Sassetti Chapel, Santa Trinità
(?) Contessina	Bust	Donatello	Bargello
(?) Fioretta Gorini	Painting	Botticelli	Pitti
Pope Leo X	Painting (with Cardinals Giulio de' Medici and Liugi de' Rossi	Raphael	Uffizi
Pope Leo X	Fresco (proceeding through Florence)	Vasari	Palazzo della Signoria
Pope Leo X	Fresco (creating thirty Cardinals)	Vasari	Palazzo della Signoria
Pope Clement VII	Painting	Bronzino	Medici–Riccardi Palace
Duke Alessandro	Painting	Vasari	Medici–Riccardi Palace
Ippolito	Painting	Titian	Pitti
Caterina	Painting (aet 21)		Poggio a Caiano
Caterina	Painting (aet 40)	Pourbus	Uffizi
Giovanni di Pierfrancesco	Painting	Vasari	Palazzo della Signoria
Caterina Sforza	Painting	Vasari	Palazzo della Signoria
Giovanni della Bande Nere	Statue	Bandinelli	Piazza San Lorenzo
Giovanni della Bande Nere	Painting	Titian	Uffizi
Maria Salviati	Painting	Vasari	Palazzo della Signoria
Cosimo I	Painting (aet 12)	Attrib. Ridolfo Ghirlandaio	Medici–Riccardi Palace
Cosimo I	Painting (as a young man)	Pontormo	Medici–Riccardi Palace
CosimoI	Painting (the Election)	Francesco and Jacopo Ligozzi	Palazzo della Signoria
Cosimo I	Painting	Vasari	Uffizi
Cosimo I	Painting (in armour)	Bronzino	Uffizi
Cosimo I	Equestrian Statue	Giambologna	Piazza della Signoria
Cosimo	Bust	Callini	Bargello
Cosimo I	Painting (wearing crown and robes of state)	Bronzino	Uffizi

335

THE PRINCIPAL MEDICI PORTRAITS

Subject	Work	Artist	Location
Eleonora Toledo	Painting	Bronzino	Studiolo di Francesco I, Palazzo della Signoria
Eleonora Toledo	Painting (with Giovanni	Bronzino	Uffizi
Isabella	Painting	Bronzino	Uffizi
Garzia	Painting	Bronzino	Uffizi
Cardinal Giovanni	Painting	Sustermans	Poggio a Caiano
Pietro	Painting	Bronzino	Uffizi
Francesco I	Painting	Veronese	Pitti
Joanna of Austria	Painting (with Filippo)		Uffizi
Bianca Capello	Painting	Bronzino	Pitti
Eleonora (daughter of Francesco I)	Painting	Pulzoni	Pitti
Maria (daughter of Francesco I)	Painting	Bronzino	Uffizi
Caterina (daughter of Francesco I)	Painting	Bronzino	Uffizi
Ferdinando I	Painting	Alessandro Allori	Pitti
Christine of Lorraine	Painting	Scipione Pulsone di Gaeta	Medici-Riccardi Palace
Christine of Lorraine	Painting (*aet* 55)	Sustermans	Corsini Gallery
Claudia (daughter of Ferdinando I)	Painting	Sustermans	Uffizi
Cosimo II	Painting (*aet* 12)	Sustermans	Poggio a Caiano
Cosimo II	Painting	Sustermans	Corsini Gallery
Cosimo II	Painting	Sustermans	Uffizi
Maria Maddalena	Painting	Sustermans	Corsini Gallery
Margherita (daughter of Cosimo II)	Painting	Sustermans	Poggio a Caiano
Francesco (son of Cosimo II)	Painting	Sustermans	Poggio a Caiano
Anna (daughter of Cosimo II)	Painting	Sustermans	Pitti
Ferdinando II	Painting (*aet* 14)	Sustermans	Pitti
Ferdinando II	Painting	Sustermans	Poggio a Caiano
Mattias	Painting	Sustermans	Pitti
Cardinal Leopoldo	Painting		Uffizi
Cardinal Leopoldo	Bust		Uffizi
Vittoria della Rovere	Painting (as a young womam)	Carlo Dolci	Pitti
Vittoria della Rovere	Painting (in middle age)	Carlo Dolci	Pitti

Subject	Work	Artist	Location
Cosimo III	Painting (as a canon of the Lateran)		Medici-Riccardi Palace
Marguerite Louise	Painting		Uffizi
Anna Maria Luisa	Painting (with Elector Palatine)	G. F. Douven	Pitti
Anna Maria Luisa	Painting (with gun and dogs)	G. F. Douven	Pitti
Violante Beatrice	Painting		Uffizi
Gian Gastone	Painting		Uffizi
Gian Gastone	Bust		Uffizi

BIBLIOGRAPHY

Acton, Harold,	*The Last Medici,* Methuen, 1932; rev. edn, 1958; reprinted, 1973.
	Tuscan Villas, Thames & Hudson, 1973.
Ady, Cecilia M.,	*Lorenzo dei Medici and Renaissance Italy,* English Universities Press, 1955.
Allodoli, Ettore,	*I Medici,* Florence, 1928.
Andriani, Giovanbattista,	*Istoria de' suoi tempi,* 1583.
Antal, Friedrich	*Florentine Painting and its Social Background,* Routledge & Kegan Paul, 1948.
Anzilotti,	*La costituzione interna dello Stato Fiorentino sotto il Duca Cosimo I de' Medici,* 1910.
Armstrong, Antonio Edward	*Lorenzo de' Medici and Florence in the Fifteenth Century,* 1911.
Baccini, Giuseppe,	*see* Orlando
Barfucci, Enrico	*Lorenzo de' Medici e la società artistica del suo tempo,* Florence, 1945.
Baron, Hans	*The Crisis of the Early Italian Renaissance,* rev. edn, Princeton University Press, 1966
Baroni, Costantino	*Bramante,* Bergamo, 1944.
Bayley, C.C.,	*War and Society in Renaissance Florence,* Toronto, 1961.
Becker, Marvin B.,	'The Republican City State in Florence' in *Speculum* xxxv, January 1960, pp. 39–50.
Biagi, Guido,	*The Private Life of the Renaissance Florentines,* Florence, 1896.
Booth, Cecily,	*Cosimo I,* Cambridge University Press, 1921.
Borsook, Eve,	*The Companion Guide to Florence,* Collins, 1966.
	The Mural Painters of Tuscany, 1960.
Bossi	*see* Roscoe
Bowra, Maurice,	'Songs of Dance and Carnival' in *Italian Renaissance Studies,* ed. Jacob.
Bracciolini, Poggio,	*Istoria dall'origine di Firenze al 1454,* Florence, 1598.
Brandi, Karl,	*The Emperor Charles V,* trans. C.V. Wedgwood, Jonathan Cape, 1965.

Brion, Marcel, The Medici: A Great Florentine Family, trans. Gilles and Heather Cremonesi, Elek, 1969.

Brown, Alison M., 'The Humanist Portrait of Cosimo de' Medici Pater Patriae' in Journal of the Warburg and Courtauld Institutes, XXIV, 1961.

Brucker, Gene A., 'The Ciompi Revolution' in Florentine Studies, ed. N. Rubinstein.
Florentine Politics and Society, 1343–1378, Princeton, 1962.
'The Medici in the Fourteenth Century' in Speculum, XXXII, January 1957, pp. 1–26.
Renaissance Florence, Wiley, 1969.

Burckhardt, Jacob, The Civilization of the Renaissance in Italy, trans. S.G.C. Middlemore, 1890, new edn, 2 vols., introduction by Benjamin Nelson and Charles Trinkaus, Harper Torchbooks, 1958.

Burke, Peter, Culture and Society in Renaissance Italy, Batsford, 1972.

Burnet, Gilbert, Some letters containing an Account of what seemed most remarkable in travelling through Switzerland, Italy, etc., 1689.

Caggese, Romolo, Firenze dall decadenza di Roma al Risorgimento d'Italia, Florence, 1912–13.

Camugliano, G. Niccolini di, The Chronicles of a Florentine Family 1200–1400, 1933.

Cantagalli, Roberto, La Guerra di Siena, Siena, 1962.

Capponi, G.A., Storia della repubblica di Firenze, 2 vols., Florence, 1875.

Carden, R.W., The Life of Giorgio Vasari, 1910.

Catalogue of the Medici Archives, Christie, Manson & Woods, 1919.

Cavalcanti, Giovanni, Istorie Fiorentine, 2 vols., Florence, 1838–9.

Cecchi, Emilio, Lorenzo il Magnifico, Rome, 1949.

Cellini, Benvenuto, Autobiography, trans. George Bull, Penguin Books, 1956.

Chabod, Federico, Machiavelli and the Renaissance, trans. David Moore, Bowes & Bowes, 1958.

Chamberlin, E.R., Everyday Life in Renaissance Times, Batsford, 1965.

Chastel, André, Art et Humanisme à Florence au temps de Laurent le Magnifique, Paris, 1961.
'Vasari et la légende Médicéene: L'école du jardin de Saint Marc' in Studi Vasariani, Florence, 1952.

Cochrane, Eric, Florence in the Forgotten Centuries 1527–1800, Chicago University Press, 1973.
The Late Italian Renaissance, Harper & Row, 1970.
'The Florentine Background of Galileo's Work' in Galileo: Man of Science, ed. Ernan McMullin, Basic Books, 1967.

339

Commines, Philip de,   *The Memoirs of Philip de Commines, Lord of Argenton*, ed. Andrew R. Scobie, 2 vols., 1906.
Conte, Giuseppe,   *Firenze dai Medici ai Lorena*, Florence, 1907.
Cronin, Vincent,   *The Florentine Renaissance*, Collins, 1967.
    The Flowering of the Renaissance, Collins, 1969.
Cruttwell, M.,   *Verrocchio*, 1904.

Dami, Brunetto,   *Giovanni Bicci dei Medici*, Florence, 1899.
Dati, Gregorio,   *Istoria di Firenze dal 1380 al 1450*, Florence, 1735.
Deiss, Joseph Jay,   *Captains of Fortune: Profiles of Six Italian Condottieri*, Gollancz, 1966.
Delaborde, H.F.,   *L'Expédition de Charles VIII en Italie*, Paris, 1888.
Dini-Traversari, A.,   *Ambrogio Traversari e i suoi tempi*, Florence, 1912.
Doren, Alfred,   *Le arti florentine*, trans. Klein, 2 vols., Florence, 1940.
Dorini, Umberto,   *I Medici e i loro tempi*, Florence, 1947.

Ehrenberg, Richard,   *Capital and Finance in the Age of the Renaissance*, trans. H.M. Lucas, 1928.
Einem, Herbert von,   *Michelangelo*, trans. Ronald Taylor, Methuen, 1973.
Ewart, K.D.,   *Cosimo de' Medici*, 1889.

Ferrara, Mario, (ed.),   *Savonarola: Prediche e scritti*, Florence, 1952.
Ferrai, Luigi Alberto,   *Cosimo I de' Medici, Duca di Firenze*, 1882.
Fischel, Oscar,   *Raphael*, trans. Bernard Rackham, 2 vols., Kegan Paul, 1948.

Gadol, Joan,   *Leon Batista Alberti: Universal Man of the Early Renaissance*, University of Chicago Press, 1969.
Gage, John,   *Life in Italy at the time of the Medici*, Batsford, 1968.
Galluzzi, Riguccio,   *Istoria del Granducato di Toscana sotto il governo della Casa Medici*, 7 vols., Florence, 1820–1.
Gaye, G.,   *Carteggio inedito d'artisti dei secoli XIV, XV, XVI*, Florence, 1839–40.
Gilbert, Felix,   'Florentine political assumptions in the period of Savonarola and Soderini' in *Journal of the Warburg and Courtauld Institutes*, XX, 1957, pp. 187ff.
    'Guicciardini, Machiavelli and Valori on Lorenzo Magnifico' in *Renaissance News*, IX, 1958, pp. 107–14.
    Machiavelli and Guicciardini: Politics and History in Sixteenth-century Florence, Princeton University Press, 1965.
Gill, Joseph,   *The Council of Florence*, Cambridge University Press, 1959.
Goldthwaite, Richard A.,   *Private Wealth in Renaissance Florence*, Princeton University Press, 1968.

Gombrich, E.H., 'The Early Medici as Patrons of Art' in *Italian Renaissance Studies*, ed. Jacob.

Grayson, Cecil, 'Lorenzo, Machiavelli and the Italian Language' in *Italian Renaissance Studies*, ed. Jacob.

Guicciardini, Francesco, *Carteggi*, ed. P.G. Ricci, Rome, 1954–62. *Storia d'Italia*, ed. Costantino Panigada, 5 vols., Bari, 1929; English edition, ed. Sidney Alexander, Collier-Macmillan, 1969.

Gutkind, Curt S., *Cosimo de' Medici: Pater Patriae, 1389–1464*, Clarendon Press, Oxford, 1938.

Hale, J.R., 'The End of Florentine Liberty: The Fortezza da Basso' in *Florentine Studies*, ed. Rubinstein. *Machiavelli and Renaissance Italy*, English Universities Press, 1961. *Renaissance Europe 1480–1520*, Fontana, 1971. 'War and Public Opinion in Renaissance Italy' in *Italian Renaissance Studies*, ed. Jacob,

Hay, Denys, (ed.), *The Italian Renaissance in its Historical Setting*, Cambridge University Press, 1961. *The Renaissance Debate*, Holt, Rinehart & Winston, 1965.

Higgins, John R., *A Historical Guide to Florence*, Robert Hale, 1973.

Holmes, George, *The Florentine Enlightenment, 1400–50*, Weidenfeld & Nicolson, 1969. 'How the Medici became the Pope's Bankers' in *Florentine Studies*, ed. Rubinstein,

Hook, Judith, *The Sack of Rome, 1527*, Macmillan, 1973.

Horne, Herbert, *Alessandro Filipepi Commonly Called Sandro Botticelli Painter of Florence*, 1908.

Horsburgh, E.L.S., *Girolamo Savonarola*, 1901.

Hyett, Francis A., *Florence: Her History and Art to the Fall of the Republic*, 1903.

Imbert, G., *La vita Fiorentina nel Seicento*, Florence, 1906.

Jacob, E.F., (ed.), *Italian Renaissance Studies*, Faber, 1960.

Janson, H.W., *The Sculpture of Donatello*, 2 vols., Princeton University Press, 1957.

Joannides, P., 'Michelangelo's Medici Chapel: Some new Suggestions', *Burlington Magazine*, CXIV, pp. 542–6.

Krautheimer, Richard, *Lorenzo Ghiberti*, Princeton University Press, 2 vols., 1970.

Landucci, Luca, *A Florentine Diary from 1450–1516*, trans. Alice de Rosen Jervis, 1927.

Laven, Peter,
Renaissance Italy, 1464–1534, Batsford, 1966.
Lettere di Lorenzo il Magnifico al Sommo Pontefice Innocenzo VIII, Florence, 1830.

Lorenzino de' Medici
Opere, ed. Simioni, 2 vols, Bari, 1913.
Scritti e documenti, Milan, 1862.

Lucas-Dubreton, J.,
Daily Life in Florence in the Time of the Medici, trans. A. Lytton Sells, Allen & Unwin, 1960.

Lungo, Isodoro del,
I Medici Granduchi, 1896.

Lyall, Archibald,
Companion Guide to Tuscany, Collins, 1973.

McCarthy, Mary,
The Stones of Florence, Heinemann, 1959.

Machiavelli, Niccolò,
Istorie Fiorentine, Opere, ed. Antonio Panella, vol. 1, Milan, 1938.

Macinghi negli Strozzi, Alessandra,
Lettere di una gentildonna fiorentina del secolo XV ai figliuoli esuli, ed. Cesare Guasti, Florence, 1877.

Maguire, Yvonne,
The Private Life of Lorenzo the Magnificent, 1936.
The Women of the Medici, 1927.

Mallett, Michael,
Mercenaries and Their Masters: Warfare in Renaissance Italy, Bodley Head, 1974.
'Pisa and Florence in the fifteenth century' in *Florentine Studies*, ed. Rubinstein.

Marks, L.F.,
'The Financial Oligarchy in Florence under Lorenzo' in *Italian Renaissance Studies*, ed. Jacob.

Martines, Lauro,
Lawyers and Statecraft in Renaissance Florence, Princeton University Press, 1968.
The Social World of the Florentine Humanists 1390–1460, Princeton University Press, 1963.

Masson, Georgina,
Companion Guide to Rome, Collins, 1965.
Italian Villas and Palaces, Thames & Hudson, 1959.

Mattingly, Garrett,
Renaissance Diplomacy, Jonathan Cape, 1955.

Minor, Andrew C., and Mitchell, Bonner,
A Renaissance Entertainment: Festivities for the Marriage of Cosimo I, University of Missouri Press, 1968.

Morassi, Antonio,
Il Tesoro dei Medici, Milan, 1963.

Morisani, Ottavio,
Michelozzo architetto, Einaudi, 1951.

Müntz, E.,
Les Collections des Médicis au XVe Siècle, Paris, 1888.

Murray, Peter,
The Architecture of the Italian Renaissance, Thames & Hudson, 1969.

Murray, Peter, with Linda Murray,
The Art of the Renaissance, Thames & Hudson, 1969.

Nagler, Alois Maria,
Theatre Festivals and the Medici, 1539–1637, trans. G. Hickenhoyer, Yale, 1964.

Nardi, Jacopo,
Istoria della città di Firenze, 1888.

Noble, Mark,
Memoirs of the Illustrious House of Medici, 1797.

Origo, Iris,
'The Domestic Enemy: The Eastern Slaves in Tuscany

	in the 14th and 15th centuries', *Speculum*, 1955, pp. 21–66.
	The Merchant of Prato, Jonathan Cape, 1957.
Orlando, Filippo, and Baccini, Giuseppi (eds.),	*Bibliotechina Grassoccia*, Florence, 1886–98.
Palmarocchi, Roberto,	*Lorenzo de' Medici*, Turin, 1941.
	La politica italiana di Lorenzo de' Medici, Florence, 1973.
Pampaloni, Guido,	*Palazzo Strozzi*, Rome, 1963.
Panella, Antonio,	*Storia di Firenza*, Florence, 1949.
Partner, Peter,	'Florence and the Papacy in the Early Fifteenth Century' in *Florentine Studies*, ed. Rubinstein.
Pastor, Ludwig von,	*History of the Popes from the Close of the Middle Ages*, ed. R. F. Keir, 1899–1910.
Pellegrini, F. C.,	*Sulla repubblica fiorentina al tempo di Cosimo il Vecchio* Pisa, 1880.
Perrens, F.-T.,	*Histoire de Florence depuis la domination des Médicis jusqu'à la chute de la république*, 9 vols., Paris, 1877–88.
Piccolomini, Aeneas Silvius,	*Memoirs of a Renaissance Pope: The Commentaries of Pius II*, trans. Florence A. Gragg, ed. Leonora C. Gabel, 1959.
Picotti, Giovanni Battista,	*La giovinezza di Leone X*, Milan, 1927.
Pieraccini, Gaetano,	*La Stirpe de' Medici di Cafaggiolo*, 3 vols., Florence, 1924; 2nd edn, 1947.
Plumb, J. H.,	*The Horizon Book of the Renaissance*, American Heritage Publishing Co., 1961.
Pope-Hennessy, John,	*Italian High Renaissance and Baroque Sculpture,* Phaidon, 1963.
	Paolo Uccello, Phaidon, 1950.
Prescott, Orville,	*Princes of the Renaissance*, Allen & Unwin, 1970.
Randolph, G.,	*Florentine Merchants in the Age of the Medici*, 1932.
Reumont, Alfred von,	*Lorenzo de' Medici*, Leipzig, 1874; London, 1876
Ricchioni, Vincenzo,	*La costituzione politica di Firenze ai tempi di Lorenzo il Magnifico*, Siena, 1913.
Richards, Gertrude R. B.,	*Florentine Merchants in the Age of the Medici*, Harvard University Press, 1932.
Ridolfi, Roberto,	*The Life of Francesco Guicciardini*, trans. Cecil Grayson, Routledge & Kegan Paul, 1967.
	The Life of Girolamo Savonarola, trans. Cecil Grayson, 1959.
	The Life of Niccolò Machiavelli, trans. Cecil Grayson, 1963.
Robiony, Emilio,	*Gli ultimi dei Medici*, Florence, 1905.
Rochon, André,	*La Jeunesse de Laurent de Médicis*, Paris, 1963.
Rodocanachi, E.,	*Le Pontificat de Léon X*, Paris, 1931.

343

Roeder, Ralph,   'Lorenzo de' Medici' in Plumb, *The Horizon Book*
Roover, Raymond de,   'Labour Conditions in Florence around 1400: Theory
                                Policy and Reality' in *Florentine Studies*, ed. Rubin-
                                stein.
                                The Rise and Decline of the Medici Bank, 1397–1494,
                                Harvard University Press, 1963.
Roscoe G., and Bossi, L.,   *Vita e Pontificato di Leone X*, Milan, 1816–17.
Roscoe, W.,   *Life of Leo X*, 1846.
                                Life of Lorenzo de' Medici, new edn, 1872.
Ross, Janet,   *Florentine Villas*, 1901.
                                Florentine Palaces and Their Stories, 1905.
                                Lives of the Early Medici as told in their correspondence, 1910.
Roth, Cecil,   *The Last Florentine Republic*, 1925.
Rubinstein, Nicolai,   'Florentine Constitutionalism and Medici Ascendancy in
                                the Fifteenth Century' in *Florentine Studies*, ed. Rubin-
                                stein.
                                (ed.) *Florentine Studies: Politics and Society in Renaissance
                                Florence*, Faber, 1968.
                                The Government of Florence under the Medici 1434–1494,
                                Clarendon Press, new edn, 1968.
                                'Politics and Constitution in Florence at the end of the
                                Fifteenth Century' in *Italian Renaissance Studies*, ed.
                                Jacob.
Rud, E.,   *Vasari's Life and Lives*, London, 1964.

Salvini, R.,   *Botticelli*, Milan, 1958.
Scaife, Walter,   *Florentine Life During the Renaissance*, 1893.
Schevill, Ferdinand,   *History of Florence from the Foundation of the City through
                                the Renaissance*, Harcourt Brace, 1936.
                                The Medici, Harcourt Brace, 1949.
Segni, Bernardo,   *Storie Fiorentine*, 1728.
Shepherd, William,   *The Life of Poggio Bracciolini*, 1837.
Sinibaldi, Giulia,   *Il Palazzo Vecchio di Firenze*, Rome, 1950.
Sismondi, J.C.L.,   *History of the Italian Republics during the Middle Ages*, ed.
                                William Boulting, n.d.
Solerti, Angelo,   *Musica, Ballo e Drammatica alla corte Medicea dal 1600 al
                                1637*, Florence, 1905.
Spini, Giorgio,   *Cosimo I de' Medici e la indipendenza del Principato Med1ceo*,
                                Florence, 1945.
Strong, Roy,   *Splendour at Court: Renaissance Spectacle and Illusion*,
                                Weidenfeld & Nicolson, 1973.
Symonds, John Addington,   *The Renaissance in Italy*, 1875–86.

Tenenti, Alberto,   *Firenze dal Comune a Lorenzo il Magnifico*, Milan, 1970.
Tolnay, Charles de,   *Michelangelo*, Princeton University Press, 1943–60.

Valori, Niccolò,   *Laurentii Medicei vita*, Florence, 1756.
Varchi, Benedetto,   *Storia fiorentina*, 3 vols., 1838–41; new edn, Florence,
                      1963.
Vasari, Giorgio,   *Le vite dei più eccellenti pittori, scultori ed architetti*, 9 vols.,
                      Florence, 1906.
                      The Lives of the Artists, trans. George Bull, Penguin
                      Books, 1965.
Vaughan, Herbert M., *The Medici Popes*, 1908.
Vaussard, Maurice,   *La Vie quotidienne en Italie au XVIIIe Siècle*, Hachette,
                      1959; trans. Michael Heron, Allen & Unwin, 1962.
Vespasiano da Bisticci, *Vite di Uomini Illustri*, ed. D'Ancona and Aeschlimann,
                      Milan, 1951.
                      The Vespasiano Memoirs, trans. George & Waters, 1926.
Villani, Giovanni,   *Chronica di Giovanni Villani*, ed. Dragomanni, 4 vols.,
                      Florence, 1844–5.
Villani, Matteo,   *Chronica di Matteo Villani*, ed. Dragomanni, 2 vols.,
                      Florence, 1846.
Villari, P.,   *La storia di Girolamo Savonarola*, Florence, 1877.

Wadia, Bettina,   *Botticelli*, Hamlyn, 1968.
Weil-Garris Posner,   'Comments on the Medici Chapel and Pontormo's
  Kathleen,   Lunette at Poggio a Caiano' in *Burlington Magazine*,
                      cxv, pp. 641–9.
Weinstein, Donald,   'The Myth of Florence' in *Florentine Studies*, ed. Rubin-
                      stein.
                      Savonarola and Florence, Princeton University Press, 1970.
                      'Savonarola, Florence and the millenarian tradition' in
                      Church History, 1958, pp. 291–305.
Weiss, Roberto,   *The Renaissance Discovery of Classical Antiquity*, Black-
                      well, 1969.

Young, G.F.,   *The Medici*, 2 vols., 1909.

INDEX

INDEX

INDEX

Government—*contd*
Signoria, method of forming, 26; organization, 27; and the 15th century Albizzi-Medici conflict, 32, 42, 49, 52–3, 55–8; manipulation of elections, 60; and foreign affairs, 79; honour Cosimo Pater Patriae, 98; and the Medici, 106, 187; seal of, 109; and the Volterran riots, 126; and ecclesiastical appointments, 130; and the Pope, 148, 149; Lorenzo the Magnificent and, 153; its authority limited, 157; Piero di Lorenzo and, 186; get Medici jewels, 187; Charles VIII and, 190; *Accoppiatori* and, 191; watch the bonfire of vanities, 192; Alexander VI and, 197; and Savonarola, 198, 200; and Cardinal Giovanni, 208; war drains the resources of, 210; and a national militia, 211; and Lorenzo di Piero's title, 220; abolition of, 264; and the Medici library, 316
Gorini, Simonetta, 233
Gozzoli, Benozzo (*c.* 1420–97), 67, 110–12, 320–1
Grandi, and government of Florence, 28; and Cosimo di Giovanni, 43; Medici declared to be, 52; become eligible for election to office, 61
'Great Schism', the (1378–1417), 34
Greek Orthodox Church, 64, 65, 67
Grocyn, William (*c.* 1446–1519), 170
Grosso, Niccolò, 76, 318
Guadagni family, 58
Guadagni, Bernardo, 49, 51–2
Guasconi family, 58
Guicciardini family, 58
Guicciardini, Francesco (1483–1540), 315; on Cosimo Pater Patriae, 63; on Lorenzo the Magnificent, 146, 157; on Capponi and Charles VIII, 190; on the French in Naples, 193; on French artillery, 195; on the sack of Prato, 213–14; on Giulio de' Medici, 233; on Giovanni delle Bande Nere, 242; on Clement VII, 243; on Cardinal Passerini, 248; on the aftermath of the siege of Florence, 251; eulogizes Alessandro de' Medici, 254; leader of the *Palleschi*, 256, 257; and Cosimo I, 257, 258, 264; Varchi on, 263
Guicciardini, Giovanni, 55, 56
Guicciardini, Luigi, 160
Guicciardini, Piero, 56
Guilds, trade, Florentine, 25–6; and Signoria, 26; cloth and wool, 33; Arte del Cambio, 33, 73; Arte di Por Santa Maria, 71; and the Cathedral dome, 72; commission statues for Orsanmichele, 73; and number of working-days per year, 119; on verge of ruin, 210; of the Calimala, 319–20

Hadfield, Charles, 325
Handel, George Frederick (1685–1759), 300
Hanno, *elephant belonging to* Pope Leo X, 226

Henry VIII, King of England (1491–1547), 239, 247–8
Henry II, King of France, *see* Orléans, Henri de Valois, Duke of
Henry IV, King of France (1553–1610), 281
Holy Leagues, Florence, Milan, the Pope and Venice, 85; Alexander VI's, 194; mercenaries in battle, 195; Savonarola and, 196; League of Cambrai, 207, 223; Julius II's, 208, 209, 211–12, 214
Humanists, Cosimo Pater Patriae, 37–8; Albizzi and, 43–4; friends of Cosimo Pater Patriae, 43, 46, 47; Piccolimini and Parentucelli, 88; and vernacular poetry, 170

Imola, 107, 128, 129, 131, 132
Insignia, of Florence, 26, 33, 313; of the Medici, 30, 48, 102, 111, 313, 319, 323; of Arte della Lana, 33; of Cosimo Pater Patriae, 76, 111; of the Medici bank, 87; Valois lilies, 102; seal of the Signoria, 109; standard of Lorenzo the Magnificent, 117; of citizens of Florence, 215; Cardinal Giovanni's personal device, 216; of Del Cimento, 284; Peruzzi family emblem, 315; arms of Piero di Cosimo, 320; the Castracani leopard, 321; Francesco I and the Medici emblem, 331

Jews, 129, 279, 297, 307
Joanna, Archduchess of Austria, *see* Medici, Joanna de', Grand Duchess
John VII Paleologus, Emperor of the East (*r.* 1425–48), 83; and the Pope, 64; enters Florence, 66; and the Council of Florence, 67, 68; and the Florentine-Milanese alliance, 83; Gozzoli and, 110

Kallistos, Andronicus, 122
Knights of St John of Jerusalem, 267
Knights of Santo Stefano, 266

La Badia, monastery of, 73
Ladislaus, King of Naples, 35
Lama, Guaspare di Zanobi del, 109
Landini, Taddeo, 328
Landino, Cristoforo, 103, 122
Landucci, Luca, on Italian warfare, 151; on the attack on Colle, 152; on an alleged assassin, 158; and the influence of Savonarola, 193; on the burning of Savonarola, 200; on the national militia, 211; his confidence, 211–12
Lannoy, Charles de, 241
Lascaris, Giovanni, *called* Rhyndacenus (*c.* 1445–1535), 169, 228
Latimer, William, 170
Latino, Cardinal, 116
Lenzi, Lorenzo, 185
Leonardo da Vinci (1452–1519), 168, 228, 240, 324
Leoni, Piero, 173, 174

INDEX

Mino da Fiesole, 331
Mirandola, Pico della, see Pico della
Mirandola, Count Giovanni
Moncada, Don Ugo di, 241
Montaigne, Michel Eyquem de (1533–92),
276
Monte Cassino Abbey, 202, 324–5
Montefeltro, Federigo da, see Urbino,
Federigo Montefeltro, Duke of
Montesquieu, Charles, Baron de la Brède et
de, 279
Montpensier, Anne-Marie-Louise d'Orléans,
Duchesse de, called Mademoiselle, 292
Morello, the horse of Lorenzo the Magnificent,
114
Museums and galleries,
Galleria dell' Accademia Carrara,
Bergamo, 325
Isabella Stewart Gardner Museum,
Boston, 325
Metropolitan Museum, New York, 330
Musée de Sèvres, 330
Musée du Louvre, Paris, 320, 330
Museo degli Argenti, 328
Museo dell' Accademia, 319, 326
Museo dell' Opera del Duomo, 320
Museo dell' Opera di Santa Croce, 315,
321
Museo Horne, 313
Museo Nazionale, 313
Museo Nazionale di Storia della Scienza,
331
National Gallery, London, 315, 320
Pallavicini collection, Rome, 325
Uffizi, look under Florence
Victoria and Albert Museum, London,
320, 330

Naples, 34, 87, 158, 169
Naples and Sicily, Kingdom of, strife in, 27–
8; Sforza a condottiere for, 81; Florentines
expelled from, 83; France and, 84, 183,
186; declares war on Florence and Milan,
84; and Florence, 106, 150, 152, 155;
Orsini estates in, 116; Lorenzo the
Magnificent's mission to, 152–5; Sixtus IV
and, 159; Charles VIII in, 193; Spain and,
208; Leo X's plans for, 219; Francis I and,
222
Napoleon I, Emperor of France, 330
Nardi, Jacopo, 213, 254
Nasi, Bartolommea dei, 146
Nemours, Duchess of, see Philiberte of Savoy,
Princess
Nemours, Duke of, see Medici, Giuliano di
Lorenzo de'
Neroni, Dietisalvi, 104, 105, 106, 124
Niccoli, Niccolò, his personality and inter-
ests, 44–5; and Bracciolini, 45, 46; Bruni
disapproves of, 46; and Traversari, 47; and
Filelfo, 47, 48; his books, 69; and Dante's
poetry, 171
Nocera, Bishop of, 244

Nori, Francesco, 137, 138

Orange, Philibert, Prince of (r. 1502–30), 242,
244, 250
Orcagna, Andrea, prop. Andrea di Cione
(c. 1308–68), 314
Orléans, Henri de Valois, Duke of, later
Henry II, King of France (1519–59), his
marriage, 252
Orsanmichele, church of, commerce in the
neighbourhood of, 20; Ghiberti's St
Matthew for, 73, 317; Donatello's work
commissioned for, 90; historical note on,
312; Ghiberti's bronzes in, 317
Orsini family, 116–17, 149
Orsini, Alfonsina, see Medici, Alfonsina de'
Orsini, Clarice, see Medici, Clarice de'
Orsini, Isabella, née Medici, Isabella di
Cosimo de', 269, 273, 277
Orsini, Jacopo, 114
Orsini, Paolo, 184
Orsini, Paolo Giordano, 269, 277–8
Orsini, Rinaldo, Archbishop of Florence, 130
Orsini, Troilo, 277
Orvieto, episcopal palace of, 247

Pageants, see Festivals
Palazzi,
Alessandri, 117
Altoviti, 314
Antinori, 330
Bardi, 39, 58, 75
Bellini, 280, 331
Capponi, 313
Corsini, 314
Davanzati, 313
degli Acciaiuoli, 315
dei Giudici, 330, 331
della Signoria (later renamed Palazzo
Vecchio, q.v.), Cosimo Pater Patriae in,
19, 49, 51, 58, 83; Alberghettino, 15, 19,
200; Priori live in, 26; the Vacca, 27, 50,
57, 139, 186, 254; Albizzi plans to attack,
55–6; Soderini at, 104; and festival of St
John the Baptist, 120; Princess Eleonora
of Naples at, 121; and the Pazzi con-
spiracy, 138–40, 141; Piero di Lorenzo at,
186; the bonfire of vanities opposite, 192;
celebrations for the election of Leo X,
218; re-named, 257; historical note on,
312; Donatello's works in, 318;
Michelangelo's David in front of, 326
Ferranti, 66
Gianfigliazzi, 314, 325
Guadagni, 315
Guicciardini, 315
Martelli, 57
Medici, building of, 75–6; courtyard of,
90; Donatello, 91–2; Filippo Lippi, 93;
Della Robbia, 108; Ucello, 108;
Pollaiuolo, 108; Botticelli, 109; Gozzoli,
110; Lorenzo the Magnificent's wedding
celebrations, 117–18; Princess Eleonora

INDEX

INDEX